The Postcolonial Contemporary

The Postcolonial Contemporary

Political Imaginaries for the Global Present

Jini Kim Watson and Gary Wilder, Editors

FORDHAM UNIVERSITY PRESS

NEW YORK 2018

Fordham University Press gratefully acknowledges financial assistance and support provided for the publication of this book by New York University.

Visit us online at www.fordhampress.com.

Library of Congress Cataloging-in-Publication Data available online at https://catalog.loc.gov.

Printed in the United States of America

20 19 18   5 4 3 2 1

First edition

CONTENTS

The Postcolonial Contemporary

Thinking the Postcolonial Contemporary

Jini Kim Watson and Gary Wilder

The Postcolonial Contemporary

To invoke the "postcolonial contemporary" is simultaneously to offer a proposition and to raise a question. It is an invitation to recognize and reflect on the emphatically postcolonial character of the contemporary conjuncture as well as to inquire into whether postcolonial criticism can adequately grasp it. We begin with the belief, on the one hand, that new historical situations require different analytic frameworks and, on the other, that grasping the political present requires close attention to historical continuities, repetitions, and reactivations.[1] Neither simply *for* nor *against* postcolonialism, the volume seeks to cut across this false alternative. Our aim is to think *with* and *beyond* postcolonial theory about political contemporaneity.

The violent, asymmetrical, and crisis-ridden character of global politics we are witnessing today belies many of the progressive promises of the twentieth century: decolonization, social democracy, state socialism, and liberal internationalism. The converging pressures of unsustainable extraction, neoliberal privatization and financialization, permanent austerity, wars-without-end and refugee flows, xenophobic nationalism, and ascendant oligarchies are rapidly reshaping the institutions and arrangements around which the postwar global order was organized. Persisting and emergent forms of capitalist imperialism are entering into new configurations that warrant scholarly and political attention. Meanwhile, the consolidation of right-wing populist movements and regimes worldwide—in the United States, Europe, Israel, Russia, Turkey, India, Philippines, and Egypt—mark an intensification of, and a possible turning point in, these developments. Yet we observe that intellectuals are struggling to find the language, concepts, and frameworks with which to grasp the contemporary political situation.

Our reflections in this introduction start from two propositions. First, a postcolonial optic remains crucial for any attempt to grasp the contours of our post–Cold War present. If the latter is largely a product of imperial pasts and afterlives, it is also producing novel imperial arrangements. And it can be understood only through approaches that decenter or unthink traditional Western paradigms that were themselves bound up with forms of colonial power, whether as cause or consequence. Second, if any history of the present should, in some sense, be postcolonial, it should also reconsider and revise many of the frameworks that were developed within the field of postcolonial studies. Such frameworks were largely developed between the 1970s and 1990s, during what we may now recognize as the twilight of the postwar period. The very spirit of postcolonial reflexivity calls on us to rethink such frameworks in relation to unfolding developments and current political challenges. The postcolonial task is therefore not to apply existing approaches to current conditions. It is to identify those critical aspects of postcolonial inquiry that may be invaluable for grasping what is postcolonial about our political present and reworking them accordingly.

We frame this volume in terms of "the postcolonial contemporary," a concept that flows from these opening propositions. The phrase raises questions about both the postcolonial character of the contemporary situation and the contemporaneity of postcolonial thinking. As such, it seeks to move beyond the habitual oppositions that have often characterized the field, such as universal versus particular, Marxism versus postcolonialism, and politics versus culture. At another level it raises questions about how both postcolonial theory and the postcolonial present may invite us to reflect more deeply on the very concept of contemporaneity, that is, on relations between past, present, and future, on the supposed self-presence of historical periods, on conventional approaches to periodization, on the peculiar temporal dynamics of contemporary global politics, and on the spatiotemporal matrices through which political lives are shaped and lived today.

We approach these issues in an interrogatory fashion. This volume is not a comprehensive survey of current approaches to postcolonial studies. It does not pretend to cover the wide range of regions, topics, frameworks, and methodologies that identify with, align with, or are informed by an engagement with postcolonial theory. Nor are the essays meant to cohere into a single programmatic position. Rather, we hope to intervene by assembling a group of thinkers whose work, despite differences and disagreements, emerges from and engages with the set of questions we are associating with "the postcolonial contemporary." That is, this intervention is less a polemic launched from the outside than a work of collective self-reflection. Most of the authors included here have been profoundly influenced by postcolonial theory and the debates thereby generated. In different ways, the pieces collected both recognize the indispensability of a certain postcolonial orientation and point beyond some of the limitations of its existing frameworks, whether implicitly or explicitly.

In broad terms, we identify three crucial dimensions of postcolonial critique that broadly orient the work of this project, although each may or may not be combined within any given piece of scholarship. First, we understand "postcolonial" as a formal temporal designation that refers to the period, processes, and formations that came into being after the end of colonialism—whether in former metropoles or colonies. (One could debate whether the concept should refer only to the "after" of modern European colonial imperialisms, whether it should also refer to the "after" of early modern Iberian imperialism, or whether it should refer to the "after" of any colonial or imperial epoch, order, regime.)

Second, "postcolonial" is a substantive historical claim about such aftermaths; it signals that the "after" is overdetermined by the before. "Postcolonial" indicates that (and asks how) social formations and subjectivities that follow colonialism are shaped, haunted, or suffused by the preceding colonial era, practices, processes, arrangements. Here *postcolonial* may refer to the persistence, repetition, or resurgence of older forms of domination (whether or not in different registers), to the ongoing harms perpetrated by those colonial pasts and experienced in the postcolonial present (or which present actors must work to repair or overcome), or to the emergence of new forms that are linked to, enabled by, or resemble those earlier forms (e.g., neocolonialism, nationalism, xenophobia, humanitarianism, etc.). Postcolonialism thus indicates aftermaths, the persistence of pasts in the present, and the enduring character of colonial transgressions, which is to say, the impossibility—and undesirability—of drawing definitive lines between a before and after.

Third, "postcolonial" also refers to the epistemological implications of the first two designations. It indexes how colonial assumptions, logics, and arrangements shaped the Western concepts through which a purportedly universal (social) science claimed to produce knowledge of the (non-Western) world during the colonial epoch, and may continue to do so in postcolonial periods that are still structured and haunted by that colonial past. It is also a claim about the instrumental power of such colonial or Eurocentric epistemologies to mediate, mystify, or legitimize colonial and postcolonial forms of domination. Thus, "postcolonial" refers to the critical perspective that recognizes and challenges such colonial conditions of knowledge production, their ongoing legacies in postcolonial periods, and their power to produce and reproduce systems of inequality within and between nations, societies, continents. It also refers to the need for, or the development of, concepts, frameworks, and ways of knowing that refuse, decenter, dismantle, bypass, or substitute for precisely those colonial (derived) epistemologies and their worldly effects. A postcolonial perspective is therefore one that recognizes, refuses, or replaces such colonial forms of thinking and bodies of knowledge.

In sum, despite the wide variety of scholarship that is identified with this field of inquiry—and its sometimes furious internal debates—a postcolonial orientation or postcolonial critique makes some combination of claims about: that which follows the formal end of colonialism, the ongoing presence of the past in the present, and their implications for producing knowledge about the world. From the perspective of these basic criteria, postcolonial criticism cannot possibly have reached an end point. It remains a vital and relevant project whose work cannot be complete. The question we address in this volume is how to revisit and revise the ways that postcolonial scholarship has tended to address

these three issues, especially given the world-historical transformations that have occurred since the initial emergence of the postcolonial project.

Contemporary Postcolonialism

In this section, we look back over the trajectory of the scholarly field that developed largely
in the wake of Edward Said's *Orientalism* (1978) and underscore the fact that postcolonial
studies has never been a homogeneous intellectual project with a fixed object or theory.[2]
It has not so much defined a particular approach as delimited a scene of debate over domination, emancipation, and knowledge production with regard to colonial pasts and the
present. In the 1980s and 1990s, its founding interventions became quickly bound up with
the more general "culture wars"—debates across the human sciences about Enlightenment
rationality, liberal universality, progressive history, and Eurocentric epistemology. Postcolonialists were often aligned with a set of poststructuralist concerns, for example:
critiques of essentialism and philosophy of the subject, attention to power-knowledge
dynamics, and elaborating an antifoundational politics of difference.[3]

Some proponents reasoned that if colonialism devalued or erased native culture, the
latter's (textual or discursive) recovery must be the proper task of postcolonial critique.
Others focused on the culturally particular and colonially refracted character of Western
epistemologies. They traced how these forms of knowledge both enabled domination and
were unable to grasp the cultures they purported to explain. Thus an enduring tendency
emerged among postcolonial scholars to emphasize cultural location, alterity, and incommensurability. Some equated cultural expression among non-Europeans with a politics of
resistance. Others produced Western cultural genealogies of the supposedly universal categories of modern social science. In both approaches, postcolonial criticism was associated
with a search for non-Western, or non-self-alienating, ways of knowing the world, representing society, and narrating history.[4]

Yet an equally robust countertendency within postcolonial theory criticized Western
discourses about the Middle East, Asia, and Africa for insisting on their absolute or categorical difference from Europe.[5] Also informed by poststructuralism and equally concerned with the colonial genealogies of modern analytic categories, they tended rather to
emphasize the link between colonial histories and cultural processes of mobility, hybridity, and intersectionality. Anthony Appiah thus identified African "postcoloniality" with
a critique of nativism and nationalism that sought to transcend the colonial binaries of
Self and Other or Africa and the West.[6] Stuart Hall regarded postcolonial critique as a
way to displace the "political binaries" that grounded both colonialism and anticolonialism.[7] Hall explained that that "the term 'post-colonial' re-reads 'colonisation' as part of an
essentially transnational and transcultural 'global' process—and it produces a decentered,
diasporic, or 'global,' rewriting of earlier, nation-centered imperial grand narratives."[8]
Scholars working from this perspective also emphasized the postcolonial character of *metropolitan* societies and culture, especially during the late-colonial and post-independence
eras of mass migration to Western cities.[9]

In turn, as a response to this general focus on the *cultural* entailments and legacies of colonialism, many Left critics of imperialism challenged the new scholarship for abandoning materialist analysis, class perspectives, and a focus on capitalism.[10] They regarded postcolonial thinking as overly identified with (European) high theory, too focused on literary and cultural analysis, and more concerned with "epistemic violence" than concrete domination and political struggles.[11] Others writing about racism and colonialism were concerned that the catchall term "postcolonial" was too singular, general, and abstract to be analytically useful. Because the diverse cases and studies grouped under its rubric often had little in common, they believed that the task of specifying diverse forms of power in the postcolonial era would be obscured by this framework. Likewise, positing a clear divide between the colonial past and the postcolonial present seemed to risk minimizing imperial continuities, effacing the ongoing forms of domination within (what was then called) the Third World and between it and the West.[12]

We might recall that a cohort of historians and anthropologists that we would now retrospectively identify with the postcolonial project actually situated themselves in a field of interdisciplinary "colonial studies." They too were concerned with the power-knowledge relations that subtended both colonial rule and post-Enlightenment science. But they primarily used the term "postcolonial" (often with a hyphen) to refer not to their own critical practice but to the states and societies that followed the end of colonial rule, or the new subjects of these societies and their cultural productions.[13] For them "postcolonial" was a descriptive rather than analytic category, a periodizing adjective rather than the name of a condition or critical orientation. At most it referred to a subfield of literary studies concerned with writers and texts from or about former colonies.

Nevertheless, many thinkers found "postcolonial" to be a useful analytic term, to refer to a particular sociohistorical situation, a certain kind of critique—of Western self-understanding, Eurocentric epistemology, and the constitutive character of colonial pasts in shaping the modern world—as well as a set of challenges associated with living and thinking in and against (the aftermaths of) colonialism. Gayatri Chakravorty Spivak, for example, spoke about the "deconstructive predicament" posed by a postcolonial situation in which subjects must engage in a "persistent critique" of those modern rational goods that they "cannot not want to inhabit."[14] Similarly, Partha Chatterjee wrote about the "postcolonial misery" that rests in a "surrender to the old forms of the modern state."[15] From a different perspective, Edward Said invoked the "tragedy" of a certain kind of "post-colonial experience" among non-Western intellectuals who were vilified for attempting to criticize both past colonial rule and present postcolonial states in the name of "intertwined and overlapping histories" in an unavoidably "interdependent" world.[16]

Dipesh Chakrabarty and Gyan Prakash began to explicitly describe as "postcolonial" the subaltern studies project of finding ways that Indian intellectuals could write histories, represent their own pasts, and specify non-Western forms of subjectivity that were not overdetermined by power-knowledge complexes that had authorized British *and* nationalist rule.[17] In their view, liberalism, nationalism, and Marxism all depended on colonial-inflected epistemologies that implied Eurocentric views of society, history, and politics; none of these could serve as reliable grounds for overcoming the kind of ongoing hierarchies, inequalities, and exclusions that postcolonial criticism identified. In a period when, in many places, colonial independence seemed only to mark the beginning of new forms of domination (whether by the West or Westernized elites), the progressive assumptions and promises of these emancipatory discourses appeared especially suspect to a new cohort of postcolonial critics. For them, questioning Marxism was not a renunciation of politics but an aspect of their political intervention.

In a different vein, Stuart Hall in 1996 argued that "postcolonial" meant not only coming *after* but going *beyond* a colonialism that, among other things, created "pluralities and multiplicities" even as it offered an impoverished "idea of a world of separate identities, of isolated or separable and self-sufficient cultures and economies." For Hall, "postcolonial" analysis examines precisely these "forms of relationship, interconnection, and discontinuity" that "colonization set into play" but were "downgraded" in its "official narrative."[18] He too defended postcolonial thinking against its crude Marxist critics. But he did so by pursuing a nuanced Marxian understanding of postcolonial processes and situations, inflected by noneconomistic, politically contingent, and culturally mindful factors.

Despite, or precisely because of, such differences, postcolonialism during the 1990s had clearly shifted from being a descriptive to an analytic term that referred at once to a type of historical situation or predicament, a kind of critical orientation, and a field of debate. David Scott captured this new status when, in 1996, he referred to "postcolonial criticism" as "a conceptual space that many of us [are] finding useful to think *in*, think *about*: a space opened up, we would argue, in Said's seminal work, *Orientalism*."[19] Scott identified with its "*general* project of reinterrogating colonialism" in order to "expose the implication of ideological projects in the making of forms of knowledge still dominant in the present" and "to produce the counter-space for the practice of constructing alternative histories of the present."[20] He was sympathetic to the charge that liberalism, Marxism, and nationalism were bound up with the very forms of colonial power-knowledge that needed to be challenged. But in his view, their political limitations for a postcolonial politics were as much historical as cultural. In other words, Scott was less concerned with indicting the geographic or cultural origins of these Euro-modern ideologies, than with the fact that the political moment in which socialism and nationalism had once been viable anticolonial pathways had passed. He thus attempted to transcend the debate between (anti-imperial) Marxists and (poststructuralist) postcolonialists by asking a different set of questions: What kind of political project could correspond to existing conditions, possibilities, and demands? What kind of political critique could adequately address the specific forms of power that defined the postcolonial present? What kind of political futures could be imagined in a world now defined by "the aftermaths of sovereignty" in the Third World, the collapse of really existing socialism in the Soviet Union, and the rise of neoliberal capitalism in the West?[21]

Indeed, by the mid-1990s, with the end of the Cold War and resurgence of U.S. imperial power (signaled by the first Gulf War), the dismantling of Fordist social democracy and the intensification of global economic interdependence, new sets of questions arose about the relationship between "globalization" and postcolonialism, that is, between new forms of postcolonial power and existing forms of postcolonial critique. This was precisely when postcolonial studies was consolidating as an academic field in North America, Europe, and Australia, with an emergent canon, primary source readers, scholarly anthologies and primers, academic journals, and premature postmortems. It was not clear whether these epochal shifts in capitalism, state form, and worldwide social interconnection and mobility called for renewed postcolonial analysis or marked the end of the conditions that had called forth postcolonial studies. Was "globalization" the new name for what postcolonial studies had been concerned with, or might it signal that postcolonial critique had become outmoded?

Already in 1993, Masao Miyoshi had suggested that under "today's global configuration of power and culture," the academic preoccupation with "postcoloniality" looked like an "alibi" for "transnational corporatism."[22] From positions that were more sympathetic to postcolonial criticism (and transformations associated with globalization), Arjun Appadurai emphasized the cultural dimensions of globalization for postcolonial societies while Michael Hardt and Antonio Negri invoked an emergent deterritorialized Empire around which global politics would be organized.[23] Other postcolonial scholars challenged such discourses of epochal rupture. Michel-Rolph Trouillot characterized the term "globalization" itself as a "North Atlantic universal" that obscured the long history, in places like the Caribbean, of global flows and interconnection that had always been bound up with capitalist imperialism.[24] Questioning postcolonial theory's anti-universalist claims in a world marred by devastating inequality and poverty, Simon Gikandi noted that "citizens of the postcolony are more likely to seek their global identity by invoking the very logic of Enlightenment that postcolonial theory was supposed to deconstruct."[25]

Not coincidentally, it was during this period that the "Global South" came properly into focus as an ambiguous geopolitical player and academic designation. A regionalization that follows the breakdown of the Cold War "Three Worlds" system, it largely maps onto postcolonial regions and recognizes the disparities between developed and developing nations. The Global South is thus part signifier of entrenched underdevelopment and part geo-imaginary for new anti-imperialist solidarities. But if the Third World was now subsumed under the category of "Global South"—with its implicit interlocutor the "Global North"—was postcolonial critique adequate for its analysis? As Arif Dirlik pessimistically noted, "The issue is no longer overthrowing colonialism or finding a 'third way of development,' but the *inclusion* of voices of the formerly colonized and marginalized in a world that already has been shaped by a colonial modernity to which there is no alternative in sight."[26]

Such questions about the geopolitics, histories, and forces of globalization generated further discussions about the units, scales, and locations of postcolonial critique. Many questioned the limitation of national frameworks for understanding colonial pasts and postcolonial presents. Debates unfolded about the relative merits of internationalism, cosmopolitanism, and transnationalism or diaspora for grasping postcolonial situations and pursuing postcolonial futures.[27] Some criticized postcolonial theory for being an artifact of the Western academy or the preoccupation of elite Third World intellectuals living in Western metropolises. Scholars associated with the Latin American Subaltern Studies group questioned postcolonialism's tendency to focus on nineteenth- and twentieth-century

Northern Europe.[28] Meanwhile, other scholars expanded the typical purview of postcolonialism to raise new questions from within fields such as classics, medieval and Renaissance studies, American studies, and East Asian studies.[29] The relation between postcolonial theory and Black studies—variously overlapping, intersecting, parallel, and divergent—has been persistent.[30] For better or for worse, postcolonialism has made it possible to regard many past colonial situations as already *post*colonial and places that had never been colonized as nevertheless post*colonial*.

In short, postcolonial studies continued to develop as a site of contested efflorescence. Yet even as its basic tenets became more widely accepted, world events rendered the field at once more urgently relevant *and* potentially moribund. Ania Loomba and her colleagues pointedly asked, "What . . . is the value of postcolonial studies in our globalizing world, and does it have a viable future beyond its existing life span, identified by Vilashini Cooppan . . . as the period from Edward Said's *Orientalism* (1978) to Michael Hardt and Antonio Negri's *Empire* (2000)?"[31] Their volume, *Postcolonial Studies and Beyond* (2005), was also a work of self-reckoning that assessed the status and efficacy of postcolonial thinking following the 9/11 attacks and the U.S. invasions of Afghanistan and Iraq. In the wake of these events, discourses of an irreconcilable "clash of civilizations" deepened; a self-devouring global capitalism teetered during the 2008 financial crisis, then returned from the brink; and the so-called Arab Spring embodied both the postcolonial world's greatest hopes and fears. The wager of a new deterritorialized empire à la Hardt and Negri seems to have been refuted by the intensification of direct forms of imperial invasion and occupation, resource wars, mounting nativist violence, the hardening of both Islamic fundamentalism and Islamophobia, and the redrawing of Cold War battle lines. Europe, Australia, and America, meanwhile, reprise colonial-era racialisms in the face of the flow of migrants fleeing unending war, poverty, and persecution. The West has become newly entwined with the rest of the world not only through war, financialization, and immigration but through the prospect of imminent environmental catastrophe, the rise of national-popular authoritarian regimes, and the spread of anti-austerity and Occupy-type mass movements. This constellation of interrelated developments has continued to unmake the postwar order, restructure global power relations, and realign axes of division and conflict.[32]

In light of these contemporary developments, we believe David Scott's penetrating questions about the demands of criticism for the political present have become only more acute. In what ways might the postcolonial analytic be able to address both the mutations and the continuities of such imperialist-capitalist forces, the simultaneous novelty and sense of inevitability of many of these configurations? What can it say, for example, about the possibilities of South-South solidarity in the face of intensified competition for development and the new paradigm of "jobless growth"?[33] Recent work by Talal Asad, for example, on liberal secularism, humanitarian violence, and Islamophobia clearly indicates the ongoing relevance of a postcolonial theoretical orientation.[34] Likewise, scholarship on critical international law, settler colonialism, and indigeneity.[35] But the contemporary political situation seems also to call for a rethinking of the relation between postcoloniality, global capitalism, and Marxian analysis. A new generation of critics and activists is increasingly interested in issues that had already seemed to be outmoded when postcolonial studies first entered the academy: anarchist tactics, socialist imaginaries, anti-imperial inter-nationalisms, and traditions of mass protest and popular resistance. Twenty-first-century developments are also raising new concerns about the urgency and possibilities for translocal solidarity, postnational democracy, and planetary politics.

Are metropole-colony frameworks, the analysis of power-knowledge complexes, and cultural genealogies of Western forms of knowledge able to grasp these new dynamics of domination and prospects for politics? If the now-mainstream concepts that were indispensable for the formation of the field—"Orientalism," "subaltern resistance," "hybridity," "epistemic violence"—are no longer sufficient, what new concepts for our postcolonial present must now be theorized? Given both its healthy history of internal debates and con-testations and the radical transformations of our neoliberalized and precarious world, what kinds of critique might the postcolonial project advance?

We do not intend to answer these questions directly. In this collection, we are less in-terested in defining what the postcolonial *is* than in what it can *do* in our current conjunc-ture. We do not limit postcolonial studies' remit to the unmasking of Western imperialist designs and epistemologies, or the unearthing of native resistance—as much as we ac-knowledge the usefulness and necessity of those intellectual projects. Put simply, the es-says collected here mobilize the self-reflexive critical practices that we believe have best characterized the sprit of postcolonial critique. Taking as their starting points a variety of historical and political situations, the following essays do not express a single theoretical orthodoxy or methodological dogma. Rather, they seek to reframe essential inquiries, ex-pand terrains for postcolonial thinking, and move beyond binaries that have shaped many of the debates outlined above (universalism versus particularism, hybridity versus differ-ence, capitalist versus colonial domination, globalization versus postcolonialism, direct versus epistemic violence, politics versus culture, situations versus experience).

It is clear to us that we cannot grasp the way that local, regional, and global politics are unfolding without thinking them in relation to colonial legacies and ongoing imperial arrangements, whether or not one prioritizes neoliberal capitalism, uneven development, U.S. hegemony, UN internationalism, the interstate system, the global war on terror, and so on. Yet it is far from clear that existing currents of postcolonial criticism can adequately address either the political specificity of these dynamics or the curious mix of imperial persistence, repetition, aftermath, reinvention, and emergence that characterizes them. Part of the challenge is to raise such questions without contributing to the academic back-lash "against" postcolonial theory—whether on the grounds that it is outmoded, out of steam, or overrepresented. It is precisely because we recognize postcolonial studies, within which we locate our own work, as a field of ongoing debate that we chose to frame this volume under the rubric "the postcolonial contemporary."

Postcolonial Temporality

Our emphasis on the postcolonial contemporary does not mean that we are interested in investigating only the latest forms of injustice and domination. Nor is our interest in colonial histories motivated only by the desire to find precedents or produce genealogies. We look back at earlier anti-imperialist thinkers and conjunctures to ask, for example, what might it mean to treat B. R. Ambedkar, W. E. B. Du Bois, Durban's 1970s Black Consciousness Movement, or superannuated Singaporean Communists as our contemporaries? Our approach to the postcolonial contemporary thus seeks to move beyond both presentism and historicism. We are less interested in privileging either the past or the present than in examining how the very phenomena associated with postcoloniality (along with corresponding modes of postcolonial criticism) might allow or compel us to reconsider conventional notions of past and present and their relation.

Among the most important issues raised by postcolonial theory, whether explicitly or implicitly, concerns historical temporality or the contemporaneity of its critique. Postcolonial criticism has long directed our attention to the ongoing power of colonial pasts to shape and haunt the present supposed to follow. The "post" has always signaled both the something that comes after and the before that remains internal to the after. Have existing frameworks of postcolonial inquiry adequately called into question conventional notions of time and history that would allow the relation between past and present to be rethought along the lines that postcolonial critique invites? If not, how can the heterodox temporal implications of postcolonial criticism be specified more explicitly and elaborated more fully? Is the postcolonial political present bound up with new types of temporal processes and experiences that might require concepts or approaches beyond those developed within postcolonial theory? As David Scott reminds us, if we are to escape "melancholic silence and paralysis," the situated political upheavals of the postcolonial world (in particular, the Haitian and Grenadan revolutions to which he attends) demand new interrogations of time, narrative form, and modes of remembrance.[36] In this collection, a number of essays rethink the very notion of contemporaneity in relation to specific revolutionary moments in the postcolonial world.

Anthony Alessandrini's essay, for example, reflects on Foucault's and Fanon's engagements with revolutions as ways for us to "reexamine our intellectual framework" and assess our own uncertain, post–Arab Spring moment. Rejecting the kind of thinking that used historical hindsight to dismiss Foucault's "mistake on Iran," Alessandrini meticulously reviews the philosopher's writings on the 1979 revolution, revealing the way Foucault and Fanon shared an intellectual openness to unfolding events and an insistence that "full respect for the singularity of such moments demand[s] new forms of thinking." To refuse final conclusions and resist preemptory declarations of success or failure become sound lessons for our political present. What intellectuals *can* do, Alessandrini suggests, is to rethink the very categories through which we view change.

Laurie R. Lambert and Sharad Chari chart, respectively, the temporal stakes of the Grenada Revolution and the radical struggles in 1970s–80s Durban, South Africa. Lambert assesses Dionne Brand's poetic and novelistic memories of the 1983 Grenada Revolution. She demonstrates how Brand, by offering a "queer chronicle" of its events, not only responds to the revolution's apparent failures, but makes visible its *other* tragedy: the noninclusion of women and sexual minorities from black radical movements. Opening up a space in which to think queer love as a form of politics, Lambert revises the long history of black radical thought and praxis, "mak[ing] it speak into silences where queer blacks struggle within and alongside the revolutionary collective." In his reassessment of unfulfilled revolutions and the present political conjuncture, Chari looks back to South Africa's "multifaceted revolutionary opening in the 1970s and 1980s," especially as manifested in four dialectically intertwined moments of struggle in South Durban's industrial basin. Using theoretical insights from C. L. R. James and Stuart Hall, he elaborates on what he calls "the moment of the disqualified," in which some militants, in some places, are marginalized by processes of political reconciliation that benefit only particular sections of society and space. Chari argues that enduring racial and spatial distinctions make the Black radical tradition significant for the critique of racial capitalism to the postcolonial present. In other words, Black politics is vital to our planetary future.

These essays evince how postcolonial theory might reflect differently on the social organization of time, lived and remembered experiences of revolution, temporal ideologies of success and failure, and figurations of history as crucial dimensions of the (post) colonial problematic. In a similar spirit of openness to past futures, Adam Spanos argues for the literary as a valuable resource for thinking political temporality. Focusing on the Arab avant-garde literary movement and the Egyptian writer Idwar Al-Kharrāt, Spanos seeks to transcend the stale binary between Western and postcolonial avant-gardisms. At the same time, in attending to the movement's open-ended experimentalism rather than self-professed stylistic rupture, such literature demonstrates the tentative and indeterminate nature of political struggle. If neoliberal security states "rule in the name of no future" and deny citizens their ability to determine a future beyond precarity, might Al-Kharrāt's literary politics of futurity suggest a political alternative? Such interventions underscore the fact that postcolonial theory should pay explicit attention to the temporal aspects of the worlds, processes, practices, and discourses it analyzes. We believe that such temporal self-reflexivity will help postcolonial studies grapple both with the contemporary situation as a postcolonial phenomenon and with the contemporaneity of postcolonial thinking in relation to it.

Just as it needs to avoid the temporal reifications imposed by abstract clock time and conventional historicism, postcolonial criticism should also avoid the spatial reifications imposed by statist logic, methodological nationalism, and varieties of nativism and culturalism, as we discuss in the final section below. Supposedly disparate spaces are no less entangled with one another than seemingly disparate times are. We believe that analyses that start from the actualities of entanglement are more likely to see beyond the conceptual limitations of traditional scholarship (regarding both temporal assumptions about pasts and futurities *and* territorial beliefs about lifeworlds, ethnicity, identity, membership, and political subjectivity). In short, a concern with "the postcolonial contemporary" invites us to ask whether the assumed temporal and spatial logics of anticolonialism or postcoloniality can continue to do the analytic and political work we need them to in our historical present.

Deprovincializing the Global South

As we outlined above in our brief taxonomy, we might say that postcolonial theory has demonstrated a consistent interest in the cultural, ideological, and epistemological conditions and processes that mediated colonial domination. Like feminism, queer studies, and critical race studies, it opened the way for a radical shift not only in *what* we (think we) know, but *how* we (think we) know—largely by calling that very "we" into question. It has provoked a thoroughgoing reconsideration of not only what and how Euro-America "knows" other places, peoples, cultures, and histories, but also what and how it knows itself, or indeed any self. Postcolonial scholarship has thus posed fundamental challenges not only to that which has always been (literally) beyond the West's knowledge and understanding, but to the West's own most cherished certainties, norms, and values.

As a consequence, diverse strands of postcolonial scholarship have frequently been linked by (1) a critique of how European colonial and racial violence has been entwined with the West's humanist epistemologies and ideologies, self-understanding, and self-presentation, and (2) a corresponding affirmation of difference in the face of the West's dubious claims to produce universal forms of knowledge, to exemplify universal forms of life, to initiate universal processes of human development, and to promote universal accord (through reason and rights, freedom and equality) for all of humanity (as abstract humans).

The affirmation of difference in postcolonial studies has never been strictly one-sided. In relation to the presumptive universality of Western concepts and experiences—reason, individuality, humanity, freedom—postcolonial scholars have identified and valorized non-European lifeworlds, forms of consciousness, discursive and embodied traditions. At the same time, in relation to Western racial, Orientalist, and civilizational discourses and practices, postcolonial scholars have also insisted on the fundamental humanity, irreducible modernity, spatial and temporal co-presence/coexistence of non-European peoples and societies often figured as inhabiting an absolutely other time and space. Postcolonial studies has thus often navigated the waters between, on the one hand, affirming the irreducible singularity and incommensurable cultural integrity of non-European peoples and, on the other, developing an antifoundationalist critique of cultural essentialism and primordial identities. Thus postcolonial theory's well-known attention to processes of historical co-constitution, cultural entanglement, creolization, and hybridity. Claims about multiple or alternative rationalities and modernities may be read as attempts, however problematic, to integrate both positions.

In recent years, however, postcolonial theory's center of gravity seems to have shifted toward an emphasis on the incommensurable singularity and cultural alterity of non-European forms of life. Here we might think of Chakrabarty's antihistoricist call to provincialize Europe, Talal Asad's postsecular focus on discursive and embodied traditions, Walter Mignolo's (along with Enrique Dussel's and Anibal Quijano's) "decolonial" preoccupation with non-Western epistemologies, and Frank Wilderson's ontological conception of "Afro-pessimism."[37] Such approaches certainly foreground the potentialities of hitherto marginalized lifeworlds and subjectivities, mobilizing them as valuable resources for a variety of political struggles. Yet the increasing emphasis on untranslatable singularities and axial differences risks reproducing the very civilizational thinking and its associated binaries—based on foundational assumptions about "normal" alignments between territory, ethnicity, subjectivity, and consciousness—that postcolonial thinking initially sought to overturn. That is, this work often figures the world in terms of categorical divisions between regions, cultures, religions, races, or forms of reason (for example, West/non-West, History 1/History 2, Christian/Islam, secular/religious, white/black, Enlightenment/indigenous).

The risk of this tendency toward binary thinking within postcolonial studies has several unfortunate consequences. Most obviously, it perversely mirrors imperial Europe's own civilizational worldview. Such an image also works to externalize internal divisions; the contradictions, unevenness, and plurality that characterize a given social formation are transposed into stable (territorial, ontological, epistemological) differences between one-dimensional entities. Once this simplified picture of the world is accepted as given and taken for granted, the work of critique is narrowed to protecting and policing those putative boundaries from outside interference, contamination, or complication. Taken to its logical conclusions, the very territorial and cultural reifications that should be historicized (worked through) are reproduced (acted out). Sadia Abbas's essay in this collection provides just such a "working through" of reified conceptions. Exploring the "constitutive porosity of Europe and West Asia," she unsettles the usual alignments of *chronos*, *topos*, and *demos* that have legitimated both imperialist and postcolonial nationalist projects of "unmixing people," and that underpin the long-standing geographical imagination of Europe's opposition to Africa and Asia. Her study of Greek and Urdu novelists Stratis Myrivilis and Qurratulain Hyder puts pressure on national narratives through attention to the literary technique of ekphrasis (the verbal description of aesthetic objects). In tracing a network of mixedness across West Asia and Europe—typically omitted by postcolonial studies' invocation of the stable concept of the "West"—Abbas provides new ways to think through not only past imperialist and nationalist projects, but the current entanglements of the European Union regarding refugee migration, the German-Turkish alliance, and the Greek debt crisis.

Intellectual projects such as Abbas's thus move beyond a tendency within postcolonial criticism to become preoccupied with identifying shadows, residues, or traces of what appear to be "Western," universalist, humanist, or liberal concepts or assumptions, in order to dismiss (as compromised, illegitimate, power-laden) the object or phenomenon in question—treating such "discoveries" as punch lines rather than starting points, and substitutes for inquiry. In this way, social and epistemological critique, through which to try to think *through and beyond* the actual dilemmas posed by "the postcolonial contemporary," is displaced by always already settled-upon critique. This moral rejection of a one-dimensional Western modernity risks backing postcolonial thinking into a political and analytic corner in which critique can only be negative, while the project to imagine and create less alienated and more just social arrangements, and to reconcile plurality and humanity, are taken off the table.[38] The idea that we should abandon or banish concepts that have mediated the West's racial violence and colonial domination implies a fictive belief in pure or innocent concepts whose provenance or novelty would not allow them to be instrumentalized. Conversely, it implies an absolutist belief that actually existing Western or bourgeois forms (of freedom, democracy, humanism, universal, etc.) exhaust the political potentialities of these concepts. Such viewpoints impoverish intellectual understanding and obstruct political possibilities. They also make it difficult to appreciate those (post) colonial actors, movements, thinkers, processes whose anticolonial/postcolonial engagement starts with the unavoidable facts of entanglement and refuses such categorical thinking.

To be clear, we are not suggesting that the risk of civilizational thinking in recent postcolonial theory be counteracted by an uncritical affirmation of abstract humanism and post-Enlightenment universality. On the contrary, we need to transcend the sterile debate between one-sided conceptions of universalism and particularism. Rather than embrace one or the other as the privileged standpoint of critique, the task is to displace the opposition itself as an imperial artifact that is empirically unfounded, analytically limited, and politically self-undermining. Important postcolonial scholars have recently directed our attention in just such a direction. We might think here of Gayatri Chakravorty Spivak's recent attention to planetarity, Paul Gilroy on postcolonial conviviality and the politics of cosmopolitan dis-identification, Robert Young on toleration and *convivencia*, and Achille Mbembe on universal community, the *in-common*, and the need to "build a world we share."[39] It is important to note that these thinkers arrive at such positions through a rigorous critique of racialization and an understanding of humanity as profoundly rooted and differentiated.[40]

We believe that one way to move beyond this impasse would be to link the indispensable project of provincializing Europe with the equally important task of deprovincializing the Global South. Scholars have rightly demonstrated that many of the purportedly neutral and universal frameworks through which the human sciences seek to know the world emerged out of particular European historical contexts and cannot adequately grasp many dimensions of non-European lifeworlds and experience. Such work has usefully revealed the covert particularism that so often masquerades as universal. But such interventions should be paired with work that also questions the status of the universal or the human as European property and challenges the idea that actually existing forms of abstract humanism and post-Enlightenment universalism are the only possible forms they can assume. In her delineation of B. R. Ambedkar's complex anticaste politics included here, for example, Anupama Rao not only corrects the elision of anticaste thought in much South Asian postcolonial theory but also situates Dalit politics within the framework of *global* responses to dehumanization. Caste is thus read alongside, and through, U.S. postemancipation critiques of slavery and Marxist theorizations of labor. Reading caste for its potential commensurability with these concepts—for its very modernity rather than supposed timelessness—Rao posits a radical deprovincialization of caste against and with which notions of race and class might also be productively reread. The wager is to think the universal precisely from the embodied, negated experience of the Dalit.

There are thus several paths along which such deprovincializing work may proceed. We could, for example, examine how many supposedly "Western" categories are in fact quintessentially *modern* categories that emerged through capitalist and imperial encounters. Insofar as they were implicitly and explicitly coproduced by colonized and non-Western peoples, the latter are their rightful heirs. A deprovincializing critique would demonstrate what should be self-evident, yet seems to require repeating, namely that colonial situations in non-European societies also produced global thinkers of world-historical problems who were concerned not only with their own conditions and experiences but with (such supposedly Western) concepts as freedom, autonomy, democracy, humanity, equality, and justice on world-wide scales. Critiques such as Wilder's recent study of Césaire's and Senghor's visions for nonnational forms of decolonization—and his examination of Du Bois's radical humanism in this volume—show that such thinkers are heirs to intellectual traditions that reflect on the good, the true, and the beautiful, on what it means to be truly human and live a full human life.[41] Moreover, the significance of these reflections extends beyond the specific context, the provincial forms of life, from which they emerged and to which they certainly refer, but not exclusively. Such inquiries would begin effectively to globalize intellectual history and critical theory; not only to expand the canon or recognize non-European intellectual traditions, but to do so in ways that call into question the deeply entrenched territorialist and culturalist assumptions (concerning place, ethnicity, consciousness, and political subjectivity) that continue to overdetermine these fields of reflection. Such an approach would challenge methodologies that depend on unreflective notions of origin, tradition, and context.

On a different front, deprovincializing should also lead us to examine how processes, contradictions, and struggles in the Global South (concerning, for example, privatization, austerity, shantytowns, resource struggles, authoritarian statism) may be viewed as harbingers of worldwide shifts, crucibles for new forms of worldwide social conflict, and situations from which to theorize the contemporary global situation.[42] We can analyze how the rapid changes unfolding in places like China, Singapore, and Mumbai are creating new global standards and serving as aspirational models for peoples around the world (including former imperial centers),[43] as well as new avenues for thinking political and aesthetic modernity (see Hitchcock in this volume). This work would also entail attending to new practices of imperialism or internationalism *within* the Global South, to new forms of South-South relations, whether as sources of inequality or solidarity. The critique of Western power, Eurocentric epistemology, and persistent imperial assumptions (about civilization, humanity, legality, etc.) remains a pressing contemporary task. But at a moment when global forms of interpenetration and interdependence have never been more determining, when "the West" is rapidly losing its control over the world economy and geopolitics, and when the need to think about democracy, solidarity, and justice on planetary scales has never been more urgent, such a critique cannot be based on reified territorial, cultural, or identitarian assumptions.

In sum, the work of deprovincializing the Global South requires us to reject monolithic models and one-dimensional analyses of epochs, regions, and civilizations. It means, for example, disaggregating "modern," "Western," and "liberal" from one another. It means attending as much to differences within, and the multiplicities that characterize, a given time, place, religion, or culture as to differences between them. It means following the lead of colonized and non-Western historical actors who regularly sought *within* existing social formations resources and allies through which to engage in anti-imperial struggles, craft new norms, enter into new configurations. It means understanding "tradition" in expansive political rather than narrow cultural terms, and expanding our conceptual matrices of the political. In other words, deprovincializing work entails dialectical thinking, immanent critique, and identifying objects of analysis as non-self-identical. Such an approach should lead us to reconsider the supposed distance between Marxist and postcolonial critiques.

Beyond Marxism versus Postcolonialism

We have been describing the ways in which the current political and intellectual conjuncture have resulted in a pronounced difficulty in defining emancipatory projects and envisioning postcapitalist and postimperial forms of life. One symptom of this impasse is the renewed indictment of postcolonial theory's incompatibility with Marxist critique, a charge illustrated in Vivek Chibber's *Postcolonial Theory and the Specter of Capital* (2013). In this polemic, Chibber vehemently takes issue with the particularizing claims of the subaltern studies project against a capitalist universalism. The latter, he argues, can only be countered by a universalist theorization of liberation rooted in the Enlightenment tradition. Enacting current mainstream anxieties over incompatible civilizations, broadsides like this rehearse the familiar standoffs between universalism and particularism, foundationalism and relativism, reason and tradition, class and race, secularism and faith, European modernity and subaltern subject positions. The book retreads the methodological debates characterized by earlier Marxist critiques of postcolonialism[44] while all but ignoring substantial and continued scholarly efforts to show the entangled nature of the two fields.[45]

Given the contemporary moment of interrelated financial crises, imperial wars, debt capture, and uneven development (between the West and the Global South but also within each), we maintain that the critical approaches embodied in varieties of Marxism and postcolonial theory constitute two indispensable and necessarily overlapping intellectual traditions. Both have provided powerful critiques of modernity and theories of liberation from occluded standpoints, *each of which entails the other*.[46] While new mutations in capitalism and changing formations of imperialism require us to rethink aspects of each tradition, both remain invaluable resources for understanding the political present.

From the start, many currents of postcolonial theory worked toward new syntheses of Marxism, poststructuralism, anti-imperialism, and non-European political traditions. But at a certain point, as we suggested above, Marxism was increasingly indicted alongside liberalism for its Eurocentric epistemology and theory of history. This drift was perhaps best exemplified by the influential distinction that Dipesh Chakrabarty made between the universal and Eurocentric history of capitalism (History 1) and the refractory currents of local non-Western history (History 2) that resisted being subsumed within the logic, power, and purview of the former.[47] Recent postcolonial scholarship, however, has attempted to develop a more integrated understanding of capitalism and colonialism (or Marxism and anticolonialism). Thus Rahul Rao suggests that attending to the intersections of postcolonial and Marxist methodologies means "finding ways of thinking about different forms of injustice together."[48] He calls for a kind of critical thinking "that is situated in a position of productive ambivalence with respect to both postcolonialism and Marxism on account of its refusal to accord any one axis of subordination analytical or normative priority."[49]

In a similar vein, Sandro Mezzadra reconciles Marxist and postcolonial approaches around the analytic of labor. Rather than the alternative modernities approach—"with distinctive and stable features making up their 'cultural' specificity"[50]—Mezzadra stresses the multiplicity emerging from capitalism as it shapes and uses labor in a wide variety of forms. That "free" wage labor may not characterize the majority of workers in the postcolonial world (given the persistence of informal, unpaid, or indentured labor) leads not to an assertion of a space of cultural difference; it is rather evidence of "the multiple ways in which labor power is commodified, and subsumed under capital."[51] Mezzadra seeks to rethink the foundational concepts of political modernity—capital, state, labor—from the standpoint of imperial processes that have proved all too compatible with capitalist ones. Yet he refuses to choose one—either imperialism or capitalism—as the privileged analytic, moving us beyond the false "choice" between either Marxist or postcolonial methods.

Vinay Gidwani too develops an integrated analytic approach. In *Capital Interrupted*, he does not regard capitalism and colonialism as separate axes of subordination. But he does extend Chakrabarty's postcolonial critique of Marxist historicism to challenge any conception of (non-European) capitalism as a complete totality or organic unity that unfolds according to a necessary logic. Gidwani's historical geography of the "agrarian question" in Gujarat India demonstrates how capitalism's "economic rationality is always contaminated by other (potentially interruptive) cultural logics" and "value-creating" practices. For Gidwani, this heterogeneity reveals the limitations of orthodox Marxism to grasp agrarian capitalism. He also indicates, however, that it is the very source capitalism's power and must be understood in Marxian terms.[52]

The attempt to overcome the opposition between Marxism and postcolonial critique, in order to grasp non-European capitalism on its own terms, has been pursued with special insight by Kalyan Sanyal and Harry Harootunian. In *Rethinking Capitalist Development: Primitive Accumulation, Governmentality, and Post-colonial Capitalism* (2007), Sanyal reconceptualizes the postcolonial world's apparent "failure" to develop by reconsidering the Marxist category of primitive accumulation. Rather than a sequential narrative of precapitalism that must give way to capitalism—or remain forever arrested at the moment of transition—he theorizes the continued coexistence of capital and noncapital in a complex configuration he terms the "post-colonial economic." Although positing a different formation of capitalist development in the postcolonial world, Sanyal's point is not to retrieve "an original and authentic space entirely outside the reach of development,"[53] whose subjects intuitively oppose the modernizing West. Rather, his "rendition of development as a complex hegemonic space, in which tradition and modernity, capital and pre-capital, converge, coalesce, and constitute each other, makes visible a terrain of counterhegemonic politics within the space of development itself."[54] In short, Sanyal offers a rigorous, comprehensive theorization of *postcolonial capitalism*—a notion that cannot be conceptualized without the Marxian concept of primitive accumulation or the situated production of economic knowledge in postcolonial India.

In *Marx after Marx* (2015), Harootunian explicitly criticizes the culturalist orientation of postcolonial studies and postwar Frankfurt School Marxism.[55] Both, he argues, mistakenly viewed capitalism through a Eurocentric lens; neither properly grasped its uneven, hybrid, and global character. Like Sanyal, Harootunian argues that primitive accumulation was not a founding event, but an ongoing aspect of modern capitalism. Through "formal subsumption" global capitalism has always been able to incorporate, without transforming, seemingly archaic or incommensurable forms of life and modes of production to the accumulation process. For this reason capitalist and colonial domination cannot be grasped apart from each other. Yet for Harootunian, the coexistence within a single uneven present of multiple forms of production and their different temporalities creates transformative possibilities that can point toward radically different futures. He recounts that while capitalist modernization led European Marxists to gradually lose sight of this original Marxian understanding, non-Western Marxists continued to attend to capitalist unevenness and to therefore reject progressive, teleological, and stagist conceptions of history. Among them were thinkers from the European periphery (Lenin, Luxemburg, Lukàcs, Trotsky) and from the Global South (José Carlos Mariátegui, Yamada Yoritaro, and Uno Kozo). Harootunian thus frames his intervention as an attempt to "deprovincialize Marxism." He may be an outspoken critic of postcolonial theory, yet his work—his attention to the indissociable character of imperialism and capitalism, his attempt to move beyond both postcolonial anti-Marxism and Western forms of Eurocentric Marxism, his call to deprovincialize critical theory, and his attention to multiple temporalities—is indispensable to any attempt to rethink postcolonial theory for the global present.

In a similar spirit, several essays in our collection can be understood as part of the broader intellectual current that rejects the false opposition of these two methodologies. Like the thinkers just mentioned, they do not seek a zero-sum game between Marxism's "universal truths" and postcolonialism's incommensurable differences. Rather, the two discourses are allowed to contaminate and restructure, "to confront and enliven each other"[56] in the attempt to grasp the postcolonial contemporary and its resurgent forms of imperial value extraction. Thus, a number of the essays that follow use situated histories of anticapitalist thought and practice to advance new articulations of postcolonial Marxism, retooling and retemporalizing the concept along the way. Gidwani epitomizes such generative thinking in his piece for this volume, which addresses the "multiform waste hub" of Madanpur Khadar in Delhi. Combining a deep engagement with Marx's writings on waste with an ethnographic study of the lives of waste-pickers—whose "infrastructural work" maintains and reproduces the urban economy—his essay thinks through the intersections of labor, ecology, and waste under India's neoliberal conditions of a "future without work."

In a different key, Gary Wilder's piece undertakes a deep interrogation of W. E. B. Du Bois's radical humanist thought and the attempt "to conjugate Marxism with the Negro Problem." Reading via a theoretical chiasmus (to use a literary figure), Wilder recharts Du Bois's intellectual trajectory by showing how he "used Marx to challenge the orthodox Left and used the (black) American historical situation to rethink orthodox Marxism." Meanwhile, Rao reads the problem of caste through early twentieth-century discourses of international Marxism (as well as of slavery and race), and Lambert considers memories of Grenada's black radical tradition and revolution through a queer analytic. Watson offers an anachronistic reading of the forgotten Marxists repressed and exiled by model Asian capitalist postcolonies, Singapore and South Korea, while Chari rethinks the "mysterious" and nonteleological contours of radical South African anti-apartheid urban movements.

Postcolonial Spatiality and New Political Imaginaries

Paralleling the tendency to falsely pit Marxism and postcolonialism against each other, otherwise diverse currents of criticism have tended to figure the global order and imperial domination in binary terms. Such approaches—whether organized around center/periphery, metropole/colony, West/non-West, West/East, or North/South poles—often map political subjectivity onto geographic or cultural location. Such oppositions typically obstruct rather than illuminate the complexity and dynamism that exist within colonial situations, the larger frames within which such situations need to be understood, and the relationship between colonial pasts and postcolonial presents. However unintended, such criticism has often betrayed a preoccupation with metropolitan forms, influences, and recognition and thereby reinscribed some of the invidious biocultural distinctions, through supposedly neutral territorial divisions, it was meant to contest.

The various regional emphases of the essays collected here do not attempt any sort of global "coverage." Nor is our logic merely to extend postcolonial studies into regions hitherto outside its purview. Rather, the diversity of the problematics undertaken here help make visible new analytical and methodological frameworks beyond those sedimented in binary territorial or civilizational terms. These essays signal an attempt to reckon with new and persisting postcolonial predicaments by reconsidering the relationship between geographic/spatial configuration and political imagination. A postcolonial approach to the contemporary conjuncture must, for example, engage with the question of mass democracy in the Global South. Recent interventions along these lines include Partha Chatterjee's conceptions of "political society" and "the politics of the governed," James Holston's reflections on "insurgent citizenship," Timothy Mitchell's genealogy of "carbon democracy," Asaf Bayat's conceptions of "contentious politics" and "social nonmovements" in the Middle East, and Behrooz Ghamari-Tabrizi's reconsideration of the Iranian Revolution through the lens of "political spirituality."[57] In this volume, Forment's rich ethnography of the Buenos Aires Salada Market (or "the poor people's shopping mall") furthers these interventions. He demonstrates that existing categories such as Chatterjee's "political society," populism, or rentier democracy are inadequate to capture the contours of new moral economies and political formations now emerging under conditions of austerity and neoliberalism in the Global South. Through his concepts of "plebeian democracy" and "plebeian citizenship," Forment reveals the market as a stage for complex struggles over "mimetic" production and consumption, labor and rights, thus reconfiguring ethicopolitical practices and notions of selfhood. Such investigations enlarge postcolonial studies' more typical focus on center-periphery relations, orienting the field instead toward creative contestations of substantive democracy.

Especially salient here are the political landscapes of Latin America, a region long ignored by the field's focus on African and Asian decolonization. As Fernando Coronil has pointed out, not only does the inclusion of Latin America expand the field's geographical and temporal scope and reveal the roots of capitalism and modernity "as a global process" since the sixteenth century,[58] it also prioritizes two aspects of postcolonialism often subordinated in its backward glances: those "historical transformations after political independence, and the analysis of contemporary imperialism."[59] Thus, studies like Forment's are valuable for moving beyond negative critique—the anatomy of imperial/capitalistic violence and exploitation—in order to begin to posit what more substantial democracies, equitable societies, and unalienated life-forms look like. Such scholarship makes subaltern social actors not just figures of resistance, but resources for contemporary political thinking.

The study of mass democracy in the Global South overlaps analytically with the study of postcolonial urbanism, a phenomenon often cast as either apocalyptic (for example, Mike Davis's 2006 *Planet of Slums*) or the site of potential entrepreneurialism to be fostered by neoliberal developmental initiatives.[60] A bipolar object that has incited both the most optimistic and pessimistic of visions, the postcolonial city is a complex entity made up of historical, economic, aesthetic, and ecological forces that cannot but exceed the categorical thinking of East/West, traditional/modern, native/foreign.[61] Yet despite the fact that postcolonial cities are sites of cultural entanglement and the co-production of urban modernities par excellence, analyses of them have often been subordinated to either the empiricism of urban studies (spatial uses, districts, typologies) or the master signifiers of economic development, growth, and investment. In contrast, the Global South metropolis may best be seen as the spatial form that, like a palimpsest, most directly mediates between colonial legacies and global futures.[62] Peter Hitchcock's essay, epitomizing such a spirit, breaks with dominant empiricist analytical categories to think the postcolonial city in relation to one of its most ambiguous qualities: velocity. Attending especially to its aesthetic dimensions, Hitchcock offers a new framework and vocabulary for the city such as the analytics of "the speed of place" and "the space of time." His evocative reading of "postcolonial obsolescence" in Jeet Thayil's novel *Narcopolis* (2012) links histories of colonial urban temporality with a postcolonial critique of speed.

The speed of environmental violence has become a key concept within the vast scholarly explosion in ecological criticism. Postcolonial thinkers such as Rob Nixon (2011), Upamanyu Pablo Mukherjee (2010), George B. Handley and Elizabeth Deloughrey (2011), and Dipesh Chakrabarty—who has boldly called for new "nonontological ways of thinking of the human" in order to grapple with humanity's role in the Anthropocene (2012),[63]—have helped define a growing body of work. In it, they theorize the profound alignments between imperialist (and increasingly militarist) extractive technologies and the environmental devastations of the postcolonial world. Like the study of mass democracy and postcolonial urbanism, postcolonial ecological thinking offers a potentially rich vantage point from which to theorize translocal solidarities and to articulate new political demands. Because of both the disproportionate ecological impact on indigenous populations and the new forms of imperialist extraction—"sometimes through outright, unregulated plunder, sometimes under camouflage of developmental agendas"[64]—it is clear that environmental politics in the Global South will not and cannot follow the contours of earlier anticolonialist imaginaries, nor strategies of cultural self-determination. Stephen Muecke's essay in our collection, situated in the struggles of the Goolarabooloo people of northwestern Australia, contributes to a rethinking of a politics of the present by moving beyond the preoccupations of settler colonial theory to consider global discourses of transnational mining companies in relation to indigenous politics. Muecke views the struggle waged by local communities against both mining companies and the Australian corporate state as evidence not of an authentic indigenous episteme to be preserved—the "usual dialectic of modernization and its critique"—but indicative of struggles over networked institutions in the face of "global colonialism." The space of the local, native, or indigenous is not merely one of uncontamination, but is revealed to be a complex and resilient resource for negotiating the institutional arrangements of science, technology, and modernity.

A final emerging spatial-political problematic may better be described by a question: What happens to the assumed territorial analytics of postcolonial studies when we shift configurations of decolonization away from Third World national and regional formations that have generated the most attention in the field (typically, South Asia, Africa, and the Caribbean), complicating the presumed binary between peripheral nation-states and the imperial domination of the center? More specifically, what happens if we rethink postcolonialism with and through the Cold War and postsocialism, as Sharad Chari and Katherine Verdery have suggested,[65] and think decolonization through an aligned, rather than unaligned, political lens? In recent years the field of Cold War studies has seen a shift from the study of an abstract power struggle between the United States and the Soviet Union to the conflict's social and microhistories, Cold War subject formation, and the interplay between decolonization, the Third World, and the rise of the American Empire. Works such as Odd Arne Westad's *Global Cold War* (2005), Chen Kuan-hsing's *Asia as Method* (2010), Heonik Kwon's *The Other Cold War* (2010), and Jodi Kim's *Ends of Empire* (2010) have suggested that the processes of decolonization, crossed by the binarism of Cold War politics, result in an influential structure of domination that mobilizes bodies, facilitates transnational engagements, and builds global imaginaries in ways that overlap with those already mapped out by postcolonial theory—but are not identical to them.

The point, again, is not that postcolonial scholarship ought to abandon the interrogation of Western colonial forms and their aftermaths and replace this concern with Cold War binarisms. The wager is, rather, that if the distinct ideological and geographical tensions of the Cold War were the very *form* that decolonization took in certain regions, such forms help us understand the complexity of our postcolonial present as simultaneously configured by Cold War imaginaries and aftermaths. The Cold War's specific character of state militarism, competitive nationalisms, socialist utopianism and vehement anticommunism dramatically shaped alignments and forged new moral and political boundaries across decolonizing nations in East and Southeast Asia and beyond that continue to structure our postcolonial contemporary.[66] Like Abbas's theoretical revision of postcolonial studies that troubles the reification of "Western" and "non-Western" cultural and political artifacts (discussed above), viewing the Cold War *as* decolonizing process complicates the story of European colonial tyranny versus non-European national liberation, center versus periphery, Western hegemony versus Eastern subordination. Reading Tan Pin Pin's documentary on Singaporean political exiles and Hwang Sŏk-yŏng's novel on the 1980 Gwangju Uprising, Jini Kim Watson's essay here shows how the "failed" Marxist longings of East and Southeast Asia's decolonization processes interrupt exemplary state narratives of hyper growth. Meanwhile, both Alessandrini's and Lambert's essays return to the uneasy Cold War revolutionary conjunctures of Iran and Grenada, respectively.

In sum, the essays collected here engage creatively with the conjuncture and problematic of the postcolonial contemporary. In their different ways, they point beyond some of the spatial, temporal, and political binaries that have subtended many of the debates in the field. Whether it is Arabic avant-garde literature, South Africa's unredeemed anti-apartheid struggles, the untimeliness of Grenada's socialist revolution, or thinking Foucault with Iran, these essays are both indebted to, and move beyond, those concepts of history, race, culture, empire, and capital that postcolonial studies has so forcefully made available to analysis. It is our hope that the essays collected here offer some beginnings for rethinking postcolonial theory for our belated, anticipatory, uneven, and wholly interconnected world.

NOTES

1. A parallel set of questions has recently been raised in Ann Laura Stoler, *Duress: Imperial Durabilities in Our Times* (Durham, N.C.: Duke University Press, 2016). She too incites scholars to pay close attention to the continuities and discontinuities across the colonial divide.

2. Some of the founding interventions include Talal Asad, "Two European Images of Non-European Rule," in *Anthropology and the Colonial Encounter*, ed. Talal Asad; Edward Said, *Orientalism* (New York: Pantheon Books, 1978); Said, *Culture and Imperialism*; Ashis Nandy, *The Intimate Enemy: Loss and Recovery of Self under Colonialism* (Oxford: Oxford University Press, 1983); Guha, *Elementary Aspects*; Chandra Talpade Mohanty, "Under Western Eyes: Feminist Scholarship and Colonial Discourses," *boundary 2* (1984): 333–58; Lata Mani, "The Production of an Official Discourse on Sati in Early Nineteenth-Century Bengal," in *Europe and its Others*, ed. Francis Barker et al. (Colchester: University of Essex, 1985), 1:107–27; Mani, "Contentious Traditions," 119–56; Abdul R. JanMohamed, "The Economy of Manichean Allegory: The Function of Racial Difference in Colonialist Literature," *Critical Inquiry* 12, no. 1 (1985): 59–87; Henry Louis Gates, ed., *Race, Writing and "Difference"* (Chicago: University of Chicago Press, 1986); Chatterjee, *Nationalist Thought*; Bernard S. Cohn, *An Anthropologist among the Historians and Other Essays* (Oxford: Oxford University Press, 1987); Gayatri Chakravorty Spivak, *In Other Worlds: Essays in Cultural Politics* (New York: Routledge, 1987); Spivak, "Can the Subaltern Speak?"; Benita Parry, "Problems in Current Theories of Colonial Discourse," *Oxford Literary Review* 9, no. 1 (1987): 27–58; Guha and Spivak, eds., *Selected Subaltern Studies*; Timothy Mitchell, *Colonizing Egypt* (Berkeley: University of California Press, 1988); Sara Suleri, *Meatless Days* (Chicago: University of Chicago Press, 1989); Gauri Viswanathan, *Masks of Conquest: Literary Study and British Rule in India* (Oxford: Oxford University Press, 1989); Bill Ashcroft, Helen

Tiffin, and Gareth Griffiths, eds., *The Empire Writes Back: Theory and Practice in Post-Colonial Literature* (London: Routledge, 1989); Gilroy, *The Black Atlantic*; Bhabha, *The Location of Culture*.

3. See, for example, Gayatri Chakravorty Spivak, "Subaltern Studies: Deconstructing Historiography," in *Selected Subaltern Studies*, ed. Guha and Spivak; Robert J. C. Young, *White Mythologies: Writing History and the West* (New York: Routledge, 1990).

4. Guha, *Elementary Aspects*; Spivak, "Can the Subaltern Speak?"; Mani, "Contentious Traditions"; Talal Asad, *Genealogies of Religion: Discipline and Reasons of Power in Christianity and Islam* (Baltimore: Johns Hopkins University Press, 1993); Chakrabarty, "Postcoloniality and the Artifice of History."

5. Said, *Orientalism*; Cohn, *Anthropologist among the Historians*; Bhabha, *Location of Culture*; V. Y. Mudimbe, *The Invention of Africa: Gnosis, Philosophy, and the Order of Knowledge* (Bloomington: University of Indiana Press, 1988); James Clifford, *The Predicament of Culture: Twentieth-Century Ethnography, Literature, and Art* (Cambridge, Mass.: Harvard University Press, 1988); Achille Mbembe, "Provisional Notes on the Postcolony," *Africa* 62, no. 1 (1992): 3–37; Gilroy, *Black Atlantic*; Stuart Hall, "Cultural Identity and Diaspora," in *Identity: Community, Culture, Difference*, ed. *Jonathan Rutherford* (London: Lawrence and Wishart, 1990); Mary Louise Pratt, Imperial Eyes: Travel Writing and Transculturation (New York: Routledge, 1992).

6. Kwame Anthony Appiah, "Is the Post- in Postmodernism the Post- in Postcolonial?" *Critical Inquiry*, 17, no. 2 (1991): 336–57.

7. Hall, "When Was 'The Post-Colonial'?" 244.

8. Ibid., 247. Hall was less concerned with Western knowledge's inability to grasp other cultures on their own terms than with the way its "binary forms of narrativization" erased these transcultural processes (251).

9. See, for example, Stuart Hall et. al., *Policing the Crisis: Mugging, the State and Law and Order* (London: Palgrave Macmillan, 1978); Paul Gilroy, *There Ain't No Black in the Union Jack: The Cultural Politics of Race and Nation* (Chicago: University of Chicago Press, 1987); Etienne Balibar, "Is There a Neo-Racism," and Etienne Balibar, "Racism and Nationalism," both in *Race, Nation, Class, Ambiguous Identities*, ed. Etienne Balibar and Immanuel Wallerstein (New York: Verso, 1991); Salman Rushdie, *Imaginary Homelands: Essays and Criticism, 1981–1991* (New York: Penguin, 1991); Rob Nixon, *London Calling: V.S. Naipaul, Postcolonial Mandarin* (Oxford: Oxford University Press, 1992); Maxim Silverman, *Deconstructing the Nation: Immigration, Racism and Citizenship in Modern France* (London: Routledge, 1992); Said, *Culture and Imperialism*; Edward Said, *Reflections on Exile and Other Essays* (Cambridge, Mass.: Harvard University Press, 2000); Tyler Stovall, *Paris Noir: African Americans in the City of Light* (New York: Houghton Mifflin, 1996); Stoler and Cooper, eds., *Tensions of Empire*; Antoinette Burton, *At the Heart of the Empire: Indians and the Colonial Encounter in Late-Victorian Britain Hardcover* (Berkeley: University of California Press, 1998); Ian Baucom, *Out of Place: Englishness, Empire, and the Locations of Identity* (Princeton: Princeton University Press, 1999); Ann Laura Stoler, "Racist Visions for the Twenty-First Century: On the Cultural Politics of the French Radical Right," *Journal of the International Institute* 7, no. 1 (1999): 1–20; Catherine Hall, *Civilising Subjects: Metropole and Colony in the English Imagination, 1830–1867* (Chicago: University of Chicago Press, 2002).

10. Shohat, "Notes on the 'Post-colonial'"; Ahmad, *In Theory*; Dirlik, *Postcolonial Aura*; Miyoshi, "Borderless World?"

11. On "epistemic violence," see Gayatri Chakravorty Spivak, "The Rani of Sirmur: An Essay in Reading the Archives," *History and Theory* 24, no. 3 (October 1985): 247–272; Spivak, "Can the Subaltern Speak." See also Asad, ed., *Anthropology and the Colonial Encounter*; Nicholas B. Dirks, ed., *Colonialism and Culture* (Ann Arbor: University of Michigan Press, 1992); Bernard S. Cohn, *Colonialism and Its Forms of Knowledge: The British in India* (Princeton: Princeton University Press, 1996).

12. Ann McClintock, "The Angel of Progress: The Pitfalls of the Term 'Post-Colonialism'," *Social Text* 31/32 (1992): 84–98; Ann Laura Stoler and Frederick Cooper, "Between Metropole and Colony: Rethinking a Research Agenda," in *Tensions of Empire*, ed. Stoler and Cooper; John L. Comaroff and Jean Comaroff, *Of Revelation and Revolution*, vol. 2: *The Dialectics of Modernity on a South African Frontier* (Chicago: University of Chicago Press, 1997).

13. Among them were Bernard S. Cohn, Ranajit Guha, and the first generation of works associated with the Subaltern Studies Collective, Jean and John Comaroff, Fernando Coronil, Nicholas Dirks, Thomas C. Holt, Sidney Mintz, Michel Rolph-Trouillot, Mrinalini Sinha, Ann Laura Stoler, Louise White, Eric Wolf, and Megan Vaughn. As late as 1997 Stoler and Cooper situated their widely read volume *Tensions of Empire* explicitly against the new discourse of "postcoloniality . . . because it homogenizes a power relationship whose limitations and contingencies need to be examined" and "it suggests an essential quality to the fact of having been colonized, implying that colonialism was the only thing of importance to people who live in what were once colonies" ("Between Metropole and Colony," 33). In the essays collected in *Selected Subaltern Studies* as well as *Elementary Aspects of Peasant Insurgency in Colonial India* (1988), *Nationalist Thought and the Colonial World* (1989), *Rethinking Working-Class History* (1989), and *The Construction of Communalism in Colonial North India* (1992), Guha, Chatterjee, Chakrabarty, Gyanendra Pandey and their colleagues only used the term "postcolonial" as a periodizing marker to indicate the societies or states that developed after the end of colonial rule.

14. Gayatri Chakravorty Spivak, *Outside in the Teaching Machine* (New York: Routledge, 1993), 50, 70; Gayatri Chakravorty Spivak, "Bonding in Difference: Interview with Alfred Arteaga (1993–94)," in *The Spivak Reader: Selected Works of Gayatri Chakravorty Spivak*, ed. Donna Landry and Gerald Maclean (New York: Routledge, 1996), 28. For exemplary elaborations of this dilemma, see Chatterjee, *Nationalist Thought*, and Chatterjee, *The Nation and its Fragments*. On the challenge that this emergent postcolonial critique began to pose for the human sciences see Edward Said, "Representing the Colonized: Anthropology's Interlocutors," *Critical Inquiry* 15, no. 2 (1989): 205–25; Carol A. Breckenridge and Peter van der Veer, *Orientalism and the Postcolonial Predicament Perspectives on South Asia* (Philadelphia: University of Pennsylvania Press, 1993); James Clifford and George E. Marcus, eds., *Writing Culture* (Berkeley: University of California Press, 1986).

15. Chatterjee, *Nation and Its Fragments*, 11.

16. Said, *Culture and Imperialism*, 18.

17. Chakrabarty, "Postcoloniality and the Artifice of History"; Gyan Prakash, "Postcolonial Criticism and Indian Historiography," *Social Text* 31/32 (1992): 8–19; Gyan Prakash, "Subaltern Studies as Postcolonial Criticism," *American Historical Review* 99, no. 5 (1994): 1475–90.

18. Hall, "When Was 'The Post-Colonial'?" 253.

19. David Scott, "The Aftermaths of Sovereignty," *Social Text* 48 (Fall 1996): 1–26.

20. Ibid. We can see this crystallization of postcolonialism as an analytic term that describes a field of study in Leela Gandhi, *Postcolonial Theory* (New York: Columbia University Press, 1998).

21. Scott, "Aftermaths of Sovereignty."

22. Miyoshi, "Borderless World?" See also Frederic Jameson and Masao Miyoshi, eds., *The Cultures of Globalization* (Durham, N.C.: Duke University Press, 1998); John L. Comaroff and Jean Comaroff, *Millennial Capitalism and the Culture of Neoliberalism* (Durham, N.C.: Duke University Press, 2001); Timothy Brennan, "From Development to Globalization: Postcolonial Studies and Globalization Theory," in *The Cambridge Companion to Postcolonial Literary Studies*, ed. Neil Lazarus (Cambridge: Cambridge University Press, 2004); Benita Parry, *Postcolonial Studies: A Materialist Critique* (London: Routledge, 2004).

23. Appadurai, *Modernity at Large*; Hardt and Negri, *Empire*. See also Gopal Balikrishnan, ed., *Debating Empire* (New York: Verso, 2003). Spivak increasingly attempted to think the relation

between globalization and postcolonialism in, for example, *A Critique of Postcolonial Reason* (Cambridge, Mass.: Harvard University Press, 1999) and *Death of a Discipline*.

24. Trouillot, *Global Transformations*. Like Stuart Hall and Paul Gilroy, Trouillot questioned Western scholarship's tendency to disavow the centrality of this mixture in the making of the modern world but suggested that new processes of globalization might allow critics to recognize the mismatch between conventionally bounded categories of social analysis (e.g., peoples, cultures, nations, states) and the heterogeneous (postcolonial) world they confronted.

25. Simon Gikandi, "Globalization and the Claims of Postcoloniality," *South Atlantic Quarterly* 100, no. 3 (2001): 627–58, 630.

26. Dirlik, "Global South," 19; emphasis added. Note also the increased interest in South-South solidarity and cultural transmissions as manifested in recent studies of the Bandung, the Afro-Asian solidarity moment, and its afterlives. See, for example, Christopher J. Lee, ed., *Making a World after Empire: The Bandung Moment and Its Political Afterlives* (Athens: Ohio University Press, 2010); Hala Halim, "*Lotus*, the Afro-Asian Nexus, and Global South Comparison," *Comparative Studies of South Asia, Africa and the Middle East* 32, no. 3 (2012): 563–83.

27. Timothy Brennan, *At Home in the World: Cosmopolitanism Now* (Cambridge, Mass.: Harvard University Press, 1997); Pheng Cheah and Bruce Robbins, eds., *Cosmopolitics: Thinking and Feeling beyond the Nation* (Minneapolis: University of Minnesota Press, 1998); Bruce Robbins, *Feeling Global: Internationalism in Distress* (New York: New York University Press, 1999); Carole Breckenridge, Sheldon Pollock, Dipesh Chakrabarty, and Homi K. Bhabha, eds., *Cosmopolitanism* (Durham, N.C.: Duke University Press, 2002).

28. See, for example, Ileana Rodriguez and María Milagros López, eds., *The Latin American Subaltern Studies Reader* (Durham, N.C.: Duke University Press, 2001), and Mabel Moraña, Enrique D. Dussel, Carlos A. Jáuregui, eds., *Coloniality at Large: Latin America and the Postcolonial Debate* (Durham, N.C.: Duke University Press, 2008).

29. Martin Hose, "Postcolonial Theory and Greek Literature in Rome," *Greek, Roman, and Byzantine Studies* 40 (1999): 303–26; Jeffrey Jerome Cohen, ed., *The Postcolonial Middle Ages* (New York: Palgrave, 2000); Ania Loomba and Martin Orkin, eds., *Post-Colonial Shakespeares* (New York: Routledge, 2002); Bruce W. Holsinger, "Medieval Studies, Postcolonial Studies, and the Genealogies of Critique," *Speculum* 77 (2002): 1195–1227; Lisa Lowe, *Immigrant Acts: On Asian American Cultural Politics* (Durham, N.C.: Duke University Press, 1996), Sandra Buckley, "Japan and East Asia," in *A Companion to Postcolonial Studies*, ed. Henry Schwarz and Sangeeta Ray (Oxford: Blackwell, 2000); Jung-Bong Choi, "Mapping Japanese Imperialism onto Postcolonial Criticism," *Social Identities* 9, no. 3 (2003): 325–39; Leo Ching, *Becoming Japanese: Colonial Taiwan and the Politics of Identity* (Berkeley: University of California Press, 2001); Deborah L. Madsen, ed., *Beyond the Borders: American Literature and Post-Colonial Theory* (London: Pluto Press, 2003); Ann Laura Stoler, ed., *Haunted by Empire: Geographies of Intimacy in North American History* (Durham, N.C.: Duke University Press, 2006); Mayfair Mei-hui Yang, "Postcoloniality and Religiosity in Modern China: The Disenchantments of Sovereignty," *Theory, Culture and Society* 28, no. 2 (2011): 3–45.

30. This can be seen in the debate over postcolonial readings and appropriations of Frantz Fanon. Homi Bhabha, "Remembering Fanon: Self, Psyche, and the Colonial Condition," introduction to *Black Skin, White Masks*, by Frantz Fanon (London: Pluto Press, 1986); Bhabha, "What Does the Black Man Want," *New Formations* 1 (Spring 1987): 118–30; Bhabha, "Framing Fanon," introduction to *The Wretched of the Earth*, by Frantz Fanon (New York: Grove Press, 2004); Henry Louis Gates, "Critical Fanonism," *Critical Inquiry* 17, no. 3 (1991): 457–70; Lewis R. Gordon, *Fanon and the Crisis of European Man: An Essay on Philosophy and the Human Sciences* (New York: Routledge, 1995); Ato-Seyki Oto, *Fanon's Dialectic of Experience* (Cambridge, Mass.: Harvard University Press, 1996); Lewis R. Gordon, T. Denean Sharpley-Whiting, and Renee T. White, eds., *Fanon: A Critical Reader* (Oxford: Wiley Blackwell, 1996); David Scott, "Fanonian Futures,"

in *Refashioning Futures: Criticism after Postcoloniality* (Princeton: Princeton University Press, 1999); Neil Lazarus, *Nationalism and Cultural Practice in the Postcolonial World* (Cambridge: Cambridge University Press, 1999).

31. Ania Loomba, *Postcolonial Studies and Beyond* (Durham, N.C.: Duke University Press, 2005), 2.

32. Bayat and Dabashi, for example, may disagree about how revolutionary the Arab Spring really was, but they each suggest that it underscored the need to rethink assumptions about revolutionary anti-imperialism and postcolonial politics in our post–Cold War moment. Hamid Dabashi, *The Arab Spring: The End of Postcolonialism* (London: Zed Books, 2012); Asaf Bayat, "Revolution in Bad Times," *New Left Review* 80 (March–April 2013): 47–60.

33. On South-South solidarity, see Isabel Hofmeyr and Michelle Williams, "South Africa-India: Historical Connections, Cultural Circulations, and Socio-political Comparisons" in *South Africa and India: Shaping the Global South*, ed. Isabel Hofmeyr and Michelle Williams (Johannesburg: Wits University Press, 2011).

34. See, for example, Asad, *Formations of the Secular;* Asad, *On Suicide Bombing* (New York: Columbia University Press, 2007); Asad, "Thinking about Terrorism and Just War," *Cambridge Review of International Affairs* 23, no. 1 (2010): 3–24; Asad, "Reflections on Violence, Law, and Humanitarianism," *Critical Inquiry* 41, no. 2 (2015): 390–427; Asad, "Thinking about Tradition, Religion, and Politics in Egypt Today," *Critical Inquiry* 42, no. 1 (2015): 166–214.

35. See, for example, Antony Anghie, *Imperialism, Sovereignty, and the Making of International Law* (Cambridge: Cambridge University Press, 2007); Kevin Bruyneel, *The Third Space of Sovereignty: The Postcolonial Politics of U.S.-Indigenous Relations* (Minneapolis: University of Minnesota Press, 2007); Lorenzo Veracini, *Settler Colonialism: A Theoretical Overview* (London: Palgrave Macmillan, 2010); Jodi Byrd, *Transit of Empire: Indigenous Critiques of Colonialism* (Minneapolis: Minnesota University Press, 2011); Audra Simpson, *Mohawk Interruptus: Political Life across the Borders of Settler States* (Durham, N.C.: Duke University Press, 2014); Glen Coultard, *Red Skin, White Masks: Rejecting the Colonial Politics of Recognition* (Minneapolis: University of Minnesota Press, 2014); Aileen Moreten-Robinson, *The White Possessive: Property, Power, and Indigenous Sovereignty* (Minneapolis: University of Minnesota Press, 2015).

36. Scott, *Omens of Adversity*, 116. See also David Scott, *Conscripts of Modernity: The Tragedy of Colonial Enlightenment* (Durham, N.C.: Duke University Press, 2004).

37. See Chakrabarty, *Provincializing Europe*; Asad, *Formations of the Secular*; Walter Mignolo, *The Darker Side of Western Modernity: Global Futures, Decolonial Options* (Durham, N.C.: Duke University Press, 2011); Frank Wilderson, *Red, White, and Black: Cinema and the Structure of U.S. Antagonisms* (Durham, N.C.: Duke University Press, 2010).

38. On the paradox of an anticapitalist left that does not know what to desire, see Fernando Coronil, "The Future in Question: History and Utopia in Latin America (1989–2010)," in *Business as Usual: The Roots of the Global Financial Meltdown*, ed. Craig Calhoun and Georgi Derluguian (New York: New York University Press, 2011).

39. See Spivak, *Death of a Discipline*; Paul Gilroy, *Postcolonial Melancholia* (New York: Columbia University Press, 2005); Robert J. C. Young, "Postcolonial Remains," *New Literary History* 43 (2012): 19–42; Mbembe, *Critique de la Raison Nègre*.

40. Note that these positions seek to relate postcolonial criticism to the emerging political challenges of our historical present. Such moves thus differ, for example, from recent attempts by Partha Chatterjee and Dipesh Chakrabarty to move beyond the existing frameworks created by the Subaltern Studies Collective. Chatterjee has turned to ethnographic localism (as a corrective to methodological nationalism) and an affirmation of sovereign national states (against the imperialism of liberal internationalism). Chakrabarty has moved in the other direction, analyzing globalization in terms of climate change and the Anthropocene in ways that effectively sidestep the political questions concerning imperial asymmetries, global entanglement, human differentiation,

and planetary solidarity that postcolonial thinking needs to address today. See Partha Chatterjee, "After Subaltern Studies," *Economic and Political Weekly* 47, no. 35 (2012): 44–49; and Dipesh Chakrabarty, "The Climate of History: Four Theses," *Critical Inquiry* 35, no. 2 (2009): 197–222.

41. See Gary Wilder. *Freedom Time: Negritude, Decolonization, and the Future of the World* (Durham, N.C.: Duke University Press, 2015). See also Crystal Parikh, *Writing Human Rights* (Minneapolis: University of Minnesota Press, 2017).

42. See Jean Comaroff and John Comaroff, *Theory from the South* (Boulder, Colo.: Paradigm, 2012), and Mbembe, *Critique de la Raison Nègro*.

43. See Ong and Roy, *Worlding Cities* and Jini Kim Watson, "Aspirational City: Desiring Singapore and the Films of Tan Pin Pin," *Interventions: International Journal of Postcolonial Studies* 18, no. 4 (2016): 543–58.

44. Ahmad, *In Theory*; Dirlik, "Global South."

45. Young, *Postcolonialism*; Bartolovich and Lazarus, *Marxism, Modernity, and Postcolonial Studies.*

46. Cf. Cedric Robinson, *Black Marxism: The Making of the Black Radical Tradition* (Chapel Hill: University of North Carolina Press, 1983).

47. Chakrabarty, *Provincializing Europe*, 47–71.

48. Rao, "Recovering Reparative Readings of Postcolonialism and Marxism," 10.

49. Ibid., 9.

50. Mezzadra, "How Many Histories of Labour?" 156.

51. Ibid., 159.

52. Vinay Gidwani, *Capital Interrupted: Agrarian Development and the Politics of Work in India* (Minneapolis: University of Minnesota Press, 2008), xxiv, xix.

53. Kalyan Sanyal, *Rethinking Capitalist Development: Primitive Accumulation, Governmentality and Post-Colonial Capitalism* (New York: Routledge: 2007), 93.

54. Ibid., 92.

55. Harry Harootunian, *Marx after Marx: History and Time in the Expansion of Capitalism* (New York: Columbia University Press, 2015).

56. Vinay Gidwani. "The Lumpen, Again! Notes (from India and Elsewhere) on Postcolonial Capitalism" (lecture, CUNY Graduate Center, New York, N.Y., April 4, 2014.

57. Partha Chatterjee, *The Politics of the Governed: Reflections on Popular Politics in Most of the World* (New York: Columbia University Press, 2004); James Holston, *Insurgent Citizenship: Disjunctions of Democracy and Modernity in Brazil* (Princeton: Princeton University Press, 2008); Timothy Mitchell, *Carbon Democracy: Political Power in the Age of Oil* (New York: Verso, 2011); Asaf Bayat, *Life as Politics: How Ordinary People Change the Middle East*, 2nd ed. (Stanford: Stanford University Press, 2013); Bayat, "Plebeians of the Arab Spring," *Current Anthropology* 56, no. S11 (2015): 533–43; Behrooz Ghamari-Tabrizi, *Foucault in Iran: Revolution after the Enlightenment* (Minneapolis: University of Minnesota Press, 2016).

58. Coronil, "Latin American Postcolonial Studies," 239.

59. Ibid.

60. See Kanekanti Chandrashekar Smitha, ed., *Entrepreneurial Urbanism in India: The Politics of Spatial Restructuring and Local Contestation* (Singapore: Springer Singapore, 2017).

61. See Ryan Bishop et al., *Postcolonial Urbanism: Southeast Asian Cities and Global Processes* (New York: Routledge, 2003).

62. See Abidin Kusno, *Behind the Postcolonial: Architecture, Urban Space, and Political Cultures in Indonesia* (London: Routledge, 2000); Zeynep Çelik, *Urban Forms and Colonial Confrontation: Algiers under French Rule* (Berkeley: University of California Press, 1997); Ato Quayson, *Oxford Street, Accra: City Life and the Itineraries of Transnationalism* (Durham, N.C.: Duke University Press, 2014); Anne-Maria Makhulu, *Making Freedom: Apartheid, Squatter Politics, and the*

Struggle for Home (Durham, N.C.: Duke University Press, 2015). See also Ong and Roy, *Worlding Cities.*

63. Dipesh Chakrabarty, "Postcolonial Studies and the Challenge of Climate Change," *New Literary History* 43, no. 1 (2012): 1–18, 13.

64. Nixon, *Slow Violence*, 37.

65. See Sharad Chari and Katherine Verdery, "Thinking between the Posts: Postcolonialism, Postsocialism, and Ethnography after the Cold War," *Comparative Studies in Society and History* 51, no. 1 (2009): 6–34.

66. See also Monica Popescu, *South African Literature beyond the Cold War* (New York: Palgrave Macmillan, 2010).

BIBLIOGRAPHY

Ahmad, Aijaz. *In Theory: Classes, Nations, Literatures.* London: Verso, 2008.

Appadurai, Arjun. *Modernity at Large: Cultural Dimensions of Globalization.* Minneapolis: University of Minnesota Press, 1996.

Asad, Talal. *Formations of the Secular: Christianity, Islam, Modernity.* Stanford: Stanford University Press, 2003.

Asad, Talal, ed. *Anthropology and the Colonial Encounter.* Amherst, N.Y.: Humanity Books, 1973.

Bartolovich, Crystal, and Neil Lazarus. *Marxism, Modernity, and Postcolonial Studies.* Cambridge: Cambridge University Press, 2002.

Bhabha, Homi. *The Location of Culture.* New York: Routledge, 1994.

Chakrabarty, Dipesh. "Postcoloniality and the Artifice of History: Who Speaks for 'Indian' Pasts?" *Representations* 37, Special Issue: Imperial Fantasies and Postcolonial Histories (Winter 1992): 1–26.

———. *Provincializing Europe: Postcolonial Thought and Colonial Difference.* Princeton: Princeton University Press, 2000.

Chatterjee, Partha. *The Nation and Its Fragments: Colonial and Postcolonial Histories.* Princeton: Princeton University Press, 1993.

———. *Nationalist Thought in the Colonial World: A Derivative Discourse.* London: Zed Books, 1986.

Cohn, Bernard S. *An Anthropologist among the Historians and Other Essays.* Oxford: Oxford University Press, 1987.

Coronil, Fernando. "Latin American Postcolonial Studies and Global Decolonization." In *The Cambridge Companion to Postcolonial Literary Studies*, edited by Neil Lazarus, 221–40. Cambridge: Cambridge University Press, 2004.

Dirlik, Arif. "Global South: Predicament and Promise." *Global South* 1, no. 1–2 (2007): 12–23.

———. *The Postcolonial Aura: Third World Criticism in the Age of Global Capitalism.* Boulder, Colo.: Westview, 1998.

Gilroy, Paul. *The Black Atlantic: Modernity and Double Consciousness.* Cambridge, Mass.: Harvard University Press, 1993.

Guha, Ranajit. *Elementary Aspects of Peasant Insurgency in Colonial India.* London: Zed Books, 1983.

Guha, Ranajit, and Gayatri Chakravorty Spivak, eds. *Selected Subaltern Studies.* Oxford: Oxford University Press, 1988.

Hall, Stuart. "When Was 'The Post-Colonial'? Thinking at the Limit." In *The Postcolonial Question*, edited by Iain Chambers and Lidia Curti. London: Routledge, 1996.

Hardt, Michael, and Antonio Negri. *Empire.* Cambridge, Mass.: Harvard University Press, 2000.

Loomba, Ania, Suvir Kaul, Matti Bunzl, Antoinette Burton, and Jed Esty. "Beyond What? An Introduction." In *Postcolonial Studies and Beyond*, edited by Ania Loomba, Suvir Kaul, Matti Bunzl, Antoinette Burton, and Jed Esty, 1–39. Durham, N.C.: Duke University Press, 2005.

Mani, Lata. "Contentious Traditions: The Debate on Sati in Colonial India." *Cultural Critique* 7 (Fall 1987): 119–56.

Mbembe, Achille. *Critique de la Raison Nègre*. Paris: La Decourverte, 2013.

Mezzadra, Sandro. "How Many Histories of Labour? Toward a Theory of Postcolonial Capitalism." *Postcolonial Studies* 14, no. 2 (2011): 151–70.

Miyoshi, Masao. "A Borderless World? From Colonialism to Transnationalism and the Decline of the Nation-State." *Critical Inquiry* 19, no. 4 (1993): 726–51.

Nixon, Rob. *Slow Violence and the Environmentalism of the Poor*. Cambridge, Mass.: Harvard University Press, 2011.

Ong, Aiwha, and Ananya Roy, eds. *Worlding Cities: Asian Experiments and the Art of Being Global*. Malden, Mass.: Wiley-Blackwell, 2011.

Rao, Rahul. "Recovering Reparative Readings of Postcolonialism and Marxism." *Critical Sociology* (2016): 1–12.

Said, Edward. *Culture and Imperialism*. New York: Vintage, 1993.

———. *Orientalism*. New York: Pantheon Books, 1978.

Scott, David. *Omens of Adversity: Tragedy, Time, Memory, Justice*. Durham, N.C.: Duke University Press, 2014.

———. *Refashioning Futures: Criticism after Postcoloniality*. Princeton: Princeton University Press, 1999.

Shohat, Ella. "Notes on the 'Post-colonial.'" *Social Text* 31/32 (1992): 99–113.

Spivak, Gayatri Chakravorty. "Can the Subaltern Speak?" In *Marxism and the Interpretation of Culture*, edited by Cary Nelson and Lawrence Grossberg. Champaign: University of Illinois Press, 1988.

———. *Death of a Discipline*. New York: Columbia University Press, 2004.

Stoler, Ann Laura, and Frederick Cooper, eds. *Tensions of Empire: Colonial Cultures in a Bourgeois World*. Berkeley: University of California Press, 1997.

Trouillot, Michel-Rolph. *Global Transformations: Anthropology and the Modern World*. New York: Palgrave, 2003.

Young, Robert J. C. *Postcolonialism: An Historical Introduction*. Malden, Mass.: Wiley Blackwell, 2001.

O N E

Foucault, Fanon, Intellectuals, Revolutions

Anthony C. Alessandrini

> My theoretical ethic is . . . "antistrategic": to be respectful when a singularity
> revolts, intransigent as soon as power violates the universal. A simple choice, a
> difficult job: for one must at the same time look closely, a bit beneath history, at
> what cleaves it and stirs it, and keep watch, a bit behind politics, over what must
> unconditionally limit it. After all, that is my work; I am not the first or the only
> one to do it. But that is what I chose.
>
> —MICHEL FOUCAULT, "Useless to Revolt?"

What Comes after the Postcolonial?

The task we have been set here, as I understand it, is to think through what the editors of this volume have aptly described as "the postcolonial contemporary"—to attempt to map its contours or, at the very least, to help bring its horizons into focus. In this spirit, I am tempted to begin by asking for a moratorium (at the very least, a temporary one) on the very term "postcolonial." Given the amount of ink that has been spilled for or against the entity that has variously been called "postcolonial studies," "postcolonial theory," or sometimes simply "postcolonialism" (the last of these most often used by hostile critics who see it as an ideology rather than as a disciplinary or theoretical formation), there is something refreshing about the idea of stepping out into a different space altogether. My contribution to this conversation is intended to be a move, even if a preliminary one, in this direction.

If I nevertheless continue to use the word "postcolonial" in what follows, it is in the way I understand the term as it has emerged from readings of the work of thinkers and participants in the decolonization struggle such as Frantz Fanon and Edward Said: not as a sphere that is somehow separate from the hideous legacy of colonialism, and certainly not as a theoretical or ideological platform to which one must swear allegiance, but instead, as a temporal marker denoting a present that is not identical to the era of high colonialism but is nevertheless saturated by this past. The goal of thinking the postcolonial present, in other words, is to continue to ask the question that underwrites the work of

Fanon and Said (among many others): What might come *after* the postcolonial, and how can the continuing struggle for decolonization bring this future into the present?

To ask this question is also to invite a series of related questions about our postcolonial present. For example: How do we think through the ongoing popular struggles in the Middle East and North Africa that have collectively come to be known as "the Arab Spring," as well as the counterrevolutionary wave of state repression that has followed—especially at a moment when attention to the latter threatens to obliterate any attempts to remember the former?[1] And this invites another question: How can such a process of thinking through "the Arab Spring" contribute to a larger reexamination of our intellectual frameworks for understanding revolutions, particularly those revolutions that used to be (and still might be) thought of as part of the struggle for decolonization? Our ability to begin to address such questions goes to the very heart of asking what political solidarity and engaged intellectual work might mean today.

It should be said that the relationship between the revolutions and popular uprisings of the Arab Spring, on the one hand, and of actually existing postcolonial studies, on the other hand, is hardly a simple one, and has already been the cause of more than a little debate.[2] Should these popular uprisings and revolutions be considered as revolts against neocolonial regimes? Should they be understood more properly outside of national contexts, as part of a global movement against neoliberalism? How should the uprisings of 2011 be understood alongside previous revolutionary uprisings in the region—for example, the Egyptian Revolution of 1952, the Algerian Revolution, the Iranian Revolution of 1979 and the subsequent Green Revolution, and the decades-long struggle against settler colonialism in Palestine—many of which were (and in some cases, continue to be) articulated as specifically anticolonial or anti-imperialist struggles? How should the Arab Spring be understood in the aftermath of the U.S.-led wars and occupations in Iraq and Afghanistan, which continue to have massively destructive repercussions throughout the region, as well as the various forms of resistance to these occupations?

To suggest definitive answers to any of these questions would be foolish. There have, however, been attempts to view the Arab Spring specifically through the lens of postcolonial studies. The most ambitious is Hamid Dabashi's *The Arab Spring: The End of Postcolonialism* (2012), which argues, as its title implies, that these popular revolts should be seen as breaking out of the ideological contexts that have defined our thinking about the condition of postcoloniality. Describing the Arab Spring (as well as the Green Revolution in Iran, which he sees as its immediate precursor) as a process of "delayed defiance," Dabashi argues for understanding these uprisings as representing "liberation movements that are no longer trapped within postcolonial terms of engagement and are thus able to navigate uncharted revolutionary territories."[3] The new itineraries of such emergent uprisings, in other words, need a new framework of understanding, outside those provided by traditional notions of colonialism/postcolonialism. There are limitations to Dabashi's formulation, but it has the great advantage of reminding us that the postcolonial is, at best, a temporal holding area; contemporary political struggles are in part attempts to move into a different space altogether. Within this framework, the uprisings of 2011 (and the continuing struggles that they have inspired) provide an ongoing challenge to our thinking about the postcolonial contemporary.

"An Educated (though Stupid) White Man"? Rereading Foucault on Iran

Why, then, revisit the work of Michel Foucault as part of this attempt to engage with the revolutions of our moment as they "navigate uncharted revolutionary territories," to use Dabashi's words? After all, critics have noted that Foucault had relatively little to say about colonialism and anticolonial struggles, in any direct way, throughout most of his body of work. I have nothing to add to this more general point regarding the Eurocentrism of Foucault's work, except perhaps a proposal to place it within two larger contexts. The first is the general (and continuing) lack of engagement with postcolonial studies within French scholarship more generally; Achille Mbembe, among others, has described this as a form of provincialism within French thought from which we might, at last, begin to break away today.[4] The second context is the complex and layered history, still being told, of the interconnections between poststructuralist thought and French colonialism, especially in North Africa. As Robert J. C. Young pointed out twenty-five years ago (although many critics still have not managed to assimilate the point), "If so-called 'so-called poststructuralism' is the product of a single historical moment, then that moment is probably not May 1968 but rather the Algerian War of Independence."[5] Indeed, it is the *conjunctural* nature of poststructuralist thought, emerging as it did in a historical moment saturated by struggles for decolonization in Algeria (and elsewhere), that makes it particularly valuable for us to think with in a contemporary moment equally saturated by revolutionary (and counterrevolutionary) impulses and uprisings.

In what follows, I propose to revisit, not just Foucault's writings on Iran and the Iranian Revolution, but also the more recent body of work that responds to the period referred to by his hostile critics as Foucault's "Iranian adventure." It is important to specify what I am *not* proposing to do in this essay. For one thing, I am not suggesting that Foucault's Iranian writings can simply and directly be applied to the task of understanding the revolutions and uprisings of the Arab Spring. I'm not at all convinced that they can, and in any case, it is equally not my intention to somehow "make sense of the Arab Spring" through a reading of Foucault. Nor am I going to weigh in on the "correctness" of Foucault's analysis of the Iranian Revolution. Indeed, I am not even going to do an extended close reading of Foucault's writings on Iran, a task that has already been performed thoroughly and brilliantly by Behrooz Ghamari-Tabrizi in *Foucault in Iran: Islamic Revolution after the Enlightenment* (2016). Instead, I simply ask us to turn our attention to one aspect of Foucault's self-described "antistrategic" theoretical ethos as it is expressed in his writings on Iran. What makes these texts exemplary for a reinvigorated form of postcolonial studies today, I suggest, is precisely their openness to the singularity of ongoing revolutions, which allows Foucault to remain attuned to the possibilities that might emerge from revolutions in the process of their unfolding (this includes attention to those possibilities that he already suspects will subsequently be foreclosed, at least in the short term). The hostile reception accorded to these writings, by contrast, suggests the temptation to subject ongoing revolutions to the standards of our already existing theories of what revolutions "should" be. For a postcolonial studies that wishes to remain open to understanding, and thus supporting, new forms of resistance that have the potential to arise from ongoing revolutions like those of the Arab Spring, then, Foucault's writings, while they do not bear a one-to-one relationship to our postcolonial present, nevertheless contain some vitally important lessons.

Doing such work means, perhaps paradoxically, beginning with the reception of Foucault's writings on Iran before moving to his actual texts—that is, beginning from where we find ourselves nearly four decades after his texts were first published. The key text here is Janet Afary and Kevin B. Anderson's 2005 book *Foucault and the Iranian Revolution: Gender and the Seductions of Islamism*, which advertises itself as providing the first complete English translation of Foucault's journalistic writings and interviews on Iran from 1978 and 1979, as well as responses (mostly hostile) from other French commentators. As for Afary and Anderson's own analysis, the subtitle "the seductions of Islamism" reveals a great deal about their larger approach, not only to Foucault on Iran, but to his body of work more generally. Babak Rahimi, in his detailed review of *Foucault and the Iranian Revolution*, sums up Afary and Anderson's reading of Foucault: "Having depicted a belligerent and even (yes!) an anti-modern Foucault, who was allegedly unapologetic for the Islamists' atrocities after the revolution, . . . the book misleadingly presents Foucault as an educated (though stupid) white man who was naively seduced by the obscurantist features of Khomeini and Islamism."[6]

My intention is not to pursue a full reading of *Foucault and the Iranian Revolution* here; in any case, Jonathan Rée (2005), Richard Lynch (2007), and, especially, Rahimi have provided thorough critiques of Afary and Anderson's simplified and partial readings of Foucault's work, and have skillfully noted the authors' own deep-seated Eurocentric attitude toward what they interchangeably describe as "Islam" and "Islamism."[7] Overall, however, their book's general attitude toward Foucault's writings on the Iranian Revolution has taken hold to such an extent that when Slavoj Žižek makes reference to these writings in his 2009 book *In Defense of Lost Causes*, he feels unconstrained in referring simply to Foucault's "mistake" on Iran and in subsequently comparing Foucault's engagement with the Iranian Revolution to Heidegger's affiliation with the Nazi Party (thereby echoing Afary and Anderson's tendency to equate "Islamism" with fascism).[8] Žižek's particular pseudodialectical turnabout involves the suggestion that Foucault's "blunder"—in a parallel way (in his reading) to Heidegger's commitment to Nazism—subsequently compelled him "to radicalize his thought": "Foucault's Iranian engagement, like Heidegger's Nazi engagement, was in itself (in its form) an appropriative gesture, the best thing he ever did, the only problem being that it was (as to its content) a commitment in the wrong direction."[9] Despite this 180-degree turn, however, Žižek does not question the fundamental basis of Afary and Anderson's assumptions regarding Foucault's "mistake"; the suggestion that Foucault's writings on Iran constitute a clear and dangerous error is simply taken for granted.

I will return to this question of Foucault's "mistake" regarding the Iranian Revolution and how a different reading of his writings on Iran can, paradoxically, teach us something about approaching the ongoing uprisings and revolutions of our time (although I should reiterate that I am *not* suggesting that Foucault's observations regarding the Iranian Revolution can be simply or directly applied to the revolutions of our time). But in fact, the full lesson for us lies not only in Foucault's writings, but also in their reception by his critics. We might begin with the particular *tone* of the dismissals of Foucault on Iran, beginning with and subsequently inspired by Afary and Anderson's book. It is identical to the tone found in a more recent book, Vivek Chibber's *Postcolonial Theory and the Specter of Capital* (2013), which presents itself as a broadside against the limitations of postcolonial theory, although Chibber's specific target is the Subaltern Studies school, and even more specifically, the work of Partha Chatterjee, Ranajit Guha, and Dipesh Chakravarty.[10] What is striking about the tone of these books is their dismissive attitude toward the theorists and texts on which they lavish their attention, combined with a sense of ill-disguised glee when they find "errors" that support their dismissiveness. Reading such books is a strange experience, since these authors have clearly spent years undertaking a close study of texts that they often appear to abhor; as Rée puts it, "Although Afary and Anderson have spent ten years working on their book, it has not been a labor of love."[11] Not surprisingly, the readings that they produce, in addition to being consistently hostile, can most charitably be described as selective.

But if such books amount to attempts to dismiss, and thus silence, certain lines of thinking (and it is difficult to see them otherwise), what is this being done in the name of, and with what end in mind? This brings us to the strange sense of glee that one finds therein. Here I will risk a simplification of my own, for I believe that *Foucault and the Iranian Revolution* and *Postcolonial Theory and the Specter of Capitalism* both share a mission with a number of similar texts produced in the last few years, which has been to ask, impatiently: Can we please be done with the "posties"?—that is, those thinkers variously described (described so as to be dismissed) in such texts as "poststructuralists," "postcolonialists," or "postmodernists." Dismissing Foucault's writings on Iran, or postcolonial theory, or the work of the Subaltern Studies group, is in such cases an attack carried out in the name of a return to ideas or principles that are alleged to be themselves under attack and mortally endangered by such "posty" thinkers. For Afary and Anderson, these endangered principles include secularism, modernity, democracy, and feminism (the last of these is understood to encompass the first three principles—that is, feminism for them must be by its nature secular); Chibber would endorse all of these and would include the Enlightenment tradition and class analysis of a recognizably orthodox nature. Their understanding and articulation of the subjects addressed by their "posty" theoretical opponents—whether it is the Iranian Revolution or post-independence South Asian historiography—are, needless to say, explicitly framed by their allegiance to these principles. The glee found in these books, then, results from a sense of a job well done; having exposed the errors of the posties, they can happily return to what Chibber describes as "more pressing subjects." "This is not a book I was especially keen to write" are the first words of Chibber's text, in a depressing preview of what is to come.[12] Truly, such books are anything but labors of love.

Foucault and Fanon on Intellectuals and Revolutions

It is striking that in these attacks on "posty" figures such as Foucault, a figure often mobilized as an ally is Frantz Fanon. Afary and Anderson and Chibber, in their respective books, reach repeatedly for claims regarding Fanon and his work in order to bolster their own arguments. Afary and Anderson, in calling for "a more porous, fluid, and hybrid interchange between the East and the West" than they find in Foucault's work (I cannot resist pointing out the taken-for-granted categories "East" and "West" in such a formulation), cite Fanon as an alternative; later, they describe "Islamism," which they accuse Foucault as espousing, as "far closer to fascism than to the socially progressive politics of a Sandino, a Fanon, a Lumumba, a Mandela, or even a Gandhi."[13] Chibber, in his book, arrays Fanon against postcolonial theorists by grouping him in with "important leader[s] in the anticolonial tradition" such as Ho Chi Minh and Che Guevara; in the book's conclusion, he presents Fanon, together with Cabral and Nkrumah, as inheritors of "the socialism of Lenin or Marx."[14] The very fact that Fanon can be placed among such a diverse company (from Gandhi to Ho Chi Minh to Nkrumah to Lenin), and for such varied reasons, suggests something very disturbing about such appropriations. In such instances, it seems, there is no need to actually *read* Fanon's work; rather, he can simply be invoked by name (neither of these books actually quote from or cite any of Fanon's writings) as the "authentic" voice of Third World revolution against one's theoretical foes, especially when such a foe is a white European thinker such as Foucault.[15]

Elsewhere, I have written at some length about the productive possibilities in thinking Fanon and Foucault together, and about some of the surprising parallels between them and their work.[16] This connection might begin from the fact that they were almost exact contemporaries, continuing through some striking similarities in their intellectual and political itineraries: For example, they nearly crossed paths at the University of Tunis, where Fanon was a lecturer from 1959 to 1960 and Foucault from 1966 to 1968 (this was of course after Fanon's untimely death in 1961).[17] Although it would be absurd to downplay the significant differences—intellectual, political, theoretical, and vocational—between Foucault and Fanon, one useful way of thinking them together from within our postcolonial present is around their understanding of the nature of intellectual work, and how this work might be related to popular struggles. To put it differently, they have some strikingly similar things to say about intellectuals and revolutions.

To start with, here is Foucault, in May 1984, shortly before his death:

> The work of an intellectual is not to form the political will of others; it is, through the
> analyses he does in his own domains, to bring assumptions and things taken for granted
> again into question, to shake habits, ways of acting and thinking, to dispel the familiarity
> of the accepted, to take the measure of rules and institutions and, starting from that
> re-problematization (where he plays his specific role as intellectual) to take part in the
> formation of a political will (where he has his role to play as citizen).[18]

We might, a bit provocatively, bring together Foucault's formulation of "the work of an intellectual" (together with his lifelong refusal to engage in polemics),[19] with Fanon's declaration, in the opening words of *Black Skin, White Masks*, about what he will and will not do in that book:

> This book should have been written three years ago. But at the time the truths made our blood boil. Today the fever has dropped and truths can be said without having them hurled into people's faces. They are not intended to endorse zealousness. We are wary of being zealous. . . . Zealousness is the arm par excellence of the powerless. Those who would heat the iron to hammer it immediately into a tool. We would like to heat the carcass of man and leave. Perhaps this would result in Man's keeping the fire burning by self-combustion.[20]

Of course, there are undeniable differences between these two statements: an obvious rhetorical one, for starters; an experiential one, without question; and, not least, the temporal gap of three decades, marked by events that Fanon would not live to see. But there is also a shared, stubborn refusal of a particular sort of intellectual vanguardism, in favor of an alternative, no less engaged but differently articulated sense of the intellectual's vocation amid the struggle toward what Foucault calls "the formation of a political will" and Fanon, in his more existential vein, refers to as "keeping the fire burning."

It might of course be objected that their actual engagements with revolutions were diametrically opposed: Fanon embracing the revolutionary party in Algeria and throwing himself, mind, body, and soul, into what he thought of and named "the African Revolution"; Foucault standing aside as the consummate observer and analyst, never trusting any party or political formation completely, embracing as his own the maxim he attributes to Jean Daniel: "'not to put trust in any revolution,' even if one can 'understand every revolt.'"[21] For example, the word "citizen," invoked by Foucault as one of the roles to be played by the intellectual in the statement above—surely this would be anathema to Fanon's more revolutionary conception of intellectual vocation? But Foucault's own notion of what such "citizenship" might look like, and what rights and responsibilities it might entail, is a complex one that is clearly not rooted in national belonging; here he is in a statement against "international piracy," written in 1979 as part of his involvement in a movement on behalf of political migrants in Europe:

> There exists an international citizenry that has its rights, that has its duties, and that is committed to rise up against every abuse of power, no matter who the author, no matter who the victims. After all, we are all ruled, and as such, we are in solidarity. . . . We must reject the division of labor so often proposed to us: individuals can get indignant and talk; governments will reflect and act. It's true that good governments appreciate the holy indignation of the governed, provided it remains lyrical. . . . The will of individuals must make a place for itself in a reality of which governments have attempted to reserve a monopoly for themselves, that monopoly which we need to wrest from them little by little and day by day.[22]

Fanon might recognize something of this notion of "international citizenry"; after all, it is easy to forget that his embrace of national liberation in Algeria—such that by the end of his life he would come to use the phrase "we Algerians"—was in every way the taking up of a struggle that, according to the ordinary dictates of nationalism, was not his own.[23]

As Darryl Li reminds us, the decision to take up "other people's wars," then as now, is a matter of great controversy and contestation, liable to get one labeled "terrorist," "foreign combatant," or "mercenary."[24] A critic such as Albert Memmi will indeed come to view Fanon's rejection of his "organic" filiation with the Antilles in favor of this chosen affiliation with Algeria as bordering on pathology.[25] Against this claim, we might instead use the word that Li uses for "foreign fighters" such as Fanon, which is also the word Foucault invokes to explain his vision of international citizenship: solidarity.

To claim that all those who are ruled are therefore in solidarity, as Foucault does in this statement, is to risk the possibility of the very word "solidarity" becoming so broad as to be rendered meaningless. But in fact—to return to the problem of our postcolonial present—isn't this already the case, to a great extent? Today, declarations of "standing in solidarity with X" are all too easy to come by; realistically, such declarations should probably be better understood as vague expressions of sympathy rather than the actual taking up of the causes and struggles of others. So from our present moment, the complex and expanded (though hardly identical) notion of solidarity that can be read out of the work of both these thinkers has a great deal to offer.

This has everything to do with our own understanding of what constitutes meaningful intellectual work today. I would suggest that an important aspect of such work involves engaging with earlier thinkers such as Fanon and Foucault from within our contemporary political and intellectual challenges and struggles, appropriating those aspects of their work that can help illuminate continuing struggles. Nigel Gibson's *Fanonian Practices in South Africa: From Steve Biko to Abahlali baseMjondolo* provides one powerful model of such an effort, bringing Fanon's work to bear on the continuing political struggles being carried on by Abahlali baseMjondolo and other members of the shack-dwellers' movement (along with other emergent political movements) in postapartheid South Africa. The goal, in Gibson's words, is to use Fanon's work to help "amplify the voices of the new movements among the damned of the earth, and to challenge committed intellectuals . . . to search for, listen to, and develop new concepts."[26]

This focus on using our intellectual work to "amplify" ongoing struggles and emergent movements might in turn send us back to Foucault's own complex engagement with a variety of political movements. Foremost among these is the Groupe d'Information sur les Prisons (Prison Information Group), together with other work done by Foucault with members of the prison movement (as well as his work in defense of individual prisoners, such as Roger Knobelspiess).[27] But it is also important to remember Foucault's varied engagements with international and transnational movements, in keeping with his statement about the responsibilities of international citizenship. Throughout the 1970s and 1980s, he was involved in multiple campaigns and initiatives with figures such as Jean Daniel, Yves Montand, and Simone Signoret, along with Bernard Kouchner, a founder of Médecins du Monde. In addition to more general activist work defending the rights of political migrants, he was particularly galvanized by campaigns on behalf of Vietnamese refugees and in support of dissidents in Poland and the Soviet Union.[28] In September 1975, three years before his trips to Iran, he was part of a solidarity delegation that traveled to Madrid to read a statement demanding the release of eleven political activists who had been condemned to death; Foucault and the other members of the delegation were subsequently detained and deported by Franco's police.[29]

These engagements provide the larger context for understanding Foucault's writings on Iran, and, more broadly, his turn during the late 1970s toward a particular form of "philosophical journalism"—although, as he slyly noted, the link between philosophy and journalism could in fact be traced as far back as Kant's famous response to a question asked by a Berlin newspaper in 1784: What is Enlightenment?[30] In a text intended to introduce a new investigative series for the Italian newspaper *Corriere della sera*, Foucault wrote in 1978:

> The contemporary world is teeming with ideas . . . on a world scale, among people and minorities that, until now, history has not accustomed to speaking or making themselves heard. . . . We have to be present at the birth of ideas, and at the explosion of their force, not in the books that formulate them, but in the events in which they manifest their strength, in the struggles led by ideas, for or against ideas. Ideas do not rule the world. But it is precisely because the world does have ideas (and that it continuously produces lots of them) that the world is not passively ruled by its rulers or by those who want to teach them what to think once and for all.[31]

It is worth thinking Foucault's articulation of the role of the intellectual as needing "to be present at the birth of ideas" alongside Fanon's own meditations on the role of the intellectual in revolutionary times. This is set out most eloquently (and not without a romanticism that he will, later in the book, undercut) in the opening chapter of *The Wretched of the Earth*. In these early pages, Fanon narrates the moment when radical urban intellectuals, driven from the city due to the collusion between mainstream nationalist parties and the colonial authorities, encounter the supposedly conservative "peasant masses," who immediately greet them with "the question for which they are not prepared: 'When do we start?'"[32]

"The Dice Are Still Rolling": Struggling toward Singularity

So there is much of value today in this strand of Foucault's work, engaged as it is with what we might call the question of international solidarity. Foucault's writings on Iran come directly out of his larger questions about the role of intellectuals and their responsibility to the emergence of new ideas and new struggles. An interview with the Iranian writer Baqir Parham, conducted during his first trip to Iran in September 1978, stands as a good entry point for understanding Foucault's engagement with the Iranian Revolution. Not surprisingly, Foucault's first words in the interview address the political grounding of intellectual work: "I do not think that we could give a definition of an intellectual unless we stress the fact that there is no intellectual who is not at the same time, and in some form, involved with politics."[33]

While space does not permit a detailed reading of this full body of work, even a cursory glance at the articles Foucault published about Iran in 1978 and 1979 reveals a sense of intellectual openness toward unfolding events. In his self-proclaimed mode of philosophical journalism, he presents us with the voices of students, union leaders, army officers, religious figures, and many others—neither privileging nor undermining any of these voices, but rather juxtaposing them over the series of texts. For this reason, a reader would search in vain for some overarching, preexisting theoretical framework or argument that unites these articles. Indeed, the one thread that runs through them is an attempt to challenge some of the preconceptions that Foucault imagines in his European readers—preconceptions that he also takes pains to identify in himself as he encounters his interlocutors. In the earliest pieces for *Corriere della serra*, he works to undo simple assumptions among Western observers about the decisive role of the Iranian army[34] and challenges the idea that Iran was going through "a crisis of modernization" (and a return to "traditional society"), arguing instead that "recent events did not signify a shrinking back in the face of modernization" but rather the rejection "of a *modernization* that is itself an *archaism*."[35] He takes pains to suggest that "the European is probably wrong" in his preconceptions about the role of religion in political struggles in Iran—carefully marking the need to overcome his own tendency to ask the wrong questions in the face of these struggles.[36] By November 1978, his observation of the role played by cassette tapes that circulated among protesters leads him to question larger presuppositions about the fate of the revolution: "It is said that order is slowly being reestablished in Iran. In fact, the whole country is holding its breath."[37]

As events continued to unfold, Foucault was scrupulous about not positing any final conclusions; in February 1979, for example, he goes no further than suggesting that perhaps the "historic significance" of "this nonviolent uprising of a whole people that overthrew an all-powerful regime—an incredibly rare outcome for the twentieth century"—might eventually come to be found "not in its conformity to a recognized 'revolutionary' model, but instead in its potential to overturn the existing political situation in the Middle East and thus the global strategic equilibrium."[38] Although Foucault actively eschewed attempts to predict the future, it is hard to quarrel with the accuracy of that last statement regarding the Iranian Revolution's overturning of the global strategic equilibrium.[39]

The best-known (or, in some circles, most infamous) aspect of Foucault's writings on Iran has to do with his observations regarding the role of what he would come to call "political spirituality" in the Iranian Revolution.[40] What is less often noted is the extent to which this analysis contains important continuities with his larger, ongoing questions about the role of intellectual solidarity and his engagements with international and transnational struggles elsewhere. For example, in "What Are the Iranians Dreaming About?" published in *Le Nouvel Observateur* in October 1978, Foucault describes the movement for Islamic governance "as a form of 'political will'"—a phrase that, as we have seen, is crucial to Foucault's understanding of the role of intellectual work in political struggles. The work of various political movements in Iran, Foucault wrote, "impressed me in its effort to politicize structures that are inseparably social and religious in response to current problems. It also impressed me in its attempt to open a spiritual dimension in politics" ("I can already hear the French laughing, but I know that they are wrong," he added wryly).[41] In his writing on Iran, as in his other engagements with political struggles, Foucault shows himself to be engaged with what he sees as the work of the intellectual—"to bring assumptions and things taken for granted again into question . . . to dispel the familiarity of the accepted"—without imagining that the intellectual's work involves in any direct way "form[ing] the political will of others." It is a distinction made clear in an article written shortly before the fall of the shah:

> The question today is no longer whether or not Muhammad Reza will leave. Except in the unlikely case of a complete turnabout in the political situation, he will leave. Instead, it is a question of knowing what form this naked and massive will would take, this will that for a long time has said no to its ruler and which has finally disarmed him. It is a question of knowing when and how the will of all will give way to politics. It is a question of knowing if this will wants to do so and if it must do so. It is the practical problem of all revolutions and the theoretical problem of all political philosophies. Let us admit that we Westerners would be in a poor position to give advice to the Iranians on this matter.[42]

In short, there is a very clear link between Foucault's writings on Iran and his larger questions regarding intellectuals and revolutions, raised amid his engagements with local political struggles in France as well as with struggles in many other parts of the world.

One of the many problems with Afary and Anderson's reading of Foucault on Iran is that they insistently refuse to acknowledge this connection between Foucault's engagement with Iran and his other international engagements. They apply a very strange standard to enforce their separation of Iran from his other political interventions during the 1970s and early 1980s. On the one hand, they argue that his engagement with political struggles in Poland and for the rights of refugees from Viet Nam (the only two of Foucault's political commitments that they mention explicitly, although of course there were many others) "were part of a broad shift within the French intellectual Left," and thus that "he did not carve out much of a distinctive position on these issues." On the other hand, they insist that Foucault's writings on Iran made him a total outlier among this same intellectual left: "On Iran, however, Foucault stood virtually alone." They even go so far as to make the ad hominem claim (typical of their mode of argumentation) that Foucault "may in fact have used these interventions [vis-à-vis Poland and Viet Nam] to regain his standing in the Parisian intellectual world after the embarrassment of the Iran episode of 1978–79"—although this supposed "embarrassment" is largely an invention of their own embellished narrative.[43]

Afary and Anderson's version is largely belied by contemporary accounts: Jean Daniel, for example, spoke of Iran as "the mistake we made together," and the journalist Serge July, a founder of *Libération* and a thinker at the heart of the French intellectual left, noted that he thought and wrote much the same things about Iran as Foucault did.[44] David Macey, in the second of two biographical works on Foucault, puts it this way: "There was a fairly widespread belief in far-left circles in Europe . . . that forces like the Mujahideen guerrillas would emerge to lead a people's revolution."[45] This is not to say that Foucault's position was identical to that of others on the left or that he wasn't concerned with questioning many of the left's presuppositions involving Iran, but simply to note that, as with Foucault's other international engagements, his writings on Iran were part of a collaborative conversation with other intellectual and political voices. Indeed, Afary and Anderson's account of the supposed subsequent isolation of Foucault from the left as a result of his positions on Iran—such that, according to them, his "standing in the Parisian intellectual world" was endangered—does not withstand scrutiny. At the same time as he was writing about Iran, Foucault remained active in a number of other causes (and was constantly sought after to serve as a public advocate for these causes), sometimes alongside those who criticized him most harshly for his positions on Iran. For example, Claudie Broyelle, who together with Jacques Broyelle published one of the most savage critiques of Foucault on Iran in March 1979, was also a participant in a press conference organized by Foucault in defense of the rights of Vietnamese refugees in June 1979.[46]

But Afary and Anderson have an ulterior motive for isolating Foucault's writings on Iran from his other political activity during this period. It is made clear from the very first pages of their book, which set the terms of the engagement to come:

> Instead of merging his Iran episode with these other, less controversial, political interventions, we therefore emphasize its *singularity*, to use a favorite term of Foucault's. We believe that, except for his more intensive and long-term organizing activities in the prisoner support movement during the early 1970s, his writings on Iran represent the most significant and passionate political commitment of his life. It was an episode that ended in failure, as he himself seemed to recognize in his silence on Iran after May 1979.[47]

There are a number of questionable points here, including their failure to distinguish between "singularity" (a term consistently used by Foucault for the consideration due to particular struggles) and "singling out," which is what they are in fact doing here. In this passage can be found the framework for their entire reading of Foucault: "Foucault's experience in Iran left a lasting impression on his subsequent oeuvre and . . . one cannot understand the sudden turn in Foucault's writings in the 1980s without recognizing the significance of the Iranian episode and his more general preoccupation with the Orient. . . . The Iran writings express characteristic aspects of Foucault's worldview."[48] The progression of their argument thus reveals itself. Foucault's engagement with Iran was different from, and more important than, all of his other political engagements—it was, they tell us, the defining political interest of his life. His writings on Iran provide the key to understanding the development of his later work (and, indeed, his "worldview" as a whole). Foucault's engagement with Iran "ended in failure" (they use variations on this phrase several times in the book); his writings on Iran amount to an extended mistake. Thus, we are left to conclude (what other conclusion is possible, given the framework?) that Foucault's body of work is equally and fatally flawed. To borrow the words of Baudrillard's infamous essay, we are implicitly exhorted by Afary and Anderson to quite simply "Forget Foucault."[49]

Although I absolutely contest this simplified reading of Foucault's engagement with Iran, I also have no intention of suggesting that Foucault's analysis of the Iranian Revolution is without error. Indeed, one additional and unexpected connection between Foucault and Fanon is around the "errors" that they made in their readings of those revolutions about which they wrote in the midst of their unfolding. Fanon certainly fell into "error" more than once in his engagement with what he named and imagined as the African Revolution. He was badly mistaken in believing that Guinea under Sekou Touré would "crystallize the revolutionary potential" of its neighboring countries; he was even more disastrously mistaken in backing an uprising in Angola that was crushed by the Portuguese army, resulting in the deaths of twenty to thirty thousand people; he failed to anticipate the forces arrayed against Patrice Lumumba in the Congo before Lumumba's assassination in January 1961.[50] Indeed, one of Fanon's comrades from the Algerian Revolution, in a tribute published a decade after Fanon's death, declared (albeit with some exaggeration): "Fanon is one of the greatest revolutionaries that Africa has ever known, and yet almost none of his theories proved to be accurate."[51] Interestingly, this is a statement that very likely seemed truer in the 1970s than it does today.

But even citing the things that Fanon and Foucault, in their different contexts, got "wrong" in their attempts to think through ongoing revolutions (not to mention the many things that they got right) acts as a rebuke to critics such as Afary and Anderson and Chibber, who write with a nostalgia for the categories and principles that they see as having preceded "posty" thinking. For what we find in Fanon's and Foucault's respective engagements with ongoing revolutions in Algeria and Iran is an attempt to write what Foucault famously called "the history of the present" without relying on already existing categories to predefine the new events unfolding before them.[52] And here, I think, is where the larger spirit underlying these writings holds such value for us today, in the midst of the still-unfolding revolutions our time. Foucault makes this clear in one of his most significant articles on Iran, "The Mythical Leader of the Iranian Revolt" (Foucault's proposed title was *"La Folie de l'Iran"*), published in late November 1978:

> I cannot write the history of the future, and I am also rather clumsy at foreseeing the past. However, I would like to try to grasp *what is happening right now*, because these days nothing is finished, and the dice are still rolling. That may be what a journalist's work is, but it is true that I am just a neophyte.[53]

I have modified one important phrase in the translation that Afary and Anderson include as part of their book: it renders the phrase "les dés sont encore en train de rouler" as "the dice are still being rolled."[54] It is a small difference, but extremely important. "The dice are still being rolled" suggests the usual analysis of power politics: who's on top, who's throwing the dice, who's betting, who's winning. "The dice are still rolling" captures more accurately what Foucault is up to in his attempts to grasp *"what is happening right now"*—that is, to write the history of the present. It is an effort to capture a moving image, while acknowledging that the contemporary moment one is writing about may be changing faster than the analysis can be articulated. It may be that the dice will eventually stop rolling, at least in this particular time and place; but until they do, one must be attentive to all possibilities and not simply rely on tried and true formulas—the very formulas that are so often used to define, and thus delimit, "the history of the future."

Embedded in this engagement with the history of the present, found in both Foucault and Fanon, is a deep sense of intellectual responsibility, coupled with a tone of humility.[55] It is a very particular form of humility, however, one that often seems to take the form of its opposite, since it involves insisting that existing frameworks of understanding cannot be applied in any simple or straightforward ways to unfolding revolutions. In Fanon, this can be readily identified in his lifelong "stretching," to use his term, of psychoanalysis and psychology, Marxism, existentialism, and other forms of analysis in order to engage with the depredations of racism and colonialism, as well as the revolutionary efforts to overthrow them that for him constitute decolonization. The most striking example is his famous statement regarding class analysis in the colonial context in the opening pages of *The Wretched of the Earth*: "In the colonies the economic infrastructure is also a superstructure. The cause is the effect: You are rich because you are white, you are white because you are rich. This is why a Marxist analysis should always be slightly stretched when it comes to addressing the colonial issue."[56] Foucault's exhortation "to be respectful when a singularity revolts," with which I began this chapter, partakes of this same spirit, which was central to his body of work as a whole.[57] In declaring his own theoretical ethic to be "antistrategic," Foucault asserts the political and intellectual challenge of respecting the singularity of particular struggles, rather than attempting to assimilate them to some larger, already known framework for understanding revolutions. This, as I have suggested, is the ethos that can be found throughout his engagement with the Iranian Revolution.

Indeed, against the Foucault who is so often caricatured as a simple pessimist regarding the possibilities for revolutionary social change, we find throughout his work—especially in his late work, including his writings on Iran—an insistence on paying close attention to the particular forms of revolt that again and again arise in history. This is an ethos captured in "Useless to Revolt?" written in May 1979 and described by Afary and Anderson (and subsequently by other critics) as his "last word" on the Iranian Revolution—whereas I see it as absolutely consistent with Foucault's ongoing articulation, in other pieces he wrote at the time and subsequently until his death in 1984, of the political role of the intellectual vis-à-vis emerging struggles:[58]

> People do revolt; that is a fact. And that is how subjectivity (not that of great men, but that of anyone) is brought into history, breathing life into it. A convict risks his life to protest unjust punishments; a madman can no longer bear being confined and humiliated; a people refuses the regime that oppresses it. That doesn't make the first innocent, doesn't cure the second, and doesn't ensure for the third the tomorrow it was promised. And by the way, no one is obliged to stand in solidarity with them. No one is obliged to find that these confused voices sing better than the others and speak the truth itself. It is enough that they exist and that they have against them everything that is dead set on shutting them up for there to be a reason to listen to them and to see what they mean to say.[59]

The second half of this quote is particularly noteworthy, since it provides a strong rebuke to those (like Afary and Anderson) who suggest that Foucault was somehow an "advocate" for the Iranian Revolution and, thus, for "Islamism." To attend to the coming of particular kinds of subjectivity into history is not in and of itself to advocate for those particular forms of subjectivity. But it is to insist that a full respect for the singularity of such moments demands new forms of thinking. This is true even in those moments when the position of the analyst moves from documentation to ethical response. Afary and Anderson take Foucault to task for his supposed refusal to denounce "Islamic government" in and of itself. But an open letter to Prime Minister Mehdi Bazargan, written in April 1979, shows that Foucault's critique of power delves deeper than they might care to go, striking at the very nature of traditional notions of "government" in and of itself: "Concerning the expression 'Islamic government,' why cast immediate suspicion on the adjective 'Islamic'? The word 'government' suffices, in itself, to awaken vigilance."[60]

"Misunderstandings Are the Medium in Which the Noncommunicable Is Communicated": Intellectuals and Revolutions Today

In short, the great lesson that Foucault and Fanon have to teach those of us working to understand the unfolding revolutions of our postcolonial present is a simple one: Revolutions change things, and among the things that they change, or should change, are the categories through which we view such changes. New subjectivities and new singularities demand new frameworks, both of understanding and of solidarity; thus Foucault's attempt, in his writings on Iran, to confront the misconceptions of "the European" as his own, and to engage with multiple actors within the struggle in order to help forge new categories of analysis. Against this Foucauldian ethos, Afary and Anderson, reading "Useless to Revolt?" as the culmination of Foucault's writings on Iran, can only conclude that what they describe as "Foucault's support for the new wave of Islamic uprisings that started in Iran in 1978" was part of "his aim . . . to set out a new theory of revolution that could be widely embraced" (among other things, this reflects their stunning inability to understand, or willful refusal to acknowledge, what Foucault referred to as the "singularity" of the Iranian Revolution). Consequently, they see this alleged project of setting out "a new theory of revolution" as "an utter failure," since "it gained him no followers."[61] This is a strange—one might even say perverse—standard of "success" for revolutionary thought. Far from using the Iranian Revolution as an opportunity to develop new frameworks of analysis, the Revolution, at least as portrayed by Afary and Anderson, does nothing but affirm those things that they already believe to be true. Not finding a single, "correct," new theory of revolution in Foucault's work, they offer nothing but a simple return to older theories.

Revolutionary times demand better than nostalgia for older, and ostensibly simpler, forms of analysis. In an article published soon after the climactic events of February 1979, Foucault provides a brilliant caricature of the story of the Iranian Revolution that might all too easily be told using already existing categories of what a revolution looks like (or is supposed to look like) to describe the unfolding events in Iran:

> On February 11, 1979, the Iranian Revolution took place. I have the impression that I will read this sentence in tomorrow's newspapers and in the history books of the future. . . . History just placed on the bottom of the page the red seal that authenticates a revolution. Religion's role was to open the curtain; the mullahs will now disperse, taking off in a great flight of black and white robes. The décor is changing. The first act is going to begin: that of the struggle of the classes, of the armed vanguards, and of the party that organizes the masses, and so forth.
>   Is this so certain?[62]

In the traditional mode of analysis that Foucault parodies here, the singularity of the popular uprisings in Iran, over a series of months and years, is subsumed into the same old narrative of what a "revolution" must look like. And when things do not follow the necessary pattern (as they inevitably won't), they can be attributed to a failed or inauthentic revolution; those seen to have "promoted" this revolution, as Afary and Anderson claim Foucault did in Iran, can then be denounced as having been in error. The nostalgia for older ways of seeing and doing things can then safely be asserted, and we can all happily return to Chibber's "more pressing subjects"—hugging close, that is, our old, accustomed way of doing things.

Like Foucault, Fanon asserted his sometimes savage irony against this nostalgic viewpoint, the very opposite of a revolutionary attention to singularity. Halfway through *The Wretched of the Earth*, the revolutionary struggle for decolonization he documents has reached a point of deep confusion and uncertainty. At this point, even the division between colonizer and colonized cannot be trusted, since, in Fanon's words, "some blacks can be whiter than the whites," and, similarly, there are Europeans who have gone over to the "native" side. In this context, Fanon suggests, there can be no single, simple form of analysis, only a responsibility to the singularity of what is beginning to emerge, even though such realizations are "galling, painful, and sickening." He represents the bewilderment of this situation with one of his many moments of irony: "And yet everything used to be so simple before: the bad people were on one side, and the good on the other."[63] It is this nostalgia for a "simpler" time, and a simpler set of categories, that he, like Foucault, insistently refuses.

There is a lesson here for those attempting to understand the unfolding revolutions of our time—for example, the still-ongoing struggles of the Arab Spring—even in the midst of developments that are too often "galling, painful, and sickening." It is a lesson that has become more and more crucial as we have moved from one set of conventional accounts of the "Arab Spring" to another, at least in the English-speaking world, in the time that has passed from 2011: from the initial simplistic understanding that these uprisings represented a brief, completely nonviolent, telegenic, social-media-based revolution that achieved their ends in about the period of time necessary to binge-watch a TV series; to the subsequent simplistic understanding, following a wave of counterrevolutionary repression, that the "Arab Spring" names a noble but misguided failure that has brought the region nothing but death, destruction, and ISIS.[64] Both accounts have more to do with a set of already existing expectations of what a revolution "should" look like (and how quickly it should achieve the ends prescribed for it by those observing it) than with the actual, still-unfolding realities of the region.

These unfolding realities demand new categories of thought and new forms of analysis—precisely the opposite of the nostalgia for older categories espoused by those who stand against the "posties" (although in many cases, their declared political sympathies may in fact lie with these revolutions). Resisting the rush to judge the "errors" of Foucault and Fanon in their engagements with the Iranian and Algerian Revolutions in no way involves letting them off the hook for the consequences of some of their decisions and formulations. It does, however, involve admitting that intellectuals who insert themselves into struggles wherein "the dice are still rolling" (as against simply using these struggles as testing grounds for their already held beliefs) inevitably risk such mistakes.

Indeed, among the things we need today is a more complex and nuanced set of theories for engaging with the misunderstandings that inevitably arise in analyses like Fanon's and Foucault's, as attempts to understand and intervene in events while the dice are still rolling. We might begin by taking to heart the words of Theodor Adorno, in a late essay on Walter Benjamin: "The recourse to 'misunderstandings' as a means of explaining the effect of intellectual phenomena does not lead very far. It presupposes that there is an intrinsic substance, often simply equated with the author's intention, which exists independently of its historical fate. . . . Misunderstandings are the medium in which the non-communicable is communicated."[65]

To be true to the larger effort to write the history of the present—with all the risks this implies—in order to engage with the revolutions and uprisings of our time, means eschewing the temptation to wait long enough to act as the arbiter of events and struggles that (appear to be) safely completed. This has been, for example, a role that far too many commentators have shown themselves willing to play regarding the "fate" of the Egyptian Revolution today, whereas a more engaged intellectual and political position would be to continue to engage with events as part of the larger unfolding of this ongoing revolution.[66] Such a position involves embracing the sense of risk articulated by the editor of an important new collection of essays, which places the ongoing Egyptian Revolution in an international context:

> As academics and students, we exist within structures of power- and knowledge-making that enable us to influence significantly the way in which policymakers, journalists, and investors deal with the people of the area we study—in this case, ninety million Egyptians. All the contributions in this volume, in their effort to understand what is going on now, and not later, are informed by a commitment to those people and their struggles.[67]

True intellectual and political responsibility to the revolutions or our postcolonial present involves exactly this sort of commitment. And true responsibility to the singularity of unfolding revolutions involves asking difficult, sometimes unanswerable (as of yet), questions. The first question to ask might not be, "Did such and such a revolution succeed or fail?" but rather, "What is the current state of this revolution, and how do we understand and respond to it?" This includes the Iranian Revolution itself; given the power of the Green Revolution and of continuing popular movements in Iran, it may be premature to even say that the Iranian Revolution is *over*, never mind to adjudicate which analysis was "correct" or "in error."[68] We might more usefully include it among the revolutions of our age to whose singularity, following Foucault, we owe our respect, and our solidarity.

NOTES

1. I am using the term "Arab Spring" as a recognizable shorthand here, even though it is a term mostly used by outside observers to describe events in the region since late 2010. Many participants in the uprisings themselves, as well as many sympathetic analysts and activists, have rejected the term "Arab Spring," preferring instead to refer to the events of 2010–2011 and their

aftermath as the Arab Uprisings or the Arab Revolts. This is not simply an argument regarding terminology; rather, it is part of the larger question of how to address the specificity of these uprisings, given that analysts have, since the inception of the uprisings, debated the proper theoretical and political frameworks for understanding them. As will become clear, my argument in this chapter is that any attempt to try to define these uprisings as either meeting or departing from the definition of "authentic" revolutions goes against the valuable attempts of Fanon and Foucault to think the history of the present, calling into question our terms of analysis accordingly. For a sense of some of these debates around the "Arab Spring" (in English), see Amar and Prashad, *Dispatches from the Arab Spring*; Haddad et al., *Dawn of the Arab Uprisings*; Lynch, *Arab Uprisings Explained*; McMurray and Ufheil-Somers, *Arab Revolts*; and Prashad, *Arab Spring, Libyan Winter*.

2. I have addressed some of these debates elsewhere. See Alessandrini, "Arab Spring 2011."

3. Dabashi, *Arab Spring*, ix–x.

4. Mbembe, "Provincializing France?" For a contemporary example that does exactly the sort of work called for by Mbembe, see Wilder, *Freedom Time*.

5. Young, *White Mythologies*, 1. Young has returned to both restate and refine this point in "Subjectivity and History: Derrida in Algeria" (in his *Postcolonialism*, 411–26). For more recent takes on the influence of Algeria specifically, and colonialism more generally, on poststructuralist thought, see Goodman and Silverstein, *Bourdieu in Algeria*; Wise, *Derrida, Africa, and the Middle East*; and Ahuluwalia, *Out of Africa*. All three of these texts are analyzed in two fine review essays by Muriam Haleh Davis; see Davis, "Algeria's Impact" and "Justifications of Power."

6. Rahimi, "Review," 3.

7. Rée, "Treason of the Clerics" and Lynch, "Review." For a recent, excellent consideration of Foucault's writings on Iran within the larger scope of his later work, see McCall, "Ambivalent Modernities." For a brief but suggestive reading of Foucault on Iran specifically within his late work on "counterconduct," see Bargu, *Starve and Immolate*, 63–70. For a complex engagement with the philosophical and political underpinnings of "Islamism" in Iran, including the influences of a number of strands from European philosophy, which belies the simplistic version presented by Afary and Anderson, see Mirsepassi, *Political Islam, Iran, and the Enlightenment*. However, the most significant engagement in English with Foucault's writings on Iran has been by Behrooz Ghamari-Tabrizi in "In Defense of Foucault," extended in *Foucault in Iran*.

8. Žižek, *In Defense of Lost Causes*, 107.

9. Ibid., 108.

10. Vivek Chibber's *Postcolonial Theory and the Specter of Capitalism* is a text that deserves a longer discussion than I can provide here, since its criticisms of postcolonial theory should be acknowledged as fundamental to many of the conversations we are having in this book, though it has of course already been the subject of a tremendous and ongoing debate. Some of this debate has entailed close readings of Chibber's book, although many responses, to be frank, have focused not so much on the book as on Chibber's public interventions since the book was written, such as an interview with *Jacobin* soon after the book's publication (see Chibber, "How Does the Subaltern Speak?"). A widely shared (via online video) debate between Chibber and Partha Chatterjee unfortunately generated more heat than light on the matters discussed. In the critical debate that followed the book's publication, Chibber's tendency to respond polemically to his critics was in keeping with the tone of the book itself; see, for example, his response to Bruce Robbins's generally sympathetic review of the book, originally published in *n+1* (Robbins, "Subaltern-speak"; Chibber, "Subaltern Mythologies"; Robbins, "Response to Vivek Chibber"). For two close but critical assessments of the book and its shortcomings (the former focusing on its failure to deal with the legacy of anticolonial thinkers such as Fanon and Said and their influence on postcolonial studies, the latter on the nondialectical nature of Chibber's analysis), see Andersson, "Obscuring Capitalism," and Taylor, "Not Even Marxist"; for one of the harshest takes on the book (together

with one of the strongest defenses of the sorts of literary and cultural approaches that Chibber disdains), see Spivak, "Review"; for a plethora of dissenting views on the book, ranging from deeply admiring to deeply critical, along with a response by Chibber himself, see the book review symposium published in the *Journal of World-Systems Research* 20, no. 2 (2014).

11. Rée, "Treason of the Clerics."

12. Chibber, *Specter of Capital*, xi.

13. Afary and Anderson, *Foucault and the Iranian Revolution*, 21, 169.

14. Chibber, *Specter of Capital*, 153, 290. In his thoughtful and thorough critique of Chibber's book, Chris Taylor notes Chibber's larger refusal to engage with "anticolonial Marxist thinkers whose work was foundational for, or retroactively incorporated into, the postcolonial canon" (including figures such as Fanon, C. L. R. James, Amilcar Cabral, and Walter Rodney), and how this allows him to make a simplified division between "Marxism" on the one hand and (anti-Marxist) "Postcolonial Theory" on the other (Taylor, "Not Even Marxist"). Axel Andersson, meanwhile, offers an excellent reading of Fanon's experience as a psychiatrist in Algeria, as a way to come at some at Chibber's blind spots in dealing with the specificities, both material and psychic, of the colonial condition (Andersson, "Obscuring Capitalism"). Both these critiques, of course, involve an actual *reading* of Fanon's work, rather than simply an invocation of a figure called "Fanon" to bolster one's argument.

15. This particular use of Fanon, it should be said, is not new: in the mid-1980s, Homi Bhabha had already diagnosed "the ritual respect accorded to the name of Fanon" among those on the left who did not bother to actually read or engage with Fanon's work (Bhabha, "Remembering Fanon," xxi).

16. Alessandrini, *Future of Cultural Politics*, 75–100.

17. For overviews of the time spent by Fanon and Foucault at the University of Tunis, see Mirzoeff, "Fanon's Lectures in Tunisia" and "Foucault on Tunisia," respectively. Foucault's own discussion of his time in Tunis, and in particular the student protests of 1968, can be found in Foucault, *Remarks on Marx*. Robert J. C. Young has discussed the influence of Foucault's time in Tunisia on his work, especially *The Archaeology of Knowledge*, which he wrote during his time there and which was first presented as lectures at the University of Tunis (Young, *Postcolonialism*, 395–410).

18. Foucault, *Foucault Live: Interviews, 1961–1984*, 462–63.

19. See his explicit articulation of this point in the interview titled "Polemics, Politics, and Problematizations," in Rabinow, *Essential Works*.

20. Fanon, *Black Skin, White Masks*, xiii.

21. Foucault, "For an Ethic of Discomfort" (originally published in *Le Nouvel Observateur*, April 1979), in Faubion, *Essential Works*, 447.

22. Foucault, "Confronting Governments: Human Rights" (originally published in *Libération*, June 1984), in Faubion, *Essential Works*, 474–75; translation slightly modified.

23. This tension is at the heart of Fanon's relationship to anticolonial nationalism amid the struggle for decolonization in Algeria. As David Macey notes, while Fanon's conception of national culture involves the idea of the nation as "the product of the will," the actual Algerian Code of Nationality, adopted after Fanon's death in 1962, was quite a different thing: "Had he lived, Fanon would no doubt have been granted Algerian citizenship and an Algerian passport, but in a sense he would always have remained an honorary Algerian." See Macey, *Frantz Fanon: A Biography*, 377, 389.

24. Li, "Shades of Solidarity."

25. Memmi, "Impossible Life of Frantz Fanon."

26. Gibson, *Fanonian Practices in South Africa*, 5–6. For more on some of these movements in contemporary South Africa, see Makhulu, *Making Freedom*.

27. See Eribon, *Michel Foucault*, 267–69. For a more recent and more detailed discussion of Foucault's engagement with the GIP, see Zurn and Dilts, *Active Intolerance*.

28. Macey, *Lives of Michel Foucault*, 436–56.

29. Eribon, *Michel Foucault*, 263–66.

30. Foucault, "For an Ethic of Discomfort," 443.

31. Qtd. in Macey, *Lives of Michel Foucault*, 406.

32. Fanon, *Wretched of the Earth*, 29.

33. Foucault, "Tehran: Faith against the Shah," 183.

34. Foucault, "Army—When the Earth Quakes" 189–94, 191.

35. Foucault, "Shah Is a Hundred Years behind the Times," 194–95.

36. Foucault, "Tehran: Faith against the Shah," 199.

37. Foucault, "Revolt in Iran Spreads on Cassette Tapes," 216. There is an interesting comparison that might be made between Foucault's observations in "Revolt in Iran Spreads on Cassette Tapes" and those of Fanon in "'This Is the Voice of Algeria,'" a chapter of *L'An V de la Révolution Algérienne* on the role of the radio in the Algerian Revolution. See Fanon, *A Dying Colonialism*, 69–98.

38. Foucault, "Powder Keg Called Islam," 241.

39. One manifestation of this was to be the horrific, Western-sponsored Iran-Iraq war—for those living in the region, the first "Gulf War"—whose global repercussions remain with us, very palpably, today (see Tripp, *History of Iraq*, 215–33). This was not, of course, an outcome directly foreseen by Foucault, but that is the whole point: the only certainty is that things will not remain the same, and our analyses have to evolve accordingly.

40. Ghamari-Tabrizi provides a useful overview of reactions to Foucault's reflections on political Islam in "In Defense of Foucault."

41. Foucault, "What Are the Iranians Dreaming About?" 208–9.

42. Foucault, "Revolt with Bare Hands," 213.

43. Afary and Anderson, *Foucault and the Iranian Revolution*, 8.

44. Eribon, *Michel Foucault*, 289.

45. Macey, *Michel Foucault*, 128.

46. Macey, *Lives of Michel Foucault*, 414. The title of the Broyelles' article, *"A quoi pensent les philosophes?"* ("What are the philosophers thinking?") was meant as a play on Foucault's earlier article *"A quoi rêvent les Iraniens?"* ("What are the Iranians dreaming?"). Afary and Anderson's book translates the Broyelles' article as "What Are the Philosophers Dreaming About? Was Michel Foucault Mistaken about the Iranian Revolution?" (the subtitle is their own invention). See Broyelle and Broyelle, "What Are the Philosophers Dreaming About?"; Foucault, "What Are the Iranians Dreaming About?"

47. Afary and Anderson, *Foucault and the Iranian Revolution*, 8–9.

48. Ibid., 3–4, 9.

49. Baudrillard, *Forget Foucault*.

50. Macey, *Frantz Fanon: A Biography*, 383, 391, 435.

51. Ibid., 28–29.

52. Foucault, *Discipline and Punish*, 30–31.

53. Foucault, "Mythical Leader," 220; translation modified, italics in original.

54. Didier Eribon (in Betsy Wing's English translation) and David Macey, who both cite this passage in their biographies of Foucault, also render it as "the dice are still rolling" (Eribon, *Michel Foucault*, 288; Macey, *Lives of Michel Foucault*, 407).

55. It is noteworthy that the recent work of David Scott, a thinker influenced by both Fanon and Foucault, invokes these same two principles: humility and responsibility. Scott's most recent book, a careful reconsideration of the emergence and downfall of the Grenada Revolution of 1979–83—a period roughly contemporary with Foucault's writings on the Iranian Revolution—provides another important intertext for analysts of the ongoing revolutions of today (see Scott, *Omens of Adversity*). This double emphasis on humility and responsibility in turn might be

compared with the still-all-too-common way of reading Fanon's work, which Scott had critiqued years earlier as the tendency to "read Fanon as though we were about to join him in the trenches of the anticolonial liberation struggle" (Scott, *Refashioning Futures*, 199).

56. Fanon, *Wretched of the Earth*, 5.

57. Foucault, "The Revolt in Iran Spreads," 453.

58. For two examples of this late writing, see, for a start, Foucault, "For an Ethic of Discomfort" and "So Is It Important to Think?" (Originally published in *Libération*, May 1981), in Faubion, *Essential Works*.

59. Foucault, "Useless to Revolt?" (originally published in *Le Monde*, May 1979), in Faubion, *Essential Works*, 452; translation slightly modified.

60. Foucault, "Open Letter to Mehdi Bazargan" (originally published in *Le Nouvel Observateur*, April 1979), in Faubion, *Essential Works*, 261.

61. Afary and Anderson, *Foucault and the Iranian Revolution*, 133.

62. Foucault, "Powder Keg Called Islam," 239.

63. Fanon, *Wretched of the Earth*, 93–94.

64. I have made this point about the shifting reception of the "Arab Spring" in more detail elsewhere; see Alessandrini, "Arab Spring Never Happened."

65. Adorno, *Prisms*, 232.

66. I have made a version of this point at greater length in Alessandrini, "Egyptian Revolution."

67. Abou-El-Fadl, "New Texts Out Now"; see also Abou-El-Fadl, *Revolutionary Egypt*.

68. For some of the best takes on the development and continuing struggles of the Green Movement and other subsequent political movements in Iran, see Abrahamian, "I Am Not a Speck of Dirt"; Postel, "Revolutionary Prefigurations"; Dabashi, *Green Movement in Iran*; Raha Iranian Feminist Collective, "Solidarity and Its Discontents"; Kadivar, "New Oppositional Politics"; and Mottahedeh, *#iranelection*.

BIBLIOGRAPHY

Abou-El-Fadl, Reem. "New Texts Out Now: Reem Abou-El-Fadl, *Revolutionary Egypt: Connecting Domestic and International Struggles*." *Jadaliyya*, July 2, 2015. http://www.jadaliyya.com/pages/index/22037/new-texts-out-now_reem-abou-el-fadl-revolutionary-.

Abou-El-Fadl, Reem, ed. *Revolutionary Egypt: Connecting Domestic and International Struggles*. New York: Routledge, 2015.

Abrahamian, Ervand. "I Am Not a Speck of Dirt, I Am a Retired Teacher." *London Review of Books*, July 23, 2009. http://www.lrb.co.uk/v31/n14/ervand-abrahamian/i-am-not-a-speck-of-dirt-i-am-a-retired-teacher.

Adorno, Theodor W. *Prisms*. Cambridge, Mass.: MIT Press, 1990.

Afary, Janet, and Kevin B. Anderson. *Foucault and the Iranian Revolution: Gender and the Seductions of Islamism*. Chicago: University of Chicago Press, 2005.

Ahuluwalia, Pal. *Out of Africa: Post-Structuralism's Colonial Roots*. New York: Routledge, 2010.

Alessandrini, Anthony C. "Arab Spring 2011." In *Encyclopedia of Postcolonial Studies*, edited by Sangeeta Ray and Henry Schwarz. Cambridge, Mass.: Wiley-Blackwell, 2016.

———. "The Arab Spring Never Happened (in English)." *Jadaliyya* (16 February 2017).

———. "The Egyptian Revolution and the Problem of International Solidarity." In Abou-El-Fadl, *Revolutionary Egypt*, 279–98.

———. *Frantz Fanon and the Future of Cultural Politics: Finding Something Different*. Lanham, Md.: Lexington Books, 2014.

Amar, Paul, and Vijay Prashad, eds. *Dispatches from the Arab Spring: Understanding the New Middle East*. Minneapolis: University of Minnesota Press, 2013.

Andersson, A. "Obscuring Capitalism: Vivek Chibber's Critique of Subaltern Studies." *Los Angeles Review of Books*, November 6, 2013. https://lareviewofbooks.org/review/obscuring -capitalism-on-vivek-chibbers-critique-of-subaltern-studies.

Bargu, Banu. *Starve and Immolate: The Politics of Human Weapons.* New York: Columbia University Press, 2014.

Baudrillard, J. *Forget Foucault.* Translated by Phil Beitchman, N. Dufresne, Lee Hildreth, and Mark Polizzotti. New York: Semiotext(e), 2007.

Bhabha, H. K. "Remembering Fanon: Self, Psyche, and the Colonial Condition." Foreword to *Black Skin, White Masks*, by Frantz Fanon. Translated by C. L. Markmann. London: Pluto, 1986.

Broyelle, Claudie, and Jacques Broyelle. "What Are the Philosophers Dreaming About? Was Michel Foucault Mistaken about the Iranian Revolution?" In Afary and Anderson, *Foucault and the Iranian Revolution*, 239–41. Originally published in *Le Matin*, March 24, 1979.

Chibber, Vivek. "How Does the Subaltern Speak? An Interview with Vivek Chibber." *Jacobin*, April 10, 2013. https://www.jacobinmag.com/2013/04/how-does-the-subaltern-speak/.

———. *Postcolonial Theory and the Specter of Capital.* New York: Verso, 2013.

———. "Subaltern Mythologies." *Jacobin*, January 3, 2014. https://www.jacobinmag.com/2014/01/ subaltern-mythologies/.

Dabashi, Hamid. *The Arab Spring: The End of Postcolonialism.* London: Zed, 2012.

———. *The Green Movement in Iran.* New Brunswick, N.J.: Transaction, 2011.

Davis, Muriam Haleh. "Algeria as Post-Colony? Rethinking the Colonial Legacy of Post-Structuralism." *Journal of French and Francophone Philosophy* 19, no. 2 (2011): 136–52.

———. "Algeria's Impact on French Philosophy: Between Poststructuralist Theory and Colonial Practice." *Jadaliyya*, June 6, 2011. http://www.jadaliyya.com/pages/index/1764/algerias-impact -on-french-philosophy_between-posts.

———. "'Justifications of Power': Neoliberalism and the Role of Empire." *Jadaliyya*, March 25, 2014. http://www.jadaliyya.com/pages/index/17067/justifications-of-power_neoliberalism-and -the-role.

Eribon, Didier. *Michel Foucault.* Translated by Betsy Wing. Cambridge, Mass.: Harvard University Press, 1991.

Fanon, Frantz. *Black Skin, White Masks.* Translated by Richard Philcox. New York: Grove, 2008.

———. *A Dying Colonialism.* Translated by Haakon Chevalier. New York: Grove, 1967.

———. *The Wretched of the Earth.* Translated by Richard Philcox. New York: Grove, 2004.

Faubion, James D., ed. *Power*, vol. 3 of *Essential Works of Foucault.* New York: New Press, 2000.

Foucault, Michel. "The Army—When the Earth Quakes." In Afary and Anderson, *Foucault and the Iranian Revolution*, 189–94. First published in *Corriere della serra*, September 1978.

———. "Dialogue between Michel Foucault and Baqir Parham." In Afary and Anderson, *Foucault and the Iranian Revolution*, 183–89. First published in *Nameh-yi Kanun-I Nevisandegan*, Spring 1979.

———. *Discipline and Punish: The Birth of the Prison.* Translated by Alan Sheridan. New York: Vintage, 1977.

———. "For an Ethic of Discomfort." In Faubion, *Power*, 443–49. First published in *Le Nouvel Observateur*, April 1979.

———. *Foucault Live: Interviews, 1961–1984.* Edited by Sylvère Lotringer. New York: Semiotext(e), 1996.

———. "The Mythical Leader of the Iranian Revolt." In Afary and Anderson, *Foucault and the Iranian Revolution*, 220–23. First published in *Corriere della serra*, November 1978.

———. "A Powder Keg Called Islam." In Afary and Anderson, *Foucault and the Iranian Revolution*, 239–41. First published in *Corriere della serra*, February 1979.

———. *Remarks on Marx: Conversations with Duccio Trombardori.* Translated by R. James Goldstein and James Cascaito. New York: Semiotext(e), 1991.

———. "The Revolt in Iran Spreads on Cassette Tapes." In Afary and Anderson, *Foucault and the Iranian Revolution,* 216–20. First published in *Corriere della serra,* November 1978.

———. "A Revolt with Bare Hands." In Afary and Anderson, *Foucault and the Iranian Revolution,* 210–13. First published in *Corriere della serra,* November 1978.

———. "The Shah Is a Hundred Years behind the Times." In Afary and Anderson, *Foucault and the Iranian Revolution,* 194–98. First published in *Corriere della serra,* October 1978.

———. "Tehran: Faith Against the Shah." In Afary and Anderson, *Foucault and the Iranian Revolution,* 198–203. First published in *Corriere della serra,* October 1978.

———. "Useless to Revolt?" In Faubion, *Power,* 451–53. First published in *Le Monde,* May 1979.

———. "What Are the Iranians Dreaming About?" In Afary and Anderson, *Foucault and the Iranian Revolution,* 203–9. First published in *Le Nouvel Observateur,* October 1978.

"Foucault on Tunisia." *History Is Made at Night,* March 6, 2011. http://history-is-made-at-night .blogspot.com/2011/03/foucault-on-tunisia.html.

Ghamari-Tabrizi, Behrooz. *Foucault in Iran: Islamic Revolution after the Enlightenment.* Minneapolis: University of Minnesota Press, 2016.

———. "When Life Will No Longer Barter Itself: In Defense of Foucault on the Iranian Revolution." In *A Foucault for the 21st Century: Governmentality, Biopolitics and Discipline in the New Millennium,* edited by Sam Binkley and Jorge Capetillo. Cambridge: Cambridge Scholars Press, 2009.

Gibson, Nigel. *Fanonian Practices in South Africa: From Steve Biko to Abahlali baseMjondolo.* New York: Palgrave, 2011.

Goodman, Jane E., and Paul A. Silverstein, eds. *Bourdieu in Algeria: Colonial Politics, Ethnographic Practices, Theoretical Developments.* Lincoln: University of Nebraska Press, 2009.

Haddad, Bassam, Rosie Bsheer, and Ziad Abu-Rish, eds. *The Dawn of the Arab Uprisings: End of an Old Order?* London: Zed Books, 2013.

Kadivar, Mohammad Ali. "A New Oppositional Politics: The Campaign Participants in Iran's 2013 Presidential Election." *Jadaliyya,* June 22, 2013. http://www.jadaliyya.com/pages/index/ 12383/a-new-oppositional-politics_the-campaign-participa.

Li, Darryl. "Shades of Solidarity: Notes on Race-talk, Intervention, and Revolution." *Jadaliyya,* March 12, 2011. http://www.jadaliyya.com/pages/index/876/shades-of-solidarity_notes-on -race-talk-interventi.

Lynch, Marc, ed. *The Arab Uprisings Explained: New Contentious Politics in the Middle East.* New York: Columbia University Press, 2014.

Lynch, R. Review of *Foucault and the Iranian Revolution: Gender and the Seductions of Islamism,* Janet Afary and Kevin B. Anderson. *Foucault Studies* 4 (2007): 169–76.

Macey, David. *Frantz Fanon: A Biography.* New York: Picador, 2000.

———. *The Lives of Michel Foucault.* New York: Pantheon, 1993.

———. *Michel Foucault.* London: Reaktion Books, 2004.

Makhulu, Anne-Maria. *Making Freedom: Apartheid, Squatter Politics, and the Struggle for Home.* Durham, N.C.: Duke University Press, 2015.

Mbembe, A. "Provincializing France?" *Public Culture* 23, no. 1 (2011).

McCall, C. "Ambivalent Modernities: Foucault's Iranian Writings Reconsidered." *Foucault Studies* 15 (2013): 27–51.

McMurray, David, and Amanda Ufheil-Somers, eds. *The Arab Revolts: Dispatches on Militant Democracy in the Middle East.* Bloomington: Indiana University Press, 2013.

Memmi, A. "The Impossible Life of Frantz Fanon." Translated by T. Cassirer and G. M. Twomey. *Massachusetts Review* 14 (1973): 9–39.

Mirsepassi, Ali. *Political Islam, Iran, and the Enlightenment: Philosophies of Hope and Despair.* New York: Cambridge University Press, 2010.

Mirzoeff, Nicholas. "Fanon's Lectures in Tunisia (1959)." *"We Are All Children of Algeria": Visuality and Countervisuality, 1954–2011.* February 9, 2012. http://scalar.usc.edu/nehvectors/mirzoeff/Lectures-in-Tunis-1959?path=Fanon.

Mottahedeh, Negar. *#iranelection: Hashtag Solidarity and the Transformation of Online Life.* Durham, N.C.: Duke University Press, 2015.

Postel, D. "Revolutionary Prefigurations: The Green Movement, Critical Solidarity, and the Struggle for Iran's Future." *New Politics* 13, no. 1 (2010).

Prashad, Vijay. *Arab Spring, Libyan Winter.* Oakland, Calif.: AK Press, 2012.

Rabinow, Paul, ed. *Essential Works of Foucault*, vol. 1: *Ethics: Subjectivity and Truth.* New York: New Press, 1997.

Raha Iranian Feminist Collective. "Solidarity and Its Discontents," *Jadaliyya*, February 19, 2011. http://www.jadaliyya.com/pages/index/683/solidarity-and-its-discontents.

Rahimi, B. Review of *Foucault and the Iranian Revolution: Gender and the Seductions of Islamism*, by Janet Afary and Kevin B. Anderson. *H-Gender-MidEast.* October 2006.

Rée, Jonathan. "The Treason of the Clerics." *Nation*, July 28, 2005. http://www.thenation.com/article/treason-clerics/.

Robbins, B. "Response to Vivek Chibber." *n+1*, January 9, 2014.

———. "Subaltern-speak." *n+1* 18 (Winter 2013).

Scott, David. *Omens of Adversity: Tragedy, Time, Memory, Justice.* Durham, N.C.: Duke University Press, 2014.

———. *Refashioning Futures: Criticism After Postcoloniality.* Princeton: Princeton University Press, 1999.

Spivak, Gayatri Chakravorty. Review of Vivek Chibber, *Postcolonial Theory and the Specter of Capital. Cambridge Review of International Affairs* 27, no. 1 (2014): 184–98.

Taylor, Chris. "Not Even Marxist: On Vivek Chibber's Polemic against Postcolonial Theory." *Of C. L. R. James*, April 29, 2013. http://clrjames.blogspot.com/2013/04/not-even-marxist-on-vivek-chibbers.html.

Tripp, Charles. *A History of Iraq.* 3rd ed. New York: Cambridge University Press, 2007.

Valayden, Diren. "The Dangers of Liberalism: Foucault and Postcoloniality in France." *Jadaliyya*, March 17, 2014. http://www.jadaliyya.com/pages/index/16940/the-dangers-of-liberalism_foucault-and-postcolonia.

Wilder, Gary. *Freedom Time: Negritude, Decolonization, and the Future of the World.* Durham, N.C.: Duke University Press, 2015.

Wise, Christopher. *Derrida, Africa and the Middle East.* New York: Palgrave Macmillan, 2009.

Young, Robert J. C. *Postcolonialism: An Historical Introduction.* Cambridge, Mass.: Blackwell, 2001.

———. *White Mythologies: Writing History and the West.* New York: Routledge, 1990.

Žižek, Slavoj. *In Defense of Lost Causes.* New York: Verso, 2009.

Zurn, Perry, and Andrew Dilts, eds. *Active Intolerance: Michel Foucault, The Prisons Information Group, and the Future of Abolition.* New York: Palgrave Macmillan, 2016.

When Revolution Is Not Enough: Tracing the Limits of Black Radicalism in Dionne Brand's *Chronicles of the Hostile Sun* and *In Another Place, Not Here*

Laurie R. Lambert

Finding a Grammar for Revolution

Near the end of her fifth poetry collection, *Chronicles of the Hostile Sun* (1984), Dionne Brand writes, "I'm sick of writing history / I'm sick of scribbling dates."[1] The poem expresses the poet-speaker's feelings of frustration after witnessing the end of the Grenada Revolution and the U.S. invasion of Grenada in October 1983. The "sickness" the poet-speaker feels in writing is caused by the blow of losing friends and colleagues to the violence of that month and her attempts to process her own trauma as a witness to and survivor of the military invasion. Her sickness is also the dread she experiences in having to use her art as a venue for correcting North Americans' misconceptions about the Caribbean that come about as a result of American imperialism. And yet in the tradition of many Caribbean writers before her, this writing of history is part of the task that the Trinidadian-Canadian Brand takes on as she documents her time as a participant in the Grenada Revolution. She is a chronicler of history and dates: Her work is art, protest, and pedagogy.

In *Historical Thought and Literary Representation in West Indian Literature* (1998), the literary critic Nana Wilson-Tagoe describes how colonial and postcolonial experiences keep Caribbean writers tethered to questions of historicity, the representation of subjectivities shaped by uneven development, and the difficulty of escaping the colonial past even as one claims the postcolonial contemporary. "Traumatized by history, the West Indian writer is yet continually haunted by its specter and perpetually engaged with redefining it," Wilson-Tagoe argues.[2] Indeed, Caribbean literature is home to a tradition of writers revisiting, correcting, and resisting versions of history derived from archives with colonial roots. This tradition has developed in part because of the Caribbean's position as a site of colonial and neocolonial conquest, and it remains an ongoing legacy today even as most of the region can be defined as "postcolonial." Brand's writing situates the Grenada Revolution as part of a black radical tradition whose many iterations across history (including the Haitian Revolution and slave resistance across the Americas, as well as African liberation movements and the Black Power movement) contributed to the pursuit of freedom on the part of black people the world over. For Brand revolution has always been part of the discourse on and practice of black freedom.

To speak of the postcolonial in the Anglophone Caribbean, in particular, is to glean simultaneously the vestiges of colonialism that remain and the strategies employed by Caribbean people for creating a contemporary moment that lives alongside these vestiges without being consumed by them. Brand's writing on Grenada is an example of this strategy played out in literary form. Her work spans multiple genres, including poetry, essay, and fiction. In each genre she grapples with the Grenada Revolution while imagining different relationships between history and the present. Brand's work explores the limits of revolution as radical praxis by examining revolutionary aftermaths. She is interested in who experiences these aftermaths, under what conditions, and where. In *Chronicles* Brand writes about returning to Canada as a result of the U.S. invasion of Grenada. The Canada she returns to is simultaneously foreign and familiar. The irony of Canada's neocolonial reach into the Caribbean is not lost on Brand, when she considers that Canada is itself a former colony of both Britain and France. It is also the place she had originally migrated to as a teenager from Trinidad in search of a better life. After Grenada she experiences Canada as a place of exile. But exile is not only a physical place, it is also a condition, such that in Brand's work Grenadians who remain in the country might also be read as exiled in the sense that the American invasion tries to prevent them from establishing sovereignty over their nation. Grenadians are citizens of a nation that is politically independent by law; however, because of the invasion, they have experienced violations of this independence that served to remind them of how the colonial remains embedded in the postcolonial. Acknowledging this simultaneous experience of sovereignty and nonsovereignty, this chapter examines the liminal spaces Brand creates in her writing to account for the messiness of a revolution that was both a success and a failure. To create these liminal spaces she represents historical events, refracting them through the genres of poetry and fiction. This process of refraction gives Brand room for invention and imagination, to remember specifically the lives of black women, including black queer women, whose radicalism may not fit within traditional definitions of Caribbean revolution.

Chronicles of the Hostile Sun captures the innocence, energy, optimism, and anger that characterized both the revolution in Grenada and the early stages of Brand's career as a writer. By the end of this poetry collection, however, the violence that marked the collapse of the People's Revolutionary Government (PRG) and the American invasion of Grenada destroys the sense of possibility the revolution initially generated. This violence would continue to haunt Brand's writing. *In Another Place, Not Here* (1996), her first novel, is Brand's most sustained meditation on Grenada following *Chronicles*. In a mode of positive critique, the novel sets forth a vision of queer love as a site of revolution. Set on an un-named island that resembles Grenada in its history and geography, *In Another Place* is nar-rated from the perspectives of two women—one a Caribbean Canadian activist who returns to the island to participate in the revolution as a labor organizer and the other a sugarcane fieldworker, abandoned by her parents as a child and living with an abusive man as an adult. The women characters narrating *In Another Place* occupy a space distinctly on the margins of the Grenada Revolution even as they are living and working in its midst. *In Another Place* positions black queer love as a constitutive part of political revolution at the same time that it resists the heteronormativity of revolution as it is conventionally defined. Brand explores how and why certain bodies (typically black, female, and poor bodies or black and queer bodies) are always already inscribed at the margins of the black radical tradition. From the margins these people often serve as a form of collateral dam-age in the name of a pursuit of black freedom. Their contributions to freedom struggles typically depend on a silencing or suppression of their gender, sexuality, or class in the name of the greater good of a black collective. Where some aspect of their identity clashes with the ideals of the revolution, their suffering (if visible at all to the masses) is deemed necessary for the promotion of the greater revolutionary project, which tends to be em-bodied in the figure of the upwardly mobile, straight, black male subject. For the women represented in Brand's later text the end of the violent revolution is not so much a surprise as it is a recursion, albeit on a spectacular scale, of the hardships and trauma they have faced their entire lives. This is an important difference between the experience of the after-math of revolution as she writes it in *Chronicles* and *In Another Place*. Through an analysis of these two texts I explore how Brand's relationship to revolution and literary represen-tation changes.

Poetry offers Brand an immediacy and distillation of thought that sharpens the feeling of trauma in the immediate aftermath of the revolution. Several years later when she turns to fictional prose, she introduces an alternate vision of "grace," as she calls it, to her repre-sentation of the revolution. When Brand publishes *In Another Place*, she is in a different moment of postcolonial history. This temporal distance, coupled with the discursiveness of fiction as a genre, provides a more expansive canvas for Brand to reimagine what hap-pened in Grenada. Together *Chronicles* and *In Another Place* draw on similar historical sources on the Grenada Revolution while exhibiting radically different voices and formal outcomes. Brand's insistence on the narrative multiplicity of Grenada as represented in two different texts decenters the colonial, patriarchal idea of a master narrative.[3] Brand's return to similar material at different moments also shows us how intellectuals and art-ists reinterpret the meaning of revolution over time. These texts reflect her numerous attempts to contribute to a discourse on revolution that is not entirely served by the historical method. She allows us to consider revolution and resistance as creative pro-cesses. In her work dual definitions of revolution as radical break and as cyclical condition are important. She returns to representations of the Grenada Revolution because even in its failure, this revolution is continuously generative of both thought and action. Her writing forms part of a postcolonial and black feminist archive of revolution that is constantly rethinking how and why revolutions of the past remain a part of our ongoing present.

By the early 1980s Brand had a serious problem with the Black Power movement in Canada. Immigrating to Toronto as a young adult in the 1970s, she was drawn to the collective movement for black empowerment and politicization that had been gathering support in Montreal and Toronto. This movement allowed her to connect with blacks from Canada, the Caribbean, Africa, and the United States. She eventually became disenchanted with the phallocentric rhetoric and tone of this militant activism, however, because it did not provide any significant platforms for women and queer people of color. Unable to see a space for herself in the Black Power movement in Canada, Brand turned to Grenada—newly immersed in revolution—as a frontier of radical possibility. In some ways travel to Grenada was one of Brand's earliest acknowledgments of the limits of the black radical tradition. Grenada was small and its scale gave her the opportunity to do more impactful work than was possible in Canada. She imagined being able to get on with the business of building the revolution without having to contend with North American racism.[4] From the beginning of 1983 Brand lived in Grenada, writing reports on foreign-funded agriculture projects.[5] She remained in Grenada for ten months until the assassination of Grenadian Prime Minister Maurice Bishop and his allies and the subsequent U.S. invasion. She survived the U.S. military assault and returned to Canada embittered after witnessing firsthand the tragedy and trauma of neocolonialism. As the revolution came to a grinding halt with Bishop's assassination, the American government seized the tragedy as an opportunity to invade Grenada, citing the need to protect American medical students on the island. This was a transparent ruse. Since the revolution's inception the U.S. government had been deeply uncomfortable with the Grenadian government's close ties to Cuba. The Grenada Revolution represented, in part, a victory for Cuban internationalism and the willingness of a tiny, newly independent nation to chart its own course in the world. In the contexts of the Cold War, the tail end of both the Black Power movement, and the wave of decolonization across the Third World, the United States was anxious about what the revolution's success would indicate to the rest of the region, particularly the recently independent Anglophone nations.

Brand's literary accounts of the revolution are poetic archives and attempts to find a grammar for postcolonial revolution. She describes the hypocrisy of the Global North and the double bind faced by small countries in the Global South who are forced to compete on the uneven playing field created by globalization in the postcolonial era. For Caribbean writers she provides an example of how to create a counterpoetics that insists on regional particularity as opposed to North Atlantic universality.[6] Within this counterpoetics she not only writes against imperialist histories of the Caribbean, but also establishes a strategy for using the historicity of imaginative writing to counteract colonizing epistemologies. By using literature to document history Brand troubles the distinction between literary invention and historical truth. Can literary work be thought of as a historical source for Caribbean nations whose ability to produce more conventional histories is often thwarted by the collusion of historical convention with imperialist oppression? This is an especially pertinent question for Grenada where Brand would have witnessed the destruction of troves of revolutionary government documents as the U.S. military bombed Grenadian government buildings.[7] Brand's poetry and fiction expose a complex relationship between imperialism, postcolonialism, and black radicalism. In her work Caribbean people suffer trauma, not only as a result of imperialism but also in the experience of revolution as a response to imperialism. Revolution itself visits a certain amount of violence on the very populations it purports to serve, and that violence is often pushed out of consciousness in order to forward the revolutionary project. Her writing is a space of confrontation and reconciliation, where readers face this dual violence.

Chronicling Revolution

There is an explicit relationship between history and literature in *Chronicles*. Several of the poems' titles include dates and the names of places Brand traveled to when she worked for the PRG. With titles such as *"Night—Mt. Panby Beach—25 March 1983," "Diary—The grenada crisis,"* and *"October 19th, 1983,"* she documents life within a revolution and the new sets of possibilities she saw emerging and destroyed in those months. These place-names and dates force the reader to look back on a specific place and time. Brand's use of the poet-speaker to witness makes a simple but important statement: This happened. I was there. The poems offer a sense of how one continues to live with those facts. Divided into three sections—Languages, Sieges, Military Occupations—the poems in *Chronicles* are not only discrete pieces that stand on their own but also fragments of a larger project that seeks to narrate the revolution from the perspective of a Caribbean national who has traveled between the region and North America. The term "chronicle" carries multiple connotations that effectively describe this work. Insofar as the collection gives an account of Brand's return to the Caribbean from Canada, the title can also be read as a biblical allusion to the two books of Chronicles, a historical account of the genealogy of Adam and the early Israelites, the exile of the Jewish people in Babylon, and finally their return from exile.[8] Brand's move from Canada to Grenada echoes the journey of the Israelites from Babylon to the "Promised Land." The *Oxford English Dictionary* defines chronicle as "a detailed and continuous register of events in order of time; a historical record, especially one in which the facts are narrated without philosophic treatment, or any attempt at literary style" and "[a] record, register, [or] narrative, account."[9] Brand's use of the diary mode, citing dates and place-names, fits with the first part of this definition, but the presentation of her account, her chronicle, in the poetic form engages the question of literary style and philosophic treatment directly. It is not always clear to readers what material in her poems is fact or invention, or how to interpret the license that Brand affords herself given the genre she has chosen. The impossibility of clarity on these terms is precisely the point for Brand, I argue: Whether it purports to be or not, all information in circulation about Grenada and the revolution is narrated with a philosophic treatment and literary style to suit the intended audience. The "facts" and narrative are altered according to who is telling the story, and to what purpose. In essence Brand's work challenges readers to consider that no historical account can be produced independent of ideology, philosophy, or literary style. As she writes a poetic account of the Grenada Revolution, her formal choices point to the possibility of plural voices and thus plural personal histories. The multiplicity of these accounts challenges the U.S. master narrative on Grenada. In this way *Chronicles* critiques the power of U.S. imperialism to dictate facts about the Global South, and the Caribbean in particular.

At the same time as her text emerges from the North American publishing industry (*Chronicles* was published by the Toronto-based Williams-Wallace Publishers), it offers a corrective to U.S.-narrated versions of the revolution. The authority it carries is different, therefore, from the government narratives it disputes because she invites readers to engage the poems of *Chronicles* as versions of the revolution narrated from specific and singular subject positions. While Brand refuses North Atlantic discourses on the "facts" about Grenada, her poems carry the weight of the eyewitness account. They stand as an important record of the revolution specifically because they do not claim to speak to a universal experience. They are her own ethnographic account of the events she and others experienced.

Poems from the section titled "Languages" address the need for a counterpoetics of revolution in Grenada, the desire for a language and perspective that would portray the revolution as a unique experience while putting Grenada (and the wider Anglophone Caribbean) in the context of late twentieth-century radicalism in Latin America and the Spanish- and French-speaking Caribbean. During this period Caribbean and Latin American radicalism often took the form of socialist (or socialist-inspired) governments and political parties who saw themselves as of a kind with the nations of the Non-Aligned Movement. The Non-Aligned Movement, composed largely of formerly colonized nations of the Global South, focused on the goal of creating south-south alliances to oppose imperialism.[10] The diversity of the nations involved in the Non-Aligned Movement meant that while most were opposed to capitalism because of its inherent links to colonial oppression, there was no widespread commitment to communism among these nations. Nonalignment was an important position for postcolonial nations navigating Cold War politics. Brand's poems locate Grenada in the context of such diffuse resistance to imperialism where governments of the Third World were in search of a "third way"—some direction in which to steer their nations beyond the capitalist/communist dichotomy.

The opening poem in *Chronicles*, "Night—Mt. Panby Beach—25 March 1983," describes an exercise in which members of the Grenadian militia, including the poet-speaker, are staked out overnight on a beach, practicing a maneuver in preparation for a possible military invasion.[11] The poem is a statement about how one embodies the ongoing struggle to preserve the freedoms won via independence. It is a poem about how to be postcolonial in a Caribbean region thrust into the Cold War. Throughout the poem Brand repeats the phrase "this night may make it to a poem," drawing attention to the process whereby she edits her memories of the revolution to produce poetry. There is a documentary aspect to the poem, a sense that it gives readers access to events that Brand actually witnessed. She lays bare the apparatus of historical invention by making readers hyperaware of her authorship and situating the poem as a metatext. The poem introduces the Grenada Revolution as if it were a Grenada-U.S. conflict. She describes the threat "of american war ships in barbados" ready to approach Grenada.[12] Throughout the revolution the PRG repeatedly warned the nation that a U.S. invasion of Grenada was likely. They knew that they were under U.S. government surveillance. They were also aware of an American Navy maneuver (code-named "Amber and the Amberdines") performed near Puerto Rico where marines practiced invading a fictional island nation.[13] On the stark difference between the Reagan administration and the Grenadian militia she writes: "They are comfy at Camp David / we are wet and always startled / though for once we have guns."[14] The "we" Brand constructs using the first person plural in this poem (and several others) suggests a collective Grenadian people, represented in characters she refers to such as the "boy" and "Rose." "Rose belongs to the militia," she writes, and so does the boy who "must put on his boots and his greens and wake me up at 4 a.m."[15] The poet-speaker sees herself as part of this community signaling a broader Caribbean solidarity. In this poem Grenadians experience the revolution as an opportunity to arm and protect themselves against the threat of American imperialism. As such, the writer is positioned with a weapon, raising the question of what it might mean for the writer turned revolutionary to pull the trigger. This is a question that surfaces throughout Brand's writing on Grenada, on the engagement of the artist in violent struggle and the simultaneous desire to document and to act. Through her attention to historical detail in the midst of poetic invention Brand establishes the poem as an alternate source of history and thus a window into the particularity of the Grenadian experience. Brand examines the radical alterity of Grenada vis-à-vis the North Atlantic, which was decidedly antirevolutionary during the late twentieth-century Cold War. In her work one can read a commitment to black radicalism as a strategy for the advancement and protection of local epistemologies and political practices even as the threat of imperialism looms. These are not poems about the pursuit of independence, but rather portraits of how Grenadians sought to make independence meaningful in a post-colonial context. These are poems about the preservation of sovereignty.

The Problem of Press Freedom

In the poem "On eavesdropping on a delegation of conventioners at Barbados Airport," Brand offers a defense for the PRG's 1979 decision to close down the *Torchlight*, a local, privately owned newspaper.[16] The poet-speaker calls out critics of the PRG as hypocrites who accept control of North American and British print media by a select group of wealthy, white men, while coming down on the Grenadian government for disrupting the freedom of the press. The poem specifically indicts media moguls Rupert Murdoch and Kenneth Thomson for their monopoly of North Atlantic media.[17] Brand writes:

> because your wrist watches are one hour behind
> the whole damn Caribbean must wait
> because you do not know that Murdoch and Thompson [*sic*]
> owning all the newspapers in the world
> is a violation of free speech,
> we cannot close down the Torchlight.[18]

Her argument is that the media in the First World is constrained by the interests of a select few and that their grip on the public is hegemonic, masking the scope and reach of
their power. That is, in terms of media production, the nations of the North Atlantic are
not as democratic as they purport to be. The domination of the media by a few powerful
individuals is an example of the violation of free speech, she contends, but it remains invisible because it occurs in the First World. The very concept of the First World evokes a
society that is shielded from such violations because it upholds particular values, including democracy and free market economics. She references time to stress the need to
recognize temporal differences between Caribbean and North Atlantic realities. This
difference is what makes First World ideas of "development" in the Third World (including IMF loans, structural adjustment, and open markets), so unpalatable and oppressive
for many in the Caribbean. The poet-speaker points out that when North Atlantic governments violate the sovereignty of Caribbean and Latin American nations by interfer-
ing in their politics, the actions of these governments are either ignored or reported on
uncritically by the American and English media. She repeats the refrain "where were you,"
taking to task the Associated Press, Reuters, and other "liberal" North Atlantic organizations for not speaking on instances of political injustice in Latin America and the
Caribbean:

> you law unions and conventions of wellwishers
> looking to be delighted at problems
> where were you when they assassinated Allende
> and when El Mercurio tried to steal the people's revolution
> and when the gleaner shot down that timid Jamaican,
> Manley[19]

Her accusatory "you" creates an angry tone that expresses the sense of combativeness
against American imperialism from those supportive of various forms of socialist government in the Global South. As she evokes Salvador Allende's Socialist Party of Chile and
Michael Manley's People's National Party (which tried to bring democratic socialism to
Jamaica), the implications here are threefold: First, that the governments of Chile, Jamaica,
and Grenada, while possessing varied postcolonial histories, shared a common political
project of guarding their nations from neocolonial oppression; second, that political opposition, aided by the American government, deployed *El Mercurio* and the *Jamaica Gleaner*
to destabilize leftist governments in Chile and Jamaica respectively; and third, that a similar tactic was deployed in the case of Grenada via false reports printed in the *Torchlight*
newspaper.[20] She uses personification to represent the *Gleaner* as the violent agent that
"shot down" Manley's vision of social democracy in Jamaica. Brand's characterization of
Manley as "timid," however, suggests that the forces of imperialism are not solely to blame
in the events that led to the departure of the PNP from government, and that the social
democracy project failed in Jamaica in part because of Manley's own personal failings. I
have argued elsewhere that the *Torchlight* was unfairly censored by the PRG.[21] Although I
disagree with Brand's evaluation of the *Torchlight*-PRG conflict, her poem highlights the
frustration the PRG experienced at not being able to sufficiently control the narrative of

the revolution given the international and local forces at play.[22] They feared that American efforts to destabilize leftist governments in Chile and Jamaica could be repeated in Grenada, and these fears were valid. Brand's poem sheds light on the pressure experienced by Caribbean governments confronting a new set of issues accompanying their postcolonial status. The power of the American public sphere to manipulate Caribbean politics bleeds into a Caribbean literary imaginary where artists and intellectuals such as Brand use the outlets available to them to respond to the American media.

The poem represents North American convention-goers as only coming to the Caribbean for the sun.[23] Unwilling to recognize the particularity of Caribbean people and politics, North Americans and Europeans instead expect to import into the Caribbean politics and values rooted in North Atlantic historical experiences. According to Brand this North Atlantic hegemony in the Caribbean creates a context where "truth is free to be fiction" and "counting is not an exact science."[24] At stake here are radically different definitions of freedom and truth. For Brand the "truth" of the Global North is often fiction when translated in a Caribbean context. The maps to freedom and sovereignty proposed by the United States for the Caribbean, with the promise of greater democracy and development, often lead to greater U.S. influence in the region without improving the lives of Caribbean citizens. Discourses on economics and "objective" reporting can become as subjective as literary language when these North Atlantic universals are thrust on the Caribbean region.

Writing in the Fractures of Revolution

In the final section of *Chronicles*, subtitled "Military Occupations," Brand details the end of the revolution. She continues with the concept of poetry as chronicle, however, the surveillance here shifts from the image of national surveillance to a personal evaluation of the politics of self in the midst of national crisis. The poems in "Military Occupations" convey a sense of urgency in their titles, rhythm, and sequencing. They announce themselves as if diary entries on the revolution's collapse: "Diary—The grenada crisis," "October 19th, 1983," "October 25th, 1983," "October 26th, 1983," "October 27th, 1983," "October 27th, 1983—evening." Again the poet-speaker is eager to correct the neocolonial record, to strike back against American imperialism and its colonizing epistemologies. With an emphasis on dates marking the assassination of Maurice Bishop (October 19) and the American invasion (October 25), these poems signal the forestalled time of the revolution—the inability of Grenadians to move forward with their project of freedom making. "Military Occupations" offers the sense that the postcolonial contemporary, this time in the aftermath of a destroyed revolution, is experienced as a period of trauma. The loss of the promise of the revolution becomes something that its survivors, including Brand, must face every day. This is what the anthropologist David Scott calls "ruined time," the experience of "temporal insecurity and uncertainty," where those deemed postcolonial subjects can never quite get to that horizon just beyond postcolonial.[25] Instead, these subjects are stuck in a neoliberal paradigm that tries to coerce them to disavow their revolutionary process by deeming it unjust or undemocratic. This state of ruined time inaugurates what Scott deems "an aftermath without end."[26] In *Chronicles* the invasion of Grenada is a harrowing example of how colonialism survives, and perhaps even reentrenches itself, even as postcolonial time is upon us. These are poems immersed in the pain of aftermaths.

"Diary—The grenada crisis" describes the scene of the U.S. invasion from a vantage point near St. George's, Grenada's capital.[27] Hours after Bishop was assassinated, a new organization, the Revolutionary Military Council (RMC), claimed to have taken over the island's governance.[28] The RMC imposed a twenty-four-hour "shoot-to-kill" curfew on the nation. The country was in total shock and chaos. Grenadians were frightened for their lives and made to feel that external forces were necessary to restore order. For most Grenadians the restoration of order meant ending the curfew and bringing to justice those responsible for Bishop's death: That was more urgent than the need to protest an unlawful military invasion. A large percentage of Grenadians accepted the American invasion because they saw U.S. and regional intervention as the only way to restore order to the nation, but some also resisted. Brand represents the invasion as a war, stressing the often overlooked fact that invading American forces met with armed resistance from Grenadians.[29] The Reagan administration sold the invasion to the American public as an effort to rescue American medical students at St. George's School of Medicine and to liberate the Grenadian people from the clutches of communism. A *New York Times* article from October 22, 1983, cites a Department of Defense official who claimed that U.S. Marines were being sent to Grenada to protect the 1,200 American citizens on the island.[30] Another *Times* article quotes Reagan referring to Grenada as a "'Soviet-Cuban colony being readied' to export terrorism."[31] The U.S. government prevented their own journalists and other foreign reporters from traveling to Grenada until several days into the invasion, when the initial military assault was completed.[32] In so doing the American government and military could dictate the narrative of the invasion, focusing on images of Grenadians and American medical students welcoming the marines. This narrative of rescue did not recognize the complexity of the situation facing Grenadians, the majority of whom had supported the revolution and were aghast both at the deaths of October 19 and at the military invasion. The images offered by Brand communicate the banality, fear, and shock that the violence of invasion brings to Grenada. The incursion of American military personnel by sea and air seems out of place in the picturesque beauty of the island. The Grenada that is familiar to the poet-speaker is destroyed by the invasion:

the ship and the cement drop against the metal skies
a yankee paratrooper strangles in his sheet.

prayers for rain,
instead again this wonderful sky;
an evening of the war and those of us looking with our mouths open
see beauty become appalling,
sunset, breaths of grey clouds streaked red,
we are watching a house burn[33]

The hostile sun is evoked in the image of the "wonderful sky" that provides the backdrop for the invasion. Here the sun's hostility is defined in the way it produces a clear day for the invaders instead of the rain that the poet-speaker hopes would interrupt the progress of the American forces. The sky is not only "wonderful" but also somehow "metal," transformed by the machinery of war. But Grenadians are not the only victims of the hostile sun. American paratroopers are strangled in their parachutes, falling like Icarus too close to the sun.

Throughout the poem the shock of invasion and the onset of a neocolonial reality is represented as keeping Grenadians in a liminal state between sleep and wakefulness, not unlike the feeling of the militia on the practice maneuver in "Mt. Panby Beach." In the second to last stanza the poet-speaker refers to "the last evening" of the war and the feeling of suffocation experienced by the survivors: "no air comes up,/we have breathed the last of it."[34] The revolution was like oxygen for Grenadians, and it was sucked up by the invasion, marking the end of freedom and national sovereignty. The poet-speaker describes a process of keeping vigil throughout the war, but there seems to be a combination of astonishment and inertia which prevent the speaker and those described in the poem from resisting. They are static, crunched in defensive positions as they hope to stay alive.[35] That an internal government conflict would set the stage for an American invasion is not something many Grenadians would have expected. The American military was facing a completely fractured nation and a population that quickly resigned itself to a fate of neocolonial dominance once their revolutionary government crumbled.

The sense of resignation to a tragic fate is communicated in the poem "October 19th, 1983."[36] The poem's opening translates shock as the inability of words to sufficiently account for the situation. At the same time, since words are not enough, they must be put in service of all the emotions that the end of the revolution triggers:

> this poem cannot find words
> this poem repeats itself
> Maurice is dead
> Jackie is dead
> Uni is dead
> dream is dead[37]

Brand does not equate the revolution with Bishop, Jacqueline Creft (minister of education), Unison Whiteman (minister of foreign affairs), and Vincent Noel (a union organizer); however, she suggests that the betrayal of trust that led to their deaths initiated the end of the revolution. The construction "is dead" appears to remove fault or agency from the act of their murders and instead emphasizes the finality of the fact. Further down, however, the poet-speaker names four other members of the New Jewel Movement (NJM), the revolution's political party, and holds them accountable for the violence:

> Bernard, Phyllis, Owusu, H.A.!
> what now!
> back to jails in these antilles!
> back to shackles! back to slavery![38]

In naming Bernard Coard (deputy prime minister), Phyllis Coard (deputy minister of Foreign Affairs), Liam "Owusu" James (member of the Central Committee), and Hudson Austin (Army General), the poet-speaker, echoing Grenadian public opinion, holds the surviving members of the NJM leadership responsible for the deaths of Bishop and his colleagues. Brand uses the term "fratricide" to describe the assassinations where black revolutionaries had turned against each other and the nation.[39] It is one of the rare moments in *Chronicles* in which she complicates her critique of the United States by acknowledging the problems arising from within the NJM itself.[40] The moment is important to the poem and to the wider text because it clears space to acknowledge tragic and fatal violence within the revolution. Here she not only names those who many Caribbean people believed were responsible for Bishop's assassination, but also assesses the fate that now awaits Grenadians and the Caribbean more broadly in the wake of their rash actions—that is a return to imprisonment, foreign encroachment, and servitude. This, too, is the postcolonial. The self-inflicted violence under which the PRG collapsed left the Caribbean open to further violation by imperialist interests. The poem repeats itself just as the cycle of empire repeats itself. The metaphorical shackles the region is returned to echo the shackles of slavery, but this time the fault is shared (if unequally) between the proponents of the revolution and the forces of empire. The poet-speaker refers to the poem self-reflexively as a funeral song for the revolution, "a dirge sung for ever / and in flesh."[41] The survivors and the collective memory of those who died embody the mournful quality of the literary dirge. Opening the collection with a poem about the militia, Brand is working through how the atmosphere for violence was embedded in the culture of the revolution. Reading backward allows us to situate the violent end of the revolution in a broader repertoire of violence that can be linked to histories of colonial slavery and the plantation.[42] Still, the collection overall betrays a sense of shock that the revolution could turn against itself in this way. It is a sudden disappointment for the poet-narrator who was fully immersed in the revolution. Although the poems of *Chronicles* document the poet's sense of an ever-unfolding tragic aftermath, during the years between the publication of *Chronicles* and *In Another Place*, Brand's perspective on how revolution rehearses the violent patterns of colonialism shifts, and she turns to the representation of black queer love as a site of revolution.

Engendering Revolution

In Another Place moves toward, and in many ways past, the tragedy of the revolution by recognizing the ongoing marginalization of women and sexual minorities from black radical movements even as they participate in these movements. Brand's novel provides a meditation on the limits of the black radical tradition in a way that her poetry does not. Although she could have easily labeled Grenada a site of disappointment where her idealism clashed with her reality and stopped writing about the revolution after publishing *Chronicles*, instead Brand continues to write Grenada into a literary imaginary using the revolution as a site for articulating a black, feminist, queer politics. This movement can be read as an attempt to address the unfulfilled promises of previous revolutionary moments when liberation for all was pledged but not achieved. Brand's writing in *Chronicles* stresses urgency and the violation of sovereignty, but her work in *In Another Place* emphasizes the coexistence of the intimate and the political, demonstrating how the two spheres are necessary to register black women's experiences in the Caribbean.[43] A crucial part of Brand's revision of revolution in this novel is her attention to the politics of gender and sexuality in the postcolonial Caribbean and her quest for what the literary critic Donette Francis calls sexual citizenship. In *Fictions of Feminine Citizenship: Sexuality and the Nation in Contemporary Caribbean Literature* (2010), Francis outlines sexual citizenship as a means of accounting for "the political significance of the intimate sphere as a cornerstone of imperialists' and nationalists' projects and thus the private sphere's importance to understandings of colonial and postcolonial subjectivity and citizenship."[44] Within this framework the concept of citizenship (in the contexts of nation and diaspora) is seen as being indelibly shaped by sexuality, sexual intimacy, and the private sphere. With *In Another Place*, Brand outlines the intersectionality of race, class, gender, and sexuality as they inform the circumstances under which black queer women are excluded from full citizenship in Canada and the Caribbean. This exclusion is part of what underscores the relationship that develops between Verlia and Elizete, the novel's protagonists. The novel tells the story of a same-sex relationship between the two women, describing how their love makes them outlaws in the midst of revolutionary politics. Brand draws outside of the lines of a patriarchal black radical tradition, making the women the center of a novel that is a queer chronicle of revolution. The text shifts between the perspectives of the two lovers, Elizete, a peasant laborer who works in the sugarcane fields, and Verlia, an expatriate who, having lived and worked in Canada for several years as part of the Black Power movement, returns to the unnamed island in order to contribute to the revolutionary movement. Here the revolution intersects with narrative strands on immigration, African Canadian life, and the translocal circuits of activism that animate the African Diaspora in the late twentieth century. Queer desire pulls all of these narrative strands together. This desire demands a feminist decolonizing politics to expose the exclusion of poor and queer black women from the discursive practices of black radicalism and revolution.

In Another Place does not represent revolution from the usual stock characters of heroic men. Thinking through the lens of gender and sexuality, Brand finds that the site of revolution needs revolutionizing itself. She explores the way the gender divide in day-to-day Caribbean life and politics functions as a microcosm of the center-periphery power dynamics that define the relationship between the microstates of the Caribbean and imperial forces to the north. Brand's writing situates gender and sexuality as truly radical components of the revolution. Her centering of sexual citizenship is radical in the sense that it represents a departure from the issues that are typically emphasized in nationalist, revolutionary struggles.

Elizete's is the most demanding and fearless voice in the novel: Through her we understand peasant life on the island. By offering a large part of the narrative through Elizete's perspective, Brand opens up the range of possibilities as to why and how the otherwise anonymous masses participated in the revolution. Her representation of Elizete depicts the development of inarticulate movements within the Grenada Revolution. Elizete is not a political leader, but she is a worker and a lover. In her view, the importance of politics and love are intertwined. Elizete and the other cane workers are not much interested in revolutionary leadership in the conventional sense; instead they view Verlia as a leader who matters. They can identify with her anonymity and her work ethic. As Elizete explains, "I suppose not only me see rescue when she [Verlia] reach."[45] There is something intriguing about Verlia as a woman who comes to the field to cut cane with them and who arrives with an eagerness to learn from the workers. By framing Verlia as a leader, even on a microscale, Brand sidesteps the need to make the novel about central figures in the revolution's history such as Maurice Bishop, whom she assigns the pseudonym Clive. Elizete never mentions Clive, or the government, for that matter, and Verlia mentions him only briefly toward the novel's end. It is the women themselves who serve as the central site of revolutionary praxis in this text, a crucial shift from *Chronicles* and a sign that Brand's work in the novel is to identify alternatives to the traditional representation of black radicalism that has shaped dominant historical narratives of the Grenada Revolution.

The novel opens with Elizete's desire for Verlia after first sighting her in the cane fields. Brand gives the first pages over to Elizete's description of the sheer beauty she sees in Verlia:

> Grace. Is grace, yes. And I take it quiet, quiet, like thiefing sugar. From the word she speak to me and the sweat running down she in that sun, one afternoon as I look up saying to myself, how many more days these poor feet of mine can take this field, these blades of cane like razor, this sun like coal pot. Long as you have to eat, girl. I look up. That woman like a drink of cool water. The four o'clock light thinning she dress, she back good and strong, the sweat raining off in that moment I look and she snap her head around, that wide mouth blowing a wave of tiredness away, pulling in one big breath of air, them big white teeth, she, falling to the work again, she falling into the four o'clock sunlight. I see she. Hot, cool and wet.[46]

Brand engulfs her readers in the full force of Elizete's gaze and her account of Verlia's physicality. Although Elizete's political consciousness does not seem much affected by the revolution in progress (she imagines that she will work under the hostile sun as long as she needs to eat), she does experience herself as a self-possessed and erotic being in relation to Verlia. Seeing Verlia, Elizete does not forget that she is a field laborer, but she remembers that there are other openings for pleasure that she can seize. The literary critic Omise'eke Natasha Tinsley calls for an engagement with women who love women as both lovers and "activists in their erotic and sexual practices."[47] Drawing on the work of Audre Lorde, Tinsley maintains the importance of eroticism and sexuality in black women's efforts to reclaim possession of their bodies. Within the matrix of colonial slavery black women were denied personhood and therefore womanhood. "They were not supposed to feel," Tinsley writes.[48] Their eroticism, love, and feeling (both of and for each other) is a way of rejecting the commodification of their bodies as "the exclusive property of white men."[49] At the beginning of *In Another Place* Elizete was caught in an abusive relationship with a man named Isaiah. Adela, the woman who raised Elizete after her parents abandoned her as a small child, handed Elizete over to Isaiah, as if she were mere property. Several times Elizete attempted to run away from Isaiah but she never got farther than the village junction. When Verlia arrives, however, Elizete is suddenly able to envision her liberation—not only political liberation, but also a sensual and emotional liberation. She finally recognizes her true self in her desire for Verlia. In his reading of *In Another Place*, the literary critic Ronald Cummings considers Verlia and Elizete's relationship a space of "erotic maroonage." Cummings defines "erotic maroonage" as "private erotic acts of desire and remembering between women."[50] Both Cummings and Tinsley note the double meaning of Elizete's reference to "thiefing sugar," as both a practice of theft that the enslaved and the maroons used to resist the plantation and as a turn of phrase to describe "the sweetness" of desire and eroticism.[51] Reimagining Grenada in this sense, Brand subverts heteronormative discourses on revolution. Her novel places political and economic liberation (via the worker-friendly policies of the revolution) in dialogue with queer sexuality and emotional liberation. Elizete's desire for Verlia is taboo, but no less urgent and lifesaving for her. The sovereignty she displays over her mind, body, and spirit in her embrace of this desire is, for Brand, a quiet triumph that cannot be ignored.

Drawing on the more archaic definition of "radical," relating to roots and fundamental processes that are deemed vital, we can consider how Brand's approach with this novel reframes gender and sexuality as foundational aspects of revolutionary discourse. Understood in this way, attention to sexual citizenship is essential to new framings of Caribbean revolution. This is not to say that sexual citizenship is a new component of Caribbean revolution, but rather that it becomes newly emergent when we turn to postcolonial narratives produced on the margins of revolution. In her revised narration of the Grenada Revolution she creates a space where a black, queer, revolutionary subject can embody and inspire revolution as effectively as the more commonly accepted Caribbean heterosexual male subject. Her writing allows readers to encounter Grenada not as a utopia, but rather as a place from which to work through ideas of sovereignty and citizenship as they play out in a postcolonial context. Brand wants revolution to *mean* something for the farmer and the diasporic black activist, for people across genders—for it to be truly radical for queer and straight subjects, for citizens and immigrants. Queering the black radical tradition, Brand's writing on Grenada rejects the Cold War binaries in order to envision the broader frameworks of decolonization and postcolonialism within which the Grenada Revolution can be read. These frameworks reflect certain patterns of postcolonial political formations as outlined in the introduction to this volume, including the "persistence, repetition, or resurgence of older forms of domination" that keep formerly colonized nations in cycles of revolution.[52]

Through the narration of the relationship between these two women Brand offers a vision of queer revolution. In this recasting of Caribbean resistance women embody the possibility for liberation in both a collective and an individual sense. Here liberation is a process more than an end point. She writes characters that explore possibilities for being and belonging. In Brand's writing women are best able to outline the contours of this liberation because they understand that the path of this particular expression of freedom must cut through and around a thicket of intersecting oppressions. Elizete imagines women as conduits to liberation using the metaphor of a bridge. She thinks:

> A woman can be a bridge, limber and living, breathless, because she don't know where the bridge might lead, she don't need no assurance except that it would lead out with certainty, no assurance except the arch and disappearance. At the end it might be the uptake of air, the chasm of what she don't know, the sweep and soar of sheself unhandled, making sheself a way to cross over. A woman can be a bridge from these bodies whipping cane. A way to cross over.[53]

Elizete's stream of consciousness reads like a manifesto for feminist liberation. Brand focuses on the vitality of scenes of revolution that involve women taking possession of their own bodies and minds. This can be a radical form of action, allowing themselves and others to "cross over." Again, the act of crossing over is not linked to a predetermined destination. The movement of crossing over, errant as it might be, is itself the revolutionary praxis. The fulfillment of radical potential is in the recognition that all possibilities are present in this black feminist movement. Verlia is Elizete's bridge away from "whipping cane" and into a space of possibility—another place, not here.

Revising the Black Radical Tradition

In the formulation that is a loving and radical bond between Elizete and Verlia, Verlia is the skeptic. Where Elizete finds their intimacy liberating, Verlia struggles to reconcile her investment in the revolution proper with her investment in Elizete. She worries that falling in love with Elizete will only distract her from the work of the revolution and is not as sure as Elizete that their love can survive within the boundaries of nationalist revolution. "I am not a man," Verlia tells Elizete. "I cannot take care of you like that; a man can promise things that will never happen not because he is lying but because they are within his possibilities in the world."[54] Verlia's rejection of seduction in the midst of the affair allows Brand to explore the limits of romantic conventions of love for peasant and working-class queer Caribbean women. Throughout the novel Elizete and Verlia confront restraints on both their love and their politics; at the same time they come to understand love as a form of politics. One way to read Brand's depiction of this relationship is to think of how Elizete and Verlia work to build their relationship and express their desire outside of the confines of heteronormative romantic love. As Verlia points out, they are always already outside of that framework. Together they model a vision for revolutionary praxis in their pursuit of their mutual desires on the margins of a black radical political movement. They learn to value and appreciate their shared love even from a place of nonbelonging. From these margins women such as Verlia and Elizete understand that the revolutionary project cannot be completed without the liberation of subjects situated at the intersection of multiple oppressions. This realization breeds apprehension within them about the black radical tradition, where they often participate in black revolutionary movements, while at the same time bracing themselves for the fallout or the moment when a line is drawn that says their identities must conform to certain strictures in order for them to be properly "revolutionary." Often this line is drawn at the place where the revolution stumbles on its own exclusionary and oppressive policies.

Verlia is an important contrast to Elizete because Verlia wants desperately for national revolution to be sufficient for her liberation. She is terrified of the freedom represented in her love of Elizete. On the day of the U.S. invasion, when both Elizete and Verlia form part of the Grenadian resistance forces, Elizete observes Verlia and sees how deeply Verlia wanted the revolution to succeed: "She bet all of she life on this revolution. She had no place else to go, no other countries, no other revolution, none of we neither. That day we all went to dreaming, imagining, trying to shoot jet fighters from the skies with shotguns and curses."[55] Elizete empathizes with Verlia's pursuit of revolution as a way of belonging in the diaspora; however, she herself has no such romantic attachments to the project. For Verlia, as with the poet-speaker in "October 19th, 1983," the U.S. invasion and the end of the revolution is akin to a return to colonial enslavement because it destroys the place where she was seeking belonging. It brings her back into a conception of diaspora as a space of negation, the "not here" of the novel. At the novel's end Verlia runs toward a cliff. An unnamed voice behind her (Elizete, perhaps?) encourages her, "Comrade, run! Comrade, sister, lover, run, not today, not today."[56] At the edge of the cliff Verlia leaps. Brand offers the description of bodies falling down the cliff, breaking bones, but then suddenly taking flight across the sea. The scene marks Brand's rewriting of two earlier moments in Grenadian history. On October 19, 1983, members of the People's Revolutionary Army opened fire on a crowd of Grenadians who were rallying in support of Prime Minister Bishop at Fort Rupert. In a chaotic exchange of fire between the military and the prime minister's supporters several civilians jumped from the fort to their deaths in an attempt to flee the bullets. The scene also echoes an incident in Grenada's colonial history in 1652 when a group of forty Caribs, indigenous to the island, jumped to their deaths from a cliff on the northern tip of the island, rather than submit to the rule of French colonizers.[57] This cliff is now appropriately named Sauteurs or Carib's Leap, a reminder of how colonial histories remain in the contemporary moment. Brand's representation of Verlia and others jumping is a way of remembering the Grenadian dead who have not been accounted for in many histories. It echoes the diasporic trope of flying Africans who find their way back to Africa out of slavery and oppression in the Americas.[58] The passage from the novel also feels like a compression of time in which readers are invited to contemplate different historical events at once. Brand recasts these histories in Verlia's queer likeness, allowing Verlia to cross over to another place once she confronts the end of the revolution. There is something liberatory in Verlia's leap even as it leaves Elizete alone to contend with the aftermath. Elizete's sense of loss in this moment is tied to Verlia's transition from the land of the living to a place of the ancestors. It is a bittersweet loss that is distinct from the trauma of the end of the political process of revolution. As a result, Elizete is not negated or otherwise forestalled by tragedy at the end of the revolution unlike the poet-speaker of *Chronicles*. She experiences trauma, yes, but she has also witnessed Verlia's "crossing over," and this makes a difference. In the wake of the revolution Elizete travels to Canada seeking traces of Verlia as she makes sense of the aftermath of their affair and the revolution. The healing work of this novel is in the redirection of mourning, not necessarily for what the revolution had achieved but rather for the possibilities that it represented in its best and brightest moments, and in the lives of those whose work was to keep expanding the horizon of possibility of whom the revolution would work to liberate.

Whereas *Chronicles* was focused on the agenda of the revolutionary government, *In Another Place* reflects Brand's turn away from revolutionary politics shaped by governments and her embrace of the politics of queer desire. This shift in her writing, thirteen years after the fall of the revolution, constitutes a reevaluation of what was truly possible in Grenada. David Scott has argued that the violent end of the Grenada Revolution was inevitable given the neoliberal impulse to stifle political formations that fail to replicate liberal visions of freedom, transparency, and democracy.[59] Brand acknowledges American liberalism's will to power in the postcolonial Caribbean, and she turns to the intimate lives of women in order to map a way out of tragedy and trauma and in search of something beyond political sovereignty.

The idealization of the Grenada Revolution that is apparent throughout *Chronicles* is a product of the time and place out of which the book emerges; the constant modes of comparison between the north and the south are reflective of Brand's diasporic condition. As her focus shifts from an analysis of the destabilization of revolutionary politics via U.S. intervention in the Caribbean, to an intimate account of revolutionary projects forged beyond the reach of U.S. imperialism, Brand asks us to consider what modes of repair can be enacted when postcolonial revolution is not enough? A primary achievement of *In Another Place* is its positioning of the intellectual, Verlia, alongside and on equal footing with the peasant, Elizete. This relationship illustrates Brand's vision for how black radicalism must continue to evolve. Her writing revises the black radical tradition to broaden its scope and make it speak into silences where black queer folks struggle within and alongside the revolutionary collective.

NOTES

Adapted from L. Lambert, "The Sovereignty of the Imagination: Poetic Authority and the Fiction of North Atlantic Universals in Dionne Brand's *Chronicles of the Hostile Sun*," *Cultural Dynamics* 26, no. 2 (2104): 173–94. Copyright © 2014 by the Author. Reprinted by permission of SAGE Publications, Ltd.

1. Brand, *Chronicles of the Hostile Sun*, 65.

2. Wilson-Tagoe, *Historical Thought*, 2.

3. Descriptions of her time in Grenada appear in several texts by Brand, including *Chronicles* (1984), *No Language Is Neutral* (1990), *Bread Out of Stone* (1994), *In Another Place, Not Here* (1996) and *A Map to the Door of No Return* (2001). Each of these texts articulates a different relationship to postcolonial revolution and trauma, and a constantly shifting vision of what Caribbean sovereignty looks like in the aftermaths of colonialism. I focus on *Chronicles* and *In Another Place* as the two texts that are dedicated primarily to representations of the Grenada Revolution.

4. Brand, *Bread Out of Stone*, 59.

5. Ibid., 12–13.

6. I borrow the term "North Atlantic universals" from Trouillot, *Global Transformations*, 29–46.

7. The U.S. military seized those Grenadian government documents that survived the bombings.

8. Coogan et al., *New Oxford Annotated Bible*, 503–80.

9. *Oxford English Dictionary Online*. www.oed.com.

10. Prashad, *The Darker Nations*, 13.

11. Brand, *Chronicles*, 7.

12. Ibid.

13. Meeks, *Caribbean Revolutions*, 168.

14. Brand, *Chronicles*, 7.

15. Ibid.

16. Ibid., 20.

17. Rupert Murdoch is an Australian American media titan and CEO of News Corporation. His holdings include the *Wall Street Journal*, Twentieth Century Fox, Harper Collins, the *Times*, the *Sunday Times*, and *New York Post* (Shawcross, *Murdoch*). The late Kenneth Thomson was a Canadian businessman whose company Thomson Corporation sold the *Times* to Murdoch in 1981 (Stewart, *History of the Times*). Thomson also owned several smaller newspapers in Canada, as well as the *Globe and Mail*, Canada's largest national newspaper.

18. Brand, *Chronicles*, 20.

19. Ibid.

20. Salvador Allende was elected president of Chile in 1970. An avowed socialist, he enacted several social reforms in Chile that were met with resistance from the Chilean elite. Allende's government was overthrown by the U.S.-supported General Augusto Pinochet in 1973. *El Mercurio*, a right-wing Chilean newspaper, received funds from International Telephone and Telegraph (ITT), an American corporation working directly with the CIA in order to destabilize Allende's government. The role of ITT in cooperating with the CIA in order to oust Allende is detailed in "The Church Report: Covert Action in Chile 1963–1973" and published by the U.S. Department of State in December 1975. Michael Manley was first elected Prime Minister of Jamaica in 1972, leading the People's Nationalist Party (PNP). A democratic socialist, his plans for social reform met much resistance from the United States (Black, *Life and Debt*). *The Gleaner* is a Jamaican newspaper noted for representing Manley as a communist and deriding him for his relationship with Fidel Castro. See Meeks, *Narratives of Resistance*, 125. Manley eventually took legal action against the *Gleaner* for claiming he "sold Jamaica to Cuba." See "Manley to Sue Gleaner," 5.

21. Lambert, "The Revolution and Its Discontents," 143–53.

22. I describe the shifting relationship between the PRG and the *Torchlight* in the second chapter of my dissertation on the Grenada Revolution. Although the *Torchlight* was run by members of Grenada's business class, I have not found any evidence to suggest that the newspaper was funded in any part by the U.S. government or any American agencies. Lambert, "Worlds Real and Invented," 71–119.

23. The danger of having an economy that is overly dependent on tourism is a topic covered by many Caribbean writers. See Kincaid, *A Small Place*; Moss, "Derek Walcott"; and Nixon, *Resisting Paradise*.

24. Brand, *Chronicles*, 20.

25. David Scott, *Omens of Adversity*, 12.

26. Ibid., 21.

27. Brand, *Chronicles*, 37–39.

28. Reports of a rift between Bishop and Coard appeared on October 15, 1983, on the front page of the *Trinidad Guardian*. Although Coard resigned from his office of Deputy Prime

Minister in order to quell the rumors that he was behind a plot to assassinate Bishop, it was obvious to the public that a power struggle was taking place within the party once Bishop was placed under house arrest on October 14, 1983. On October 19 the *Guardian* printed another article reporting that Unison Whiteman (Minister of Foreign Affairs), Lynden Ramdhanny (Minister of Tourism), Norris Bain (Minister of Housing), George Louison (Minister of Education), and Jacqueline Creft (Minster of Education) had all resigned from office on October 18, 1983. The article also quoted Whiteman claiming that Coard was now running the country. On October 21 the *Guardian* reported that Hudson Austin was heading the RMC and that he had announced over Grenada's national radio station that "security forces" had killed Bishop, Whiteman, Creft, Bain, and union leaders Vincent Noel and Fitzroy Bain. During this time Coard and his wife Phyllis remained in hiding.

29. Cuban construction workers who were staying at the airport construction site in Point Salines also put up armed resistance, but this fact has been overreported, I would argue, in publicized U.S. accounts of the invasion. A CIA "Grenada Situation Report" from October 22, 1983, conceded that "the Cubans may have been suspicious of Coard and [did] not have a clear picture of the new regime's intentions." In sizing up the resistance American military personnel could expect to meet in Grenada, the document reports that the RMC was "mobilizing the remainder of the Army and the 2,000 to 4,000 member militia." In the parts of this document that have not been redacted, no mention is made of Cuban (or any other) military forces. Another CIA document dated October 30, 1983, cites Cuban media reports that there were approximately 784 Cubans in Grenada at the time of the U.S. invasion, including 636 construction workers and 43 military advisers.

30. Ayres Jr., "U.S. Marines Diverted."

31. Taubman, "The Reason for Invading."

32. Farrell, "Reporters to Go to Grenada."

33. Brand, *Chronicles*, 38.

34. Ibid., 39.

35. Ibid.

36. Ibid., 40.

37. Ibid.

38. Ibid., 41.

39. Ibid.

40. A similar moment occurs in the poem "Eurocentric" where she writes, "(even male revolutionaries refuse to radicalise their balls)" (*Chronicles*, 21). This line, however, points to gender problems in radical political movements generally, as opposed to identifying gender issues within the Grenada Revolution specifically. For an analysis of women's roles during the revolution, including attention to some of the problems they faced from within the NJM, see Phillip, *Women in Grenadian History*.

41. Brand, *Chronicles*, 41.

42. Thomas, *Exceptional Violence*, 4.

43. For recent critical contributions about the links between the personal and the political in Caribbean women's writing, see Donnell, *Twentieth-Century Caribbean Literature*; Francis, *Fictions of Feminine Citizenship*; Scott, *Caribbean Women Writers*; and Smith, *Sex and the Citizen*.

44. Francis, *Fictions of Feminine Citizenship*, 1–2.

45. Brand, *In Another Place*, 9.

46. Ibid., 3.

47. Tinsley, *Thiefing Sugar*, 20.

48. Ibid.

49. Ibid., 21.

50. Cummings, "Queer Theory," 329.

51. Ibid., and Tinsley, *Thiefing Sugar*, 3.
52. Jini Kim Watson and Gary Wilder, introduction to this volume.
53. Brand, *In Another Place*, 16.
54. Ibid., 72.
55. Ibid., 114–15.
56. Ibid., 245.
57. Brizan, *Grenada*, 23.
58. For a discussion of flying Africans, see Gomez, *Exchanging Our Country Marks*, 117–120; Savannah Unit, *Drums and Shadows: Survival Studies among the Georgia Coastal Negroes*. Other contemporary novelists to take up the trope include Lovelace, *Salt*, and Morrison, *Song of Solomon*.
59. Scott, *Omens of Adversity*, 127–64.

BIBLIOGRAPHY

"Army in Full Control." *Trinidad Guardian*, October 21, 1983.

Ayres, Drummond B., Jr. "U.S. Marines Diverted to Grenada in Event Americans Face Danger." *New York Times*, October 22, 1983.

Black, Stephanie, director. *Life and Debt*. Kingston, Jamaica: Tuff Gong Pictures Production, 2001.

Brand, Dionne. *Bread Out of Stone: Recollections, Sex, Recognitions, Race, Dreaming, Politics*. Toronto: Coach House Press, 1994.

———. *Chronicles of the Hostile Sun*. Toronto: Williams-Wallace, 1984.

———. *In Another Place, Not Here*. New York: Grove Press, 1996.

———. *A Map to the Door of No Return: Notes to Belonging*. Toronto: Doubleday Canada, 2001.

———. *No Language Is Neutral*. Toronto: Coach House Press, 1990.

Brizan, George. *Grenada: Island of Conflict*. 1984. London: Macmillan, 1998.

Central Intelligence Agency. "Grenada Situation Report as of 1700 22 October 1983." Freedom of Information Act Electronic Reading Room. Document Number: 0000401538. https://www.cia.gov/library/readingroom/home.

Coogan, Michael D., Marc Z. Brettler, Carol Newson, and Pheme Perkins, eds. *The New Oxford Annotated Bible*. Augmented 3rd ed. New York: Oxford University Press, 2007.

Cummings, Ronald. "Queer Theory and Caribbean Writing." In *Routledge Companion to Anglophone Caribbean Literature*, edited by Michael Bucknor and Alison Donnell, 323–31. New York: Routledge, 2011.

Donnell, Alison. *Twentieth-Century Caribbean Literature: Critical Moments in Anglophone Literary History*. New York: Routledge, 2006.

Farrell, William E. "U.S. Allows 15 Reporters to Go to Grenada for Day." *New York Times*, October 28, 1983.

"Five Ministers Resign. Whiteman: Coard Running the Show." *Trinidad Guardian*, October 19, 1983.

Francis, Donette. *Fictions of Feminine Citizenship: Sexuality and the Nation in Contemporary Caribbean Literature*. New York: Palgrave Macmillan, 2010.

Gomez, Michael A. *Exchanging Our Country Marks: The Transformation of African Identities in the Colonial and Antebellum South*. Chapel Hill: University of North Carolina Press, 1998.

Kincaid, Jamaica. *A Small Place*. New York: Farrar, Straus, Giroux, 1988.

Lambert, Laurie. "The Revolution and Its Discontents: Grenadian Newspapers and Attempts to Shape Public Opinion during Political Transition." *The Round Table: The Commonwealth Journal of International Affairs*, Special Issue "The Invasion of Grenada 30 Years On: A Retrospective" 102, no. 2 (2013): 143–53.

———. "World Real and Invented: The Grenada Revolution and the Caribbean Literary Imaginary." PhD diss., New York University, 2013.

Lovelace, Earl. *Salt*. London: Faber and Faber, 1996.

"Manley to Sue Gleaner." *Torchlight*, September 26, 1979.

Meeks, Brian. *Caribbean Revolutions and Revolutionary Theory: An Assessment of Cuba, Nicaragua and Grenada*. Mona, Jamaica: University of the West Indies Press, 1993.

———. *Narratives of Resistance: Jamaica, Trinidad, and the Caribbean*. Mona, Jamaica: University of the West Indies Press, 2000.

Morrison, Toni. *Song of Solomon*. New York: Penguin Books, 1997.

Moss, Stephen. "Derek Walcott: The Oxford Poetry Job Would Have Been Too Much." *Guardian*, May 3, 2012. http://www.guardian.co.uk/books/2012/may/03/derek-walcott- interview.

Nixon, Angelique. *Resisting Paradise: Tourism, Diaspora, and Sexuality in Caribbean Culture*. Oxford: University Press of Mississippi, 2015.

Phillip, Nicole Laurine. *Women in Grenadian History, 1783–1983*. Kingston, Jamaica: University of the West Indies Press, 2010.

Prashad, Vijay. *The Darker Nations: A People's History of the Third World*. New York: New Press, 2007.

Savannah Unit, Georgia Writer's Project, Work Projects Administration. *Drums and Shadows: Survival Studies among the Georgia Coastal Negroes*. 1940. Athens: University of Georgia Press, 1986.

Scott, David. *Omens of Adversity: Tragedy, Time, Memory, Justice*. Durham, N.C.: Duke University Press, 2014.

Scott, Helen. *Caribbean Women Writers and the Globalization Fictions of Independence*. Burlington, Vt.: Ashgate, 2006.

"See Saw 'Coup' in Grenada: Bernard Coard Resigns." *Trinidad Guardian*, October 15, 1983.

Shawcross, William. *Murdoch: The Making of a Media Empire*. New York: Simon & Schuster, 1997.

Smith, Faith, ed. *Sex and the Citizen: Interrogating the Caribbean*. Charlottesville: University of Virginia Press, 2011.

Stewart, Graham. *The History of the Times: The Murdoch Years, 1981–2002*. New York: Harper Collins, 2005.

Taubman, Philip. "The Reason for Invading." *New York Times*, November 1, 1983.

Thomas, Deborah. *Exceptional Violence: Embodied Citizenship in Transnational Jamaica*. Durham, N.C.: Duke University Press, 2011.

Tinsley, Omise'eke Natasha. *Thiefing Sugar: Eroticism between Women in Caribbean Literature*. Durham, N.C.: Duke University Press, 2010.

Trouillot, Michel Rolph. *Global Transformations: Anthropology and the Modern World*. New York: Palgrave Macmillan, 2003.

Wilson-Tagoe, Nana. *Historical Thought and Literary Representation in West Indian Literature*. Gainesville: University of Florida Press, 1998.

THREE

Mysterious Moves of Revolution: Specters of Black Power, Futures of Postcoloniality

Sharad Chari

During the celebrations of the independence of Ghana in 1957, I met some Pan-African young men from South Africa who told me that my book had been of great service to them. I wondered how and they explained to me. A copy was in the library of the Black university in South Africa, though they didn't know anything about it until a white professor there told them: "I suggest that you read *The Black Jacobins* in the library; you may find it useful." Eagerly they got the book, read it and found it a revelation, particularly in the relation between the blacks and the mullatoes. That relation they found very important for understanding the relation between the Black South Africans and the Coloureds who are people of mixed race, black and white. They typed out copies, mimeographed them and circulated the passages from *The Black Jacobins* dealing with the relations between the blacks and the mixed in Haiti. I could not help thinking that revolution moves in a mysterious way its wonders to perform.

—C. L. R. JAMES, 1980 foreword to *The Black Jacobins*

Then comes a phrase which Grace [Lee Boggs] loves. I have underlined it. You can talk a lot of high-falutin' nonsense about socialism (or, if you like, God) and love and revolutionary masses, etc. etc., but this bitter process is the way—it is not worth a damn "if it lacks the seriousness, the suffering, the patience and the labour of the negative."

—C. L. R. JAMES, *Notes on Dialectics: Hegel, Marx, Lenin*, reading Hegel's *The Phenomenology of Mind*

Revolution Moves

In his 1980 foreword to *The Black Jacobins*, C. L. R. James writes that "the book was written not with the Caribbean but with Africa in mind." However, this three-page foreword in fact brings into constellation multiple space-times. The 1962 appendix, "From Toussaint L'Ouverture to Fidel Castro," had already confirmed that historical comparison was essential to his praxis. But as he thinks back more than forty years in 1980, James recalls the obvious motivation for his politico-theoretical project: his frustration with narratives of the Middle Passage that rendered slaves abject. But he also recalls the London in which he had been living since 1933 while working on the history of the Russian Revolution alongside intense Trotskyist discussion circles, before his own meeting and break with Trotsky in 1938 over "the Negro question," the same year that *The Black Jacobins* was published. And he recalls working politically with George Padmore on Pan-African and Black internationalism alongside these events. Through this dialectical kaleidoscope, James wrote a play about Toussaint L'Ouverture and the Haitian Revolution, and subsequently the book that would become an *ur*-text of Black liberation.

As he reflects on scholarship on the Haitian Revolution since his 1938 text, particularly on the political role of maroons, James reiterates his central argument, "that the slaves, gathered in hundreds at a time in the sugar factories of the north plain, had owed much of their success to the fact that they had been disciplined, united and organized by the very mechanism of factory production."[1] He contrasts these northern "Black Jacobins" with slaves in the south, "undisciplined by factory production," who had left the plantations only to be "persuaded" to return, "like any other workers in advanced countries today." After this promise of a Haitian "Southern Question," a geographically differentiated explanation of the conditions of production of revolution, James deftly subverts this expectation with a smashing of space-times: "So we now see that in the Caribbean the slaves in revolution, rural as well as urban, acted automatically as if they were in the second half of the twentieth century."[2] How do we understand this tense shift, and what do we make of "automatic action," by revolutionary slaves no less? What might we make of *these* mysterious moves?

I suggest that the movement between the quotations above hinges on a Hegelian hauntology that allows James across his oeuvre to hold onto the singularity of situated struggle while making audaciously universal claims, not just for the past but for the here and now. In what follows, I suggest that it is the archive of what Paul Gilroy calls the Black Atlantic that makes this possible.[3] Indeed, I suggest that this archive, particularly as an oceanic and submerged archive, compels what Ian Baucom calls a process of "temporal accumulation" that pushes its central question through and beyond the twentieth-century formation of Black politics.[4] "The Sea is History," Baucom thinks with Derek Walcott,[5] and its historical futures are always already uncontainable. I aim to think with Gary Wilder's astute observation in this volume that Black Atlantic criticism is located inside/outside the postcolonial canon, at once "component" and "challenge." This is a conversation that only bodes well for the postcolonial critique of the future.

To return to James and his interlocutor in the Johnson Forest Tendency, veteran Asian American activist-intellectual Grace Lee Boggs, there is more to the "labor of the negative" than documenting the accumulation of tragedy. This takes us to the importance of reading with generosity James's proposition "that in the Caribbean the slaves in revolution, rural as well as urban, acted automatically as if they were in the second half of the twentieth century."[6] From the perspective of this volume and its rethinking of "the postcolonial," is "acting automatically" not an abrogation of the quest for subaltern agency that seems essential to postcolonial thought? I mean the word "seems" deliberately. I pose this question as an opportunity. Indeed, at our moment in which the very gesture of subaltern rescue is so thoroughly implausible, even blithely elitist, and while we cannot but read this passage through Gayatri Chakravorty Spivak's recasting of subalternity as "effacement through disclosure,"[7] might we push further still, to read subalternity as precisely a work of automatization in the time of capital, in the sense that Derrida suggests:

> The capital contradiction does not have to do simply with the incredible conjunction of the sensuous and the supersensible in the same Thing; it is the contradiction of *automatic autonomy*, mechanical freedom, technical life. . . . The automaton mimes the living. The Thing is neither dead nor alive, it is dead and alive at the same time. It survives.[8]

This is also a précis of the transatlantic slave trade.

To put it differently, I suggest that we read this insight through what Cedric Robinson calls the Black radical tradition,[9] which Gilroy recasts in more supple terms as the cultural politics of the Black Atlantic, premised on the praxis (action and intellection) of chattel slaves at the historical foundations of racial capitalism.[10] Incidentally, Wilder (this volume) notes in an aside that "it is a mystery that Robinson's opus is not required reading for students of postcolonial studies." I do not think it is a mystery, alas. But I do think it is high time we read Robinson's work with the care that it deserves.

Derrida continues his line of thought to ask how automatons "whom one calls 'men,' living men, temporal and finite existences, become subjected, in their social relations, to those spectres that are relations, *equally social* relations among commodities."[11] The specter in Derrida is of course his debt to Marx. As this text works through Marx's dialectics of reality and appearance, the crux of the argument is that although Marx was "one of the first thinkers of technics," he sought in vain to exorcise the phantoms that haunt the "artifactual body" to provide an objective representation of capital.[12] Elsewhere, I argue that this deconstructive revision of Marx points to a different Marxism that engages the spectral rather than simply hoping for a good exorcism, and that this "hauntological" treatment of capital is precisely what the Black radical tradition has produced in various genres, not least "the blues."[13] In that piece, I reflect critically on the ontological turn in anthropology and related fields to argue that the Black radical tradition supports an attention neither just to historical and socially constructed difference nor to "noncapitalist" or "postcapitalist" spaces of alterity, but to capitalism's ontological instability and to the fragility of life in its wake. Toni Morrison's *Beloved* (1987), for instance, can be read for precisely this attention to ontological instability and fragile life in the wake of plantation slavery, and by analogy in other racial capitalisms since.

To return to James's *Black Jacobins*, the specter that haunts the automatization of the living in the most productive slave-based colony of the transatlantic imperial world is revolution. Much of the narrative skill in *The Black Jacobins* rests on working with this specter of revolution as it ricochets across the Atlantic, bringing strange bedfellows together and fomenting new contradictions as "revolution moves in a mysterious way its wonders to perform."[14] There is much to say about the central characters of the Haitian revolution in James's text, following the stage dramatization of Toussaint L'Ouverture played by Paul Robeson. James's attention to theater permeates the narratives of former slaves turned leaders of the revolution, including Toussaint, Dessalines, Christophe, Moïse, and Hyacinth, and their multiple struggles with slavery and forced labor, empire, and independence, all against the backdrop of shifting imperial intrigues of France, Spain, and Britain, and various class factions invested in maintaining superprofits from coercive plantation agribusiness. From play to historical polemic, Toussaint remains the central figure in the shifting terrain of struggle, his tragic life a metaphor for the most prosperous colony in the Caribbean, reduced to independence and long-term poverty and suffering.

While he dissects the complexity of struggle, and painstakingly diagnoses each "error" made by Toussaint and his compatriots, James is not content to write social history without asking, "What should Toussaint have done?"[15] His point is not just to satisfy counterfactual curiosity. Rather, the question takes us back to the point I begin this chapter with, that James was fundamentally concerned with the multiplicity of space-times that constitute the politics of the present. He must ask this question, just as he is gratified in his 1980 foreword that South African anti-apartheid activists might use his text as a tool for *their* revolution. After all, James explains, Lenin, Robespierre, and Toussaint faced similar questions in extending military victories through their respective revolutionary struggles. In all these instances, the revolutionary leader confronts the militant Left, crushes a significant uprising within the revolution, and helps efface the specific content of subalternity. For Lenin, this content was the lived experience that led to the Kronstadt revolt, in whose aftermath Lenin hastily instituted the New Economic Policy. For Toussaint it was the conditions of possibility for a revolt by ex-slaves in the north of Saint Domingue who refused to return to hard labor in postslavery plantations still owned by their former white masters. Toussaint's trusted general and adopted nephew Moïse may have led this uprising, but it is clear that he did not stop it, and Toussaint executed him for this. "What exactly did Moïse stand for?" asks James, and he immediately answers, "We shall never know." But James wagers some guesses through what he cautions are questionable sources:

> Toussaint refused to break up the large estates. Moïse wanted small grants of land for junior officers and even the rank-and-file. Toussaint favoured the whites against the Mulattoes. Moïse sought to build an alliance between the blacks and the Mulattoes against the French. It is certain that he had a strong sympathy for the laborers and hated the old slave-owners. But he was not anti-white.[16]

James argues that Toussaint had mastered the capacity to traverse vast swathes of space, with "hundreds of thoroughbred horses scattered in stables all over the country, . . . he habitually covered 125 miles a day," tirelessly engaging people in such a way that "none knew when and where the Governor would appear."[17] But by the time he found it necessary to execute Moïse and placate militant Black workers, he appears to have lost touch with people; instead, he subjected them to increasingly harsh forms of control of movement and confinement to plantations, as well as isolation from the revolutionary army, James adds, "an infallible sign of revolutionary degeneration."[18] In an engaging work of narrative history, Laurent Dubois breezes by this moment without noting that James pulls the emergency brake at this point, when the question of subalternity appears as popular knowledge and freedom of movement.[19] I argue, following Gita Patel's insights, that the insistence on the past-perfect subjunctive, to that which should have been (*jo hona tha*, in Hindi), must also be key to our contemporary revisioning of postcolonial praxis.[20] The point is not to reconstruct a better rendition of Moïse, which even the expert narrative historian cannot do given archival limitations, but rather to think as James does of political alternatives, for us, now. For James in the 1930s, this was a conversation with Lenin, which he would have explicitly with Trotsky on "the Negro question":

> Lenin in his thesis to the Second Congress of the Communist International warned the white revolutionaries—a warning they badly need—that such has been the effect of the policy of imperialism on the relationship between advanced and backward peoples that European Communists will have to make wide concessions to natives of colonial countries in order to overcome the justified prejudice which these feel towards all classes in the oppressing countries. Toussaint, as his power grew, forgot that.[21]

"Forgetting" does not do justice to the theoretical and political problem here. The problem of subalternity as "disclosure through effacement" remains key here, precisely as a tool for excavating political alternatives. This imperative is necessary for any defensible postcolonial Marxist project that is not trapped in the biopolitical hoax of twentieth-century state socialism, which never could fulfill its promise of universal access to the means of life. I call this problem "the moment of the disqualified" that, following James's insight, emerges and is repressed in all modern revolutionary movements and which, in diverse forms today, remains key to the political and theoretical project of a materialist (if not Marxist), engaged postcolonialism of the future.[22]

This has been a long prelude to the specific revolution I have been concerned with in my research since 2012. This research for a book project called "Apartheid Remains" attends to the ways in which the remains of various moments of the past persist as limits to struggle today as witnessed from a specific cross section of twentieth-century South Africa. The book is structured as a palimpsest, to provide a sense of the accumulation of space-times in the detritus of racial capitalism, through an industrial-residential patchwork landscape in the southern reaches of the Indian Ocean city of Durban. In the South Durban Industrial Basin, residents of formerly "Coloured" Wentworth and "Indian" Merebank have been consigned to life in a toxic valley that traps pollution and foists burdens of ill-health on these racialized populations. Merebank "Indians" and Wentworth "Coloureds" are porous categories that also remain in forms of fragile habitation on the borderlands of what was meant to be a white city. These are areas close to the city center and to industrial jobs, and not as marginalized from opportunity as most "African" townships and informal settlements extending out into the peri-urban hinterland. Through a historical ethnography of changing twentieth-century processes of segregation and struggle, and their accumulating effects, I diagnose how people conserve the means of struggle in novel ways. Indeed, residents of these areas have at various times and in various ways refused their immediate spatial inequalities alongside the broader struggles against racial capitalism before, during, and after apartheid.

Of several insights that have emerged through this research, I mention two linked points briefly. First, although "Indian" and "Coloured" racial and spatial interpellations stick to the skin in different ways, people's affinities to these racial terms carry other legacies as well. I try to show how people living in these areas have been formed through divergent

Indian Ocean legacies, submerged oceanic pasts that shaped forms of common life in the subaltern world of Durban of the early twentieth century.[23] These oceanic histories of space-making were also processes of "disclosure through effacement" in a particular way; former indentured laborers became "Indian" after they were dispossessed from an increasingly eugenic Indian nationalism in India for which working-class diasporas were becoming of little value by the 1930s. Indianness took root in interstitial and neglected areas, while other poor people of mixed Indian Ocean origins were becoming an increasingly transient proletariat defined, particularly in Durban, by landlessness and tenancy before they were stamped with the label "Coloured." When specific populations and territories were marked by race, as Indian Merebank and Coloured Wentworth were in the midcentury work of science fiction that was the apartheid city, these older oceanic and proletarian histories of embodiment and place-making have continued to shape urban life in subtle ways that remain difficult to affirm.[24] As the poet and cultural critic Gabeba Baderoon argues in a work of great power and insight, Indian Ocean histories of slavery, forced labor, sexual violence, and subaltern Islam haunt South African cultural life, surfacing in a variety of quotidian forms, not least in widespread violence against women, which is then pathologized as an aspect of "Coloured culture."[25]

The second point concerns the vicissitudes of Black Consciousness thought in this landscape of lived racism. Merebank and Wentworth were areas in which an important strand of youth activism refused their racialization, not by turning to the Indian Ocean but to the Black Atlantic. When the young Bantu Stephen (Steve) Biko founded what would become the Black Consciousness Movement, he did so as a Black medical student living in the Black students housing at Wentworth. The upsurge of political Blackness in the 1970s was vital to a generation of militant women and men who were by the 1980s part of an uncontrollable internal movement for change. In marked contrast, today's appeals to political Blackness take a wide array of forms from elite claims to Black empowerment to various populist calls for autochthony and essentialist Africanity. These appeals are often at odds with the experimental and coalitional forms of the Black Consciousness Movement of the 1970s.

Indeed, Black Consciousness was just one aspect of what had become a multifaceted revolutionary opening in Durban in the 1970s and 1980s. My argument, which I only sketch here, is that with the leadership of the liberation movements banned, jailed, and exiled, quite a bit more political creativity was to emerge in the country, through four distinct, dialectically interrelated moments of struggle. I call the first "the politico-theological moment" which involved a collective leap of faith into the political unknown. Beginning with dockworker strikes in 1972–73, spreading to an interconnection of Black workers' strikes across industrial Durban, student activism, and New Left Marxism, and connecting with Black theology and the nascent Black Consciousness Movement centered on Steve Biko, along with the radicalized Natal Indian Congress, formed early in the century by M. K. Gandhi, this "moment" is written about in the historiography as "The Durban Moment." What is often not as appreciated is that its internal strands were crisscrossed through shared praxis of reading, debate, protest and solidarity. What remains striking

about the Durban Moment is its openness and experimentation, in matters of friendship, solidarity, love, and movement strategy.

This moment sharply contrasts with what I call the "moment of insurrection" fueled
by the African National Congress's (ANC's) long-standing romance of rural guerrilla
warfare, despite its own abrogation of agrarian organizing by midcentury. Images of Che
and Fidel riding into Havana with AK47s on their back, and ideas from various other
Cold War anticolonial conflicts from Algeria to Vietnam fueled this strongly gendered
and militarist ideology, which resonated with communities like Merebank and Wentworth in raced and gendered ways. However, the internal *urban* struggles of the 1970s,
including the Soweto Uprising, had not in any obvious way been directed by the exiled
leadership of the ANC and South African Communist Party (SACP). This led to intense
questioning within the liberation movement organizations, and to a mythic trip by members of the ANC-SACP high command to Vietnam, where they met the legendary General Vu Nguyen Giap, who had defeated the French and Americans in military battle. In
this revolutionary parable, the legendary general impressed upon the South Africans the
importance of grassroots mass mobilization as a precondition for military advantage.
Interpretations of the Vietnam trip diverged, and the parable was used for quite different purposes. For some, it was the case for building hegemony through mass-based
organizations in the country. For others, including the Special Operations (Special Ops)
program championed by SACP leader Joe Slovo, it was an argument for fomenting a
"people's war" through intensified sabotage. These two possibilities fed into the following
two moments.

The third moment was an attempt at "resolving" the first two moments through what
I call the "moment of urban revolution," in which a small ANC-front vanguard group
sought to build hegemony in the country through the groundswell of urban civic, housing, and labor organizations, linking underground units to the exiled leadership and effectively providing a platform for the imagined return of the exiled ANC and SACP. This
vanguard was headed by the man who was until recently the finance minister of South
Africa, Pravin Gordhan. The faction of the ANC around President Jacob Zuma was connected to this moment. In a sense, they won the revolution, if for the right of the president to loot the public coffers for home improvement and a R4 billion presidential jet in a
time of deepening social crisis. When I started writing "Apartheid Remains," I was inspired by James's *Black Jacobins* to write an account of the ways in which the tools of biopolitics used to build racial segregation in the first half of the century were picked up as
instruments of struggle in the moment of urban revolution. Indeed, this way of seeing the
third moment carries the same Hegelian hauntology that James wrestled with in his
thought, but it does not do justice to those for whom "the seriousness, the suffering, the
patience and the labour of the negative" remains ongoing work. For this, the notion of
dialectics must always be spatiotemporal and open rather than "resolvable" through an
integration of thesis and antithesis; it must stay with the lived praxis of struggle.

Indeed, the means of biopolitical expertise were out of reach for many, if not most, in
the third moment. What I call the "moment of the disqualified" dwells in outlaw cultures

that remained too undisciplined to be "organized" by the ANC vanguard, too creative to be contained, and yet given the specific violent repression of Indian Ocean histories in Indian and Coloured life, also open to violence against the self and other. In strange and aleatory ways, one small, self-organized "anti-apartheid unit" from Wentworth managed to become a unit of Special Ops, formed as a consequence of the leadership's trip to Vietnam. They took matters into their own hands in a notorious car bombing of a beachfront café, an incident that brought infamy to the group that could never fully transition from terrorists to struggle heroes, or from crime to legitimate politics.

In the next section, I turn to this event within the South African revolution that remains, for many, a moment of infamy. I then interpret this "moment of the disqualified" through insights from Stuart Hall's work on "the mugger" in Britain at a roughly contemporaneous moment, as well as his consequent work on the unraveling of the notion of a coalitional Black political subject. Returning to the aftermath of apartheid in the areas I research and teach, I conclude with the ways in which this journey-through-struggle offers insights on the hauntology of Black Power for the project of reconceiving a materialist or Marxist postcolonial politics of the future, anywhere on our oceanic planet.

The Moment of the Disqualified

Former Umkhonto we Sizwe commander and now Foreign Affairs director Robert McBride on Tuesday apologized to the relatives of those killed during operations by the African National Congress' Special Operations unit in and around Durban during the early '80s. McBride was testifying in his amnesty application for a number of bombing incidents in and around the city between 1981 and 1986. In one of the incidents, McBride planted a bomb outside the Magoo's bar and the Why Not bar on the Durban beachfront. . . . McBride said reconnaissance of the Why Not bar by [Gordon] Webster, who had concluded that the place was "infested with police," had convinced him that it was legitimate target. This information was conveyed to the sub command in Botswana and he was instructed to go ahead with the bombing, McBride said. He added he had raised concerns over civilian casualties but was told by the commander of the Special Operations unit Aboobaker Ismail that in terms of the Kabwe conference and policy changes in the ANC that civilian casualties were a secondary consideration and that the main concern was to target military personnel. . . . He said on the night of the attack he was assisted by Matthew Lecordier and Greta Apelgren who were unaware of the specifics of the operation. McBride said he purchased a vehicle under a false name in which he packed the explosives, comprising SZ6 charges, in the boot of the car. Explaining the construction of the bomb, McBride said: "As per instructions, detonators were added into all the SZ6 charges so as to give the explosion a greater impact. Also as per instructions, I added shrapnel to the explosive charges. This I was able to get from for example cutting old burglar guards in my father's workshop and placing it amongst the shrapnel." McBride said this was in accordance with his instructions on how to make a car bomb.

South African Press Association, October 5, 1999

I will not allow them to stand in judgment over me. I will never be judged by the same standards as those who maintained and supported apartheid. . . . Those who committed offences in the interests of apartheid did so to perpetuate it. My actions were to destroy it. I ask the public and the TRC members to consider what their attitude would have been to the establishment of a court, or quasi court, which judged the actions of the Nazis in the same way it judged the actions of those who resisted in the concentration camps. . . . I therefore, with no prejudice to my son Robert John McBride, or any other applicants to the amnesty committee, withdraw from all proceedings relating to this committee. I will take no part in them—either as a witness, an applicant, a bystander, a civilian or a concerned South African.

Derrick McBride's statement withdrawing his application for amnesty to the Truth and
Reconciliation Commission, South African Press Association, September 25, 1999

These are retrospective statements by a son and ageing father, both anti-apartheid militants, both facing prospects of amnesty under the provisions of the Truth and Reconciliation Commission. Robert McBride, the son, comes clean on his role in "a number of bombings" in the Durban and Pietermaritzburg region between 1981 and 1986, culminating in a car bomb between the Magoo's Bar and the Why Not? Bar on the Durban beachfront, which placed him and his girlfriend-accomplice Greta Apelgren in a particular status of infamy. He apologizes to victims, notes the shift in the official line of the ANC, references his commander Aboobaker Ismail ("Rashid") of the Special Operations Unit, also called the Solomon Mahlangu Unit, established by the ANC National Executive Committee in 1979 after the trip to Vietnam, with a command structure independent of the ANC's armed wing, Umkhonto weSizwe (MK), probably as a response to the degree of infiltration of MK structures by the South African security establishment by the late 1970s. Rashid reported to ANC President Oliver Tambo and chief of staff of MK, Joe Slovo, and in time, directly to Slovo. By a twist of fate, a group of young men centered on Robert in Wentworth thought of themselves as an "anti-apartheid unit," and very quickly, had become a Special Ops unit led by Gordon Webster. In time, Robert and Gordon split their two units, and took several covert trips out of the country to ferry arms and relay instructions, sometimes with Greta and her sister Jeanette as cover. After Gordon's capture, Robert took over both units and was one person away from the MK chief of staff. Finally, Robert references that while the initial rationale for Special Ops was to target strategic military and economic installations, the policy toward civilian casualties had been relaxed and policy toward "soft targets" had become more lenient by the 1985 Kabwe Conference.[26] When it came to the car bomb, Robert says he was concerned about civilian life, and yet, he repeats, he was following instructions.

Robert recruited his father, Derrick, into many of the activities conducted by this anti-apartheid underground cell. At the highest point of their activities, when Gordon was arrested for the first time and taken to a hospital to treat injuries suffered in his ambush, Derrick and Robert conducted a masterly raid to free their captured comrade. Derrick drew up plans, conscripted several people into roles, and some even wore costumes, with Derrick dressed up as a priest supervising the operation. Apparently, the nurses cheered as they "released" Gordon, all the way until they shot a Black civilian during their get-away. This contrasts with the story of the car bomb and its afterlife, when the story of this underground cell becomes particularly murky. The father's refusal to speak confirms something about the specificity of the place from which his politics emerged, and to which many of the members of the cell would return. As I have suggested, these were "terrorists" who could never quite transition into "struggle heroes," their deeds never quite memorialized as part of the good fight for freedom and independence. Indeed, Robert has continued to have a checkered career with multiple bailouts from the highest echelons of the ANC, and this speaks to the layers of secrecy and mythmaking that continues to surround the official past of the anti-apartheid struggle.

Part of the explanation for the difference of this cell lies in the carceral space of the Coloured township of Wentworth, where young men were drawn into a world of gangs and violence. Street gangs in apartheid's townships took multiple forms, and Wentworth was by now known for its gangs in the 1970s and 1980s. These street gangs were unlike the politically oriented *amatsotsis* of Soweto in Clive Glaser's classic research.[27] The photographer Peter McKenzie, who emerged from the ganglands of Austerville in Wentworth, expresses the specific disaffection of young people during and after apartheid with particular clarity. One group of young men refused to join the gangs and created a kind of countercultural alternative in a shack behind one of their homes, where they listened to reggae, smoked greens, and decided to light a fire in a high school classroom. This was the birth of an "anti-apartheid unit" that, through a set of fortuitous connections, led to Special Ops.

Once Robert had been exposed to "political education" in trips abroad, members of this informal cell saw themselves as a revolutionary base, with Robert as "commissar." Apart from multiple acts of sabotage, and the daring and successful raid of the hospital to free Gordon Webster, Robert McBride is remembered primarily for the car bomb between the Durban beachfront bars, ostensibly to attack security personnel and also as an act of "armed propaganda." Robert and Greta's photographs were splashed in the press, a young Coloured "Bonnie and Clyde" who did not look like the racist stereotype of the terrorist. In prison, both suffered tremendously, and they were lionized by others. Did they represent, as ANC veteran Mac Maharaj suggests, a trajectory akin to Sri Lanka's Tamil Tigers or Peru's Sendero Luminoso? Told from its many participants, the story is far more complex and deeply ambiguous. What is clear is that the Magoo's bombing placed McBride in a category of infamy for white society and the mainstream press in a way that he has not been able to shake off. Members of the cell insist that this infamy is racialized and is directly linked to the fact that white civilians faced the brunt of this attack while Black civilians of other attacks, including of car bombs, have never been remembered with the same pathos.

One possibility is that there is something specific about car bombs that explains this event. Mike Davis in his history of the car bomb, the "poor man's nuclear weapon," notes that it is relatively inexpensive yet capable of surprisingly destructive "manifestoes written in the blood of others," borrowing from Regis Debray; they are just as indiscriminate and "inherently fascist" as aerial bombs used by "democracies"; and they leave very little forensic evidence while providing voice for marginal actors and even ad hoc groups.[28]

There is quite a bit of relevance to the McBride cell in this formulation, particularly given that a group of young men with tenuous connection to the exiled movement, and limited and sporadic political education, could have pulled off an event with lasting emotional effects in South Africa. Semi-autonomous cells in any modern revolutionary movement interpret messages and act on them in ways that the movement has to account for, and indeed ANC President Oliver Tambo had repeated the call from Lusaka to make South Africa "ungovernable" while also cautioning that he had "no wish to celebrate liberation day surrounded by a desolate landscape of destroyed buildings, and machines reduced to scrap metal."[29] If the leadership could cover their ideological tracks, young men from a Coloured township already stigmatized as gang-ridden had already been considered prone to crime.

The bombing of the Magoo's Bar and the Why Not? Bar, the arrest of Robert McBride and his then girlfriend Greta Apelgren, the media barrage about the seemingly respectable Coloureds killing civilians, the subsequent saga of their trials at which some of their comrades turned state witness, their very difficult time in prison, and their different ways of dealing with the Truth and Reconciliation Commission are the elements of a tale too complex to relate. Narrations change over time, perhaps because people contending with a difficult episode, for which they paid dearly, find easier ways of relating what must be an eternal return to the Magoo's bombing. Perhaps also, retrospect has made it easier to share the burden of infamy too firmly associated with Robert McBride.

I have said little about the father, Derrick McBride, whose life is altogether more complex. I spoke to this irascible ageing militant several times at the little shop he ran next to his home, while being involved in several issues from police corruption to the impossibility of land claims. Derrick spent time on Robben Island for his involvement in some of the events in his son's case. He recounted to me his first days on "the Island," where he was surprised that the ANC had not yet "sprung" Mandela, and he demanded to see the leadership, a sign of his absolute refusal of hierarchy. At another moment, he said he met the wildly popular MK leader Chris Hani and told him he could blow up all the oil tanks around Durban Airport, to which he recounts the revolutionary leader responding, "We want to inherit this country, not blow it up." The circulation of statements like this, from Tambo as from Hani, speak to the restraint rather than recklessness of militants emerging from what I call "the moment of the disqualified." McBride senior is important for his insistent theorization of the conditions that produced his militancy. Unlike the son, who has sought high office in the ANC accumulation machine, the father has remained critical of the repression of militancy within the struggle and of the shifting class politics of what I call the ANC accumulation machine. Like the figure of Moïse in the Haitian Revolution, Derrick McBride is the voice that continues to speak against revolutionary degeneration.

One figure connected to the McBride cell clarifies its difference from many other ANC activists. A young white woman from an affluent background, whose father was at one point director of an Anglo-American corporation, became centrally involved in the legal defense of Robert McBride in his darkest years on Death Row. Paula Leyden, later Paula McBride, went to Lusaka to seek assistance from the ANC to appeal for his conviction to be commuted to a term sentence, and in the process she critiqued the movement's conceptualization of the boundary between the criminal and the political activist in apartheid's prisons. With others from Lawyers for Human Rights, she lobbied the National Party as well, and as a consequence, the state lifted the death sentence alongside the unbanning of liberation movement organizations. Against the enduring ambiguities of the Magoo's car bomb, the end of the death penalty was a clear victory that would not have seen the light of day had the ANC not been pushed by Leyden and her associates. This was a victory of utopian vision beyond the program of liberation and beyond the specific outlaw culture that McBride's cell had emerged from.

This is only one instance among many in which people sought to fight apartheid's injustices without just following orders from their leadership. This is why Derrick McBride's refusal to participate in the Truth and Reconciliation Commission "as a witness, an applicant, a bystander, a civilian or a concerned South African" remains so sharp. In his fearless speech from a corner of Wentworth, at the age of eighty-three in 2015, he incarnates the specter that that continues to haunt post-apartheid racial capitalism.

Specters of Black Power

What does the "moment of the disqualified" tell us about post-apartheid South Africa, two decades after the advent of democracy, when the ANC-led political alliance appears incapable of stemming deepening capitalist social crisis? At the end of decade two, Gillian Hart identifies the crisis of ANC hegemony through processes of "de-nationalization" of South African capital, or capital flight led by South African corporations moving headquarters and dis-identifying with national development, alongside "re-nationalization" of a political project to transform territorial hegemony.[30] Post-apartheid society is in no simple sense "neoliberal," as the extension of social welfare continues to be vital to hegemony, and as the ANC continues to hold out a beacon of class mobility to the Black majority. Capital flight and growing inequality have also been a boon to the growing security industry, alongside fears and fantasies of racialized crime war crystallized in the spectacle of the Oscar Pistorius trial, with its strange brew of steroidal masculinity and disdain for the presumed Black male intruder. These elements of the ANC accumulation machine and the security industry rearticulate the second and third moments of the South African revolution to help manage an aspiring Black middle class slipping deeper into consumer debt than ever, as we know from Deborah James's important research.[31]

For many South Africans, particularly after the massacre of mineworkers at Marikana in 2012, with continued corruption at the highest levels of the ANC and the critique of "state capture" building in 2017, the century-old ANC has lost touch with its purpose.[32] Many have voiced that they have repaid their electoral debt to the ANC for the years spent shepherding the liberation movement. Although most of the ANC leadership appears to have lost sight of the widespread suffering in post-apartheid South Africa, others have turned relentlessly to it, whether through the Economic Freedom Fighters, the National Union of Metalworkers and its proposed United Front, or the alliance of students and precarious workers across South African universities in the Rhodes Must Fall and Fees Must Fall movements.

South Africa's current crises might be read productively through another text on the multifaceted capitalist crisis that attends what I have called the moment of the disqualified. *Policing the Crisis* by Stuart Hall and his colleagues contextualizes media fear and loathing of "the mugger" within scales of crisis from the global to the national, spiraling through neighborhoods like Handsworth in Birmingham, and Southall and Brixton in London.[33] The authors show how mugging is "localized" in specific sites and Black male bodies through alienation, wagelessness, and vulnerability in times of austerity.[34] In contrast to the state's attempt at "policing the crisis," the authors think from the perspective of immigrant workers and disaffected youth. In the extremely insightful final section, Hall and his colleagues show how crises converge on the backs of Black youth, in their exploitation, exclusion, and subordination.[35] These young people respond to these violations through innovative forms of praxis, by "hustling," which the authors see in relation to other kinds of criminalized informal activity around the world. The authors look to the U.S. Black Panthers for its experiments with making "hustling" a site of revolutionary politics, as personified in the lives of George Jackson, Malcolm X, and other militants transgressing the boundaries of crime and politics. The repression of the Black Panthers in the United States notwithstanding, the authors argue that "the mugger" represents something like Black youth on strike who might yet constitute a collective revolutionary project.

From the perspective of South African Black youth, and participants in the new student movement that swept the country's universities since 2015, the idea of youth on strike, refusing criminalization and bankrupt futures by demanding free and quality higher education, remains extremely prescient. In the past few years, a slow and steady phenomenon has also crept into the affluent parts of Johannesburg, as young men begging on street corners have started displaying signs mocking their criminalization, praxis that parallels shifts in Hall's work, as we will see. Although not concertedly linked events, these are creative and political responses from different class fractions of South African youth refusing what they have been dealt in the strange time after apartheid.

Stuart Hall's work did not stop with the formulation in *Policing the Crisis*. Hall argues that the politics of representation in and of Black Britain had shifted from a first moment centered on struggles over "relations of representation," where racial stereotypes are at stake, to a second moment in which Black producers sought to change the script, just as C. L. R. James sought to change the script of the Haitian Revolution, and on to a third moment in which "regimes of representation" play "a formative, and not merely an expressive, place in the constitution of social and political life."[36] In other words, in the third moment, the discursive and aesthetic aspects of representation become directive of politics. This imperative takes Hall to question the resilience of the coalitional Black politics that had been so powerful across what I call the recovering white supremacies of Britain, the United States, and South Africa. Indeed, the cultural politics of the U.S. Black Panther Party and of linked Black community and labor movements in Britain and South Africa in the 1970s and 1980s had presumed that coalitional Blackness would take a life that Hall argues has not come to be. Hall calls this moment "'the end of innocence' or the end of the innocent notion of the essential black subject."[37]

"The end of innocence" is a moment of recognition of multiple histories and forms of oppression and expression that coalitional Black politics sought to unify. Indeed, Hall and his colleagues' reinterpretation of hustling was also centered on a particular kind of Black masculine subject in the shadows of Black Power, in the wake of the repression of the Black Panther Party and parallel groups in Britain and South Africa precisely at this moment. Steve Biko had been murdered in South Africa in late 1977, not long before the publication of Hall and his colleagues' work on the mugger, and anticipating the crisis of coalitional Black politics that Hall later calls "the end of innocence." But in this hasty reformulation, Hall leaves behind the specter that continues to haunt the struggles he seeks to represent.

Indeed, we might follow Roderick Ferguson's argument that the end of the essential Black subject was not the cause but the outcome of Black feminist and queer critical and artistic production.[38] Rather than looking for another representational idiom, like ethnicity or diaspora, Ferguson asks for a diagnosis of "lateral moves" that make racial, class, gender, and sexual rearticulations possible.[39] Elsewhere, Ferguson exemplifies such moves in his thoughtful reading of James Baldwin, "suffering an impossibility of staying put and the crampedness of segregation, [who] leaves New York to write—to write against the racial and sexual definitions that 'tried to put him in his place.'"[40] What we see in Baldwin is a self-conscious quest for bodily rearticulation, but how do we understand the specters that follow Baldwin's "lateral moves," whether of American racism and homophobia, or of Black Power?

Barnor Hesse conceptualizes Black politics as "the symptom of creolization repressed in the modern institution and representation of the political," or, I would add, the political-economic.[41] Hesse's formulation suggests that representations of racial capitalism will always have to contend with "disclosure through effacement" of the creole or the mixed. A masculinist form of Black politics might be one form of disclosure, while the forms of expression from Black women blues singers in Angela Davis's work are another.[42] This formulation allows us to think of the specter as that which survives repression, and pushes new representational forms alongside the irrepressible forms creolization takes.

How might we return, in this light, to James's rendition of the Haitian Revolution in relation to Wentworth and Merebank in Durban, South Africa?[43] In none of these situations does a coalitional Black politics adequately address creolization in these divergent forms of racial capitalism. In his 1980 foreword, James has the intuition that something about "the Mulatto question" in Toussaint's Saint Domingue makes his text relevant to "the Coloured question" in apartheid South Africa, but he does not quite put his finger on what this is. We know that he was wrestling with his own relationship to what we might now call the white Marxist tradition, pushing beyond Lenin and Trotsky in ways he could not yet anticipate. The specter that haunts the Caribbean revolutionary dandy in London is not just revolution, but also, what Édouard Glissant calls *antillanité* as "a method and not a state of being."[44] Rather than separating the question of subjectivity from the abolition of racial capitalism, James's lateral moves through the labor of the negative offer a reminder not just of the incompleteness of Black Power, nor just the ghost of struggles lost, but of futures yet to be won.

Black Power as the Future

In the neighborhoods surrounded by oil refineries that I research, many if not most people continue to self-identify as Indian or Coloured, not Black. Many former activists of the Black Consciousness Movement from this area have moved on and out. People residing next to oil refineries and other polluting industries know the lethal costs of long term ill-health in this landscape, but they have refused to be moved from these areas in relative proximity to the city center and to industrial employment. The memory of apartheid's forced removals has been a potent means to mobilize people to refuse to be moved, and people know all too well that they will never inherit the beautiful bourgeois and formerly white city but would join the expanding urban periphery with the African majority. The resistance to movement is partly about loss of access to work and to the city center, but it is also entangled with anti-Black racism that militates against political Blackness.

I have put it brusquely because it does instantiate what Glissant and Hesse refuse, trouble with creolization and Blackness as "states of being." Wentworth and Merebank continue to be politically vibrant areas, and their residents suffer materially, environmentally, and also psychically, through the ongoing repression of Indian Ocean histories of creolization. Rather than pathologize these populations yet again, I suggest a mode of thought that begins with the moment of the disqualified and with "the seriousness, the suffering, the patience and the labour of the negative."

Considered in dialectical relation, the four moments of Durban's revolutionary 1970s and 1980s show us that Durban's Black Jacobins appeared to "act automatically," refusing their automatization as cogs in apartheid's racial capitalism. However, their modes of activism were not simply a product of the industrial crucible of the South Durban industrial basin, connected to the most important Indian Ocean port linked to the mining hinterland. Of the four moments of revolution, the militant praxis evident in Wentworth's outlaw cultures is the least valorized, but also the closest to the militancy of James's rendition of Moïse, the rebel slave who refused revolutionary degeneration surrounding Toussaint L'Ouverture, as others refuse the politics of the African National Congress today.

Black politics as method calls for a postcolonialism of the future, responsive not just to racial-sexual formations posited by nation-state territoriality, but to our entangled futures. Jini Kim Watson in this volume imagines postcolonial critique beyond the colonial shadow, attentive to anachronism and to "incompatible temporalities," and her essay enacts what Ferguson calls "lateral moves" necessary for thinking across multiple space-times, with multiple stakes. The cultural and political traditions of the Black Atlantic bequeathed powerful legacies for anticolonial and anticapitalist struggle. C. L. R. James tapped into these through his journey to the Haitian Revolution, his solidarity with South Africa, and his work with Padmore on the Black international. These were all "lateral moves."

An oceanic way of thinking makes these moves explicit only by bringing to light shifting processes of articulation and disarticulation, fast currents and also the stranded or marooned; the fleeting and emergent as well as the submerged and drowned. Durban lies between the powerful legacies of the Black Atlantic and the emergent forms of the Indian Ocean, with its strange brew of American, Chinese, and Indian imperial power, resource extraction, piracy, Islam, conscription, and creolization. To read this as the dawn of an "Asian Century" would be convenient for the Asia-centrism of postcolonial studies in the U.S. academy as part of U.S. racial formation. Rather, we might learn from a future-oriented discipline, demography, which predicts that by midcentury a quarter of our planet will be African, and that "more than half of global population growth between now and 2050 is expected to occur in Africa."[45] Simply put, the Earth is an oceanic and (with Public Enemy in mind) an increasingly Black planet. Against new forms of capital and imperial power, our only hope of a shared planetary future will have to be constitutive, in the sense that Sadia Abbas aptly puts it in this volume of the future forms that Black Power takes. Like James, as we labor with the negative, engaging new forms of disqualified praxis, we must have Africa in mind.

NOTES

The section "Specters of Black Power" draws from and substantially adapts arguments from Chari, "Postcolonial-Postsocialist Marxisms."

1. James, *Black Jacobins*, xvi–xvii.
2. Ibid., xvii.
3. Gilroy, *Black Atlantic*.
4. Baucom, *Specters of the Atlantic*, 325–33.
5. Ibid.
6. James, *Black Jacobins*, xvii.
7. Spivak, *Critique of Postcolonial Reason*, 310.
8. Derrida, *Specters of Marx*, 192.
9. Robinson, *Black Marxism*.
10. Gilroy, *Black Atlantic*. Gary Wilder's piece in this volume draws out important differences between Robinson and Gilroy, including their very different ways of handling intellectual and sociocultural creolization at the heart of Atlantic (and any other oceanic) circulation. I suggest that Robinson can be read through a dialectical method that insists on the entanglement of "Western" and "African" elements, and even with the broader cultural archive that Gilroy brings to bear on the problematic. I also appreciate Wilder's generous reading of DuBois, but I would call him a late-Victorian progressive (interested in classic progressivist themes like self-sufficiency, cooperativization, and "economic democracy") rather than a "postcapitalist" (not his term) or a revolutionary in the Marxist or Anarchist sense for most of his long intellectual career. I argue that his form of radicalism ought also to be seen at precisely the entangled intersection of progressivism and the Black radical tradition.
11. Derrida, *Specters of Marx*, 194.
12. Ibid., 213–14.
13. Chari, "Blues and the Damned."
14. James, *Black Jacobins*.
15. Ibid., 229.
16. Ibid., 225.

17. Ibid., 202.
18. Ibid., 226.
19. Dubois, *Avengers of the New World*, 246–47.
20. Gita Patel, personal communication, London, June 20, 2012.
21. James, *Black Jacobins*, 233.
22. My argument here is truncated of necessity. The more fully developed and substantiated version appears in my book in progress, *Apartheid Remains*.
23. Chari, "Limits to Mutuality."
24. Ibid.
25. Baderoon, *Regarding Muslims*.
26. Amnesty Committee, "2001 Ruling."
27. Glaser, *Bo-Tsotsi*.
28. Davis, *Buda's Wagon*, 8–11.
29. Goodwin, "Oliver Tambo."
30. Hart, *Rethinking the South African Crisis*.
31. James, *Money for Nothing*.
32. See the damning report on state capture by Bhorat et al., "Betrayal of the Promise."
33. Hall et al., *Policing the Crisis*.
34. Ibid., 338.
35. Ibid., 345–47.
36. Hall, "New Ethnicities," 165.
37. Ibid., 165–66.
38. Ferguson, "Lateral Moves" 118.
39. Ibid., 223.
40. Ferguson, "Parvenu Baldwin," 233.
41. Hesse, "Symptomatically Black," 58.
42. Davis, *Blue Legacies and Black Feminism*.
43. James, *Black Jacobins*.
44. Glissant, *Poetics of Relation*, xxi.
45. United Nations, *World Population Prospects*, 3.

BIBLIOGRAPHY

Amnesty Committee. "2001 Ruling on Robert McBride's Amnesty Application." *Politicsweb*. February 6, 2008. www.politicsweb.co.za/news-and-analysis/text-of-the-2001-ruling-on-robert-mcbrides-amnesty.

Baderoon, Gabeba. *Regarding Muslims: From Slavery to Post-Apartheid*. Johannesburg: Wits University Press, 2014.

Baucom, Ian. *Specters of the Atlantic: Finance Capital, Slavery, and the Philosophy of History*. Durham, N.C.: Duke University Press, 2005.

Bhorat, Haroon, et al. "Betrayal of the Promise: How South Africa Is Being Stolen." State Capacity Research Project. May 2017. http://pari.org.za/betrayal-promise-report/.

Chari, Sharad. "The Blues and the Damned: Surviving the Ontologies of Capital and Biopolitics." *Critical African Studies* 9, no. 2 (2017): 152–73.

———. "An 'Indian Commons' in Durban? Limits to Mutuality, or the City to Come." *Anthropology Southern Africa* 37, no. 3–4 (2014): 149–59.

———. "State Racism and Biopolitical Struggle: The Evasive Commons in Twentieth-Century Durban, South Africa." *Radical History Review* 108 (2010): 73–90.

———. "Three Moments of Stuart Hall in South Africa: Postcolonial-Postsocialist Marxisms of the Future." *Critical Sociology* 43, no. 6 (2017): 831–45.

Davis, Angela Y. *Blues Legacies and Black Feminism: Gertrude "Ma" Rainey, Bessie Smith, and Billie Holiday.* New York: Pantheon Books, 1998.

Davis, Mike. *Buda's Wagon: A Brief History of the Car Bomb.* London: Verso Books, 2007.

Derrida, Jacques. *Specters of Marx.* New York: Routledge, 1994.

Dubois, Laurent. *Avengers of the New World: The Story of the Haitian Revolution.* Cambridge, Mass.: Harvard University Press, 2004.

Fanon, Frantz. *The Wretched of the Earth.* 1961. New York: Grove Press, 1991.

Ferguson, Roderick A. "The Lateral Moves of African American Studies in a Period of Migration." In *Strange Affinities: The Gender and Sexual Politics of Comparative Racialization*, edited by Grace Kyungwon Hong and Roderick A. Ferguson, 113–30. Durham, N.C.: Duke University Press, 2011.

———. "The Parvenu Baldwin and the Other Side of Redemption: Modernity, Race, Sexuality, and the Cold War." In *James Baldwin Now*, edited by Dwight A. McBride, 233–61. New York: New York University Press, 1999.

Gilroy, Paul. *The Black Atlantic: Modernity and Double Consciousness.* London: Verso, 1993.

Glaser, Clive. *Bo-Tsotsi: The Youth Gangs of Soweto, 1935–1976.* Portsmouth, N.H.: Heinemann, 2000.

Glissant, Édouard. *Poetics of Relation.* Translated by Betsy Wing. Ann Arbor: University of Michigan Press, 1997.

Goodwin, Peter. "Oliver Tambo: Pretoria's Public Enemy Number One." *Gazette*, July 5, 1986.

Hall, Stuart. "New Ethnicities." In *Black British Cultural Studies*, edited by Houston A. Baker Jr., Manthia Diawara, and Ruth H. Lindeborg, 163–72. Chicago: University of Chicago Press, 1996.

Hall, Stuart, Chas Critcher, Tony Jefferson, John Clark, and Brian Roberts. *Policing the Crisis: Mugging, the State, and Law and Order.* London: Macmillan, 1978.

Hart, Gillian Patricia. *Rethinking the South African Crisis: Nationalism, Populism, Hegemony.* Durban: University of KwaZulu-Natal Press, 2013.

Hegel, G. W. F. *The Phenomenology of Mind.* London: Allen and Unwin/Macmillan, 1949.

Hesse, B. "Symptomatically Black: A Creolization of the Political." In *The Creolization of Theory*, edited by Françoise Lionnet and Shu-mei Shih, 37–61. Durham, N.C.: Duke University Press, 2011.

James, C. L. R. *The Black Jacobins.* 1938. London: Penguin Books. 2001.

———. *Notes on Dialectics: Hegel, Marx, Lenin.* Westport, Conn: Lawrence Hill, 1980.

James, Deborah. *Money for Nothing: Indebtedness and Aspiration in South Africa.* Stanford: Stanford University Press, 2015.

Morrison, Toni. *Beloved.* New York: Penguin Books, 1987.

Nuttall, Sarah. *Entanglement: Literary and Cultural Reflections on Post-Apartheid.* Johannesburg: Wits University Press, 2009.

Robinson, Cedric J. *Black Marxism: The Making of the Black Radical Tradition.* 1983. Chapel Hill: University of North Carolina Press, 2000.

South African Press Association. "McBride Apologises to Family of Those Slain in Armed Struggle." October 5, 1999. www.justice.gov.za/trc/media%5C1999%5C9910/p991005a.htm.

South African Press Association. "McBride Withdraws Amnesty Application." September 25, 1999. www.justice.gov.za/trc/media%5C1999%5C9909/p990925a.htm.

Spivak, Gayatri Chakravorty. *A Critique of Postcolonial Reason: Toward a History of the Vanishing Present.* Cambridge, Mass.: Harvard University Press, 1999.

United Nations, Department of Economic and Social Affairs, Population Division. *World Population Prospects: The 2015 Revision, Key Findings and Advance Tables.* New York: United Nations, 2015.

FOUR

Reading Du Bois's Revelation: Radical Humanism and Black Atlantic Criticism

Gary Wilder

The Black Atlantic stands in a peculiar relation to certain currents of recent postcolonial thinking.[1] The history of slavery as a founding matrix for modern capitalism, imperialism, and racism has certainly been a crucial reference point for the postcolonial critique of Euro-American modernity and its forms of knowledge. Similarly, this critique has also been deeply informed by the insights of towering Black Atlantic intellectuals, many of whom have become canonized within postcolonial theory.[2] Yet the actual content of much Black Atlantic history and criticism—irreducibly creole, translocal, intersectional—does not easily align with the territorialist and culturalist assumptions that continue to underlie broad currents of postcolonial scholarship. Insofar as the latter seeks to demonstrate the existence of singular lifeworlds or epistemologies that are incommensurable with a putatively Western modernity, it has reproduced the very civilizational thinking that postcolonial theory itself initially emerged to contest, and which broad currents of Black Atlantic history, experience, art, and critical reflection have consistently called into question (whether explicitly or implicitly).[3]

This uncomfortable fit between postcolonial critique and Black Atlantic criticism may be recognized in the figure of W. E. B. Du Bois. In many ways, of course, Du Bois is an exemplary postcolonial thinker.[4] He spent his life exploring the deep structural relations between Atlantic slavery and capitalist modernity, the color line and liberal democracy, colonial imperialism and global instability. No one has thought more deeply about the actual and possible meanings of freedom and democracy in social worlds structured by racism, about racialization and subject formation, and, to use Nahum Chandler's felicitous phrase, about "the problem of the Negro as a problem for thought."[5] Anticipating one strong impetus of postcolonial scholarship, Du Bois also attended directly to the distinctive lived experiences, forms of life, cultural expressions, and history-making practices of black diasporic and African peoples. But despite such evident affinities, Du Bois's writings also unsettle many of the binary oppositions on which postcolonial theory continues to depend: universalism versus particularism, integration versus separation, liberalism versus radicalism, Marxism versus anti-imperialism, the West versus the non-West.[6] Moreover, Du Bois regularly employed concepts and affirmed values that postcolonial criticism has often regarded as irredeemably bourgeois, liberal, or Western, such as truth, beauty, love, justice, and humanity.

In this essay, I would like to attend to the current of radical humanism that informed Du Bois's critique of historical conditions, his conception of the good life, and his vision of a more human (because self-managed, shared, and just) world for all peoples. This humanist investment, I will argue, was integral to the democratic, socialist, and internationalist synthesis that he developed during the period surrounding his 1934 resignation from the NAACP, and on which his reputation as a signal black radical thinker is rightly based. I will suggest that Du Bois's challenging thought illuminates some of the limitations of current postcolonial scholarship, whose frameworks cannot easily grasp the radical charge of his humanism or the humanist substrate of his radicalism. Conversely, I will suggest that Du Bois's radical humanism offers a valuable resource that may usefully transcend some of the lacunae and impasses of current postcolonial thinking and thereby help us think politically about the (global) historical present. The legacy of Du Bois reminds us that the Black Atlantic critical tradition may be a crucial component of any attempt to engage "the postcolonial contemporary."[7]

Du Bois's Revelation

On June 8, 1938, Du Bois delivered the commencement speech at Fisk University, his alma mater, commemorating the fiftieth anniversary of his own graduation. Scholars have paid little attention to this seemingly anomalous discourse, titled "The Revelation of Saint Orgne the Damned." David Levering Lewis, Du Bois's biographer, called it "a lengthy, rhetorically ornate, and metaphorically exuberant sermon" that was "an unforgettable example of the *sui generis*."[8] Lewis refers to this supposedly unclassifiable speech as an extension of the "autobiographical indulgence" that had accompanied his recent seventieth birthday celebration at Atlanta University where he was then a sociology professor.[9] Lewis summarizes it in three sentences as being primarily about the failures of Negro education.

But Fisk was clearly an important venue for Du Bois. It was the scene of his undergraduate education in the humanities. There he was immersed for the first time in a black majority social milieu and, as a summer school teacher, he first encountered black Southern poverty and culture. In June 1888 he had delivered the Fisk graduation speech on "the fearful power" of Otto von Bismarck as nation builder.[10] He was invited back ten years later, on June 15, 1898, to deliver a commencement address in which he spoke of the restricted career opportunities and special difficulties facing "college-bred Negroes" in America. He exhorted them, when challenged by the toils and sorrows of the working life in a racist society, to protect the high-cultural liberal arts ethos that they discovered during their university studies. He expressed his wish that their acts be guided by a commitment to work, sacrifice, and service beyond mere material improvement. This pursuit of meaningful work according to a higher vision of life, he explained, would simultaneously "serve humanity" and contribute directly to "the striving" of "the Negro people."[11] By this time, Du Bois had a PhD in history from Harvard, had studied sociology at Friedrich Wilhelm University in Berlin, and had published *The Suppression of the African Slave Trade*, *The Philadelphia Negro*, and several of his most important essays, some of which would be integrated into *The Souls of Black Folk*. When, forty years later, Du Bois again addressed a cohort of Fisk graduates, both he and the world had changed in significant ways.

He composed his 1938 address after having spent the previous eight years engaging with Marx's writings, developing a new program for black self-segregation and economic self-management in response to the Great Depression, and distancing himself the NAACP's long-term legal strategy to challenge racial segregation and obtain full citizenship for black Americans. He had also recently returned from an extended trip through Europe (including five months in Nazi Germany), the Soviet Union, China, Japan, and Hawaii. "The Revelation of Saint Orgne the Damned" therefore warrants our attention as an important and innovative expression of the particular form of black Marxism that Du Bois developed during the 1930s. It should be read as exemplary of the radically humanist vision of socialism and democracy, and the radically democratic and socialist vision of humanism, that Du Bois spent his life developing.[12]

Offered as a literary fable, Du Bois purports to relay "The Revelation," as he himself heard it, of this fictional Saint Orgne (an anagram of "Negro") regarding family, church, school, work, art, race, economics, and politics. The speech's aim, as he informed Fisk President, Thomas E. Jones, was to indicate "the path which young American Negroes today must follow if they are going to attain a secure place in modern culture."[13] On one level, the literary presentation assumes a tongue-in-cheek tone that works to undo the sober pretentions usually associated with commencement speakers, elder statesmen, stuffy professors, and philosophers—the parodic trace of Nietzsche's "Thus Spoke Zarathustra" is unmistakable. It seems also to be addressed widely to parents, educators, and pastors, to all manner of sermonizers and clerics, secular or religious, who pretend to propagate ethical maxims and orthodox dogma. At the same time, Du Bois's "Revelation" is a serious critique of black families, schools, churches, and political leaders for failing to confront directly the real ethical and political dilemmas created by what Cedric Robinson would later call "racial capitalism."[14] His "Revelation" seems also to model without irony what it means to reflect truthfully on the predicament of black youth in American society. Moreover, like Nietzsche, Du Bois may be read as offering a secular vision of the good life for modern humans; this speech is a resounding "Yes!" to life itself.

"The Revelation" is structured as an account of Saint Orgne's long and arduous journey toward enlightenment regarding the situation of the Negro in America. It unfolds as a fictional biography of trial and tribulation punctuated by saintly sermons, or "revelations" on various topics whose insights emerged through a series of difficult experiences of oppression and disillusionment. This form allows Du Bois to braid elements of his own life trajectory with the collective history of blacks in America as each moved through various ways of understanding and responding to their racial predicament. He thus implies that "revelation" is less a matter of divinely revealed truth than the ongoing discovery of social truths (about race, poverty, sociality, and democracy) through everyday practices and lived experiences. It is a story about coming to terms with the truth of what blacks were up against in America.

His address begins with the black saint asking himself whether "the dark damnation of color" is real. After "looking full at life as it is and not as it might be or haply as he would have it," he responds, yes, as an American Negro, "in truth thou art damned, and may not escape by vain imagining nor fruitless repining."[15] His prophecy quickly reveals that this is a double damnation in which racial exclusion and enforced poverty sustain one another. He relays that without money it is impossible to support a family, improve education, or reform churches. "How," he asks, "shall we have time for real knowledge; and freedom of art; and effort toward world-wide democracy, until we have the opportunity to work decently and the resources to spend, which shall enable us to be civilized human beings?"[16] Saint Orgne reveals how this double damnation is compounded by a corrupt and complicit black elite. He recounts, for example, how a group of poor black cotton farmers owned a common piece of land on which they worked collectively and whose fruits they divided evenly. But after seven years of toil they discovered that "the preacher" had mortgaged their land "behind the backs of the trusting flock and had run away with the money."[17]

But Du Bois is clear: Corrupt practices by the black elite were conditioned by the systemic problem of industrial capitalism. Saint Orgne explains that there exists sufficient wealth and economic capacity to feed, clothe, shelter, and educate the world. "If sharing of wealth were based not on owning but only on effort, and if all who are able did their share of the world's work . . . and limited their consumption to reasonable wants, we could abolish poverty."[18] Yet, he continues, in the United States workers are left "as poor as possible in order further to increase the wealth of a few." Worse, "we . . . not only . . . produce primarily for the profit of owners and not for use of the mass of people, but we have grown to think that this is the only way in which we can produce."[19] On the one hand, he recounts, "We organize industry for private wealth and not for public weal and we argue . . . that no human planning can change the essentials of this process." On the other, "The process has failed so many times . . . that we are bound to change or starve in the midst of plenty."[20] The only sane alternative, Saint Orgne preaches, is to "produce for the satisfaction of human needs and distribute according to human want."[21] He exhorts his listeners "to work not simply for individual profit but for group weal; not simply for one group but for all groups," and to enjoy "the freedom to dream and plan."[22] It will thereby be possible "to think of the time when poverty approaches abolition."[23]

Yet the Saint also decries the fact that black laborers cannot simply participate in this general struggle for economic justice and social transformation because they are "cut off from the main effort by the lesions of race; by the segregation of color; by the domination of caste."[24] As a result, "black folk of America are faced with the most difficult problem of realizing and knowing the part which we have got to play in this economic revolution."[25] Saint Orgne explains that the white labor movement in America and Europe excluded and deceived black workers. Its object "was not the uplift of all labor; it was to join capital in sharing the loot from exploited color labor. So we too, only half emancipated, hurled ourselves forward, too willing, if it had been possible, to climb up to a bourgeois heaven on the prone bodies of our fellows."[26]

On one level, the challenge was how to align in a common struggle with racist white workers who did not recognize both groups' common interests. On another level, the challenge was to specify what a multiracial working class should be fighting for. Du Bois indicates that the white labor movement and the striving black bourgeoisie deceived themselves. This collective deception then made it difficult for most American blacks to "conceive of [a] future world which is not dominated by present white nations and thoroughly shot through with their ideals, their method of government, their economic organization, their literature, and their art; or in other words, their throttling of democracy, their exploitation of labor, their industrial imperialism, and their color hate."[27]

Du Bois relays that this combination of forces—institutional racism, economic exploitation, social degradation, discrimination by the white labor movement, the failure of black leaders, and the need for black masses to support a global economic revolution—led Saint Orgne to try to create an autonomous community founded on the principles of black self-management. Accordingly, he

> organized a church with a cooperative store in the Sunday school room; with physician, dentist, nurse and lawyer to help, serve, and defend the congregation; with library, nursery school and a regular succession of paid and trained lecturers and discussion; they had radio and moving pictures and out beyond the city a farm with house and lake. They had a credit union, group insurance and building and loan association. The members paid for this not by contributions but by ten dollars a month each of regular dues and those who would join this church must do more than profess to love God.[28]

Underscoring the "irreparable harm slavery had done to the [black] *family* group," the saint also relates this program for community self-management and economic autonomy to the issue of gender inequality.[29]

In "The Damnation of Women" (1920) Du Bois had argued that American racism had the paradoxical effect of making black women more economically independent with regard to black men than white women were with regard to white men.[30] But he also indicates that the price of this relative independence was family disintegration. He concluded that black women's freedom was incompatible with what he called "married motherhood."[31] In his 1938 address, he revisits this dilemma. On the one hand, the saint regards marriage within bourgeois society as a form of domination, which he calls "martyrdom," and motherhood as a kind of trap that would obstruct women from realizing their full social and human potential.[32] On the other hand, he identifies the family as an invaluable locus for social training, cultural education, and subject formation. He insisted that black mothers did, and should, play a crucial role in cultivating habits related to comportment, ethics, and values. How then could he criticize racial capitalism from the standpoint of the normative family while also being committed to women's emancipation? The Saint does so by calling on his audience to "create a new family group . . . a cultural group" that is not "subordinate" to the "merely biological" and "blood relationship of families."[33] He thereby attempts to resolve this contradiction between gender equality and family life by separating kinship from biology and making parenting a public matter for which the cooperative community would take collective responsibility.

"The Revelation" suggests that the path to a radically different social order would be mediated by black cooperative associations. These would serve simultaneously to ensure the community's economic survival, enact a different set of social arrangements, and create a form of dis-alienated life to which self-managing blacks, now with the prospect of better realizing their human potential, could offer a whole-hearted "yes." This vision of black mutualism exceeded narrowly defined economic matters and had implications far beyond the black community. Saint Orgne explicitly links this plan for "economic revolution" to what he called "our salvation and . . . the salvation of the world."[34] He thus "preached the word of life from Jeremiah, Shakespeare and Jesus, Confucius, Buddha, and John Brown."[35] This remarkable constellation indicates the planetary scope of this attempt to relate radical reflections from diverse cultural traditions about what it means to live a human life in a just world. It pointed beyond the divisions between religious and secular revelation in order to link ethical insights, beautiful literature, insurgent politics, and exemplary practices. In order to more fully understand how this "word of life" indexed what I am calling a radical humanism we need first to understand the speech as a further iteration of the critical position and political program that Du Bois had been elaborating through the 1930s.

The Black Radical Predicament

Most accounts of Du Bois's life understandably trace an arc of increasing political radicalization from the moment he left Great Barrington to attend college at Fisk University in 1885 to his 1961 decision to join the Communist Party and then exile himself to Ghana shortly before his death two years later. His professional life is frequently divided into steps along this path. A first period (1894–1910) encompasses his early career as an academic sociologist and liberal idealist who employed rational scholarship to challenge the illogic of racial discrimination. A second period (1910–34) corresponded to his tenure as a social democratic public intellectual with the NAACP and the *Crisis*, marked by his participation in legal struggles against institutional segregation. During this time, his politics continually shifted leftward; he came to understand World War I as an inter-imperial struggle, and he confronted the refusal of Northern white liberals in government, public opinion, or labor unions to embrace full citizenship for black Americans. A third period, the focus of this essay, opened in 1934 after Du Bois resigned from the NAACP and the *Crisis*. It was marked by his increasingly militant anticapitalist, anti-imperialist, internationalist, and Pan-African commitments and interventions.

In *Dusk of Dawn*, Du Bois recounts how in the early 1930s he began "to pause and take stock" of the NAACP civil rights struggle to which he had devoted himself since 1910.[36] He recalls his "basic theory had been that race prejudice was primarily a matter of ignorance on the part of the mass of men" and that "when the truth was properly presented, the monstrous wrong of race hate must melt . . . before it. All human action to me in those days was conscious and rational."[37] Yet despite the NAACP's legal victories and advances in black education, leadership, and literature, he explained, "The barriers of race prejudice were certainly as strong in 1930 as in 1910 the world over, and in certain aspects . . . even stronger."[38] He thus came to identify the deep psychic and material substrate within which American racism was rooted. On the one hand, "we were not facing simply the rational, conscious determination of white folk to oppress us; we were facing age-long complexes sunk now largely to unconscious habit and irrational urge."[39] On the other, white "race prejudice was built and increasingly built on the basis of income which they enjoyed and their anti-Negro bias consciously or unconsciously formulated in order to protect their wealth and power."[40] In response, Du Bois recalibrated his expectations about how long the struggle against race discrimination was likely to last and on what terrain it would have to be fought. Accordingly, he shifted strategy to focus more directly on "the economic rehabilitation and defense of the American Negro."[41]

Du Bois recalls that the Russian Revolution "first illuminated and made clear this change in my basic thought"[42] by providing an example of a large nation deciding to confront poverty directly and orient state action to improve mass welfare by placing governing power in the hands of workers.[43] He also recalls his 1926 visit to the Soviet Union as a revelation: "Mentally I came to know Karl Marx and Lenin. . . . Since that trip my mental outlook . . . will never be the same."[44] But he also knew that in Jim Crow America, the task of creating a multiracial workers' democracy would confront a specific set of obstacles that orthodox Marxism did not foresee.

Du Bois had already been a member of the Socialist Party from 1910 to 1912. After quitting, he criticized American socialists for relegating black workers' struggles against the color line to a secondary concern. He warned them that in practice, socialism in America could not succeed without the support of black labor and that in principle, socialism could not move forward as a project if any social group were to be excluded from its organizations, victories, and future improvements.[45] Following World War I, he continued to grapple with the actual and possible relationship between the black freedom struggle and the American labor movement. He stated clearly that most black Americans belonged to "an exploited class of cheap laborers" who shared with white workers an interest in fighting for more "democratic control" of capital in the service of a new "industrial democracy."[46] Yet, he explained, "Practically we are not part of the white proletariat and are not recognized by that proletariat to any great extent. We are the victims of their physical oppression, social ostracism, economic exclusion and personal hatred."[47] As a result, he observed, "the Negro radical" is caught "between this devil and deep sea": capital, on the one hand, and white working-class racism, on the other.[48]

Throughout the interwar period, Du Bois continued to criticize socialists for eliminating black workers from their calculations, the American Federation of Labor for accepting unions that excluded black workers, and communists for recruiting black workers without addressing the deep racism of the mass of white workers into whose ranks they were thrown and with whom they were expected to collaborate. He also rebuked each of these groups for demonizing black workers on the grounds that they did not recognize their common interests with the white labor movement and therefore join the anticapitalist struggle. Black workers were also accused by leftist organizations of accepting various compromises with capitalism and petit bourgeois black leaders.[49] Regarding such orthodoxy, Du Bois held to his 1921 insight: "Under these circumstances how silly it would be for us to try to apply the doctrine of class struggle without modification or thought."[50]

Du Bois recognized that the Depression had made the situation of black workers especially precarious and the imperative for socialist transformation even more urgent. But it also sharpened the dilemma facing black radicals. In 1931 he was unequivocal:

> *Present organization of industry for private profit and control of government by concentrated wealth is doomed to disaster. It must change and fall if civilization survives. The foundation of its present world-wide power is the slavery and semi-slavery of the colored world including the American Negroes. Until the colored man, yellow, red, brown, and black, becomes free, articulate, intelligent and the receiver of decent income, white capital will use the profit derived from his degradation to keep white labor in chains.* There is no doubt then, as to the future, or as to where the true interests of American Negroes lie.[51]

But as long as white workers resented black competition, American unions excluded black members, and working-class "mobs" "demand the right to kill 'niggers' whenever their passions . . . are inflamed by propaganda," black militants could not simply accept the fiction of a preconstituted or unified working class.[52] Du Bois believed both that black workers were positioned to act as a revolutionary vanguard and that white masses would never follow their revolutionary initiative:

> Negroes know perfectly well that whenever they try to lead a revolution in America, the nation will unite as one fist to crush them alone. . . . Negroes perceive clearly that the real interests of the white worker are identical with the interests of the black worker, but until the white worker recognizes this, the black worker is compelled in sheer self-defense to refuse to be made the sacrificial goat.[53]

In the early 1930s Du Bois immersed himself in the writings of Marx in order to think through the contradictions of American capitalism, the limitations of actually existing socialism, communism, and trade unionism, and the predicament confronting black radicals. Although in 1926, Du Bois stated: "I stand in astonishment and wonder at the revelation of Russia that has come to me . . . if what I have seen with my eyes and heard with my ears in Russia is Bolshevism, I am a Bolshevik,"[54] nonetheless, he never simply applied Marxist dogma to the (black) American context. He both used Marx to challenge the orthodox Left and used the (black) American historical situation to rethink orthodox Marxism.

In the spring of 1933 Du Bois taught a sociology seminar at Atlanta University on "Karl Marx and the Negro Problem."[55] In May he published an article in the *Crisis* that attempted to reconsider Marx's nineteenth-century insights in relation to the changing character of twentieth-century capitalism, the peculiar conditions of the U.S. racial formation, the political conjuncture of the Great Depression, and the black freedom struggle. He begins by describing Marx as "a colossal genius of infinite sacrifice and monumental industry" and placing *Capital* alongside the Bible, Kant's *Critique of Pure Reason*, and Darwin's *Origin of Species* as "books in the world which every searcher of truth must know."[56] Du Bois suggests that recent history, defined by the Russian Revolution and the Great Depression, made Marx's writings newly relevant. Capitalism's cycles of war and economic crisis were "forcing the world to contemplate the possibilities of fundamental change in our economic methods."[57] More and more people began to believe that "whether violently or peacefully, revolution seems bound to come."[58]

Yet he also insisted that Marx's analysis needed to be rethought in relation to the changing character of capitalism itself. Here Du Bois emphasized the "world-wide organization" of the market, the acceleration of mass production on larger scales, and the emergence of a new "working-class aristocracy" of "technical engineers and managers" that occupied a position "between the older proletariat and the absentee owners of capital."[59] He notes that banks and financiers assumed a more prominent role as intermediaries between employers and workers. Additionally, "common labor in America and white Europe, far from being motivated by any vision of the possibility of revolt against capitalism, has been blinded by the American vision of the possibility of layer after layer of the workers escaping into the wealthy class and becoming managers and employers of labor."[60]

One result of these transformations, Du Bois explains, was that competition among groups had fractured the working class, "leaving the Negro at the bottom chained to helplessness . . . by the Color Bar."[61] Du Bois contends that global capitalism had come to rely ever more on imperialism and racism. By creating "a world-wide new proletariat of colored workers . . . furnishing by the lowest paid wages in modern history a mass of raw material for industry . . . capitalists have consolidated their power . . . and bribed the white workers by higher wages, visions of wealth and the opportunity to drive 'niggers.'"[62] Moreover, he contends, "the bulk of American white labor is neither ignorant nor fanatical. It knows exactly what it is doing and it means to do it."[63]

Du Bois thus indicates how the color bar was a structural and functional feature of capitalist accumulation and social regulation. On the one hand, white working-class racism was fueled by the existence of this new labor aristocracy. On the other, racism under capitalism created a strong affinity between black workers and a new group of black petit bourgeois clergyman, teachers, farm owners, professionals, and small businessmen who did not exploit labor. It followed, for Du Bois, that "the revolt of any black proletariat could not, therefore, be logically directed against this class, nor could this class join either white capital, white engineers, or white workers to strengthen the color bar."[64] In short, he believed that such conditions challenged orthodox Marxist conceptions of class as the primary axis of social differentiation and antagonism. He concluded that "there is not at present the slightest indication that a Marxian revolution based on a united class-conscious proletariat is anywhere on the American far horizon. Rather race antagonism and labor group rivalry are still undisturbed by world catastrophe."[65]

Du Bois's analysis thereby returned him to the predicament facing black radicals whose exclusion from the white labor movement was unfairly attributed to ignorance or conservatism. "In the hearts of black laborers alone . . . lie those ideals of democracy in politics and industry which may in time make the workers of the world effective dictators of civilization."[66] Yet under existing conditions "his only defense is such internal organization as will protect him from both parties [white capitalists and white workers], and . . . prevent inside the race group any large development of capitalist exploitation."[67] It was this historical crisis and strategic impasse, along with his reconsideration of Marx in relation to twentieth-century racism and capitalism, that informed Du Bois's new program for black self-segregation. He recognized that the freedom struggle had to move beyond demanding legal rights and that it needed to ally with the white labor movement to create a democratic socialist society. The challenge was to know *how* to be an antiracist leftist and a black anticapitalist in Depression-era America. What kind of movement, tactics, and strategy might best allow black Americans to pursue these transformative aims? Such questions about the relationship between the black freedom struggle and the white labor movement, as well as between Marxist theory, socialist or communist politics, and racial emancipation were the site of intense debates among a wide range of black radicals in and beyond the United States during the 1930s.

Cooperative Commonwealth

Du Bois's proposed solution to the black radical predicament was a program for cooperative self-management. He observed that the Great Depression had struck black Americans with special force, intensifying their poverty and leaving them even more vulnerable to resurgent institutional racism. Yet he also suggested that the crisis may have created a historical opening that could upend bourgeois common sense (which he called "the American assumption"),[68] radicalize American workers, and create opportunities for a multiracial movement that could radically transform social relations. This, in other words, could be a second chance to realize the revolutionary possibility that had been briefly opened by post–Civil War Reconstruction in the 1870s.[69]

Under such conditions, Du Bois insisted, the black freedom struggle had to address poverty and economic inequality directly. He also argued that racial emancipation would require large-scale societal transformation. This meant that black radicals would have to align with the U.S. Left in a broader anticapitalist struggle despite the entrenched racism of white workers, trade unions, and socialist and communist parties. He insisted that any response to this predicament must start with a clear-sighted understanding of the actual historical situation facing black communities: the failure to abolish the color line through court cases, the entanglement of economic and racial domination, the fact of institutional and social segregation, the reality of white working-class racism, and the limitations of Marxist theory to grasp this situation. This meant that he refused to proceed from either the liberal fiction of civic sameness or the communist fantasy of class unity. But neither did he think that a circumscribed black nationalism could achieve the wholesale transformation, the reconstruction of American democracy, that he believed was necessary. Du Bois looked for immanent possibilities within the existing situation. He believed that real change would require patience, endurance, and a long-term struggle on multiple fronts.[70] Learning his lesson from the 1870s, he concluded that black communities would have to assume a leading role in this process. They could not look to the U.S. government, to white liberals, or to revolutionary leftists for resources or leadership.

He later recalled concluding that "the attack upon these hidden and partially concealed causes of race hate, must be led by Negroes in a program which was not merely negative in the sense of calling on white folk to desist from certain practices and give up certain beliefs: but in the sense that Negroes must proceed constructively in a new and comprehensive plan of their own."[71] Given the unconscious substrate of the color line, the catastrophic economic conditions precipitated by the global economic crisis, and the race prejudice of the American labor movement, Du Bois explained, "Deliberate, and purposeful segregation for economic defense" had become an immediate imperative.[72] To this effect, he proposed "to use the power of the Negro as a consumer," which would serve as "a new instrument of democratic control over industry."[73]

Black economic cooperatives had a long history in the United States.[74] Du Bois had promoted them as early as 1918 when he wrote editorials about them in the *Crisis* and participated in a preliminary meeting to establish a Negro Co-Operative Guild.[75] Now, in the early 1930s, Du Bois again called for the creation of self-managing associations that would largely withdraw from the existing economy in order to establish autonomous systems of cooperative production and distribution without labor exploitation. These would require "careful planning" in order to "eliminate unemployment, risk, and profit. . . . This would be a realization of democracy in industry led by consumers' organizations and extending to planned production."[76] Further, Du Bois suggested that these cooperatives could "socialize most of [their] professional activities."[77] Banking, insurance, law, and medicine could "change from a private profit to a mutual basis."[78] Likewise, schools, colleges, publishers, and literature could be reorganized along cooperative lines. "Today we work for others at wages pressed down to the limit of subsistence. Tomorrow we may work for ourselves, exchanging services, producing an increasing proportion of the goods which we consume and being rewarded by a living wage and by work under civilized conditions."[79] In this way, he stated, "Negroes can develop in the United States an economic nation within a nation, able to work through inner cooperation, to found its own institutions, to educate its genius, and . . . to keep in helpful touch and cooperate with the mass of the nation."[80]

Most immediately, this was a realist response to the existing situation and meant to secure blacks' immediate survival during the Depression. This proposal, of course, went against the NAACP's long-term rejection of all policy that consented to any form of segregation. But in a 1933 *Crisis* article, Du Bois explained, "There is no other way; let us not be deceived. American Negroes will be beaten into submission and degradation if they merely wait unorganized to find some place voluntarily given them in the new reconstruction of the economic world."[81] And again in 1934: "The only effective defense that the segregated and despised group has against complete spiritual and physical disaster, is internal self-organization for self-respect and self-defense."[82]

Importantly, Du Bois distinguished between immediate strategies and ultimate aims, writing,

> Doubtless, and in the long run, the greatest human development is going to take place under experiences of widest individual contact. Nevertheless, today such . . . contact is made difficult and almost impossible by petty prejudice. . . . It is impossible, therefore, to wait for the millennium of free and normal intercourse before we unite . . . to accomplish his economic emancipation through voluntary determined cooperative effort.[83]

He underscored that "this plan did not . . . advocate segregation as the final solution of the race problem; exactly the contrary; but it did face the facts . . . with thoughtfully mapped effort."[84] As he said to Fisk University students in 1933, this new approach, which included a plan to promote what he called "autonomous Negro universities,"

> simply accepts the bald fact that we are segregated, apart, hammered into a separate unity by spiritual intolerance and legal sanction backed by mob law, and that this separation is growing in strength and fixation. . . . Recognizing this brute fact . . . What are we going to do about it? . . . How far and in what way can we consciously and scientifically guide our future so as to ensure our physical survival, our spiritual freedom, and our social growth? Either we do this or we die. There is no alternative.[85]

Here we can clearly see that Du Bois did not regard this program as a mere economic expedient, for he added the following: "Let us not beat futile wings in impotent frenzy, but carefully plan and guide our segregated life, organize in industry and politics to protect it and expand it and *above all to give it unhampered spiritual expression in art and literature*."[86] He thus underscored its far-reaching social, political, cultural, and spiritual implications. He explicitly linked the creation of "self-governed" communities through "economic solidarity" to "the building of a full humanity."[87] He wrote,

> Rail if you will against the race segregation here involved and condoned, but take advantage of it by planning secure centers of Negro co-operative effort and particularly of economic power to make us spiritually free for initiative and creation in other and wider fields, and for eventually breaking down all segregation based on color.[88]

He also argued that this cooperative movement would be a crucial weapon in the ongoing struggle for full citizenship.[89] Through "voluntary and increased segregation, by careful autonomy and planned economic organization," he argued, black Americans could "build so strong and efficient a unit that 12,000,000 men can no longer be refused fellowship and equality in the United States."[90]

Even more expansively, he suggested that these cooperatives could establish a new mode of democratic self-government and form the backbone of an inclusive and transformative national network.

> The Negro group in the United States can establish, for a large proportion of its members, a *co-operative commonwealth*, finding its authority in the consensus of the group [and its intelligent choice of inner leadership]. It can see to it that not only no action of this inner group is opposed to the real interests of the nation, but that it works for and in

conjunction with the best interests of the nation. It need draw no line of exclusion so long as the outsiders join in the consensus.[91]

Self-segregation would thus be the means through which black Americans could lead the effort to establish this multiracial "co-operative commonwealth" composed of self-managing collectives practicing consensus politics.[92] Du Bois called this "a special chance for a new trial of democratic development without force among some of the worst victims of force. . . . I can conceive of no more magnificent nor promising crusade in modern times. We have a chance to teach industrial and cultural democracy to a world that bitterly needs it."[93]

The aim then was not simply to withdraw and survive, nor was this merely a tactic to obtain civic equality, nor only a dream for black Americans to flourish spiritually as fully recognized humans (though it certainly was that). It was a far-reaching strategy through which to abolish the color bar, transform economic relations, and reconstruct American democracy. The program was motivated by historic opportunity and moral responsibility to demonstrate to the world what democracy could be. It would do so by founding black social cooperatives that could then be emulated and instituted on national and international scales. These mutualist practices and autonomous institutions would serve as "the economic ladder by which the American Negro, achieving new social institutions, can move *pari passu* with the modern world into a new heaven and a new earth."[94]

In sum, economic self-management would allow besieged blacks to survive the long-term struggle against economic depression and racial segregation and would better allow them to achieve their long-standing political demand of full citizenship within the republic. At the same time, it would help to fundamentally transform American economic, social, and political arrangements. It would produce alternative institutions and subjects, with new habits and values, around which a postcapitalist multiracial democracy could be organized. And these self-managing cooperative communities would serve as allies and examples for other peoples and nations. In this way black radicals could *anticipate*—by modeling and enacting, calling for and calling forth—the kind of human emancipation that Du Bois envisioned for all peoples. These social cooperatives would not only allow black radicals to move *with* the modern world; they would allow them to move the world itself closer to a new heaven and a new earth.

Scholarly discussion of Du Bois's radical turn in the 1930s, and this plan specifically, seems to revolve around the axes of assimilation versus separation, nationalism versus Marxism, race versus class, or reformism versus revolution. But his initiative sought to transcend just such false oppositions. I would argue that the key terms for his program were self-management, cooperation, and democracy. It was neither about assimilating into nor separating from the existing national society—but about radically transforming it, and through it, the world. Du Bois's focus on economic self-organization distinguished his program from the NAACP's legal and electoral orientation. His mutualist critique of private property and profit distinguished it from both Booker T. Washington's vocational accommodation with capitalism and from Marcus Garvey's entrepreneurial nationalism. And his emphasis on democratic consensus distinguished it from the centralized and hierarchical tendencies within U.S. labor unions and the American Communist Party.

Radical Humanism

If the aim of economic self-segregation was a cooperative commonwealth, what would be the aim of this commonwealth? To begin to answer this question, I suggest we return to the 1938 "Revelation" where Saint Orgne "preached the word of life." We saw that he offers a series of unambiguous socialist propositions about abolishing poverty, limiting consumption, and sharing wealth. These he linked to an equitable and interdependent form of life based on nonexploitative ways of being together. It is important to note that the Saint's call for collective arrangements, his vision of something like a cooperative commonwealth, posits material welfare as a means, not an end in itself.

The Saint relays that

> when men no longer fear starvation and unemployment . . . In such a world living begins; in such a world we will have freedom of thought and expression and just as much freedom of action as maintenance of the necessary economic basis of life permits; that is, given three or six hours of work . . . we ought to be sure of at least eighteen hours of recreation, joy, and creation with a minimum of compulsion for anybody.[95]

"Life is more than meat. . . . Living is not for earning, earning is for living. The man that spends his life earning a living, has never lived."[96] Rather, he affirms,

> Life is the fullest, most complete enjoyment of all the possibilities of human existence. . . . It is the free enjoyment of every normal appetite. It is giving rein to the creative impulse, in thought and imagination. Here roots the rise of the Joy of Living, of music, painting, drawing, sculpture and building; hence come literature with romance, poetry, and essay; hence rise Love, Friendship, emulation, and ambition.[97]

Against vulgar materialists, whether bourgeois or Marxist, who insisted on the imperative to produce and consume, he declares, the "realm of the physical need be only the smaller part of life and above it, planning, emotion and dream; in the exercising of creative power, in building, painting, and literature there is a chance for the free exercise of the human spirit."[98] Indeed the Saint identifies "the rock foundations of Democracy" as "the freedom to create within the limits of natural law, the freedom to love without limit; the freedom to dream of the utter marriage of beauty and art."[99]

Just as Du Bois's vision of humanism explodes its bourgeois integuments, his vision of democracy exceeds its degraded liberal form, which was "confined to . . . electing certain persons to power . . . [and] minor matters of administration" and excluded ordinary people from "determining what goods shall be produced, what services shall be rendered, and how goods and services shall be shared by all."[100] In contrast, Saint Orgne advocates "a broad conception of democracy" that that does not only allow "the complaints of all" to "be heard, or the hurts of the humblest healed; it is for the vastly larger object of loosing the possibilities of mankind for the development of a higher and broader and more varied human culture."[101] "Democracy . . . forms not merely a reservoir of complaint but of ability, hidden otherwise in poverty and ignorance. . . . Democracy means the opening of opportunity to the disinherited to contribute to civilization and the happiness of men."[102] Economic equality, social cooperation, substantive democracy, and the "joy of living" in the service of worldwide human emancipation and elevation are indissociable elements of Du Bois's integrated vision.

Note that Du Bois here is calling neither for racial assimilation into a unitary nation-state nor an undifferentiated family of man. Saint Orgne insists that the facts and effects of racial discrimination cannot be ignored. Black intellectuals may rightly reject the existence of natural biological races. Nevertheless:

> We American Negros form a definite group, not entirely segregated and isolated but differentiated to such a degree that we have largely a life and thought of our own. . . . Absorption into the nation, except as a slow intellectual process, is unthinkable. . . . Separated and isolated as we are, we form in America an integral group and this fact has its meaning, its worth and its values.[103]

The saint is certainly inviting black Americans to protect and celebrate their cultural distinctiveness. But just as important, he is reminding them that that these very qualities enable them to serve as leaders in a struggle for the realization of human freedom in and beyond their communities. Du Bois famously observed that the history of racial segregation and discrimination burdened black people with a disabling "double-consciousness, the sense of always looking at oneself through the eyes of others, of measuring one's soul with the tape of a world that looks on in amused contempt and pity."[104] Yet this very situation, "which yields [them] no true self-consciousness" also "gifted" them "with second sight in this American world."[105] Throughout the 1930s Du Bois implies that it is precisely this most marginalized community that has a privileged insight into the working of modern racism, capitalism, and their inextricable relations, and an invaluable perspective on the promise and contradictions of freedom and democracy. Likewise, he believed that their specific historical experience led black Americans to cultivate the political virtues and spiritual values that would allow them to be in the vanguard of any movement to reconstitute American democracy and create conditions for social justice worldwide. Saint Orgne thus declares, "we can be among the first group to help restore the idea of high culture and limited income and dispel the fable that riotous wealth alone is civilization. Acting together . . . we can be the units through which universal democracy may be accomplished."[106]

To identify Du Bois as a radical humanist is not to suggest that he was an abstract universalist whose politics were based on liberal assumptions about the fundamental, disembodied, and transhistorical sameness of generic humans as rational, sensible, or suffering beings. All of his thinking proceeded from the fact of the color line, the social predicaments thereby produced, and the forms of subjectivity, sociality, and cultural expression accordingly developed. In books like *The Souls of Black Folk* (1903) through *The Gift of Black Folk* (1924), *Black Folk, Then and Now* (1939), and *The World and Africa* (1947), he never wavered from his 1897 proposition that "the Negro people, as a race, have a contribution to make to civilization and humanity, which no other race can make."[107] But as this statement indicates, he spent his life searching for ways to affirm black cultural specificity that would promote political universality and help realize human potentiality generally. This is the perspective from which we might understand the saint's invocation of "the democracy of race," not just a place where individuals of all races are equally included but where all racial communities may develop their singular cultural capacities.[108] This commitment to "universal democracy" did not imply black self-negation. On the contrary, it pointed beyond the false opposition between universality and particularity. Note that Saint Orgne concludes his "philosophy of life" by declaring:

> Through cooperation, education and understanding the cultural race unit may be the
> pipe line through which human civilization may extend to wider and wider areas to the
> fertilization of mankind. It is to this use of our racial unity and loyalty that the United
> States impels us. We cannot escape it. Only through racial effort today can we achieve
> economic stability, cultural growth and human understanding. The way to democracy lies
> through race loyalty. . . . Selah and Amen.[109]

This was a situated universalism that sought to articulate black singularity with a "more abundant" life for all humans.

Political Legibility

Should we really read "The Revelation of Saint Orgne" as a sui generis text? Similar attempts to relate black autonomy to human emancipation are braided through most of Du Bois's major texts. The appearance of "The Revelation" between two of Du Bois's avowedly radical texts, *Black Reconstruction* (1935) and *Dusk of Dawn* (1940), certainly invites us to treat it as a further iteration of, rather than a deviation from, his Depression-era radicalism. I have tried to suggest that it both echoes and extends the radical humanist orientation that subtended his political reorientation during the 1930s. But the vision expressed in this speech and concurrent writings has been largely illegible to Du Bois's allies and interlocutors, then and since.

The fact that Du Bois's radicalism and his humanism were two sides of the same coin has not been the focus of sustained scholarly attention. The lack of critical attention to "The Revelation" seems to suggest that scholars have found it difficult to incorporate into their interpretations of his radicalization. From a liberal perspective, Arnold Rampersad provides an indispensably illuminating account of the peculiar mix of New England Puritanism, Southern Congregationalism, Harvard pragmatism, and European social reformism that informed Du Bois's morally grounded, spiritually elevated, and politically engaged scholarship and criticism. He argues that by the interwar period, Du Bois consistently attempted to triangulate "socialism, black nationalism, and liberal idealism" as interdependent concepts, "which he attempted to unify in his version of the pragmatic method."[110] But Rampersad also insists on "their tendency toward separation into competing forces" in the (more explicitly Marxist) works following *Darkwater* (1920).[111] In particular, he emphasizes the tensions between Du Bois's commitments to black cultural specificity and Marxist theory, ultimately regarding the latter as an intrusive aberration that, in the mid-1930s, temporarily diverted him from his deeper and more abiding concerns with black culture and civil rights. These are curious claims given the powerful way that Du Bois synthesizes antiracism, anticapitalism, anti-utilitarianism in his integrated vision of cooperative self-management.

From a Left perspective, Cedric Robinson finds it equally difficult to account for the kind of position that Du Bois develops in "The Revelation." For he reads Du Bois as demonstrating that being a "Black radical thinker" and "a sympathetic critic of Marx" were "irreconcilable roles."[112] Instead of focusing on Du Bois's original synthesis, Robinson tells a linear story about his intellectual evolution from bourgeois liberalism, through Western radicalism, to finally discover the black radical tradition. Robinson defines the latter as rooted in African metaphysics, embodied by a transhistorical will "to preserve the collective being, the ontological totality," and expressed in an enduring African identity that was not fundamentally shaped by New World conditions.[113] Robinson certainly recognizes the importance of Marxism to Du Bois's thinking during the 1930s but treats his embrace of the black radical tradition in *Black Reconstruction* as a sudden illumination that allowed Du Bois finally to overcome his "Westernized eyes."[114] Robinson also identifies Du Bois's Marxism in that text primarily with his account of the spontaneous revolt and self-emancipation of the enslaved black masses during the Civil War. But, as I suggest below, *Black Reconstruction*, like the rest of his writings during the thirties, wove together strands of what Robinson would call black nationalism, Western radicalism, *and* petit bourgeois ideology.

Neither of these approaches can account for a discourse like "The Revelation of Saint Orgne" in which the celebration of the singularity of black life is inseparable from a heterodox Marxism that advocates cooperative socialism, popular democracy, and a radical humanist commitment to life as "more than meat." Both approaches reify what were actually distinct facets of Du Bois's integrated approach and then treat their supposedly surprising encounter in his work as a problem to be solved or an anomaly to be explained. Instead, we should attend to how Du Bois's thinking called into question the very categorical assumptions and binary oppositions on which these interpretations are based.

The confounding character of Du Bois's radically humanist vision of a black led cooperative commonwealth also attended its inception. In a letter to President Jones of Fisk, Du Bois explained that he regarded his program for black self-management as "a method of realizing a world wide humanity."[115] But among the New Deal establishment, neither black leaders nor white liberals supported Du Bois's new orientation. His emphasis on economic restructuring, his invocation of "self-segregation," and his frank endorsement of socialist objectives were anathema to the NAACP's self-understanding and its longstanding civil rights policy. In May 1934, after several years of internal discord during which he wrote editorials criticizing the association, Du Bois finally resigned from the *Crisis* and the NAACP.[116] Immediately thereafter he accepted a regular position in sociology at Atlanta University.[117] Back in an academic setting, he immersed himself in Marx's writings and completed *Black Reconstruction in America*, on which he had been working since 1931.[118]

Given that Du Bois wrote this magnum opus precisely during the period that he reoriented his political strategy, it is useful to read *Black Reconstruction in America* and his

Depression-era writings about black self-management through economic cooperatives in relation to each other. In both cases he was preoccupied with the historical conditions of the possibility of a black-led alliance to reconstitute American society along multiracial, socialist, and democratic lines. In both, he demonstrates that there can be no racial emancipation under capitalist arrangements and no real socialism as long as a color bar exists. *Black Reconstruction* echoes Du Bois's contemporaneous reflections on a cooperative commonwealth by examining not only the fact of formal emancipation but the deeper meaning of human freedom; not only the self-liberation of the black masses but their historical opportunity to lead a multiracial movement to reconstitute American democracy; not only the opportunity to institute a noncapitalist labor regime but the purpose of a new socialist democracy; not only the prospect of realizing black citizenship but the possibility of furthering human unity.

I suggest we read *Black Reconstruction* as implicitly triangulating post–Civil War history, Marxist theory, and Du Bois's historical present. It is as much a genealogy of the Jim Crow legacy of (the missed opportunity of) Reconstruction as it is a history of emancipation and its immediate aftermath. In it, Du Bois's conjunctural analysis of what might have been possible during Reconstruction is shaped by his immediate engagement with the black radical predicament in the mid-1930s. His analysis of the latter, conversely, was informed precisely by what had been both possible and foreclosed in 1876. If the specter of Reconstruction animates Du Bois's interwar plan for cooperative self-segregation, this book might offer clues for reading interventions like "The Revelation of Saint Orgne" rather than stand as a point of (presumably more Marxist) contrast to them.

As a serious engagement with Marxism and socialism in relation to the peculiar conditions of (black) American history, *Black Reconstruction* was of a piece with the other work Du Bois began producing in the thirties. *Pace* Robinson, it neither simply marked a conversion to European Marxism nor a movement through a Marxist or socialist transitional phase in order to discover a non-Western black radical tradition. *Pace* Rampersad, Du Bois did not simply return, after a Marxist interlude, to a "liberal idealist" concern with racial uplift, black cultural experience, and citizenship rights. From this time on, he continually engaged and revised conventional understandings of Marxism, socialism, democracy, and humanism in relation to the fact of the color line in twentieth-century capitalism, which also meant in relation to black history, experience, culture, and consciousness. In doing so he certainly reframed capitalist domination in relation to the color line and anticapitalist struggle in relation to the lived experience of enslaved people and the historical agency of black masses. But like other Western Marxists, he also rejected economistic, utilitarian, and authoritarian conceptions of socialist society and human freedom. He envisioned forms of multiracial democratic socialism that would allow all humans to live more fully human lives.

So too in *Black Reconstruction*, Du Bois's radicalism and his humanism—his attention to black self-management *and* human solidarity, to cultural singularity *and* human potentiality, to democratic socialism *and* human flourishing—are inseparably entwined. He concludes his study by observing that the establishment of "a new dictatorship of property in the South through the color line" was "a triumph of men who in their effort to replace equality with caste and to build inordinate wealth on a foundation of abject poverty have succeeded in killing democracy, art, and religion."[119] Even more forebodingly, "Whatever the South gained through its victory in the revolution of 1876 has been paid for at a price that literally staggers humanity."[120] Note the multiple valences of this claim: Not only blacks seeking substantive emancipation, but all humans seeking substantive democracy were effectively disenfranchised (however asymmetrically). At stake in this defeat were not only the hope for material self-preservation and formal liberty, but for democracy, art, and religion, humans' higher selves, fuller potentialities, and spiritual lives—the good, the true, and the beautiful—that freedom and democracy are meant to serve; that which makes human lives meaningfully human were destroyed.

As in his other work at this time, this radical humanism does not imply the erasure of differences. In one of the last passages of *Black Reconstruction*, Du Bois writes, "Humanity is one and its vast variety is its glory and not its condemnation. If all men make the best of themselves, if all men have the chance to meet and know each other, the result is the love born of knowledge and not the hate based on ignorance."[121] He is referring to a differential unity composed of culturally distinct groups who serve humanity by making the best of themselves and have the opportunity to make the best of themselves under conditions of real freedom, universal democracy, socialist property relations, and relations of translocal solidarity.

Du Bois's attempt to think human freedom in terms that point beyond the false opposition between universality and particularity, by confounding rather than confirming categorical cultural distinctions, is evident in *Black Reconstruction*'s lyrical description of emancipation. Du Bois writes, "The mass of slaves . . . were in religious and hysterical fervor. This was the coming of the Lord. This was the fulfillment of prophecy and legend. . . . It was everything miraculous and perfect and promising."[122] He emphasizes the creole matrix in relation to which these scenes of ecstatic redemption are intelligible: "To these black folk it was the Apocalypse. The magnificent trumpet tones of Hebrew Scripture, transmuted and oddly changed, became a strange new gospel. All that was Beauty, all that was Love, all that was Truth, stood on top of these mad mornings and sang with the stars."[123] Here we can glimpse the thoroughly mixed and irreducibly New World or Black Atlantic character of enslaved peoples' political subjectivity. The magnificent trumpet tones of Hebrew Scripture oddly transmuted into a strange new gospel of freedom subtended by and saturated with beauty, love, and truth. Religious. Humanist? Judeo-Christian? African? African American? American? Particular? Universal? Yes. No. All. Not exactly.

Consider also Du Bois's analysis of the peculiar "song" that these suddenly freed people addressed to God, nature, history, humanity, and, surely, themselves:

> A great song arose, the loveliest thing born this side the seas. It was a new song. It did not come from Africa, though the dark throb and beat of that Ancient of Days was in it and through it. It did not come from white America—never from so pale and hard and thin a thing. . . . Not the Indies nor the hot South, the cold East or heavy West made that music. It was a new song and its deep and plaintive beauty, its great cadences and wild appeal waited, throbbed and thundered on the world's ears with a message seldom voiced by

man. It swelled and blossomed like incense, promised and born anew out of an age long past, and weaving into its texture the old and new melodies in word and in thought."[124]

Clearly Du Bois is referring not only to black music but also, through such cultural expressions, to a more profound ethical and political sensibility born of an unimaginable historical predicament that compromised a black Atlantic gift and message to the world. White Americans, he explained, neither heard nor understood this freedom song. "Yet it lived and grew; always it grew and swelled and lived, and it sits today at the right hand of God, as America's one real gift to beauty: as slavery's true redemption, distilled from the dross of its dung."[125] We can see that human freedom for Du Bois was never only the absence of slavery, the enjoyment of full citizenship, or the ability to make a living. Formal liberty was a point of departure, not arrival, that allowed free blacks to express a promise and message about human flourishing, through a sublime expression of human beauty distilled from the "dross and dung" of the New World black experience, one composed of densely interwoven cultural and historical strands.

Politically, Du Bois was concerned with analyzing the emancipatory vision that was distilled from this historical situation, experience, and praxis. He did not attempt to titrate the elemental agents that may have composed it. He was less interested in the cultural origins of slaves' actions than in their historical conditions of possibility, their political potentiality, and the different worlds that they postulated and enacted. Moreover, for Du Bois, these practices and visions, from flight and emancipation through citizenship and Reconstruction, unfolded in, and could be *fully* realized only through multiracial alliance with other progressive forces. Their aim, he underscores, extended beyond black freedom to include the realization of real democracy and human solidarity in and beyond America.

Throughout the 1930s Du Bois reclaimed and reworked categories that had been instrumentalized and degraded by existing liberal democratic and bourgeois capitalist social orders: freedom, democracy, justice; friendship, brotherhood, culture; art, beauty, love. Throughout this period he produced densely layered and braided works that were inseparably Marxist, socialist, democratic, and humanist *and* were refracted through the violent experiences and sustaining forms of sociability, solidarity, cultural expression, and resistance developed by New World blacks. These writings crystallized, in a radical form, the kind of synthesis Du Bois had long pursued.

Already in *Souls of Black Folk*, Du Bois endorses "Work-Culture-Liberty" as an integrated vision of freedom in which material security, educational equality, and full citizenship each entail one another. Social, cultural, and political aims, he explains, cannot be dissociated but must be "welded into one." Neither material well-being, nor training, nor civil rights should be pursued as ends in themselves; they are indivisible aspects of an expansive "freedom to work and think . . . to love and aspire." The aim is to promote fully developed minds, spirits, and souls free to cultivate love, imagination, and creativity. At the outset Du Bois writes, "This then, is the end of his striving: to be a co-worker in the kingdom of culture, to escape both death and isolation, to husband and use his best powers and his latent genius."[126]

In this landmark work, Du Bois suggests that black Americans in the 1890s continued to pursue this trinity of Work-Culture-Liberty. Moreover, they did so not only in order to secure their full citizenship, freedom, and humanity as emancipated Americans. By doing so through their community's distinctive set of experiences, practices, and values they would emancipate America itself from spirit-crushing racism, materialism, rationalism, and utilitarianism:

> The ideal of fostering and developing the traits and talents of the Negro, not in opposition to or contempt for other races, but rather in large conformity to the greater ideals of the American Republic. . . . All in all, we black men seem the sole oasis of simple faith and reverence in a dusty desert of dollars and smartness.[127]

The objective was not merely that blacks be included in America on a basis of economic, social, or political equality. It was to create the conditions for a different set of social arrangements through which the black community and the American nation as a whole might be elevated. In this vision, the aims of race unity, civilizational reciprocity, and human solidarity are inseparable. Du Bois was not arguing that black victims needed recognition by white oppressors or inclusion in the U.S. state, but that America (and the modern world) desperately needed the "pure human spirit" that initially informed its democratic experiment but which, in the present "dusty desert of dollars and smartness," only survived in the black community's social practices, spiritual values, and expressive culture.[128]

Far from merely affirming liberal democracy or formal liberty, this was a critique of capitalist materialism and soulless utilitarianism from the standpoint of black sociality, economic solidarity, radical republicanism, human interconnection, and "higher culture." Du Bois thus speaks of a democratic republic founded on justice, mercy, and truth—of free blacks' "longing toward a truer world."[129] Similarly, in *Darkwater* Du Bois did not only demand that socialism and democracy include all racial groups, that socialism be founded on democratic principles, and that democracy address itself to the economic sphere in order to truly pursue justice for all people. He also insisted that the aim of socialist democracy was to create a more fully human form of life for all people, one in which one works to live rather than lives to work:

> What a world this will be when human possibilities are freed, when we discover each other. . . . All humanity must share in the future industrial democracy of the world. For this it must be trained in intelligence and in appreciation of *the good and the beautiful*. . . . There must, for instance, persist in this future economics a certain minimum of machine-like work and prompt obedience and submission. . . . Its routine need not demand twelve hours a day or even eight. With World for All and All at Work probably from three to six hours would suffice and leave abundant time for leisure, exercise, study, and avocations. But what shall we say of work where spiritual and social distinctions enter? *Who shall be Artists and who shall be Servants in the world to come? Or shall we all be artists and all serve?*[130]

Here too Du Bois is not simply challenging liberal democracy from the standpoint of economic injustice, or existing socialism from the standpoint of racial exclusion. He is neither only demanding full civil rights for African Americans nor a better deal for black workers. He envisions an altogether different logic of labor and value, sociality and political association, human being and human meaning. He elaborates a radically humanist vision that integrated democracy and socialism, beyond the color bar, for a "truer world" with "abundant time" for leisure, exercise, study, and avocations, founded on justice and mercy, the good and the beautiful, in which all would be artists and all would serve. This is the perspective from which we should read *Darkwater*'s closing poem, "A Hymn to the Peoples," a secular prayer that calls on the "World-Spirit" to "make humanity divine."[131]

I am not suggesting that Du Bois's thinking remained unchanged over the years. The shifting historical situation, his immersion in Marx's writings, his attention to economic inequality, and his reflections on mutualist cooperatives led him in the 1930s to reformulate in more radical terms the kind of synthesis he had continually assayed. But one-dimensional accounts about whether, when, or why Du Bois supposedly shifted from integrationism to separatism, liberalism to Marxism, or nationalism to internationalism seem to miss some of the richest, most creative, and challenging aspects of his political thinking. We need to recognize, on the one hand, that Du Bois's increasingly leftist writings between the wars fashioned a radicalism that was irreducibly democratic and humanist, and, on the other, that his earlier "liberal" writings already pointed toward a radical critique of capitalism and an economic understanding of substantive freedom.

Over the arc of his career, Du Bois continually analyzed, in order to abolish, the color line. Likewise, he examined the specific historical experiences, social practices, consciousness, values, and cultural expressions of African and African-descended peoples, especially in the New World. Following World War I, and especially after the Great Depression, he became more convinced than ever that racism could not be overcome under capitalist conditions and that socialism could not be realized as long as a color line existed. During this time, he also became increasingly convinced that the problem of racial capitalism was global (institutionalized through imperialism) and the struggle for black freedom and human emancipation had to be international. Furthermore, he believed that any socialism worthy of its name had to be grounded on popular consensus, mutualist cooperation, and democratic self-management. But to grasp this specific iteration of black radicalism, we need to dispense with narrow understandings of humanism as necessarily bourgeois, universalism as necessarily abstract, democracy as intrinsically liberal, socialism as promoting technocratic administration, Marxism as a synonym for vulgar materialism (or state socialism), and all of them as intrinsically white or European. Here we might usefully recall Sylvia Wynter's demand that bourgeois Man not be reduced to the human as such.[132]

Du Bois's (Postcolonial) Contemporaneity

I suggest that Du Bois's intellectual and political approach, as I've tried to outline it, has become largely illegible today. Antihumanist critical theory has rightly deconstructed the philosophy of the subject, challenging assumptions about rational, autonomous individuals that have subtended liberal society and its forms of knowledge. Important scholarship has demonstrated how the very concept of a normative "humanity" enabled processes of differentiation, practices of exclusion, and the perpetration of extreme forms of violence in and by the West. More recent theoretical discussions have rightly demanded that we rethink humanity's extractive and destructive relationship to nature (including nonhuman animals). The need to challenge Western liberalism's pernicious fictions about sovereign individuals and abstract humanity has never been more urgent. There is no question that bourgeois humanism must be unconditionally opposed.

But I wonder whether the forms this opposition have taken are sufficient, as the anthropologist David Scott has asked, to meet the demands of our political present.[133] Many currents of recent critical theory restrict themselves to hunting for traces of liberalism, humanism, universalism, or Eurocentrism in our objects of study in order to denounce said objects. This morally gratifying but analytically limited unmasking operation seems implicitly to be guided by an absolutist belief in pure objects, ideal forms, and one-dimensional actors. This practice might allow academics to feel better in dark times, but it does not necessarily help readers grapple with the real predicaments that plague our political present. The latter, I suggest, require us, beyond negative critique, to risk naming the kinds of arrangements, the type of polities, and forms of life for which an antiracist and anti-imperial Left might want to struggle. Recent critics have usefully reminded us that predictions of hopeful or catastrophic futures often function to disable political dissent in the present.[134] But do the real dangers of what Lauren Berlant calls "cruel optimism" mean, as she suggests, that we should abandon all future-oriented discussions of the good life as a neoliberal trap?[135]

In contrast, the kind of radical humanism that Du Bois pursued recognizes that categories like freedom, democracy, and justice, not to mention truth, beauty, joy, and love, have authorized all manner of racial, imperial, and capitalist violence. But it treats this insight as the starting point rather than the aim of political reflection. Recognizing that future possibilities can arise only from existing arrangements, Du Bois practiced dialectical thinking and immanent critique. Rather than simply saying *no* to domination, he said *yes* to more integrated ways of being, knowing, making and relating, *yes* to democratic self-management, *yes* to social production and common property, *yes* to plural polities and planetary solidarities. His interwar project valued political imagination and utopian anticipation. It insisted that politics also entails the pursuit of a life worth struggling for, in which all people (or peoples) can live fully human lives and from which no humans may be excluded.

Du Bois's program was radical insofar as the humanism it envisioned could not be realized under existing arrangements. In other words, it was radically opposed to bourgeois humanism, abstract universalism, and Western liberalism. But rather than just reverse or negate these, he elaborated a position that points beyond many of the spurious oppositions that continue to impoverish our political thinking: concrete particular versus abstract universal, singularity versus solidarity, autonomy versus interdependence, community versus humanity, anti-imperialism versus humanism. Yet many readers continue to treat the "humanist" aspects of Du Bois's thought as signs of a residual liberalism, traces of an elite education, or an unreconstructed identification with the West. They are often automatically regarded as intrinsically incompatible with Marxism, anticolonialism, or Pan-Africanism.

I suggest that such interpretations are symptomatic of a tendency within current critical thinking to reduce the modern to the West, the West to white, and the white West to an all-encompassing liberalism. We are then left with a monocultural West and a one-dimensional modernity that can be criticized only from the standpoint of categorical cultural difference.[136]

In contrast, Du Bois's radical humanism begins with the proposition that, for better or worse, all peoples inhabit a common world, that there is no getting around entangled pasts and interdependent futures, that racism may be the defining feature of modern domination, but political conflict is not simply or only organized around self-identical cultural axes. His interventions regularly displaced conventional debates about assimilationism versus separatism, reformism versus revolution, and nationalism versus internationalism. They embraced black culture and criticized Western modernity without becoming preoccupied with whether a figure, concept, or practice was of Western origin. He was more concerned with political possibility than cultural purity.

In short, Du Bois's critical thinking points beyond the kind of binary civilizational thinking that has reappeared in recent discussions of *tradition* within some currents of postcolonial thinking.[137] These approaches have and continue to do indispensable critical work. But they leave little room for the kind of radical humanism that Du Bois developed. The latter might best be situated within a vital, elastic, and heterogeneous *political* tradition rather than a self-contained cultural tradition. Here we might recall Paul Gilroy's still timely writings about a black Atlantic "tradition of expression" that integrated politics, ethics, and aesthetics, centered its efforts on questions about "the good life," and developed a "redemptive critique" based on a "utopian move beyond ethnicity and the establishment of a new basis for community, mutuality, and reciprocity."[138]

The black radical tradition did not only will to its heirs precedents for heroic flight and mass refusal. It also left a legacy of deep reflection on the problem of freedom, the meaning of emancipation, and the project of humanizing human life. Du Bois's radical humanism may be read as a reflection on and contribution to this tradition. From this perspective we might recall that when Walter Benjamin invoked present actors' responsibility to "the tradition of the oppressed," he was not simply suggesting that past struggles be commemorated or even imitated. Rather, he opened the possibility that their vital forces might still be accessed and awakened. Benjamin argued that "every historical moment" offers a "revolutionary chance" whereby the existing "political situation" provides "the right of entry" to a "distinct chamber of the past," which "up to that point had been closed and locked."[139]

As I suggested, Du Bois himself engaged with political temporality in a similar fashion, spending his life confronting the grim legacy of an ever unrealized emancipation in the United States. He produced genealogical analyses linking the promise of freedom, the foreclosure of Reconstruction, the consolidation of segregation, and the new conditions, political challenges, and transformative possibilities that opened after World War I. He also constructed a historical constellation between the political situation of the 1870s and that of the 1930s. He sought to pursue the unrealized possibilities of Reconstruction while also recognizing that a new set of constraints would require a new political strategy. His program for black economic autonomy and cooperative self-management called for a set of anticipatory practices that would enact, model, and facilitate the future multiracial socialist democracy for which he called. As I've argued elsewhere about Aimé Césaire and Léopold Senghor, Du Bois should be read as a nonprovincial global thinker whose political insights retain a contemporaneous charge for us now.[140] Rather than ask whether or how he conforms to recent postcolonial thinking, we might better ask whether his political interventions indicate pathways beyond current impasses. In a moment when the Left seems to have ceded the struggle for ideas to reactionary revolutionaries, when fashioning new forms of translocal solidarity, emancipatory internationalism, and nonliberal universalism are imperative, and when Marxism needs to be rearticulated with postcolonial insights, we should not now leave Du Bois's radical humanist legacy in the closed chamber of a lifeless past.

NOTES

For their comments and suggests on various versions of this essay, I thank Anthony Alessandrini, Gavin Arnall, Banu Bargu, Zahid Chaudhary, Gina Dent, James Ferguson, Mayanthi Fernando, Duana Fulwilley, Jason Frank, Alexander Livingston, Lisa Malkki, Anupama Rao, Camille Robcis, Alejo Stark, Kabir Tambar, and Jini Kim Watson.

1. For the purposes of this essay I understand postcolonial scholarship to consist of work written in the wake of the pioneering interventions by a roughly defined cohort of thinkers that would include, among others, Talal Asad, Edward Said, Bernard S. Cohn, Stuart Hall, Ranajit Guha and the Subaltern Studies Collective, Gayatri Chakravorty Spivak, Homi K. Bhabha, and Paul Gilroy.

2. A partial list would include W. E. B. Du Bois, C. L. R. James, Aimé Césaire, Frantz Fanon, Édouard Glissant, Stuart Hall, Sylvia Wynter, Paul Gilroy, but could stretch on.

3. This despite the fact that postcolonial theory partly established itself through theories of hybridity and creolization that challenged identitarian thinking and that someone like Said should be considered a radical humanist.

4. A recent example is Lowe, *Four Continents*.

5. Chandler, *Problem of the Negro*.

6. For readings that evaluate Du Bois in terms of such assumed categories rather than using Du Bois to displace them, see Appiah, *Lines of Descent*; Rabaka, *Problems of the Twenty-First Century*.

7. This essay is part of a larger project on radical humanism and Black Atlantic criticism that attempts to trace critical affinities among Anglophone and Francophone Black Atlantic radical intellectuals in the United States, the Caribbean, Europe, and Africa, regarding humanism, socialism, and democracy.

8. Lewis, *Fight for Equality*, 441.

9. Ibid. On February 23, 1938, he had given an extended address titled "A Pageant in Seven Decades" [Credo] at Atlanta University commemorating his seventieth birthday.

10. Du Bois, Fisk graduation speech, June 1888. http://credo.library.umass.edu/view/collection/mums312.

11. Du Bois, "Careers Open to College-Bred Negroes," in *W. E. B. Du Bois: Writings*, 831, 833.

12. My interpretation aligns in significant respects with Manning Marable's reading of Du Bois as a cultural pluralist and radical democrat. Marable, *Black Radical Democrat*.

13. Aptheker, *Correspondence*, 165.

14. Although Du Bois did not use the term, he addressed precisely this phenomenon. Robinson, *Black Marxism*.

15. Du Bois, "Revelation of Saint Orgne the Damned," in *Writings*, 1048.

16. Ibid., 1054.

17. Ibid., 1057.

18. Ibid., 1055.

19. Ibid., 1056.

20. Ibid.

21. Ibid., 1055.

22. Ibid.

23. Ibid., 1061.

24. Ibid., 1056.

25. Ibid.

26. Ibid., 1067.

27. Ibid., 1067–68.

28. Ibid.

29. Du Bois, "Revelation," 1050.

30. Du Bois, "The Damnation of Women," in *Writings*, 965.

31. Ibid.

32. Du Bois, "Revelation."

33. Ibid., 1050.

34. Ibid., 1056.

35. Ibid., 1059.

36. Du Bois, *Dusk of Dawn*, 760.

37. Ibid.

38. Ibid., 761.

39. Ibid., 771.

40. Ibid., 770.

41. Ibid., 750.

42. Ibid., 761.

43. Here "one of the largest nations of the world made up its mind frankly to face . . . the problem of the poverty of the mass of men in an age when an abundance of goods and technical efficiency of work seemed able to provide a sufficiency for all men." He believed that "Russia was trying to accomplish this by eventually putting into the hands of those people who do the world's work the power to guide and rule the state for the best welfare of the masses." Ibid., 762.

44. Ibid., 764. For "in the face of contempt and chicanery and the armed force of the civilized world, this nation was determined to go forward and establish a government of men, such as the world had never seen."

45. Du Bois, "Socialism and the Negro Problem" (1913), in Lewis, *A Reader*, 579.

46. Du Bois, "The Class Struggle," originally published in *Crisis* (June 1921), in Lewis, *A Reader*, 555, 556.

47. Ibid., 555.

48. Ibid., 556.

49. See "The Negro and Radical Thought," originally published in *Crisis* (July 1921); "The American Federation of Labor and the Negro"; and "The Negro and Communism," originally published in *Crisis* (September 1931); all in Lewis, *A Reader*.

50. Du Bois, "The Class Struggle," 556. In response to black radical critics, such as Claude McKay, Du Bois explained, "Socialists, Communists, and trade unionists are advancing the illusory idea that we have only to embrace the working class program to have the working class embrace ours . . . and act on the equality of mankind and the abolition of the color line." In fact, he explained, black radicals first had "to convince the working classes of the world that black men,

brown men, and yellow men are human beings and suffer the same discrimination that white workers suffer." Du Bois, "Radical Thought," 533.

51. Du Bois, "The Negro and Communism," 593.

52. Moreover, contra Communist accusations that black leaders constitute a "petit bourgeois minority dominating a helpless black proletariat, and surrendering to white profiteers," Du Bois insists that the majority of black civil rights leaders have been poor salary men who have not exploited black labor and "whose foresight and sacrifice . . . [have] saved the American freedman from annihilation and degradation." Ibid., 588–89.

53. Ibid., 591. This predicament, he explains, accounts for why black leftists like himself continued "fighting doggedly on the old [legal] battleground, led by the N.A.A.C.P.," despite knowing full well that the right to vote "means increasingly less and less to all voters" and that "courts are prostituted to the power of wealth" (592). What may have appeared to be an unthinking expression of liberal bourgeois consciousness or ideology was actually a function of a contradictory historical situation.

54. Du Bois, "Russia," originally published in *Crisis* (November 1926), in Lewis, *A Reader*, 582.

55. Readings ranged from his early work on socialism and history in the 1840s to *Capital*. His notes indicate that the course was divided into one week on "the man," two weeks on "his times," five weeks on "his message," four weeks on "his critics," and four weeks on "the Negro." http://credo.library.umass.edu/view/pageturn/mums312-b064-i544/#page/1/mode/1up.

56. Du Bois, "Marxism and the Negro Problem," originally published in *Crisis* (May 1933), in Lewis, *A Reader*, 538.

57. Ibid., 540.

58. Ibid.

59. Ibid., 541.

60. Ibid., 542.

61. Ibid.

62. Ibid.

63. Ibid., 541.

64. Ibid., 543.

65. Ibid., 543–44.

66. Ibid., 544.

67. Ibid., 543.

68. Du Bois, *Dusk of Dawn*.

69. Du Bois continually revisited the period, possibilities, and failures of Reconstruction. See "Of the Dawn of Freedom," in *Souls of Black Folk* (1903) in *Writings*; "Reconstruction and Its Benefits," *American Historical Review* 15, no. 4 (1910): 781–99; "The Reconstruction of Freedom," in *The Gifts of Black Folk*; and *Black Reconstruction in America*.

70. The political and theoretical affinities between Du Bois and Antonio Gramsci, who were contemporaries, need to be further explored.

71. Du Bois, *Dusk of Dawn*, 761.

72. Ibid., 783.

73. Ibid., 706, 707.

74. Nembhard, *Collective Courage*.

75. Du Bois, *Dusk of Dawn*, 759.

76. Ibid., 709.

77. Ibid., 710.

78. Ibid.

79. Ibid., 711.

80. Du Bois, "A Nation within a Nation" (June 1935), in Lewis, *A Reader*, 568.

81. Du Bois, "On Being Ashamed of Oneself," originally published in *Crisis* (September 1933), in Lewis, *A Reader*, 1024–25.

82. Du Bois, "Separation and Self-Respect," originally published in *Crisis* (March 1934), in Lewis, *A Reader*, 559.

83. Du Bois, "Segregation," originally published in *Crisis* (January 1934), in Lewis, *A Reader*, 558. He later contrasted this strategy of "organized and deliberate self-segregation" to "the absurd Negro philosophy of Scatter, Suppress, Wait." *Dusk of Dawn*, 569, 568.

84. Du Bois, *Dusk of Dawn*, 777.

85. Du Bois, "The Negro College," originally published in *Crisis* (1933), in Lewis, *A Reader*, 1018–19.

86. Ibid.; emphasis added.

87. Du Bois, "Nation within a Nation," 568, 569.

88. Du Bois, *Dusk of Dawn*, 711.

89. Du Bois later insisted that his strategic shift did not conflict with his long-standing struggle for "political and civic and social equality": "It was clear to me that agitation against race prejudice and a planned economy for bettering the economic condition of the American Negro were not antagonistic ideals but part of one ideal." Ibid., 776–77.

90. Du Bois, "Nation within a Nation," 570.

91. Du Bois, *Dusk of Dawn*, 712; emphasis added. Du Bois appropriated and reworked the term "cooperative commonwealth." It had been the title of an 1884 "outline of socialism" for an American audience written by a German Marxist immigrant, Laurence Gronlund. It then became a rallying cry for the agrarian Populist movement in North America during the 1890s. Gronlund, *Cooperative Commonwealth*; Postel, *Populist Vision*.

92. Du Bois explained, "In the long run force defeats itself. It is only the consensus of the intelligent men of good will in a community or in a state that really can carry out a great program with absolute and ultimate authority. And by that same token, without the authority of the state, without force of police and army, a group of people who can attain such consensus is able to do anything to which the group agrees." Ibid., 715.

93. Ibid., 714–15.

94. Ibid., 715.

95. Ibid., 1061.

96. Ibid., 1060.

97. Ibid.

98. Ibid., 1061.

99. Du Bois, "Revelation," 1062.

100. Ibid., 1065.

101. Ibid., 1063–64.

102. Ibid., 1066.

103. Ibid.

104. Du Bois, *Souls of Black Folk*, in *Writings*, 364.

105. Ibid.

106. Du Bois, "Revelation," 1066.

107. Du Bois, "Conservation of the Races," in *Writings*.

108. Du Bois, "Revelation," 1049.

109. Ibid., 1069.

110. Rampersad, *Art and Imagination*, 182.

111. Ibid. For an interpretation that situates Du Bois directly in the tradition of American pragmatism, see West, *American Evasion of Philosophy*.

112. Robinson, *Black Marxism*, 240.

113. Ibid., 171. Robinson argues that "the Black radical tradition cast doubt on the extent to which capitalism penetrated and re-formed social life" and contends that "it had been as an emergent African people and not as slaves that Black men and women had opposed enslavement" (166, 171). But it is not clear that Robinson's abiding concern to separate these forms of resistance and consciousness from "Western" epistemologies, ideologies, and traditions aligns with Du Bois's immanent and dialectical analyses of the new forms of sociality, idioms of thought and action, and visions of political association that emerged precisely from within, and out of the materials provided by the historical experience of slavery in the Americas. My reading of Du Bois as an irreducibly modern Black Atlantic thinker aligns, rather, with the that of Gilroy in *The Black Atlantic*, who sees Du Bois as attending to "the interconnections between Africa, Europe, and the Americas," demonstrating "a complete familiarity with the cultural legacy of western civilization," claiming "access to it as a right for the race as a whole," and regarding "this legacy as his own personal property" (121).

114. Robinson, *Black Marxism*, 240.

115. Aptheker, *Correspondence*, 165.

116. Publicly he attributed this decision to the group's inability "to formulate a positive program of construction and inspiration," its resistance to his attempts realign the organization, and the fact that his "program for economic readjustment" was "totally ignored." Du Bois, "Dr. Du Bois Resigns" (August 1934), in *Writings*, 1260–61.

117. He had previously taught there from 1897 to 1910, during which time he had defined the constellation of intellectual and political issues that would preoccupy him for the rest of his life: slavery and modernity; the problem of Negro freedom and the prospect of multiracial democracy; race prejudice, the institutional color line, and black lived experience; black emancipation, American democracy, and world peace. On his resignation and shift to Atlanta, see Lewis, *A Reader*.

118. On the writing of *Black Reconstruction*, see Lewis, *Fight for Equality*, 350–51, 360–364. The same semester that he taught "Karl Marx and the Negro Problem," while working on this book, Du Bois also offered a course on "Negro Economic History" (http://credo.library.umass.edu/view/collection/mums312). Then in August 1933 he convened the second Amenia Conference with a younger group of black Marxist intellectuals, including Ralph Bunche, E. Franklin Frazier, Sterling Brown, Abram Harris, Charles Houston Harris, and Roy Wilkins. This cohort publicly criticized the old NAACP legal strategies for civil rights and called for closer a closer alliance between the black community and the American labor movement. Du Bois did not share their faith in the prospect of white workers' embracing black allies. But recognizing the quality of their scholarship and the importance of their insights as well as the need for a new political orientation to the color line, he included them in his conference. See *Dusk of Dawn*, 772–74; Lewis, *W. E. B. Du Bois*, xx; Singh, *Black Is a Country*, 70–79.

119. Du Bois, *Black Reconstruction*, 707.

120. Ibid., 706.

121. Ibid.

122. Ibid., 122.

123. Ibid., 124.

124. Ibid.

125. Ibid., 124–25.

126. Du Bois, *Souls of Black Folk*, 366.

127. Ibid., 370.

128. Ibid.

129. Ibid., 359, 528.

130. Du Bois, *Darkwater*, 50.

131. Ibid., 135.

132. Wynter, "Unsettling the Coloniality of Being/Power/Truth/Freedom."

133. Scott, *Refashioning Futures.*

134. Edelman, *No Future*; Adams, Murphy, and Clarke, "Anticipation."

135. Berlant, *Cruel Optimism.*

136. This longing for an external standpoint of critique may help explain recent preoccupations with affects, bodies, animals, and objects.

137. This would include work informed by Chakrabarty's argument about self-contained life-worlds which depends on a dubious distinction between "History 1" and "History 2," Walter Mignolo's emphasis on the decolonial de-linking of epistemologies, recent discussions of Islam as a discursive and embodied tradition, and transhistorical propositions about the ontology of Blackness posited by Afro-Pessimists. Dipesh Chakrabarty, *Provincializing Europe: Postcolonial Thought and Historical Difference* (Princeton: Princeton University Press, 2000); Walter Mignolo, *The Darker Side of Western Modernity: Global Futures, Decolonial Options* (Durham, N.C.: Duke University Press, 2011); Talal Asad, *Formations of the Secular: Christianity, Islam, and Modernity* (Stanford: Stanford University Press, 2003); Saba Mahmood, *The Politics of Piety: The Islamic Revival and the Feminist Subject* (Princeton: Princeton University Press, 2005), Frank Wilderson, "Afro-Pessimism and the End of Redemption," *Occupied Times*, March 30, 2016; Jared Sexton, "Afro-Pessimism: The Unclear Word," *Rhizomes* 29 (2016).

138. Gilroy, *Black Atlantic*, 29–39.

139. Benjamin, "Paralipomena," 402.

140. Wilder, *Freedom Time*, and Wilder, "Here/Hear Now Aimé Césaire." On Du Bois as a nonprovincial thinker, see Chandler, *X: The Problem of the Negro*, and Chandler, *Toward an African Future.*

BIBLIOGRAPHY

Adams, Vincanne, Michelle Murphy, and Adele E. Clarke. "Anticipation: Technoscience, Life, Affect, Temporality." *Subjectivity* 28, no. 1 (2009): 246–65.

Appiah, Kwame Anthony. *Lines of Descent: W. E. B. Du Bois and the Emergence of Identity.* Cambridge, Mass.: Harvard University Press, 2014.

Aptheker, Herbert, ed. *The Correspondence of W. E. B. Du Bois*, vol. 2: *Selections, 1934–1944.* Amherst: University of Massachusetts Press, 1976.

Benjamin, Walter. "Paralipomena to 'On the Concept of History.'" In *Selected Writings*, vol. 4: *1938–1940*. Cambridge, Mass.: Belknap Press of Harvard University Press, 2006.

Berlant, Lauren. *Cruel Optimism.* Durham, N.C.: Duke University Press, 2011.

Chandler, Nahum Dimitri. *Toward an African Future: Of the Limit of the World.* London: Living Commons Collective, 2013.

———. *X: The Problem of the Negro as a Problem for Thought.* New York: Fordham University Press, 2013.

Du Bois, W. E. B. *Black Reconstruction in America, 1860–1880.* New York: Free Press, 1998.

———. *Darkwater: Voices from within the Veil.* New York: Oxford University Press, 2007.

———. *Dusk of Dawn.* Edited by Henry Louis Gates Jr. Oxford: Oxford University Press, 2007.

———. *The Gift of Black Folk: The Negroes in the Making of America.* 1924. Garden City Park, N.Y.: Square One, 2009.

———. *W. E. B. Du Bois: Writings.* Edited by Nathan Huggins. New York: Library of America, 1986.

Edelman, Lee. *No Future: Queer Theory and the Death Drive.* Durham, N.C.: Duke University Press, 2004.

Gilroy, Paul. *The Black Atlantic: Modernity and Double Consciousness.* Cambridge, Mass.: Harvard University Press, 1993.

Gronlund, Laurence. *The Cooperative Commonwealth: An Exposition of Socialism*. Cambridge, Mass.: Harvard University Press, 1965.

Kelley, Robin D. G. *Freedom Dreams*. Boston: Beacon Press, 2002.

Lewis, David Levering. *W. E. B. Du Bois, 1868–1919*. New York: Holt, 1994.

———. *W. E. B. Du Bois: The Fight for Equality and the American Century, 1919–1963*. New York: Henry Holt, 2000.

———. *W. E. B. Du Bois: A Reader*. New York: Henry Holt, 1995.

Lowe, Lisa. *The Intimacies of Four Continents*. Durham, N.C.: Duke University Press, 2015.

Marable, Manning. *W. E. B. Du Bois: Black Radical Democrat*. New York: Routledge, 2005.

Nembhard, Jessica Gordon. *Collective Courage: A History of African American Cooperative Thought and Practice*. University Park: Pennsylvania State University Press, 2014.

Postel, Charles. *The Populist Vision*. Oxford: Oxford University Press, 2007.

Rabaka, Reiland. *W. E. B. Du Bois and the Problems of the Twenty-First Century: An Essay on Africana Critical Theory*. Lanham, Md.: Lexington Books, 2008.

Rampersad, Arnold. *The Art and Imagination of W. E. B. Du Bois*. Cambridge, Mass.: Harvard University Press, 1976.

Robinson, Cedric. *Black Marxism: The Making of a Black Radical Tradition*. Chapel Hill: University of North Carolina Press, 1983.

Scott, David. *Refashioning Futures: Criticism after Postcoloniality*. Princeton: Princeton University Press, 1999.

Singh, Nikhel Pal. *Black Is a Country: Race and the Unfinished Struggle for Democracy*. Cambridge, Mass.: Harvard University Press, 2005.

West, Cornel. *The American Evasion of Philosophy: A Genealogy of Pragmatism*. Madison: University of Wisconsin Press, 1989.

Wilder, Gary. *Freedom Time: Negritude, Decolonization, and the Future of the World*. Durham, N.C.: Duke University Press, 2015.

———. "Here/Hear Now Aimé Césaire!" special issue titled "Aimé Césaire and Negritude," edited by Michaeline Crichlow and Gregson Davis, *South Atlantic Quarterly* 115, no. 3 (2016): 585–604.

Wynter, Sylvia. "Unsettling the Coloniality of Being/Power/Truth/Freedom: Toward the Human, after Man, Its Overrepresentation—An Argument." *CR: The New Centennial Review* 3, no. 3 (2003): 257–337.

FIVE

Deprovincializing Anticaste Thought:
A Genealogy of Ambedkar's *Dalit*

Anupama Rao

It was not until the facade of the ruling Congress Party's secularism exploded in the late 1980s and early 1990s, first with Hindu majoritarianism and immediately thereafter, with the upsurge of lower-caste politics in Northern India, that caste regained the centrality that colonial rulers had long assigned it. Once again, it became an indispensable category for understanding Indian politics and society, something that nationalists had typically rejected during the era of anticolonial struggle.

Current debates about caste and Indian democracy illuminate key concerns of this essay. As is well known, caste has been equated with the Indian social *tout court*.[1] It has been attributed to deep-rooted religious conceptions and shared beliefs, such as purity and pollution, about the different castes. This form of caste's analytical valence was in fact a result of colonial-era knowledge production, whereby theory arrives first, and theory shapes actual social practice. It would be more accurate to say, however, that caste distinction precedes religious faith, and that one of religion's key purposes, if not its key purpose, is to ensure caste's reproduction.

This is not to say that caste is singular and unchanging; on the contrary, its historical transformations are extensive. These range from the emergence of regionally distinct castes associated with militarized precolonial regimes, to caste's analytic utility for colonial governance and strategies of indirect rule, and its role in structuring labor relations and the appropriation of surplus. However, a widely acknowledged telos of transformation assumes that caste is a backward or particularist category that dissolves into the universal with progressive development, thereby reprising dominant distinctions between culture and capital.

Thus Western theory has tended to treat caste as a form of nonpolitical difference and a manifestation of hierarchy that contrasts with Euro-American conceptions of equality. While scholars of South Asia have responded by historicizing caste's social pertinence and its analytic centrality, they have done so by presenting caste as a form of subcontinental difference.

This essay argues the obverse. It argues that the global conversation about caste also enabled it to attain social density and become a political identity of enduring consequence. Throughout the twentieth century, anticaste thinkers related struggles for caste equality with global movements for human emancipation. Indeed, it was through acts of political commensuration, that is, through explicit comparisons between caste and race, and later, between caste and class, that caste (and the evil of untouchability, in particular) came to be addressed as a historically determined form of quite general processes of inequality and subordination. Thus if anticolonials and social reformers provincialized caste as an intensely local form of hierarchy that offered no scope for comparison elsewhere, anticaste thinkers drew on historical comparisons between caste and other forms of inequality.

The ascendancy of capital, which correlated with a leveling of colonial subjects before imperial law, and thus with the implied denigration of both elite and everyman in the colony, spawned connections undreamt of by indigenous elites. Not surprisingly, anticaste thought was inherently global, with its leaders imagining affinities with political projects elsewhere in the world. In the process, they demonstrated the limits of anticolonial nationalism, which tended to regard caste inequality as a matter of social reform that was secondary to national independence. This upper caste prejudice, together with (and related to) the colonial-anticolonial binary that has structured South Asian postcolonial theory, has led to eliding anticaste thought from national historiography.

In this essay I focus on how debates about caste became a part of global discussions about inequality, and the relevance of anticaste thought for discussions of political subject-formation more generally. The focus is on untouchable leader and political thinker B. R. Ambedkar's (1891–1956) analysis of the *Dalit*,[2] or outcaste, as a stigmatized subject necessary to, yet derided by, the ideology of caste Hinduism. In Ambedkar's analysis Dalits were ritually condemned to stigmatized labor, reproducing their own humiliation and social exclusion while performing utilitarian tasks for the Hindu social order. His practice of negative identification, naming the outcaste *as Dalit*, was in the interest of intensifying claims on equality by positing the Dalit as the figure of a new universality. Given constraints of space, below I offer a series of snapshots about how colonial capital enabled new modes of connection and differentiation between imperial subjects who began to conceive the relationship between inequality and embodiment in unforeseen ways. The point of the exercise is to stage a conversation between Marxism and postcolonial theory before they existed as definable analytic frames counterposed against each other, as the editors of this volume note. Revisiting a moment when insurgent connections between caste and class, Ambedkar and Marx, was possible thus also illuminates alternative itineraries of subaltern radicalism and life-making whose detour through historical comparison and global connectivity was the precondition for "de-provincializing" caste .

Figures of Dispossession: Slavery and Historical Comparison

In 1863, a newly literate ex-slave from New Orleans commented on the brutal and enduring contradictions of slavery that extended beyond slave emancipation. He did so through a dialogue with the founding documents, the American Constitution, especially its Preamble, and Lincoln's Emancipation Proclamation. This Colored Man, as he referred to himself, painstakingly reproduced the text of the Constitution in his uncertain hand as though the act of writing was a way of claiming the Constitution for himself, as his right. In the margin of selections from the Constitution and the Emancipation Proclamation, he inserted commentary contrasting the emancipatory potential of the texts against evidence of whites' denial of rights to newly freed black citizens. He challenged those parts of the text where his appearance was marked by its simultaneous devaluation, the 3/5 clause. Instead, he channeled the radical democratic aspirations of the Preamble to argue: "*We* [are] the people."[3]

The Proclamation traveled. America exerted its long shadow across the Atlantic and beckoned Jotirao Phule (1827–1890), founder of the Satyashodak Samaj (Truth-Seeking Society), to write the history of caste as a history of struggle and enslavement through comparison with Atlantic world slavery. Phule's *Gulamgiri* was published in 1873, a decade after the Colored Man's scribbles. That text is structured by an imagined affinity with the Emancipation Proclamation and figures such as George Washington and the Marquis de Lafayette. For Phule, unlike for the Colored Man, American republicanism was of one piece, with the Emancipation Proclamation completing the promise of the Constitution: Phule expressed his admiration of Abraham Lincoln for rescuing American Negroes from thralldom and exhorted upper castes to do the same for their Indian brethren. Phule also recognized race as the basis of Atlantic world slavery and argued that the Aryan/Dravidian distinction played a similar role in structuring the social antagonisms of caste.[4] This was followed by Phule's efforts to produce a combined and inclusive identity for the peasant and untouchable castes and to make them visible as a demographically dense political collectivity, as the community of *shudra-atishudras*. (We see here the example of a political performative that sought to birth a new collectivity through the practice of renaming.)

Fifty years later, W. E. B. Du Bois described a postbellum America characterized by complex practices of unfreedom premised on worker discipline, acquisitive ideology, and marketized social relations. His 1935 magnum opus, *Black Reconstruction*, locates the origins of modern racial capitalism in a legislated emancipation, followed by the institution of Jim Crow, which marked the failure of the all too brief experiment in American democracy. Indeed for Du Bois, the "Negro problem" originates with the legal freedoms announced by the Thirteenth, Fourteenth, and Fifteenth Amendments. Haunted by its past, American democracy could only ever make an appearance as *abolition-democracy*: It was a name that marked the intimacy between a specific history (American slavery) and a universal idea (democracy).[5] Du Bois brought the terms into proximity with each other as a pithy reflection on the grounding contradictions of American democracy, its historical entanglement with enslavement, and unfreedom.

If *Black Reconstruction* signaled a turning point in Du Bois's thinking, so did the *Annihilation of Caste* mark a turning point in Ambedkar's oeuvre. The two texts were published a year apart in 1935 and 1936, respectively. What unites these otherwise disparate texts is their authors' discovery of the logic governing a social order, race and Hinduism, respectively. Du Bois had referred to the hardening of a "caste system" when he associated the failure of emancipation with the rise of racial capitalism and the emergence of a white and black proletariat. The *Annihilation of Caste* posited the intractability of untouchability reform when conceived within Gandhian rubrics of an ethicized Hinduism capable of doing justice to the untouchable, figured by Gandhi as *Harijan* (literally, person of God). In the extended debate with Gandhi that his text inaugurated, Ambedkar argued that the abolition of untouchability was impossible without the annihilation of Hinduism since caste and Hindu religion were mutually entailed. Ambedkar indicted the anemic and complicit responses of social reformers to caste as a social formation predicated on violence and inequality. Like Du Bois's conception of abolition democracy, caste annihilation linked a specific history, the abolition of caste, with the transformation of (Hindu) society *tout court*.

In his other writings, Ambedkar explicitly compared untouchability with the history of slavery beginning in Rome and ending with North American plantation slavery. He argued that slaves in ancient Rome were educated in keeping with their masters' status, and that they participated in the economy as scribes, performers, musicians, and skilled laborers. Plantation slavery was brutal, yet the status of a value-producing property meant that there was some incentive to protect the slave: "Being property and therefore valuable, the master for sheer self-interest took great care of the health and well-being of the slave."[6] Ambedkar argued that the slave's status as value-producing property entitled him or her to better protection than the outcaste, whose labor was degraded and devalued, and who was subject to extreme stigmatization. Ambedkar's comparison was thus meant to illustrate the severity of untouchability when measured against the legislated disenfranchisement of the American slave.

Let me stop here for a moment to highlight three points. The first is the inspiration of republicanism for Indian anticaste thinkers. The second is the creative miscommunication of specific histories (of race and slavery, or caste and capital), the flattening of their complexity as these ideas traveled so that contested historical figures such as Lincoln or Washington could become heroes in the anticaste repertoire. The last has to do with the place of slavery as the defining figure of unfreedom in republican thought and the power of its image on both sides of the Atlantic.

Figures of Dispossession: Phule's Satyashodh *and Anticaste Critique*

Phule's indictment of Brahminism as an order predicated on the intellectual enslavement of the downtrodden castes is well known. So too, his effort to rewrite history as a history of caste insult and humiliation. Phule attacked Brahmin ideology by exposing its roots in superstition, irrationality, and violence. He argued that the most powerful political challenge to Brahmin hegemony was the project of intellectual emancipation and mass intellectuality: The *satyashodak*, the truth seeker, was a warrior in the battle against superstition and inequality; the cultivation of *satyashodh*, or truth-seeking, required constant vigilance.

Equally significant is the fact that Satyashodak thought was enabled by even as it responded to the material context of caste's transformation. Phule's attention to agrarian distress as the combined outcome of native rent seeking and colonial surplus extraction is remarkable. Ironically, Phule's critique of the colonial economy, an important early intervention connecting caste and capital, was enabled by his and other non-Brahmins' entry into the colonial market through military recruitment, colonial public works, and mill labor.[7] The considerable financial security of a small non-Brahmin elite, plus their familiarity with modern infrastructure and communicative technologies, enabled the penetration of anticaste critique into areas that became the mainstay of Satyashodak, and later non-Brahmin activism.

Again, North American transformations played a key role. Problems faced by British industry in procuring Southern cotton during the American Civil War led to the opening of the Suez Canal to enable access to cotton markets via steam shipping. The cotton-producing regions of Khandesh and Berar in western India were integrated into the global cotton economy and created new linkages between the rural hinterland and the city, and between Bombay and the British Empire.[8] Second, western India's cotton economy of the late nineteenth century was indicative of deeper transformations of the agrarian countryside, including rising indebtedness. Though reinvestment of capital into agricultural production was largely nonexistent, the widespread dependence of farmers on cash loans from village moneylenders for survival indicates the degree to which social relations had been commodified: The fact that cultivators found themselves in a cycle of debt bondage in which they had little say over the sale of their crop yields suggests they were no longer in control over their own labor.

Jairus Banaji's classic study of the Deccan moneylenders addresses the centrality of debt (and rent seeking) to the colonial economy, and by so doing makes an important intervention in the Marxist "transition" debate by challenging the telos that underlies the distinction between "real" and "formal" subsumption. Through an exhaustive case study of the impact of the commodification of agriculture on the nineteenth-century Deccan, Banaji shows that the subjugation of Indian small peasantry to the usury capital of Marwari and Gujarati merchants and to a nascent capitalist class emerging from the big peasantry in the Deccan was accomplished by repurposing prior modes of production such that they could perform in a different historical environment but serve the requirements of surplus extraction nonetheless. Essentially, peasant indebtedness to local moneylenders had alienated them from the means of production, and it could be argued that like the industrial proletariat, the peasant, too, was now working for a wage. In essence agrarian indebtedness, rather than a sign of backwardness, was the historically specific mode by which "the peasant receives a wage for his own reproduction, whether in the form of an advance on the crop to be delivered or as a share of the crop. Behind all these appearances *the peasant has become dependent on the capitalist—is a worker.*"[9]

Phule described this same world of peasant struggle and survival in vivid detail. His writings are noteworthy in recognizing that modern transformations of caste also carried the potential for immanent critique. In *Gulamgiri* he notes that the Indian peasant has been "the proverbial milch cow. . . . Those who successively held sway over him cared only to fatten themselves on the sweat of his brow, without caring for his welfare or condition. It was sufficient for their purposes that they held him safe in their clutches for squeezing out of him as much as they possibly could."[10] Phule goes on to link agrarian distress with various states of transient and impoverished existence. He notes, "Many farmers who cannot subsist on their fields alone will leave home and become vagrant [*paraganda*], working for wages in a big city instead of starving."[11] The alienation of rural labor from its own labor power is depicted by figures such as the moneylender, who index the commodification of social relations in a colonial economy.

Phule offers a sustained account of the living conditions of shudra-atishudra farmers in *Shetkaryacha Asud* (Cultivator's Whipcord), describing how they live, eat, and work by drawing on a colloquial, everyday Marathi. His painstaking descriptions delineate key aspects of the agrarian sensorium: In essence this is a work of radical empiricism that seeks to describe a social totality from the perspective of the exploited and the victimized. Phule describes a world of routinized deprivation with attention to figures that embody impoverishment and vulnerability. In describing the lifeworld of an indebted, uneducated farmer, Phule is especially attentive to the bodies of young children:

> A stream of water flowing outside from the bath has formed a puddle swarming with maggots. Some of this water has trickled onto the bodies of a group of stark naked children assembled beneath a nearby white chafa tree. They are foul with itchy sores on their heads and snot falling from their noses.[12]

Not much later, a *pada* (poem) written by Pandit Kondiram, the president of the Bombay Shri Somavanshi Mitra Samaj (Association for Friends of the Somavanshi) and a key exponent of Satyashodak ideology, drew on similar imagery to communicate the horrors of untouchability. Kondiram noted that untouchables were forced to wear a black thread, and could own no new clothes or jewelry. They dressed in clothes from corpses, wore iron jewelry, ate from broken clay pots, and owned only "dogs and asses; rats and mice." They were dispossessed, shadowy figures reduced to begging and eating food unfit even for animals.

> The [Mahars'] condition is so deplorable, that they come begging
> For the rotten food scraps that have been thrown to the cows [literally, "thrown into the cow shed"]
> Which even the cattle will not touch.[13]

Kondiram ends with the powerful image of Mahar children sitting on a dung heap, their bodies covered with ash, sores on their eyes, rags covering their buttocks, their stomachs "sunken and empty." Like Phule's excruciatingly detailed picture of the cultivator's life, Kondiram's attention to the wretched condition of the Mahars utilizes social description as the practice of (social) critique.[14]

Anticaste activists contended that *jatibhed*, caste division, was not merely a social arrangement but a mode of thought, indeed a *social abstraction* along the lines of the property-personhood relation instituted by classical liberalism. For instance, Phule argued that the shudra-atishudras were denied access to critical thought, and used the metaphor of stamping, imprinting, or a weight sitting on the head to compare Brahmin dominance with intellectual enslavement.[15] In turn he advocates radical empiricism as a form of immanent critique: Naming and description were key to satyashodh; they were themselves practices of intellectual emancipation, which sharpened the experience of injustice and indifference through resonant imagery. Increasingly, these became a staple of Satyashodak public culture.

Figures of Dispossession: Caste, Class, and Marx in Maharashtra

If postemancipation America exerted a strong imaginative hold on anticaste thinkers, so did Marxist internationalism some decades later. The interwar saw an explosive expansion of communicative possibility via print capital and technologies of violence. Popular Marxism of the period was the product of a diverse comingling of energies—from the Islamic universalism that enthused proponents of Khilafat, to the religious aspirations that energized Swadeshi activists, anarchism, nonviolent technologies of the self, and revolutionary violence. Early Marxism was temporarily yoked to the Comintern and its internationalist aspiration for a brief period in the interwar, but this putative unity quickly fragmented primarily because of the war. The period saw important efforts to establish political equivalence between class struggle and anticolonial protest: Lenin's position on the affinity between "the national and colonial question" met an early challenge from Rosa Luxemburg, who countered with a commitment to internationalism, and later, by Tatar Muslim radical Sultan Galiev and Swadeshi nationalist M. N. Roy, who redirected focus to the peasant and proletarian question in the colonies by attacking the presumed "progressivism" of bourgeois anticolonialism. As is well known, Marxist thought was soon subsumed under Stalinist modernization and the party state in the Soviet Union, while the colonial world was consigned to the classification of backwardness and underdevelopment, which could be overcome through the helping hand of Western developmentalism. (Recall that colonial Communist Parties were each placed under the "guidance" of their metropolitan counterparts and that the debates about capitalist "transition" in the East appear to have regressed from the more open, multidirectional possibilities envisaged for it earlier.)

Bombay exerted a magnetic force on Dalits and lower castes, and it was a critical destination for both global Communism and the Indian Communist Party.[16] It is here, through the potent possibility of cross-caste interaction, that Marxism was "deprovincialized."[17] However, as we will see below, embodied forms of discrimination could undermine the possibility of proletarian identity without adequate praxis to respond to them.

THE POLITICS OF SPACE

Spatial politics helps explain the powerful adjacencies between caste and class that emerged in interwar Bombay. While the variable demand for cotton led to an immiseration of

Western India's peasants, the subjects of Phule's earlier descriptions, indigenous capitalists in Bombay had shifted their capital to the construction of cotton mills to produce textiles for the domestic market and yarn for the China market. This allowed them to avoid taking on subordinate positions in an international market dominated by European finance and European shipping. From 1890 until the turn of the century, the textile industry was characterized by an unstable labor supply combined with rural famine and urban epidemic, which forced an increasingly flexible mode of production. However, the two decades preceding World War I saw the stabilization of urban conditions: High labor demand was met with high labor supply, and there followed a period of rising profits.[18] This context shaped labor's sense of political possibility but also exacerbated urban precarity.[19]

The *chawls* (tenements) of the Bombay City Improvement Trust (BCIT), and later of the Bombay Development Directorate (1919–26), were important sites of Dalit activism at the time. These included marches and political processions of the Samata Sainik Dal (formed in 1924 by Dalit military pensioners to protect Ambedkar); the first celebration of Ambedkar Jayanti (Ambedkar's Birthday) on the open grounds of the B.D.D. chawls; study circles organized by Dalit Communists associated with the Delisle Road Friends' Circle; performances of Ambedkari *jalsa*, a form of pedagogic folk theater, by the Scheduled Caste Federation (formed in 1942); and the establishment of the offices of the Independent Labour Party and the Municipal Kamgar Sangh (Municipal Workers' Union). B. R. Ambedkar lived in a BCIT chawl until he moved to Dadar's middle-class Hindu Colony in 1934. He lived there with his family until the 1960s; almost all of his organizational and publishing efforts were located in this area.[20]

The area was also associated with an earlier phase of Dalit activism: struggles for public access; institutional initiatives by the Depressed Classes Mission, which started separate schools in response to Dalit students' continued inability to enter mixed government or government-aided schools; and activism of the Bombay Millhands Union, formed in 1894 by the non-Brahmin leader N. M. Lokhande. Additionally, the area was home to Non-Conformist missionaries and the nondenominational Hindu reformist organizations, such as the Prarthana Samaj. Thus a historic association between anticaste and antipoverty activism was a precursor to working-class alliance. Meanwhile, the Independent Labour Party formed by Ambedkar in 1936 had explicitly argued for a caste-class critique and mobilized workers from the Dalit castes.

The resignification of caste through its proximity with class is important in this regard. But how were such adjacencies established?

TRANSLATING CLASS

The standard translation of *Capital* appeared in Maharashtra in the 1960s. However, in the mid-1930s Ambedkar's newspaper, *Janata*, had printed translations of "Wage, Labour, and Capital," which had been translated from Communist pamphlets. *Janata* also published Soviet social realism in serialized form, especially Gorky's *Mother*, which attained iconic status. Meanwhile, the *Kamgar Vangmay Prasarak Mandali* (Organization for the Spread of Workers' Literature), established in 1931, published pamphlets on Lenin's life, the Russian Revolution, and the Paris Commune but little on Indian conditions.[21] The collectivity of caste-class was addressed in the process of translating the *Communist Manifesto*.

The Berlin-returned scientist Gangadhar Adhikari, known for his thirteen-volume *Documents of the History of the Communist Party of India*, translated the *Communist Manifesto* into Marathi in 1931 as the *Communist Jahirnama*.[22] (Adhikari had studied in Berlin between 1922 and 1928 and come under the influence of prominent Indian Communists, eventually going on to chair the Indian Association in Central Europe.) The *Jahirnama* made class legible as a new form of political collectivity through association with existing forms of social experience; terms such as *kashta* (hard work), *daridryata* (impoverishment, destitution), *bekaar* (unemployed, worthless), *bhukekangal* (pauperized); association with social forms, such as the degraded Dalit classes, *dalit varga*, Pathans (popularly associated with the "flesh trade," moneylending, extortion, and other parasitical activities that further impoverished working people), and the *mavali*, associated with the communities of the hilly Sahyadri mountain range and their traditions of banditry and guerrilla warfare. Each of these was imprecisely identified with class and constituted something like an excessively dispossessed multitude, visually identifiable rather than class-specifiable. The power of these forms of life was precisely this: to connote and conjure intimacy with the emergent category of "class." That is to say, "labor" was both underspecified and overdescribed. We see a process of de-abstraction/concretization in the *Jahirnama*: Exploitation was rendered visible through everyday language and personified in figures of predation. This act of naming cut both ways: It called up existing forms of life *on their own terms*, and by placing them beside each other forced novel associations between them. "Labor" was not the sum of its parts. Rather, naming the "difference" of labor was also an act of enframing that brought multiple constituencies together as a political force and ethical community.

Thus if one were to ask what Marxism meant, how its potential for social and political emancipation was understood, we might argue—as Andrew Sartori has recently argued with regard to "Lockeanism"—that the thought did not strictly correlate with the writings of a thinker by that name or the numerous scholarly interpretations of Marx's work.[23] Rather Marxism was powerful as a mode of thought precisely because it called up earlier images of destitution and dispossession that had a long association with anticaste thought, but which were now redefined through the analytical availability of labor as a critical concept.[24] In other words, a set of cosmopolitan aspirations and connections preceded the substance of the intellectual links that Dalits tried to establish, and remained as a placeholder for forms of praxis that had yet to come. Ironically, it is at this juncture that efforts to specify Dalit subjectivity confronted the limits of thinking through a politics of labor.

Below I briefly address such failed commensuration as a productive site for thinking in non-normative ways about the political universal, and thus uncoupling our understanding of the radical or revolutionary subject from the organizing antagonism of labor-capital.

Thinking the Remnant

Following the conceptual impasse of liberalism and the end of Communism, a group of political philosophers and social theorists has been concerned with how history might intersect with theory to reanimate or revivify conceptions of "the political." For them, the relationship between the experience of social marginality and trajectories of political enfranchisement/visibility cannot be explained through the normative language of political philosophy, which typically considers questions of freedom, liberty, sovereignty, and morality without attending to material conditions, relations of production (as also social relations), and agonism within the domain of the social. Thus Judith Butler asks, "What happens when the universal is wielded precisely by those who signify its contamination, by those socially excluded and marginalized?" Is it possible that "conventional and exclusionary norms of universality can, through perverse reiterations, produce unconventional formulations of universality that expose the limited and exclusionary features of the former . . . at the same time that they mobilize a new set of demands"?[25]

We might think with Butler in recalling figures that have claimed the place of the universal by challenging the primacy of labor universalism for accounts of political subject-formation. Jacques Ranciere speaks of philosophy's discomfort with the figure of the poor as an illustration of philosophy's discomfort with the concrete as such. In other writings, such as *Nights of Labor* (newly translated as *Proletarian Nights*), Ranciere criticizes the assumption that the divide between intellectual and manual labor is real.[26] Indeed, Ranciere is at pains to indict something like an inequality of imagination that is produced when thinkers engage in the fallacy of associating the capacity for thought with a sociological conception of status and location, thereby assuming that material destitution constrains mass intellectuality. More recently, Frank Ruda has argued that poverty is the "unthought" in Hegel's philosophy and focused on the transformation of the poor into "rabble" in Hegel's *Philosophy of Right*.[27] Or, the literary theorist Peter Stallybrass has argued that we revisit the figure of the *lumpenproletariat* in Marx's *Eighteenth Brumaire*, to see that he conceives them as a sartorial category, a visible multitude.[28] Instead, Frantz Fanon argued that the *lumpenproletariat* was "one of the most spontaneous and radically revolutionary forces of a colonized people."[29] And then there is minority identity—e.g., Negro, Dalit, Muslim, and Jew—which gained salience in the interwar in the context of imperial transition and nation-state formation.

This brief, speedily recounted inventory addresses logics internal to a Marxist accounting of political subject formation, as well as those external or exorbitant to it: It is meant to bring into view figures whose concrete particularity troubles the constitution of the social whole and whose politicality, that is, the conditions by which their actions might be viewed as properly "political" must be established rather than assumed. How, then, was this specific to Dalits?

Efforts at commensuration—caste and race, or caste and class—had been productive, but they were unstable and ultimately insufficient due to caste's relationship with Hinduism. Ambedkar's conception of the Dalit as a distinctive political subject was haunted by the connection between religion and politics. As earlier efforts to specify the civic disability of caste gave way to a concern with the past in Ambedkar's late writing, he began to argue that the Dalit was a subject of historical violence, a form of remaindered life produced by the epochal conflict between Buddhism and Brahminism. Ambedkar repeatedly distinguished Dalit genealogy from the history of the shudra castes, arguing that this fourth caste was composed of the community of degraded *Kshatriyas* (warriors) whose place in the caste hierarchy was unstable (and politically suspect) due to their aspirational mobility within caste Hinduism.

Dalit identity was also unstable, but for a different reason. Dalit history could only become grounds for a Dalit future as negative example. The outcaste was the excluded insider, simultaneously within and without Hindu society, which was organized around the unbridgeable line between the "Touchables" and the "Untouchables." Dalit stigma produced a gap between history and the future because stigma could not become the grounds for political organization: Unlike labor, it could not be "in" and "for" itself. One could argue that stigma was a limiting concept in Ambedkar's thought, a form of embodiment that could not be abstracted or universalized, that stigma was a devalued aspect of the body-self. Or, *stigma* lies at the limits of Ambedkar's thought because it is an aspect of negated personhood that is signified perceptually, through connection (and extension) with the untouchable's body, and cannot be equated with exploitation or inequality *as such*. The practice of naming the untouchable as Dalit was important: It was an effort to signal both a history of degradation and its transcendence en route to political selfhood. Yet the status of this new subject (and his or her place in regimes of worth and value) was uncertain.

Stigma, Service, and Labor, or Ambedkar, Gandhi, and Marx

How might we think more broadly about stigma as both a mark of inequality/degradation and a mechanism of its reproduction—stigma as a productive force that has no place in orthodox Marxism and yet is widespread as a means of extracting value, not synonymous/coeval with labor? What distinguished stigma from labor? In the Indic case, which was predicated on the model of sacrifice rather than of accumulation, and conceived ritual action as a form of symbolic expenditure, the untouchable was both necessary and expendable: He or she gave to caste its systemic coherence as a hierarchy of inequities, or "graded inequality," as Ambedkar referred to it, but was also extraneous to it.[30] And here the challenge of Ambedkar's great agon, M. K. Gandhi, comes into play.

Gandhi's reinterpretation of sacrificial logic was also an effort to ethicize the regime of caste and challenged the Marxian logic of accumulation and value. More important, it contrasted with Ambedkar's effort to bring the outcaste within the framework of commensuration by giving him or her pride of place in a (global) account of dehumanization. Gandhi's creative efforts to think the "labor question" in the interwar, at a time when labor had assumed salience as an administrative category and become the focus of social reform and political radicalism, is significant. His writings on shudra (manual) labor, and the relation of labor to sacrifice more generally, suggests one way to reconceive the relationship between the history of politics and a politics of the body, which comes together seamlessly as *one history* in Marx's narrative of labor's struggle against the predations of capital. For Gandhi, the ethics of sacrifice—and the generalizability of shudra labor—subsumes or enfolds the possibility of giving to labor *as such* a distinctive identity. In his view, an embodied ethicality trumped the politicality of labor.

Gandhi had begun to demand universal shudrahood before he named the Untouchable as *Harijan*, or person of god, thereby erasing the historical memory of (historic) violation that was central to Ambedkar's critique. (This is the reason for Ambedkar's abhorrence of Gandhi's term.) Gandhi argued: "If everyone regarded himself as a shudra, religion would be well rid of the concept of high and low. The principle of (voluntary) manual labor, of service, that characterized shudra dharma ought to be the governing principle of everyone's 'varnadharma.'"[31]

A generic conception of shudra labor (unlike, say, the specialized ritual labor of Brahmin or the degraded labor of the outcaste) most closely resembled the Marxist conception of universal labor. Though shudra labor stood for manual labor in general, it was incapable of becoming abstract labor power: Labor as such was subsumed within a theory of social action and sacrificial economy from which it was not easily disentangled. We will recall that castes were produced through the dismemberment of *Purusa*, originary man, and the association of distinctive body parts with the function of each caste. Thus the history of labor was embedded within a theory of (caste) duty and obligation, *varnashramadharma*, predicated on the division of laborers. (Because the outcaste was invisible in this origin myth, Gandhi could later maintain that untouchability was itself a belated and baneful addition, a historic wrong to be righted by the penitence of upper castes.) Thus it is important to recognize Gandhi's redefinition of shudra labor as social care, as *seva*, or service to the social body: This underscored the difference between *seva*, on the one hand, and accumulative logic, on the other. By translating the problem of accumulation into the performative politics of service and sacrifice, Gandhi redefined labor as social gift.

Gandhi was certainly playing on the same field as Marx with regard to the question of subaltern agency—whether shudra or proletariat. Furthermore, Gandhi was positing the occupational order of caste against the social totality of labor and capital, the logic of the gift against the violence of commodity fetishism. A generous reading of Gandhi might explore his focus on the repetition of small acts—toilet cleaning, spinning, nursing—as ethical enactment and the practice of *ahimsaic* nonviolence. If nonviolence was to be a critique of violence, it had to fully engage violence: Gandhi did so by collapsing the possibility of doing violence *to* others onto the self and redefined self-violence as sacrifice. This was sacrifice as annihilation, rather than sacrifice as restoration. In the latter case, the logic of substitution prevails: Animals are sacrificed "as if" they were humans, to reestablish cosmic order in a violent, vengeful world. In Gandhi's case, service was a "giving without return."

I have hoped to show that disembedding caste labor from the (putatively consensual) regime of caste involved engaging the ritual and the political, the negated and the universal. For Gandhi, labor history was enfolded within a theory of praxis, *varnashramadharma*, where the performance of labor was attached to descent: Shudra labor was performed by shudras because it was *shudra labor*. This subsumed labor within a theory of social action, which produced complex obstacles to disentangling labor from the economy of sacrifice. In this we can see Ambedkar and Gandhi coming at the problem of enfolded labor from different points. Ambedkar confronts stigma as having a basis in history and reads it *out* from the caste body as its necessary prosthetic. Instead, Gandhi demands universal shudrahood—we must "do" as they do, and thus become "like" them. Ambedkar sought to transvalue and sublate the political subjectivity of stigma while Gandhian ethics called for an act of imaginative identification—recall Gandhi often argued that he was an untouchable or a woman.

Like labor, stigma *was* history, yet it could not be detached or abstracted from the body.[32] Stigma could not be valorized like value-producing labor. Without political value for Dalit personhood, outcaste labor was fated to be marginalized. The response to this dilemma did not call for universalizing labor by politicizing it, via the general strike, for instance. Rather, it required dissolving the specificity of Dalit identity through commensuration and contract as a first step. Ambedkar supported socializing capital and redistributing resources, rather than abolishing the capitalist state because he understood the wage labor contract, like liberal rights more generally, as an instrument that abstracts and universalizes.[33] Universal equivalency enabled Dalits to cast off stigma, and capitalist modernity was to be applauded for this. What was required was not the retreat into subaltern alterity, or an alternate temporality: In bringing Dalits within a field of abstract mediation, the time of capital brought them within the frame of a global history of dehumanization, and took them outside the culturalism of caste.

Ideas of class exploitation and proletarian emancipation were generative, but they were insufficient. Labor was political because the identity of labor derived from its antagonism to capital. Thinking stigma through labor appeared to be productive and useful. Yet to translate caste into class would ignore caste's history as (Hindu) violence. Like religion (and Hinduism), labor, too, was ultimately only a partial force in accounting for Dalit dispossession. Labor offered a metaphor—but not a formula—for associating the identity of a collective with its experience of dispossession. Ironically, in claiming the universal, Ambedkar's project also brought into view the stubborn materiality of stigma, and the specificity of caste. By laying claim to the universal, Ambedkar's Dalit also marked the nonidentity of the subaltern subject of rights from the normative, universal rights-bearing subject.

Constitution and Conversion

Ambedkar participated in a debate on the third draft of the Indian Constitution on November 25, 1949, about two months before independent India's first Republic Day in his capacity as chairman of the Constitutional Drafting Committee. Ambedkar was famous by then for his powerful writings against untouchability, but he was even better known as a persistent critic of the upper-caste Hindu limits of Congress reformism and of Gandhi's position on untouchability. Signaling his uneasiness about the Constitution he had helped to author, Ambedkar stated:

> On 26 January 1950, we are going to enter a life of contradictions. In politics we will have equality and in social and economic life we will have inequality. . . . We must remove this contradiction at the earliest moment, or else those who suffer from inequality will blow up the structure of political democracy which this Assembly has laboriously built up.[34]

Ambedkar and his generation had done their best to make a "good" constitution through recourse to a grand exercise in comparative constitutionalism. Yet nothing could be settled by the Constitution given the enormity of its brief: to inaugurate a political democracy by eradicating caste, a millennial order of injustice and inequality.[35] Ambedkar was not above rejecting the founding document he had played a key role in birthing. He argued, "I am quite prepared to say that I shall be the first person to burn the [Constitution]. I do not want it. It does not suit anybody. If our people want to carry on, they must remember that the majorities cannot ignore the minorities by saying: 'Oh no, to recognize you is to harm democracy.'"[36] Ambedkar's reluctance reflects both his commitment to and skepticism of programs and policies instituted to produce social equality. Instead, he draws our attention to the gap between legislated redress and existential suffering, and between the founding document and the equality it imagines: The recurrent staging of these aporia underscored the difficult relationship between caste and democracy, between historical difference and equality.

Ambedkar's response was in keeping with a general tendency to invest in institutional responses while remaining skeptical of their transformative effects. Rather than excising contradiction from the field of politics, Ambedkar's actions effected a signal transformation of the political, which consisted of investing law (and Constitution) with the capacity to reveal the state's historic complicity in the extension of caste power. In Aniket Jaaware's powerful formulation, "This is what I would like to call the stamp on the forehead of the state. I mean stamp in the double sense of a bureaucratic seal of endorsement, as well as a mark of the contradiction that is, from now on, forever visible. This is, in a certain sense, an ironic inversion of the stamp of caste."[37] This "stamp" has produced the Dalit as political potentiality, and a very particular sort of historical subject. Rather than a bland universalism, we have a universalism that results from agonism, or an embodied particularism that points the way to a collective political future for which we can discern only the trajectory— the untouchable "becoming Dalit"—but not its substantive content or outlines.

The agonistic relationship between B. R. Ambedkar and Gandhi, not to mention Ambedkar's remarkable interventions around the caste question, played a crucial role in redefining untouchability as a form of social suffering and inequality, and a specter haunting Indian politics. Ambedkar's standoff with Gandhi in September 1932 over the issue of separate political representation for the "Depressed Classes" (as they were known in bureaucratic parlance) had provoked a remarkable turn of events that included Gandhi's fast unto death, followed by the compromise of the Poona Pact, which instituted reserved constituencies to enhance the political representation of the Depressed Classes. It was Ambedkar's position that Dalits were a non-Hindu minority that inaugurated the crisis of 1932: In effect, Ambedkar had used the demand for separate representation as a way to translate the negative identity of Dalits into collective political interest. As it happened, the events of 1932 marked Ambedkar's entrance on the national stage as a powerful critic of Congress nationalism, an insurgent thinker, and reluctant founding father whose ideas of radical equality were well beyond their time.

Ambedkar's Buddhist conversion on October 14, 1956, months before his death on December 6, revealed "another" Ambedkar who appeared unconvinced that Dalit redress could be legislated at all. To many, conversion seemed to be a reversal of Ambedkar's insurgent demands for a secular, political response to the violation of caste, a response captured by the self-nominalization of a disempowered and marginalized community as *Dalit* (literally, "ground down," "crushed," "broken"), a potent reminder of the historic violence of caste. Yet Ambedkar's search for a religious alternative to Hinduism had been publicly stated as early as 1935, and the Buddhist alternative had been alive among Dalit communities from the middle of the nineteenth century.[38] In justifying conversion, Ambedkar drew on his long-standing criticism of Hinduism as a "religion of rules," which lacked ethics. Instead, he argued: "A religious act may not be a correct act but must at least be a responsible act. To permit of this responsibility, Religion must mainly be a matter of principles only. It cannot be a matter of rules. The moment it degenerates into rules it ceases to be Religion, as it kills responsibility which is the essence of a truly religious act."[39] Ambedkar's reclamation of Buddhism as agonistic presence and a persistent historical force thus reverberated well beyond the immediate event of conversion where 600,000 Dalits, most of them hailing from the region of western India, converted en masse in a powerful public ceremony in Nagpur city. Though broadcast as an act of human emancipation, the conversion to Navayana Buddhism—a Buddhism of Ambedkar's making that took shape through the writing of the posthumously published *Buddha and His Dhamma* (1957)—had deep political consequences: It revealed the inseparability of caste stigma (legitimized by Hinduism) and impoverished Dalit existence via a "religious" critique of religion (read Hinduism). By locating emancipation between the Buddhist past, and an emancipated future, Ambedkar essentially produced an immanent critique of caste that held religion and politics in play as mutually entailed, each the locus of intensive agonism: Political separation and Buddhist conversion manifest that relation.

At work here is a peculiar form of secularization: The imagination of social equality was predicated on emancipation from (Hindu) religion, but religious emancipation could only ever be conceived as an act of politics. The word "secular" has to be qualified in this context: It is about showing the implication of religion with politics and challenging Enlightenment construction of the autonomy of the religious and spiritual. In this regard, Buddhist conversion was as much a practice of social withdrawal as it was the assertion of a distinctive political-ethical identity for Dalits: Conversion disclosed the necessary, if agonistic relationship between untouchability and caste Hinduism, and by so doing allowed Dalits to reassert their (negated) humanity.

In Lieu of a Conclusion

Naming and renaming was a long-standing technique in the repertoire of anticasteism, which described social oppression through approximation and analogy, that is, through acts of empathetic identification. Global imaginaries of connection and comparison were simultaneously accounts of forms of life that resisted translation. In the process, caste came to be seen as a bodily property, embodied by figures of historic violation whose experiences enlarged the conceptual matrix of political subjectivity.

Not long ago, standard theories of Indian modernization included an assumption of Sanskritization, formulated by the anthropologist M. N. Srinivas.[40] With modern development, lower castes would imitate the Brahmins in their quest for upward social mobility. In the process, the polluting characteristics of lower caste practices would winnow away, and a peaceful transition to modernity was therefore possible, Srinivas implied. Caste oppression would simply melt away in the sunshine of capitalist progress, without any need of accounting for its historic injustice, or any effort on the part of its victims to acknowledge the character of their humiliation.

One way to describe this essay, and its tacit rebuttal of Srinivas, is to rephrase a classic question in postcolonial studies: Can the subaltern think? In posing the problem in this way I am not merely foregrounding the scant attention to caste in South Asian postcolonial theory. I am also challenging the fixation on (subaltern) resistance to the exclusion of what I believe is a crucial focus of anticaste activism, namely its insistence on intellectual emancipation.

Locating the emergence of critical practice requires that we address not merely the capacity for emancipated thinking but also the enabling contexts for the emancipation so imagined. Anticaste thought was a creative response to the onset of capitalist modernity, since the latter was both an enabling condition of possibility and a significant object of analysis for anticaste thinkers. It is in the encounter between caste and capital that a "politics of caste" was produced, where caste was theorized and its end anticipated. The social abstractions to which capitalism gave rise—in this case, the dematerialization of caste relations and their subsequent reorganization—provided key openings for new forms of critique that theorized everyday life and social inequality.[41] Slave emancipation and interwar internationalism were significant historical conjunctures, conceptual openings that facilitated "new" ways of addressing older social forms. In particular they recast normative questions of enfranchisement, universality, and political affinity as requiring to be thought anew, rendered meaningful in a different time and place, and responsive to pertinent structures of degradation, destitution, and dispossession. Efforts to describe social oppression, that is, the practice of a sort of radical empiricism, which had a long history in the repertoire of anticasteism enacted empathetic convergence with other figures of destitution. Global imaginaries of connection and comparison also conjured forms of life in their historical specificity. Ambedkar's Dalit is one such figure, who comes into view as we undertake the project to deprovincialize caste and defamiliarize its more common association with tradition and social backwardness.

NOTES

1. Dirks, *Castes of Mind*.

2. Literally, crushed, ground down, broken; used as a term of militant self-identification by former untouchables.

3. Hager, "A Colored Man's Constitution."

4. For an extended discussion of Phule's rewriting of history, see Rao, *The Caste Question*, esp. chap. 1.

5. Du Bois, *Black Reconstruction*, 184–87. Abolition democracy was a way to conceive the civic and political personhood of black workers, through their education, control over capital, and political rights.

6. Ambedkar, "Slaves and Untouchables," 117.

7. Kadam, *Narayan Meghaji Lokhande*.

8. Hazareesingh, "Chasing Commodities."

9. Banaji, *Theory as History*, esp. 308–9; emphasis added. See also Harootunian, *Marx after Marx*.

10. Phule, *Shetkaryacha Asud*, 31.

11. Ibid., 242.

12. Ibid., 235–36.

13. Pandit Kondiram, "Pada," verse 4, in G. B. Valangkar, "Anarya Dosh Pariharak Mandali Petition to His Excellency the Commander-in-Chief of Bombay Presidency in Poona, July 1984." [Marathi] Khairmode Collection, Bombay University.

14. "Woman" was another densely described figure whose vulnerability to the sexual advance of lascivious Brahmin priests, not to mention irrational social dicta, was portrayed with intense anger. More important yet, Phule argued that the social reproduction of caste was predicated on the regulation of female sexuality, that the sexual division of labor was the substrate of caste hierarchy.

15. Phule, *Gulamgiri*, 83–84. Recall that Aniket Jaaware uses the branding metaphor in his discussion of Ambedkar's use of the law to indict state complicity in perpetuating caste inequality.

16. In 1921, M. N. Roy was sent to Tashkent by Lenin to head the Asiatic Bureau of the Comintern to train an army of Indian revolutionaries. The Indian Military School was closed in 1921, to be replaced by University of the Toilers of the East. In the meantime a number of muhajireens (volunteers) who had fought in the Khilafat movement had been trained there. Some were among the thirteen members of the émigré Indian Communist Party—established in Tashkent in 1920—who came to the subcontinent in 1922 only to be arrested in the Peshawar Conspiracy Case. Meanwhile, M. N. Roy had started publication of the *Vanguard of Indian Independence* by May 1922. More important, he began to communicate with Shripad Amrit Dange, a Maharashtrian Marxist, after reading Dange's text, *Gandhi versus Lenin*. The two maintained steady communication aided by the arrival of Charles Ashleigh, of the British Communist Party, in Bombay on September 19, 1922. By then, Dange had started publication of the *Socialist*. (The paper was started on August 5, 1922.)

Charles Ashleigh was joined in Bombay by Philip Spratt, who was asked in 1926 to journey to India (together with Ben Bradley and Lester Hutchinson) as a Comintern agent at the behest of Clemens Dutt, elder brother of R. P. Dutt, the well-known theorist of the British Communist Party, and author of *India Today* (1949). Spratt had been encouraged to launch regional Workers and Peasants Parties as a cover for building the nascent Communist Party of India. In Bombay, key members of the Workers and Peasants Parties managed to infiltrate the Girni Kamgar Union (Textile Workers' Union) in 1928, just before the city's historic general strike of that year. By 1929, key Maharashtrian Marxists—G. Adhikari, S. A. Dange, S. V. Ghate, and S. S. Mirajkar—had been arrested in the Meerut Conspiracy Case on the charge of treason, together with Muzaffar Ahmed, P. C. Joshi, Philip Spratt, Shaukat Usmani, and others.

17. Harootunian, *Marx after Marx*. See also Kaviraj, "Marxism in Translation."

18. Kidambi, "Contestation and Conflict," 107.

19. There were emerging fissures between peasant-workers, who maintained a link with rural land and labor regimes, and Dalits, who saw urban migration as an escape from rural exploitation, often at the hands of the same agrarian castes they reencountered in the city on the shop floor. Dalit separatism was also a response to the rise of aggressive non-Brahmin populism, and the migration of key non-Brahmin activists to the Congress by 1930. Dalits responded with claims on colonial franchise, which included mobilizing the discourse of minority in aid of separate political representation.

20. Rashid, "The House That Ambedkar Built."

21. The Lal Bavta Girni Kamgar Union (Red Flag Textile Workers' Union), Tarun Kamgar Sangh (Young Workers' Association), and the Marxist League were also affiliated with the KVPM. Members were encouraged to join by paying a rupee, which entitled them to the Mandali's publications. These included *Communist Jahirnama* (Communist Manifesto); *Russian Krantica Itihas* (History of the Russian Revolution); *Comrade Lenin* (Comrade Lenin); *Ase ka* (Why it is so), a primer for children; *Paris Commune Arthat Lal Bavtyance Pahile Rajya* (Paris Commune: The First Kingdom of the Red Flag); *Ai Bhag Ai* (Gorky's *Mother*); *Communistanca Jabab* (A short account of the Meerut testimonies); *Molmajuri ani Bhandval* (Wage, Labor, and Capital); *Kon Kasa Charitartha Calavitho Arthat Kamkaryance Arthashastra* (Who Makes Things Happen, Or The Workers' Political Economy); and *Russian Krantica Sankshipta Itihas* (A Short History of the Russian Revolution). These texts are available in the British Library's Vernacular Collection of Proscribed Literature.

22. Unlike the Marathi translation of *Capital*, which relies on an English translation, Adhikari translated the Communist Manifesto from German. The text, which was published in 1931 as the Communist Jahirnama, was proscribed in 1933. Maharashtra State Archives, "Labour Unrest and Communist Activities," Annual Lists of Proscribed Literature, 543 Series, Home (Political).

23. Sartori, *Liberalism in Empire*.

24. Peter Gay has noted Marx's ability to bring together histories of British political economy, French socialism, and German philosophical idealism in a galvanic unity. However, by so doing, Marx also drew attention to the two disconnected or disjointed histories he sought to unify: a British history of political economy that predicated liberty on property, that is, the model of classical liberalism, and another that drew from French republican ideals of equality as a response to enslavement and unfreedom. These two histories—the exclusionary right to property and the commitment to radical human equality—activate an internal tension in European intellectual history that is typically resolved by assuming the political equality of men as the enabling prior ground for disclosing the labor-capital antagonism. Thus the primacy of labor—and the proletariat as the figure of a collective universality—is historically specific, even as it is interpretively overdetermined.

25. Butler, "Restaging the Universal," 40–41.

26. Ranciere, *The Philosopher and His Poor*; Ranciere, *Proletarian Nights*.

27. Ruda, *Hegel's Rabble*.

28. Stallybrass, "Marx and Heterogeneity."

29. Fanon, *The Wretched of the Earth*, 129.

30. See Ambedkar's analysis of the transformation of the upanayam ceremony between Vedic and Puranic Hinduism (*Who Were the Shudras*), or his analysis of "surplus" women in the essay "Castes in India". Both are discussed in Rao, *The Caste Question*, chap. 3.

31. This essay is an argument translated from the Gujarati-language Harijanbandhu newspaper. Gandhi's argument that Untouchables were (once) Shudras can be found in *Young India*, February 5, 1925.

32. Marx himself addressed the heterogeneity of real labor against labor as abstraction, e.g., in the *Grundrisse*. Dipesh Chakrabarty's engagement with the heteronomous histories of capital is the most significant for the South Asian context. See Chakrabarty, "The Two Histories of Capital." A more recent argument by the late Kalyan Sanyal takes recourse to a nonculturalist account of capitalist unevenness. Sanyal defines what is outside capitalist logic as noncapital to mark a relation of nonsubsumption. See Sanyal, *Rethinking Capitalist Development.*

33. Ambedkar went beyond a procedural commitment to the protection of individual freedoms by advocating some degree of state ownership and central planning for enacting social equality. "For purpose of [legally prescribing the economic structure of society] is to protect the liberty of the individual from invasion by other individuals, which is the object of enacting Fundamental Rights." *States and Minorities,* 409.

34. Ambedkar, *Constituent Assembly Debates,* 981.

35. Members of the Constituent Assembly had renounced the Muslim separate electorate as a hangover from the colonial past against the backdrop of subcontinental Partition, "in the national interest." Meanwhile the eradication of untouchability became a central tenet of the Indian Constitution: Affirmative action policies developed a comprehensive, far-reaching response to the social and economic disabilities of caste, while the courts actively legislated Hindu equality. The Sachar Committee Report (2006) has produced troubling data on the socio-economic status Muslims, and has been a catalyst for debates for Muslim reservations [affirmative action]. http://mhrd.gov.in/sites/upload_files/mhrd/files/sachar_comm.pdf. Last accessed November 3, 2017.

36. Rajya Sabha Debates, September 2, 1953, 877. http://rsdebate.nic.in/bitstream/123456789/588187/1/PD_04_02091953_7_p844_p924_3.pdf#search=AMBEDKAR.

37. Jaaware, "Uses of Foucault and Ambedkar."

38. Geetha and Rajadorai, *Towards a Non-Brahmin Millennium.*

39. Ambedkar, "Annihilation of Caste," 75.

40. Srinivas, *The Dominant Caste and Other Essays.*

41. Whether it was seen to be continuous with capitalist modernity as a category produced by it or as a place from which to challenge alienated life or dehistoricization (in Lefebvre's words), the relationship between everyday life and capitalism's commodification of labor (and the laborer) was assumed. Harry Harootunian speaks of the everyday as a temporality rather than a geopolitical space. The everyday is enabled by, yet distinctive from capitalist modernity; it exists within the time of capital as a distinctive form of materialization that is perceived as a form of social unevenness. Harootunian, *History's Disquiet.*

BIBLIOGRAPHY

Ambedkar, B. R. *Annihilation of Caste: With a Reply to Mahatma Gandhi.* In *Dr. Babasaheb Ambedkar's Writings and Speeches,* vol. 1, edited by Vasant Moon. Bombay: Government of Maharashtra, 1979.
———. *Constituent Assembly Debates* 11 (1949): 977–981. http://164.100.47.132/LssNew/constituent/vol11p11.html.
———. "Slaves and Untouchables." In *Dr. Babasaheb Ambedkar's Writings and Speeches,* vol. 5, edited by Vasant Moon. Bombay: Education Department, Government of Maharashtra, 1979.
———. *States and Minorities: Memorandum Submitted to the Constituent Assembly on the Safeguards for the Scheduled Castes.* In *Dr. Babasaheb Ambedkar Writings and Speeches,* vol. 1, edited by Vasant Moon. Bombay: Education Department, Government of Maharastra, 1979.
Banaji, Jairus. *Theory as History: Essays on Modes of Production and Exploitation.* Chicago: Haymarket Books, 2011.
Butler, Judith. "Restaging the Universal: Hegemony and the Limits of Formalism." In *Contingency Hegemony Universality: Contemporary Dialogues on the Left,* edited by Judith Butler, Ernesto Laclau, and Slavoj Žižek. London: Verso, 2000.

Chakrabarty, Dipesh. "The Two Histories of Capital." In *Provincializing Europe: Postcolonial Thought and Historical Difference*, 47–72. Princeton: Princeton University Press, 2007.

Dirks, Nicholas. *Castes of Mind: Colonialism and the Making of Modern India*. Princeton: Princeton University Press, 2001.

Du Bois, W. E. B. *Black Reconstruction, 1860–1880*. New York: Free Press, 1998.

Fanon, Frantz. *The Wretched of the Earth*. New York: Grove Press, 1963.

Geetha, V., and S. Rajadorai. *Towards a Non-Brahmin Millennium: From Iyothee Thass to Periyar*. Calcutta: Samya, 1998.

Hager, Christopher. "A Colored Man's Constitution." *New York Times*, August 30, 2013. http://opinionator.blogs.nytimes.com/2013/08/30/a-colored-mans-constitution/?_r=0.

Harootunian, Harry. *History's Disquiet*. New York: Columbia University Press, 2000.

———. *Marx after Marx: History and Time in the Expansion of Capitalism*. New York: Columbia University Press, 2015.

Hazareesingh, Sandip. "Chasing Commodities over the Surface of the Globe." Commodities of Empire, Working Paper No. 1. http://www.open.ac.uk/Arts/ferguson-centre/commodities-of-empire/working-papers/WP01.pdf.

Immerwahr, Daniel. "Caste or Colony: Indianizing Race in the United States." *Modern Intellectual History* 4, no. 2 (2007): 275–301.

Jaaware, Aniket. "Stamping the State on Its Forehead: The Uses of Foucault and Ambedkar." Paper presented at Jawaharlal Nehru University, Munirka, New Delhi, Delhi, March 15, 2007.

Kadam, Manohar. *Narayan Meghaji Lokhande: Bharatiya Kamgar Calvalice Janak*. Mumbai: Mahatma Phule Samata Pratishthan and Akshar Prakashan, 2002.

Kaviraj, Sudipta. "Marxism in Translation: Reflections on Indian Radical Thought." In *Political Judgment: Essays for John Dunn*, edited by Richard Bourke and Raymond Guess, 172–200. Cambridge: Cambridge University Press, 2009.

Keer, Dhananjay, and S. G. Malshe, eds. *Mahatma Phule Samagra Vangmaya*. Mumbai: Maharashtra Rajya Sahitya Ani Sanskruti Mandal, 1980.

Kidambi, Prashant. "Contestation and Conflict: Workers' Resistance and the 'Labour Problem' in the Bombay Cotton Mills, c. 1898–1919." In *Labour Matters: Towards Global Histories*, edited by Marcel van der Linden and Prabhu P. Mohapatra, 106–30. New Delhi: Tulika Books, 2009.

Kramer, Paul. "Harsh Deviations: The Rise and Fall of the Caste School of American Race Relations, 1936–1948." Paper presented at a workshop on "Race, Caste, and Democracy," Columbia University, September 27–28, 2013.

Natarajan, Balmurli, and Paul Greenough, eds. *Against Stigma: Studies in Caste, Race, and Justice since Durban*. Hyderabad: Orient Blackswan, 2009.

Phule, Jotirao. *Gulamgiri* [Slavery]. In *Samagra Vangmay: Mahatma Phule Samagra Vangmay* [Collected Works of Mahatma Jotirao Phule]. 1969. 2nd ed. Edited by Y. D. Phadke. Mumbai: Mumbai Rajya Sahitya ani Samskriti Mandal, 1991.

———. *Shetkaryacha Asud* [Cultivator's Whipcord]. In *Samagra Vangmay: Mahatma Phule Samagra Vangmay* [Collected Works of Mahatma Jotirao Phule]. 1969. 2nd ed. Edited by Y. D. Phadke. Mumbai: Mumbai Rajya Sahitya ani Samskriti Mandal, 1991.

———. *Slavery: Selected Writings of Jotirao Phule*. Edited by G. P. Deshpande. Translated by Maya Pandit. New Delhi: Leftword Books, 2002.

Ranciere, Jacques. *The Philosopher and His Poor*. Edited by Andrew Parker. Translated by Andrew Parker, Corinne Ostor, and John Drury. Durham, N.C.: Duke University Press, 2004.

———. *Proletarian Nights: The Workers' Dream in Nineteenth Century France*. 2nd ed. London: Verso, 2012.

Rao, Anupama. *The Caste Question: Dalits and the Politics of Modern India*. Berkeley: University of California Press, 2009.

Rashid, Omar. "The House That Ambedkar Built Gets Scant Notice." *The Hindu*, September 8, 2015. http://www.thehindu.com/news/cities/mumbai/the-house-ambedkar-built-in-mumbai-gets-scant-notice/article7626379.ece.

Ruda, Frank. *Hegel's Rabble: An Investigation Into Hegel's Philosophy of Right*. London: Bloomsbury Academic, 2013.

Sanyal, Kalyan. *Rethinking Capitalist Development: Primitive Accumulation, Governmentality, and Postcolonial Capitalism*. London: Routledge, 2007.

Sartori, Andrew. *Liberalism in Empire*. Berkeley: University of California Press, 2015.

Slate, Nico. *Colored Cosmopolitanism: The Shared Struggle for Freedom in the United States and India*. Cambridge, Mass.: Harvard University Press, 2012.

Srinivas, M. N. *The Dominant Caste and Other Essays*. New Delhi: Oxford University Press, 1994.

Stallybrass, Peter. "Marx and Heterogeneity: Thinking the Lumpenproletariat." *Representations* 39 (1990): 69–95.

Visweswaran, Kamala. *Uncommon Culture: Racism and the Articulation of Cultural Difference*. Durham, N.C.: Duke University Press, 2010.

SIX

The Postcolonial Avant-Garde and the Claim to Futurity:
Edwar al-Kharrat's Ethics of Tentative Innovation

Adam Spanos

The Impasse of Postcolonial Studies

Writing in the U.S. periodical the *Nation* in 2014, the journalist Adam Shatz reflected on the dynamics of struggle in the Middle East and the failure of the Left to respond to recent changes:

> As the regional balance of power has shifted and American dominance wanes, I have begun to worry that an all-consuming preoccupation with America and Israel leads progressive writers to become strangely incurious about the crimes for which the West can't be blamed and the developments, such as the politicization of sectarian identity, that are shaking the region far more profoundly than the Israeli-Palestinian arena. . . . The theoretical intricacy of academic anti-Orientalism [which informs this preoccupation] . . . sometimes conceals an attempt to wish away the region's dizzying complexity in favor of the old, comforting logic of anticolonial struggle. . . . Like all old maps, it has begun to yellow.[1]

Shatz contended that observers should respect the complexity and fluidity of the contemporary Middle East rather than submit to an ideological narrative of the region's ailments. Echoing V. S. Naipaul, from whom he otherwise distanced himself, Shatz affirmed that the investigative writer should not seek to understand the region through a single filter, but should rather strive to cultivate a "readiness for adventure or revelation," an openness to the contingencies and accidents that invariably disrupt one's given frames of understanding.[2] This sentiment—that one should be wary of academic forestructures in approaching vital areas of human life like the contemporary Middle East—is a welcome one, even if it resembles Said's own critique of a similar "textual attitude" in the scholars he critiqued.[3]

Shatz's concluding assertion that recent developments in the Middle East shouldn't be viewed as the legacy of Western imperialism or Israeli settler colonialism raises a different problem. This claim is objectionable not because the Israelis, Americans, or European colonizers ought to be held responsible for all suffering in the region—clearly regional actors share a portion of the blame, if in historically mediated ways—but because it separates past from present in an unhelpful way. Disregarding the plentiful evidence that suggests continuities across successive regimes in Middle Eastern national and regional power structures, Shatz represented phenomena like the emergence of the Islamic State in Iraq and Syria and the Syrian civil war as events that upend the "teleological assumptions" of anticolonial critique. Shatz thereby disallowed recognition of what Robert Young calls "postcolonial remains": the interpenetration of past with present in such a way that potentiality—present futures—is differentially distributed along geopolitical lines inherited from colonial times.[4] Shatz overlooked not only the significance of the past as a conditioning agent of the present, but the ways that even seemingly defunct pasts can be mobilized for making alternative futures: hence the outrage among engaged Egyptian activists at Shatz's assertion in January 2012 that "the heady days of the Arab Spring have come to an end."[5]

Shatz's decision to frame his critique of the U.S. Left's positions on the Middle East with reference to Edward Said's writing on Orientalism, which, he "fear[s,] . . . has congealed into an orthodoxy," reveals a broader challenge facing postcolonial studies today.[6] The field currently occupies a bizarre temporality in which its practitioners often allege that students and the general public are not yet equipped to understand their claims as well as those made by denizens of the global South for lack of basic "transnational literacy," while nonpracticing observers in adjacent academic specializations—and those among the broader Left like Shatz—believe that the field has become anachronistic, displaced by newer concerns like world literature and ISIS. In this temporal fold of the "already/not yet," postcolonial studies currently finds itself at an impasse.

My suggestion is that attention to the various postcolonial avant-gardes can help clarify this temporal paradox and contribute to the reassertion of the field's guiding insight that the colonial past structures the present while presenting a new framework for research. Postcolonial studies, if it is to escape the charge that it is inherently backward-looking, melancholically detached from the present, even conservative, must recover the sense of futurity that animates its political interventions. The avant-garde is a repository of this futurity not because its members represent a society's most progressive forces, but because it articulates social injustice as a temporal paradox that demands future redress.

Deprovincializing the Arab Avant-Garde

The postcolonial avant-garde raises a number of interesting questions that challenge the assumptions of both Western aesthetics and the mode of thinking that aims to escape reflexive Eurocentrism. On the standard narrative, the avant-garde emerged in Western Europe and the United States as a protest against the banalization of art following its transformation from a tool of moral instruction to a commodity, a shift tacitly endorsed by liberal states, which came to understand art as a sphere of production like any other. Renato Poggioli's influential study specified a number of features of the avant-garde, including its short-lived journals and numerous manifestos, antagonistic stance and welcomed unpopularity, romanticist roots and experimentalism, opposition to the bourgeoisie and to kitsch, and fetishization of technology.[7] For the present purposes, one of his most important contributions was his assertion that the avant-garde could not exist under "totalitarian" regimes but only within the liberal regimes of nominally democratic countries. Peter Bürger deepened Poggioli's contextual analysis, claiming that the "historical avant-garde"—that set of diverse artists and provocateurs who operated in the major European capitals and New York between 1880 and 1930—was constituted by its members' rejection of the institutional setting in which they were expected to operate. For Bürger, the avant-garde targeted the entire social apparatus that mediated the public's relation to art and supplied the grounds from which art was to be understood. Bürger considered the notion of "aestheticism," or art for art's sake, as the most important precondition for the emergence of the avant-garde, for it was only with the appearance of this doctrine that "social ineffectuality stands revealed as the essence of art in bourgeois society" and the avant-garde acquired the opponent that retroactively brought it into being.[8] The avant-garde didn't simply reject its autonomous status, however, but retained from aestheticism the apolitical character of the artwork's contents, even as its form and public presentation were construed as protests against the socially mandated role of art.[9] For Bürger the avant-garde's protest was finite insofar as its spectacular acts came to be recognized as a form of art itself—hence his dismissal of the incitements of the "neo-avant-garde."

In much of the postcolonial world, the visuals arts and literature do not have the same autonomy that Western avant-gardists sought to undo, and many countries lack the national and regional markets that would allow artists to support themselves through the sale of their work and so constitute themselves as a special domain of production. In these conditions, the avant-garde must signify differently if it is to mean anything at all; we are left with the standard question asked by postcolonialist historiography since Dipesh Chakrabarty: Can this concept make sense of reality in the South, or is it only intelligible within the Western historical framework from which it emerged and of which it sought to make sense?[10]

One response to this question involves the assertion of the absolute difference separating cultural forms from different societies and the consequent need to invent new concepts for each. Such an approach disables cultural comparison, and therefore confirms an antitheoretical stance that verges on myopic empiricism at its worst. Furthermore, it overlooks the possibility of universalisms that emerge from non-Western locations or in the relation between peoples from distant places. Following Gary Wilder, then, we might instead heed the call to "deprovincialize" the cultural and intellectual production of the non-Western world in order to recognize its mutual claim to an at least potentially human level of influence.[11] In addition to searching for "original" cultural forms and narratives outside the West, this approach obliges us to examine non-Western iterations of cultural products understood as Western in order to better understand what is properly universal in each and what is merely contingent.

A second dilemma immediately arises, however, which is particular to the study of the avant-garde. On one hand, recognition of a postcolonial avant-garde offers the opportunity to foreground the capacity, exercised by all the historical avant-gardes, to initiate calls for social change, which is certainly one motivation for the few studies of the postcolonial avant-garde that exist.[12] On the other hand, the mode of agency enacted by Western avant-gardes has often been criticized for a certain kind of will to power and aggression that should make us pause before extending it to artists from postcolonial societies that were in a sense the victims of this avant-garde energy.

Raymond Williams writes that avant-garde artists, despite their expressed goal of challenging the dominant capitalist way of life, betray an investment in "that central bourgeois figure—the sovereign individual."[13] Likewise Peter Nicholls observes that the historical avant-garde engaged tropes of "global modernisation and imperialist expansion" to break with cultural decadence; these figures were valued precisely for their destructive connotations and the "fantasy of self-authoring" at their root.[14] From here the avant-garde often devolved into misogyny, as its male representatives came to see their relationships with women as a figuration of the constraints imposed by the modern polities in which they lived.[15] That the avant-garde relied on a model of subjectivity with such close ties to imperialism, sexism, and other forms of mastery should give us pause before simply assuming the universal applicability of the term. If colonial and postcolonial societies did not have recourse to such modes of aggrandizement—except in tendentious imitation of colonial power—what grounds of comparison, if any, exist for the recognition of specifically non-Western avant-gardes?

The next section attempts to answer this question by analyzing an influential artist in Egypt, Edwar al-Kharrat, whose literary and critical writings since the late 1960s have been identified as partaking in and commenting on a wider "avant-garde" movement. Although I will make the case for a certain restricted use of the avant-garde, it is worth exploring the term's connotations in Arabic in order to ground this usage in the historical and philological context that gives it meaning. *Al-ṭalīʿa* signifies "vanguard," "avant-garde," "portents," "beginnings," as well as "youth"; it derives from a root that supplies verbs, including "appear," "ascend," "break forth," and "erupt." Perhaps the most famous cultural work featuring this noun as its title is the Cairene journal edited by Lutfi al-Khuli from the mid-1960s. Although the journal published at least one volume devoted to recent literature—a special issue in 1969 with the title "This is how the young writers speak" (*Hakadhā yatakallam al-udabāʾ al-shabāb*)—its contents were generally devoted to political and social questions from a Marxist standpoint.[16] The same holds true for *Ṣawt al-Shaʿb*, the newspaper of the Parti de l'Avant-Garde Socialiste in Algeria; *Avant-Garde*, the periodical of the Union Marocaine du Travail; and another journal called *al-Ṭalīʿa*, published by the Syrian Communist Party. Without taking up the much-debated issue over the term's dual militaristic and cultural connotations, we can note that other terms have seemed to prevail in Arabic cultural criticism. Much more frequently used descriptions of innovative aesthetic practice are *al-tajrībiyya* (experimentalism), *al-ḥadīth* (the modern), and *al-jadīd* (the new). We therefore discover a second challenge on the terminological register to complement the normative one just mentioned. How do we account for Arab critics' choices of nomenclature? Should we allow an additional conceptual level, perhaps unarticulated or undertheorized, at which some of the general insights of Western cultural historiography can be applied? How can we make use of these concepts without presupposing their universality or the validity of the entire narrative that such concepts invariably condense? What other narratives do the aspirations of Arab artists and critics suggest?

Experimental Criticism

Edwar al-Kharrat has played an instrumental role in the literary renewal of Egypt—and, through his novels and criticism, much of the rest of the Arabic-speaking world—that began in the 1960s and has flourished since the 1970s. The revolution in novel-writing that al-Kharrat effected has led many readers to appreciate the family resemblance between this pioneering author and his European modernist predecessors: Marcel Proust, for the narratological and ethical role of memory in his work; James Joyce, for the fragmentation of narrative; Virginia Woolf, for the use of alliteration; André Breton, for the blending of the dream-state with consciousness and the passion for unification with others; and Alain Robbe-Grillet, whose interest in "objectivity" mirrors one of the tendencies that al-Kharrat identifies in his literary criticism with the "new sensibility" in Arabic literature.[17] Al-Kharrat's explicit endorsement of *turāth*—cultural heritage—as a resource for the affirmative dimension of his experimentation has in turn come to be understood as another key intertextual register of the work. Thus critics find al-Kharrat in conversation with the pre-Islamic *nasīb*, or the ode to lost love; the Sufi poet Ibn 'Arabi (d. 1290 CE); the grammarians al-Khalil ibn Ahmad (d. 791 CE) and Ahmad ibn Muhammad al-Razi (d. c. 1232 CE); and a variety of religious traditions and beliefs, primarily Coptic, but also Islamic.[18] Here we will be interested less in the particular sources of al-Kharrat's style and philosophical outlook than in the ways he puts these to use. Al-Kharrat's method of "pastiche" or sampling from diverse sources is a unique one that supposes notions of time and history that bear crucially on how he positions himself in literary history.[19] Al-Kharrat identifies neither with the avant-garde understood as a self-authorizing break from tradition nor with the postmodernist critique of this aspiration.

Al-Kharrat calls attention in a number of his critical writings to a general transformation in the qualities of recent imaginative works written in Arabic. In referring to this unusual literature as the product of a *ḥasāsiyya jadīda*, a "new sensibility," al-Kharrat draws on the aspiration to novelty and originality that, in conventional periodizations, has marked Western culture since the Romantic movement and Arabic literature since the so-called *nahḍa*, or Arab renaissance, in the late nineteenth century. In identifying this new sensibility as the latest instantiation of a modernizing impulse that he also found in ancient Egypt, however, he exploded those traditional chronologies. As we shall see, this amorphous and pluriform inclination cannot be reconciled to the drive toward culmination at stake in both Western modernism's utopian dreams and the negative labor of its more radical avant-garde faction.

The question of the immediate origins of this new sensibility—as a critical nomination and literary phenomenon—is a vexed one. As al-Kharrat makes clear in his major essay on the subject, the concept took hold in literary practice during the 1970s. But he enumerates a range of conjunctures that might be understood as alternative beginnings. Among these he mentions the various endeavors of the 1960s, foremost among them the journal for which he served as an editor, *Gallery 68*; the small magazines of the 1930s and 1940s—*al-Tatawwūr, al-Bashīr*, the old *al-Fuṣūl*—that were "avant-gardist" (*ṭalīʿiyya*) and "revolutionary" (*inqilābiyya*) with respect to the rules then governing the depiction of "reality"; and the socialist critic Salama Musa, whose calls for literary change in the 1930s already anticipated the claims of the "new sensibility."[20] Al-Kharrat doesn't represent himself as the author of this transformation in the history of aesthetics.[21] This sets his critical discourse apart from the traditionally grandiose self-stylization of the European avant-gardes.

Al-Kharrat's refusal to decide on a strict origin for the new sensibility, or to write with the progressive élan of the advocates of commitment and some of his postrealist contemporaries, endows his writing with a tentativeness that is fundamental to both his critical and his literary intervention. For even though he acknowledges the emergence of something new in written art, his relationship to that recognition is humble, tempered by a sense of the limits of both his knowledge and the validity of his insights, and expressed in a language that is devoid of bluster, even unsure. Al-Kharrat largely eschews the self-conviction of the avant-garde in favor of a critical style or approach that is experimental rather than declaratory. This does not mean that he lacks causes or entirely believes in the political acumen of his readership; as he has said in an interview, his goal is "to bring the reader to life, to wake him up . . . not to soothe people to sleep."[22] But his experimentalism, still activist in its intentions, differs considerably from the avant-garde aim to shock the bourgeoisie, as it leads him to continually rewrite his ideas so as to approach what still eludes his grasp. Not merely a personal eccentricity, this critical experimentalism has an intimate relationship with the kind of literature al-Kharrat advocates. Critical experimentalism, like the avant-garde manifesto form, names a way of thinking and writing about art that aspires to elicit something new for both critical discourse and literature proper; but it differs from the manifesto in that it doesn't claim the universal validity of its insights. Both presuppose the immanent nature of the discourse on literature to literature itself, but critical experimentalism remains a "perennial questioning" (*al-tasāʾul al-mustamirr*) rather than a definitive answer to an aesthetic question.[23]

Edwar al-Kharrat's Tragic Historical Vision

The structure of repetition and return presupposed by this critical ethic is also at work in al-Kharrat's fiction. His narratives, like his literary criticism, do not abide by a linear chronological schema. Even the narratological approaches pioneered by Gérard Genette and others to grapple with time in the modernist novel do not avail because al-Kharrat's narratives fail to supply the temporal prepositions and other clues that allow one to determine when achrony has been introduced or what temporal relation one scene bears to another on the linear timeline that such a narratology presupposes. This effect is related to the blurring of generic boundaries that al-Kharrat calls "transgeneric writing" (*al-kitāba 'abra al-naw'iyya*) in the sense that these syncretisms force the supremely time-conscious novel form to loosen its strictures by taking on board, for example, the meandering consciousness of lyric poetry or the recursive structures of music.[24] Al-Kharrat understands his writing as engaged in the destruction of generic boundaries, hence his claim that his critical writing and "narrative writing" are really not different,[25] his invocation of metaphors culled from the visual arts to explain his compositional practice, and his practice of labeling a given work as a "novelistic text" (*naṣṣ riwā'ī*), a "novelistic collage" (*kulūj riwā'ī*), or "novelistic miscellanies" (*tanwī'āt riwā'iyya*). Al-Kharrat's "novelistic texts" are not discrete units but tend toward "auto-intertextuality," or the repetition of characters and events among his many novels.[26] This in turn complicates the author's decision to call his first novel, *Rama and the Dragon*, part of a trilogy—itself only a small piece of al-Kharrat's extensive oeuvre—and forces consideration of the relationship between parts and wholes in terms of iterating levels rather than a simple duality. It is tempting to understand al-Kharrat's efforts to deconstruct the notion of a textual unit by appealing to multiple levels "above" and "below" the standard book-length work as an analogue of his pluralist social understanding, an affirmation of "diversity in unity" and the reverse.[27] However, he is more inclined in his interviews and autobiographical writings to figure this issue in mystical terms as the communion between the individual and the "universe" or "being" (*al-kawn*).[28]

About *Rama and the Dragon*'s "plot" or manifest content there is little that can be said other than that it centers on Mikhail, an older man who encounters a woman whom he had loved earlier in life, Rama, and with whom he now spends nine days. The renewal of their affair does not result in a change of its earlier fortune, and they part ways after some amount of argument stemming from philosophical differences about such matters as how to attain political justice and the virtues of her career as an archaeologist. Already, however, this is not a satisfactory description, as al-Kharrat revises each of these terms as the narrative proceeds in order to destabilize what readers are trained to presume are stable realities. The boundary between the narrator and Mikhail frequently dissolves, and the long passages composed as a stream of consciousness further erode the illusion that the narrator is omniscient. Likewise, Rama comes to be associated with a variety of legendary women, goddesses, and holy figures so as to render her being manifold: the Virgin Mary, Isis, Nut, Hathor, Hapi, Circe, Aphrodite, Demeter, Astarte, the Phoenix, Ishtar, and Sayyidna al-Husayn. The togetherness of Rama and Mikhail also comes into doubt, as Rama materializes and dematerializes in his consciousness, leaving him unexpectedly alone even when within proximity of her bodily presence. The failure of their relationship, its termination at the novel's end, cannot be taken as a stable description, as the affair resumes at the conference where they meet at the beginning of *al-Zaman al-Ākhar* (The Other Time), the next novel in the "trilogy."

Here I want to focus on just one moment in the text in which Mikhail articulates a highly idiosyncratic and apparently despairing view of history and the possibilities for political change in the present. This vision is connected to his assertion, made on several occasions during his debates with Rama, that a revolutionary solution to Egypt's problems cannot come to pass. We may begin from a quasi-biographical perspective and note that al-Kharrat was imprisoned in the final years of the British administration of Egypt for his participation in a Trotskyite group. He was forbidden from subsequently recollecting this time as a sacrifice for national and socialist liberation, however, as the Nasser regime imprisoned nearly the entire generation of his literary peers for leftist sympathies and continued British policies of applying pressure on artists and intellectuals to ensure their adherence to the government's agenda.[29] Although al-Kharrat construes his turn away from activism as a function of aging,[30] we can surmise he shares the general Left melancholia pervasive globally but with its own particularities in the Egyptian case. The oft-voiced disappointment of both the author and Mikhail, and their estrangement from the surrounding, relational world, should be viewed in relation to the ever-narrowing sphere of Egyptian politics and the state's mobilization of a socially destructive law of emergency to bolster its claim to rule. Of course, this depoliticization can never be completely successful, as the numerous rebellions from the 1977 Bread Intifada to the "Arab Spring" attest, but the despair that characterizes Mikhail's discussions of involvement in protests ought to be measured against the state's efforts to criminalize this and many other kinds of civic participation.

The novel's political motif, at its most explicit, takes the form of a recurring battle with the state that degenerates into a massacre. These scenes suggest that no positive change can be expected from political protest because Mikhail sees only chaos in the state's persecution of political dissidents. Mikhail observes the indeterminacy of means and ends in contemporary struggles, which means too that the dividing lines out of which politics emerge have been blurred, the transitivity that political action requires annulled. This limits his ability to narrate change, to describe how events precipitate qualitative changes in the lives of other human beings. Narrative is overwhelmed, and we are left with a pure instance of historical parataxis:

> Mikha'il said to himself: Tall al-Za'tar and Abu Za'bal, the arenas of the coliseum and the
> graveyard of Caracalla and the dungeons of the inquisition, the helmets of the Vikings
> and the dogs trained to mangle the blacks of Zimbabwe and the power of the documents
> of forgiveness [*saṭwat ṣukūk al-ghufrān*] and the statements of the political bureaus and
> central committees, Spartacus, Jesus, Husayn bin al-Mansur crucified with thieves and
> rebels and fugitives, the prison cells of the Bastille and the swords of the Crusaders
> and the chains of the Saracens [*salāsil al-ṣalāḥīn*], the prostitutes of Saigon and the victims
> of Black September, Black June and all the black months, the devil's islands no matter how
> their names differed Sing Sing Tura Robben and the Aegean Sea, the corpses floating on
> the Nile in Uganda and those stabbed with poisoned spears in Burundi and Rwanda and the
> crushed in Chile and the pulverized in Bangladesh, the snows of Argentina and the ovens
> of Dachau, the quartering of limbs and the blades of guillotines and the shattering blows
> on execution mats [*al-nuṭū'*], the Khartoum of Kitchener and the factories of Victoria in

Manchester and the Paris Commune and the fields of sugar cane and cotton in Mississippi and upper Egypt, the huts and putrid wounds that cover the face of the earth and the ghettos of Harlem and Odessa and Warsaw, the barbed wire of Siberia and the oases of the Sahara and the electrodes in women's breasts and men's penises in Algeria and Haiti, the caravans of the Qarmatians, and Baghdad falling under the hooves of Hulagu, the pyres of witches, and the white soldiers with their single wide-mouthed cannon harvesting jungles and valleys, the slave ships from Guinea and Zanzibar, the whisky syphilis opium and bullets for the red Indians and the yellow and black too, from Beirut to Guernica, from Berlin to Leningrad, from Sinai to Dayr Yāsīn, from Carthage to Constantinople, from Jerusalem to Shanghai, from Buchenwald to Munich, and from Bombay until Dinshaway, from the Huns to the Mongols, from the Hyksos to the Mandarins to Vietnam and from the Mamluks to the playboys, isn't this the story of every day? From the first day to the last day? Isn't this the rule and the law? Isn't this the story of this wise, productive, dreaming, two-legged, eloquent, rational, ravenous individual? . . . The list doesn't end and hasn't ended. The dragon is one unslain [*ghayr maqtūl*] and the lance of St. Michael is blunted [*mathlūm*] but still brandished [*musharri'an*] among the stars.[31]

This remarkable passage is reminiscent to my mind only of Derrida's "ten-word telegram" listing the "plagues" of the "new world order," but its distance-destroying transhistorical quality makes Derrida's list look narrow by comparison.[32] Its heartbreaking incantation of the wrongs of history, most but not all committed by representatives of states, demonstrates the extraordinary breadth of al-Kharrat's erudition and empathies. The names of perpetrators it inscribes cuts across the understood fractures of contemporary identity politics and confirms, in its inclusiveness, Edward Said's imploring statement that "there is suffering and injustice enough for everyone."[33] In this passage, similar versions of which occur in several of his novels,[34] al-Kharrat produces a historical tableau that flattens the various moments into a single, nonsequential list. Yet one must acknowledge that it possesses a critical function: like the "multi-millennial span" that Qurratulain Hyder uses to challenge colonial and nationalist historiography according to Sadia Abbas, al-Kharrat's lists undermine progressive narratives employed by states and development experts.[35] Al-Kharrat hasn't abandoned the attempt to make sense of history, though he has raised the stakes by dismissing facile narratives; and this transformation of history from a stable foundation that functions as "life's teacher" into a question that compels further thought distinguishes his philosophy of history from that of the European Enlightenment and its postmodern critique.[36]

Surely Mikhail's allusions to these historical crimes do not evince the "pathology distinctly autoreferential" and the "stylistic connotation" that Fredric Jameson identifies as the characteristically flattening effects of the postmodern approach to the past.[37] Unlike the nostalgia film or a historical novel by E. L. Doctorow, there is sincerity in Mikhail's list and an attempt to engage these historical events as objective determinants of a real, external world. Mikhail may feel at a loss about how to effectively respond to "the tyranny of the world"; he may even have despaired of "the basic right of counterattack"; but he has in no sense lapsed into the ironic mode of addressing the forces of order that is sometimes difficult to distinguish from capitulation to them.[38] Nor does his historical vision betray signs of the modernist fantasy of a complete break with the past, even though al-Kharrat perhaps tends here, like Ezra Pound and his peers, to a monistic understanding of the logic or moving force of history. But whereas Pound's man of action will destroy the feudal economics of usury and restore the capacity of language to transmit essential meanings, al-Kharrat's hero is ruthlessly self-questioning and fails inevitably to discover the principle that ties together all the atrocities he names. He experiences acutely the inability of language to represent a world prone to catastrophe, and the frustration of his ability to even describe the problem to be solved sends him into exile from the world of instrumental reason. This catastrophic historical consciousness must be reckoned constitutively different from the perception of "disposability" that has been identified with "modern" (Western) historical consciousness, in the sense that it doesn't afford a vantage point for either mastery of or detachment from the events constituting the history of the present.[39] Although al-Kharrat's historical vision is, like its ideal Western counterpart, an immanent one that understands humans rather than gods or fate as the determining agents, it complicates the binarism typical of this debate in its unwillingness to see this free will as an unrestricted capacity to bend history as one pleases.[40] Al-Kharrat's self-confessed "humanism" does not imply a belief that the sorrows of history he lists can be resolved, or ones like them prevented, simply through acquiring knowledge about the syntax of the list. He presents the list as a mystery, without providing its causal factors and internal relations, because the logic of willful commitment to progressive enlightenment is too facile. Al-Kharrat challenges the glibness of this historical confidence in requiring readers to contemplate the absent syntax and, in so doing, invest themselves in the relations between suffering constituencies—in the mutuality of suffering—as a precondition for an "emerging humanism."[41] This is a humanism predicated on an understanding of the violence of enlightenment, one that posits its existence in the domain of potentiality rather than the accomplished fact.[42]

The Question of Autonomy

In an article from 2003 titled "Kull minnā Multazim" (All of us are committed), al-Kharrat chafes against the dogmatic version of commitment that its adherents seek to impose on aspiring writers. Al-Kharrat would resignify the term as "the value of freedom, the freedom of the artist and the freedom of the other . . . in dialogue."[43] Art's task is not to declare the "absolute, final, conclusive truth" but to present open questions and "to bring the holy down to earth"; for it is only through free rein, independent of all preconceived notions, that art can pose a challenge to social conventions.[44] Arab writers must thus jealously guard their independence of mind, not conceding anything to the residual creed of social realism or to the state apparatus that periodically intervenes to censor works of literature.

From a certain vantage point, then, al-Kharrat's representation of new Arabic writing seems to invert Peter Bürger's narrative of the avant-garde. If for Bürger the historical avant-garde was a reaction against the doctrine of "aestheticism" that had freed art from its worldly commitments and constructed an artistic domain autonomous from other sectors of social and political life, for al-Kharrat the new writing protests the total integration of art and life championed by the advocates of commitment. Al-Kharrat is not suggesting, however, that writers should disavow their political aims and resign themselves to a position within the general division of labor. For him the problems an avant-garde must confront are the fixity of aesthetic doctrines and the subordination of art to life. Al-Kharrat has in mind a positive conception of freedom as the right to experiment in unrecognized zones of artistic and ethical endeavor. This is another way of phrasing a perennial theme in both his critical and creative interventions: the abhorrent nature of boundaries and the desire to find an open space in which communication of various sorts becomes possible.

Although it has not been my intention in this chapter to demonstrate such lines of influence, it is clear that al-Kharrat and many of his Egyptian colleagues at journals like *Gallery 68* and in groups like *Art et Liberté* were taken by the restless energies and formal experimentation of such Western projects as Surrealism.[45] Yet al-Kharrat seems to have separated literary techniques cultivated by Western artists from the specific ends to which they were put there. In his hands, "automatic writing," for example, came to function less as a means of self-knowledge than an intuitive apperception of historical wrongs too broad for any author to contain, the rectification of which would fall to the collective intelligence of readers. In calling attention to such a distinction, I do not mean to suggest that postcolonial avant-gardes are necessarily innocent of the will to power characteristic of the Western historical avant-garde, or to posit an essential difference between the two. Indeed, the historical traffic between postcolonial and metropolitan avant-gardes runs in both directions, albeit unevenly, giving the lie to any hard and fast division. My point, however, is that the avant-garde took a distinct form in the Egyptian postcolony for reasons having to do with the material constraints on its artistic institutions, the absence of an imperial instinct, and the very different needs of artists and citizens in a society subject to authoritarian—rather than consumerist—impediments to democracy.

That al-Kharrat, one of the most innovative of late twentieth-century Arabic prose artists, should have operated a break from existing literary norms through an idiom of humility and uncertainty—rather than of bombast and self-righteousness, as in the West—reveals two subsidiary insights about the avant-garde as such. The warring tone wasn't essential to the European avant-garde: Its members' posturing as radically able sovereign individuals was a contingent maneuver of compromise with a reigning European aspiration, one that led the imperial system to its apotheosis and had much to do with the Western avant-garde's collapsing fortunes. However, the indistinction between art and politics supposed by al-Kharrat and his peers, along with all of the European avant-gardes, underscores the connection of the concept to a vision of justice, even as its participants' dalliances with programs as varied as fascism and communism reminds us that commitment to justice isn't sufficient to guarantee any particular transformations in the social field.

This lack of guarantee has motivated al-Kharrat to construct a new understanding of the relationship between the historical subject, political change, and the literary text.

Although he has an outlook that I have described as catastrophic, it is important to emphasize that the continuity of these catastrophes as they ramify in historical time saps the present of its exceptional quality. In this sense al-Kharrat's catastrophism differs entirely from the Egyptian state's, which, like its counterparts in the West, claims much of its legitimacy and justifies many of its tactics through appeal to a perpetual state of emergency. And although al-Kharrat's catastrophes temper the sense of unmitigated agency driving the phantasmagoric Western sovereign subject, they do not amount to an obstacle so imposing that they would discourage action entirely. In the novel's incitement to readers to become subjects capable of autonomously discerning a logic in a list of horrors not emplotted by any figure of authority, *Rama and the Dragon* makes allowances for a future not countenanced by prior avant-gardes in which others will become capable of directing social change.

The Postcolonial Avant-Garde between Contemporaneity and Futurity

A major contemporary predicament of the postcolonial is to be denied a proper temporal position. On all sides futurity is coming to be a privilege of the powerful. States rule in the name of no future, employing securitarian logics to usurp the right of peoples to negotiate their own becoming. Neoliberalism mandates an extraordinary fiscal heteronomy that all but eliminates the ability of peoples to determine their future, redistributing risk so as to minimize the exposure of capital-holders while subjecting everyone else to the precarity of day-to-day survival. The fashions and utilitarianism of knowledge production have caused the displacement of postcolonial studies in the humanities, effectively relegating the field to the status of relic. In the name of adjusting to the new circumstances precipitated by the spread of neoliberal reason and terrorist resistance, even the Left advocates a turn away from the cultural, discursive, and antiracist orientation of postcolonial studies toward a model of power that reflects these recent challenges. In order to effect these transformations away from postcolonial approaches, the claim is often made that the colonial past is no longer relevant to the contemporary world. Confronted with logics of rule that are vehemently presentist in their attempts to regulate possible futures, and faced with this disavowal of the ongoing significance of the past, the postcolonial currently has no stable temporal position—past, present, or future—on which to ground its political interventions.

Postcolonial studies should not capitulate to logics it essentially opposes by taking up economistic or globalizing models but should instead embrace its condition and become a poetics of the anachronistic. Jini Kim Watson provides one strong model for this work through her exploration of development from "the wrong side of history," those who inhabit territories whose economies have been described as the "success stories" of modernization yet who have failed to acquiesce to the apolitical behavioral norms on which this success depends.[46] Peter Hitchcock offers signposts for another such site of inquiry, with his account of the variable velocities of transformation in the various sectors of modern life: Attention to the differing trajectories and rates of acceleration between these processes cues us in to the aporias of neoliberalism, the false universality of its promises, and shows us the contradictions that might be exploited for the sake of dejustifying its violence.[47] The postcolonial avant-garde constitutes a third anachronism from which to challenge a temporal regime that is not simply progressivist but which uses the threat of a bad future to justify extraordinary measures in the present. The postcolonial has always been invested in figures out of history, and with the complex temporal dynamics that characterize imperial expansion. Study of the postcolonial avant-garde can contribute to this project by disclosing the political and aesthetic hopes of people who understand themselves to be in some way out of sync with the time of their societies and the globalizing present.

To make the case for the anachronism of the avant-garde requires the displacement of several basic assumptions about time on which Western scholars of the phenomenon have relied. First, one must separate an understanding of anachronism from anteriority. Neither the postcolonial subject nor postcolonial studies is "behind" in the sense Johannes Fabian understood when he accused anthropologists of denying the coevalness of the non-Western subjects they studied; this is true not only because we don't accept the value judgment that this denial entailed but because time does not follow the single linear path that Fabian and modernization theorists assumed.[48] Postcolonial studies concerns itself with the anachronistic not in the sense of what is irretrievably past, or of those who have been left behind by history (understood as that unerring, forward-rushing world spirit), but as the paradoxical temporality of all those who aren't allowed access to dominant temporalities or who find their place within them unlivable—and yet who seek to experiment with "what might come *after* the postcolonial" in terms of forms of art and life.[49] Second, study of Edwar al-Kharrat reveals that the avant-garde doesn't simply reveal the future within the present, as though the avant-garde instantiated the teleological movement of artistic development; rather, the futurity expressed by the avant-garde is one that is alive to those elements of the past that weigh on the present as an encumbrance that can't easily be disposed of. The avant-garde doesn't reveal where art is going but bespeaks the desire for a different future. Finally, a postcolonial avant-garde doesn't follow the "historical avant-garde," nor do its artists experience their desynchronization from the cultural time of their societies as a calibration with Western standard time. The scope of lived times is radically plural, so that artists may find a number of possible temporal referents and rhythms suitable for the desynchronizing gesture that is fundamental to the avant-garde break. To speak of a postcolonial avant-garde—even an Arab or Egyptian avant-garde—is therefore not to focalize a single temporality, but to indicate a range of possible ways in which artists call attention to the uninhabitability of their postcolonial present(s) and call for more just futures.

NOTES

1. Shatz, "Writers or Missionaries?" 35.
2. V. S. Naipaul, *Finding the Center*, quoted in Shatz, "Writers or Missionaries?," 28.
3. Said, *Orientalism*, 92–94.
4. Young, "Postcolonial Remains."
5. Shatz, "Whose Egypt?" 15

6. Shatz, "Writers or Missionaries?" 34.

7. Poggioli, *Avant-Garde*, 21, 39, 57, 81, 138.

8. Bürger, *Avant-Garde*, 26–27.

9. Ibid., 49.

10. Chakrabarty, *Provincializing Europe*.

11. Wilder, *Freedom Time*, 10.

12. See Harney, "Postcolonial Agitations"; Kapur, "Dismantled Norms"; and Winkiel, "Postcolonial Avant-Gardes."

13. Williams, "Politics of the Avant-Garde," 55.

14. Nicholls, *Modernisms*, 78, 157.

15. Ibid., 192; cf. Williams, "Politics of the Avant-Garde," 57.

16. See Ramadan, "Sixties Generation in Egypt."

17. See Meyer, *Experimental Arabic Novel*, 213; and Caiani, *Contemporary Arab Fiction*, 67–95.

18. See Starkey, "Intertextuality," 158–59.

19. Hala Halim argues that al-Kharrat juxtaposes Western texts, particularly representations of Alexandria by writers like E. M. Forster and Lawrence Durrell, so as to "subvert their meaning." See Youssef, "Alexandria Archive," 334–36.

20. Edwar al-Kharrat, *al-Ḥasāsiyya al-Jadīda*, 14. All translations from the Arabic are my own unless otherwise indicated. On Salama Musa, see Edwar al-Kharrat, "Mashriq," 180.

21. Similarly, Elisabeth Kendall notes that the editors of *Gallery 68* did not claim to be the sole agents of the new writing but only "mother figure[s]" encouraging experimentation. See Kendall, *Journalism and the Avant-Garde*, 135.

22. Obank, "Interview with Edwar al-Kharrat," 32.

23. Al-Kharrat, *al-Ḥasāsiyya al-Jadīda*, 21.

24. Al-Kharrat, *al-Kitāba ʿabra al-Nawʿiyya*.

25. Al-Kharrat, "Avant-Garde Narration," 240; this is a translation of an interview: Edwar Al-Kharrat and Sabry Hafez, "Ḥiwār maʿ Edwar Al-Kharrat," 106. Subsequent references to the English version will be indicated by "I," followed by the Arabic version, indicated by "H."

26. I take the concept of "auto-intertextuality" from Anna Zambelli Sessona, cited in Ostle, "From Intertext to Mixed Media," 135.

27. Al-Kharrat, "Cultural Authenticity."

28. Al-Kharrat, I, 236–37/H, 101–2.

29. See Jacquemond, *Conscience of the Nation*, 16.

30. Al-Kharrat, "Foreword."

31. Al-Kharrat, *Rāma wa al-Tinnīn*, 269–70; Al-Kharrat, *Rama and the Dragon*, 251–52, translation modified. Tall al-Zaʿtar is a refugee camp in Lebanon and the site of a massacre of Palestinians by right-wing militias during the Lebanese Civil War. Abu Zaʿbal is an Egyptian town and home to a factory that the Israeli air force bombed in 1970. Caracalla was a Roman emperor (r. 198–217 CE) known for his brutality. Husayn bin al-Mansūr al-Hallāj (d. 922 CE) was a Sufi mystic executed for heresy. Black September refers to the armed conflict that broke out in Jordan between Palestinians and Jordanians in 1970. Black June is the militant Palestinian group formed by the splintering of the Palestine Liberation Organization in 1974. Sing Sing is a maximum-security prison just north of New York City. Tura is the site of a large prison complex south of Cairo. Robben Island, just off the coast of Cape Town in South Africa, is the site of a defunct political prison. Aegean Sea refers to the deserted islands where the Greek military junta of 1967–74 and other modern Greek dictatorships held political prisoners. Dachau and Buchenwald were concentration camps run by Nazi Germany during the Second World War. The Qarmatians were members of a ninth- and tenth-century CE utopian movement that raided convoys of Muslim pilgrims and sacked Mecca and Medina trying to end what they considered superstitions. Hulagu (d. 1265 CE) was a Mongol emperor who conquered much of Western Asia, including

Baghdad. Dayr Yāsīn was a Palestinian town the residents of which were massacred and dispersed by Zionist paramilitaries in the 1948 War. Dinshaway is an Egyptian town where British soldiers fired on protesting residents in 1906, propelling the Egyptian nationalist movement. The Hyksos were a group of Western Asian origin that conquered parts of Egypt in the second millennium BCE. Saint Michael defeated Satan during the war in heaven in the Book of Revelation, and is revered in Coptic Christianity.

32. Derrida, *Specters of Marx*, 100–105.

33. Said, "Bases for Coexistence," 207–8.

34. Cf. Al-Kharrat, *Stones of Bobello*, 47, 106–7, 110, 120.

35. See Sadia Abbas, this volume.

36. See, for example, Hartog, *Regimes of Historicity*.

37. Jameson, *Postmodernism*, xii, 19.

38. Al-Kharrat, *Rāma wa al-Tinnīn*, 255; Al-Kharrat, *Rama and the Dragon*, 237.

39. Koselleck, *Futures Past*, 192–204.

40. Koselleck notes that the Western voluntaristic notion of the "disposability" or "make-ability" (*Machbarkeit*) of history "obscures the potential for the surplus and surprise character of all history," and was more of an "ideological amplifier" among activists than an actual description of the human relation to historical development. See ibid., 199.

41. Al-Kharrat, "Cultural Authenticity," 24.

42. Cf. Gary Wilder's defense of the radical humanism of Frantz Fanon, W. E. B. Du Bois, and other Black Atlantic intellectuals in this volume.

43. Al-Kharrat, "Kull minnā Multazim," 73.

44. Ibid., 92, 96.

45. See Hala Halim, "Scope for Comparatism."

46. See Jini Kim Watson, this volume.

47. See Peter Hitchcock, this volume.

48. See Helgesson, "Radicalizing Temporal Difference."

49. See Anthony Alessandrini, this volume.

BIBLIOGRAPHY

Bürger, Peter. *Theory of the Avant-Garde.* Translated by Michael Shaw. Minneapolis: University of Minnesota Press, 1984.

Caiani, Fabio. *Contemporary Arab Fiction: Innovation from Rama to Yalu.* London: Routledge, 2007.

Chakrabarty, Dipesh. *Provincializing Europe: Postcolonial Thought and Historical Difference.* Princeton: Princeton University Press, 2000.

Deheuvels, Luc, Barbara Michalak-Pikulska, and Paul Starkey, eds. *Intertextuality in Modern Arabic Literature since 1967.* Manchester: Manchester University Press, 2009.

Derrida, Jacques. *Specters of Marx: The State of the Debt, the Work of Mourning, and the New International.* Translated by Peggy Kamuf. New York: Routledge, 2006.

Fabian, Johannes. *Time and the Other: How Anthropology Makes Its Object.* New York: Columbia University Press, 2002.

Halim, Hala. "Scope for Comparatism: Internationalist and Surrealist Resonances in Idwār al-Kharrāṭ's Resistant Literary Modernity." In *Arabic Humanities, Islamic Thought: Essays in Honor of Everett K. Rowson*, edited by Joseph E. Lowry and Shawkat M. Toorawa, 425–68. Leiden: Brill, 2017.

Harney, Elizabeth. "Postcolonial Agitations: Avant-Gardism in Dakar and London." *New Literary History* 41, no. 4 (2010): 731–51.

Hartog, François. *Regimes of Historicity: Presentism and Experiences of Time.* Translated by Saskia Brown. New York: Columbia University Press, 2015.

Helgesson, Stefan. "Radicalizing Temporal Difference: Anthropology, Postcolonial Theory, and Literary Time." *History and Theory* 53 (December 2014): 545–62.

Jacquemond, Richard. *Conscience of the Nation: Writers, State, and Society in Modern Egypt.* Translated by David Tresilian. Cairo: American University in Cairo Press, 2008.

Jameson, Fredric. *Postmodernism, or The Cultural Logic of Late Capitalism.* Durham, N.C.: Duke University Press, 1991.

Kapur, Geeta. "Dismantled Norms: Apropos an Indian/Asian Avantgarde." In *When Was Modernism: Essays on Contemporary Cultural Practice in India,* 365–414. New Delhi: Tulika Books, 2000.

Kendall, Elisabeth. *Literature, Journalism and the Avant-Garde: Intersection in Egypt.* London: Routledge, 2006.

Al-Kharrat, Edwar. "Cultural Authenticity and National Identity." *Diogenes* 52, no. 2 (2005): 21–24.

———. "Foreword: Random Variations on an Autobiographical Theme." In *Writing the Self: Autobiographical Writing in Modern Arabic Literature,* edited by Robin Ostle, Ed de Moor and Stefan Wild, 9–17. London: Saqi Books, 1998.

———. *Al-Ḥasāsiyya al-Jadīda: Maqālāt fī al-Ẓāhira al-Qiṣaṣiyya.* Beirut: Dār al-Ādāb, 1993.

———. *Al-Kitāba ʿabra al-Nawʿiyya: Maqālāt fī Ẓāhira "al-Qiṣṣa - al-Qaṣīda" wa Nuṣūṣ Mukhtāra.* Cairo: Dār Sharqīyyāt, 1994.

———. "Kull minnā Multazim," in *Taḥawullat Mafhūm al-Iltizām fī al-Adab al-ʿArabī al-Ḥadīth,* edited by Muhammad Barrada, 70–99. Damascus: Dār al-Fikr, 2003.

———. "The Mashriq." In *Modern Literature in the Near and Middle East, 1850–1970,* edited by Robin Ostle, 180–92. London: Routledge, 1991.

———. *Rama and the Dragon.* Translated by Ferial Ghazoul and John Verlenden. Cairo: American University in Cairo Press, 2002.

———. *Rāma wa al-Tinnīn.* 1980. Cairo: Dār wa Matābiʿ al-Mustaqbal bi-l-Fajāla wa al-Iskandariyya, 1993.

———. "The Relative and the Absolute in Avant-Garde Narration." In *The View from Within: Writers and Critics on Contemporary Arabic Literature,* edited by Ferial J. Ghazoul and Barbara Harlow, translated by Maggie Awadalla, 228–45. Cairo: American University in Cairo Press, 1994.

———. *Stones of Bobello.* Translated by Paul Starkey. London: Saqi, 2005.

Al-Kharrat, Edwar, and Sabry Hafez. "Ḥiwār maʿ Edwar Al-Kharrat: Yawm 3 Yanāyir 1982." *Alif: Journal of Comparative Poetics* 2 (Spring 1982): 90–113.

Koselleck, Reinhart. *Futures Past: On the Semantics of Historical Time.* Translated by Keith Tribe. New York: Columbia University Press, 2004.

Meyer, Stefan G. *The Experimental Arabic Novel: Postcolonial Literary Modernism in the Levant.* Albany: State University of New York Press, 2001.

Nicholls, Peter. *Modernisms: A Literary Guide.* 2nd ed. New York: Palgrave Macmillan, 2009.

Obank, Margaret. "Interview with Edwar al-Kharrat." *Banipal,* no. 6 (1999): 31–33.

Ostle, Robin C. "From Intertext to Mixed Media: The Case of Edwār al-Kharrāt." In *Modern Arabic Literature,* edited by Deheuvels, Michalak-Pikulska, and Starkey, 133–48.

Poggioli, Renato. *The Theory of the Avant-Garde.* Translated by Gerald Fitzgerald. Cambridge, Mass.: Harvard University Press, 1968.

Ramadan, Yasmine. "The Emergence of the Sixties Generation in Egypt and the Anxiety over Categorization." *Journal of Arabic Literature* 43, no. 2–3 (2012): 409–30.

Said, Edward W. "Bases for Coexistence." In *The End of the Peace Process: Oslo and After,* 205–10. London: Granta Books, 2000.

———. *Orientalism.* New York: Vintage, 1994.

Shatz, Adam. "Whose Egypt?" *London Review of Books* 34, no. 1 (2012): 15–17.

————. "Writers or Missionaries?" *Nation*. July 15, 2014. 27–35.

Starkey, Paul. "Intertextuality and the Arabic Literary Tradition in Edwār al-Kharrāt's *Stones of Bobello*." In *Modern Arabic Literature*, edited by Deheuvels, Michalak-Pikulska, and Starkey, 149–159.

Wilder, Gary. *Freedom Time: Negritude, Decolonization, and the Future of the World*. Durham, NC: Duke University Press, 2015.

Williams, Raymond. "The Politics of the Avant-Garde." In *The Politics of Modernism: Against the New Conformists*, 49–63. London: Verso, 1989.

Winkiel, Laura. "Postcolonial Avant-Gardes and the World System of Modernity/Coloniality." *Avant-Garde Critical Studies* 30 (2014): 97–116.

Young, Robert J. C. "Postcolonial Remains." *New Literary History* 43, no. 1 (2012): 19–42.

Youssef, Hala Youssef Halim [Hala Halim]. "The Alexandria Archive: An Archaeology of Alexandrian Cosmopolitanism." PhD diss., University of California at Los Angeles, 2004.

SEVEN

Neither Greek nor Indian: Space, Nation, and History in *River of Fire* and *The Mermaid Madonna*

Sadia Abbas

Voices out of the stone out of sleep
deeper here where the world darkens,
memory of toil rooted in the rhythm
beaten upon the earth by feet
forgotten.

—GEORGE SEFERIS, "Mycenae"

Those, who scoff at the idea of transfer of population, will do well to study the history of the minority problem, as it arose between Turkey, Greece, and Bulgaria. If they do, they will find these countries found that the only way of solving the minorities problem lay in exchange of population. The task undertaken by the three countries was by no means a minor operation. It involved the transfer of some 20 million people from one habitat to another. But undaunted, the three shouldered the task and carried it to a successful end because they felt the considerations of communal peace must outweigh every consideration. That the transfer of minorities is the only lasting remedy for communal peace is beyond doubt.

—B. R. AMBEDKAR, *Pakistan, or The Partition of India*

Continental Drift

Invoking the sectarian divide between Catholics and Protestants as an explanation for the treatment meted out to Greece by the Eurozone at the Summit of July 13, 2015, the French economy minister at the time, former Rothschild banker, and now president, Emmanuel Macron, is reported to have said: "The eurozone is going through a war of religion with a northern Europe that's Calvinist and that doesn't want to forgive the sinners, and a Catholic Europe in the south that wants to turn the page."[1] Striking though such a statement is, in its admission of a thriving sectarianism in the heart of secular Europe and in its apparent confirmation of T. S. Eliot's bleak speculation that no civil war ever ends, it is perhaps more significant for the way it declares the invisibility of Greece.[2] In so doing, it paradoxically reveals the challenge that Greece (and the many Hellenisms—Pan, Phil, Neo—with which it is associated) poses to the conceptual parameters of Europe and the way in which the resultant conceptual instability is a threat to the physical borders of the continent, soliciting yet again the question: "What precisely is Europe?"[3]

If Christian divisions are the emblems of sociocultural and political difference here, then this remark says little about Greece, for it simply forgets Orthodox Christianity, let alone such niceties as divisions between (say) the Exarchate and the Patriarchate. That Orthodox Christianity is rarely visible in Europe, despite its indubitable presence in many of the nations on the continent, including ones that belong in the European Union, is not surprising, but the reasons for it are significant and perhaps particularly so for postcolonial studies: Greek orthodoxy has one of its historical seats in Constantinople and is thus outside the borders of Europe (if one, a priori, sets aside the continental ambiguity of Constantinople/Istanbul); that it is, indeed, also "Eastern" in name does not help either. At the same time, the question of Orthodox Christianity's location makes visible the proximity of Islam.[4] The constitutive presence of Islam in the making of Europe, that is, *as* constitutive, by way of the Ottoman presence in Greece or (say) Moorish Spain, or the Arab presence in Southern Italy, or the Muslim populations of the Balkans . . . cannot be recognized within what is *called* "Europe."[5]

Yet it is precisely the imbrication of Asia and Europe and North Africa that the Urdu novelist Qurratulain Hyder and the Greek writer Stratis Myrivilis, whom I discuss here, make visible. As both produce critiques of nationalism and identitarianism, they present visions and conceptions of their respective countries that fundamentally undo the idea of Europe in which Europe is always defined in (sometimes *as*) opposition to Asia, Africa, Islam, et al., and which is predicated on the "unmixing" of peoples that has forged so many modern nations, including India, Pakistan, Greece, and Turkey. "Unmixing" is, of course, the dreadful term Lord Curzon is supposed to have used at the Conference of Lausanne. The thinking behind the idea was probably related to the need to manage the Indian colonial population and had already prompted the soon revoked Partition of Bengal.[6]

In Hyder's *River of Fire* (1998), her own English "transcreation" of her Urdu novel, *Ag ka Darya* (1959), and Myrivilis's *The Mermaid Madonna (I Panagia i Gorgona)* (1949), ekphrasis and narrative plays and excurses on the question of origin and time are used to challenge nation and "History," that is, history conceived teleologically and *as* European destiny.[7] Both authors trouble a teleological conception of time and space, where the history of a space is always already leading to a particular point in which all loss, ruin, and atrocity is redeemed in the name of whatever is designated the telos.[8] It is, of course, not news to say that the idea of Europe is reliant on the Hegelian telos and that that teleological impulse is also very much part of the way the nation-state partakes of the narrativization of history. In such narrativization, the particularities of any given space are always secondary and subject to the teleological drive.[9] *Chronos*, *topos*, and *demos* rarely align in accordance with this drive.[10]

One could say, then, that two kinds of teleological time-space are brought into collision in the work of these authors: the nation and the Germanic culmination of history in *The Philosophy of History* that comes to stand in for Europe *as* the end of history. For as world spirit and history travel West and North, in a movement that Samuel Pressner has called a colonial travel narrative, they are firmly located in northwestern Europe.[11] In this movement, even the European South has to be left behind, and as Roberto Dainotto argues, having posited Africa as nature and Asia as the "the prehistorical unfreedom of despotism," the South was produced as "the necessary antithesis that Hegel's Germanic north had to imagine in order to imagine itself as progress and modernity—in order, namely, to be Europe . . . [and] had to occupy the place of negativity (the 'immaturity' of history)."[12] A recognition of the epistemic and physical violence of this spatialization of history, indeed of the relation between the epistemic and the physical, is writ large in the novels I discuss here.

Both authors use visual descriptions of aesthetic objects to imagine and even spatialize time. They simultaneously perform a tension between the illusion of the legibility and accessibility of the past and the necessary opacity of that past, bringing to the fore the epistemic untenability of the demand for continuity in any teleological attempt at historical and spatial organization. I focus on a statue—the *Sudarshan Yakshini*, or Tree-spirit with a branch—in *The River of Fire* and the eponymous painting in *The Mermaid Madonna*. In the representation of each of these, the authors exploit the apparent self-evidence of images in order to suggest the very opposite of the transparency implied by the illusion of self-evidence. At stake in the representation of this tension, indeed in what one might read as the *thematization* of a fundamental tension between words and pictures in a history of Western aesthetics that encompasses Plato, Lessing,[13] and Da Vinci, is the distance between a national narration of history and the pressure that the history of precisely that space, construed in non- (or even differently) teleological terms, can exert on national narratives. The act of spatialization associated with ekphrasis, where the ambition of visualization is to instantiate and even concretize in space that which is assumed to be flattened and homogenized by the abstraction of language, brings the variant histories of the space of the nation and the narrow and deracinated historical construal of that space in tension. As we shall see, the statue persists over time, a concrete presence through millennia; the painting attempts to visualize time in the form of the fusion of divinities, providing a material representation of time, simultaneously manifesting, revealing, and attempting to overcome the abstraction that can govern life.

My placing together of Myrivilis and Hyder is not casually analogical. Although both share the milieu of global modernism, it is their exploration (Myrivilis) or critical deployment (Hyder) of the idea of Greece and its centrality to the projects of nationalism, and of the relation of those projects with the fiction of a Europe that is somehow *separable* from Asia and Africa, that interests me here.[14] This is precisely because they engage with one of the central problematics of twentieth-century modernity—the unmixing of populations, which itself draws upon the stabilizing structures of colonial taxonomies of race, ethnicity, and religion.

As the epigraph from B. R. Ambedkar suggests, each attempt at such unmixing draws on, and is connected to, previous ones. At the same time, Ambedkar's troubled assertion that the population transfer formalized in the Lausanne Convention shows that "the transfer of minorities is the only lasting remedy for communal peace is beyond doubt" reveals the terrible centrality of more or less benign notions of ethnic cleansing to the making of twentieth-century nations and to the twentieth-century imagination. Moreover, Ambedkar's invocation of the Bulgarian, Greek, and Ottoman-Turkish case as a precedent that might help justify the two-nation theory espoused by Muhammad Ali Jinnah invites a harder critical confrontation with the complex relation between postcolonial emergence and imperial dissolution. Assuming that we map this relation on to the emergence of Pakistan and the dissolution of the Ottoman empire, we may then be able to ask more difficult questions, given the Indian Muslim identification with the Turkish case and the concern of the British colonial powers for the reaction of their Indian and Near Eastern Muslim subjects: What kind of epistemic shift would we require in postcolonial studies in order to see decolonization in a European country (Greece)?[15] Within the epistemic order that constitutes Europe and the postcolonial nation in fatal embrace and the discursive economy of postcolonial studies, can a European country be postcolonial? What, then, of the East/West binarism, sometimes disavowed but nonetheless assumed, in much current thinking?

In their practice, both Hyder and Myrivilis pressure the alignment of *chronos* and *topos* and the additional tension in which that attempted alignment sits with the *demos*, which must be purified, separated, "unmixed," if bringing such a vision of space in line with the disparate populations that inhabit it is to be achieved with narrative consistency and tidiness. Moreover, as we shall see, for Hyder the chronotope of the nation is fundamentally linked to the epistemological structures of British colonialism.

Reading Hyder and Myrivilis, as they engage with nations and nationalisms, calls forth an attendant exposure of the chronotope of Europe, enabling a meditation on the paradoxes of European time-space and thus on the way in which "Europe"—a cipher for another cipher "the West"—and the idea of the nation interact violently with actually and inconveniently existing space and its once and future inhabitants. At the same time, they formally perform the very connectivity the chronotope of Europe that Europe *as* chronotope erases and appears to prohibit.

Space in Another Time

Discussing debates over the provenance of certain architectural and sculptural motifs in ancient India, the art historian Partha Mitter writes, "The honeysuckle and acanthus motif which at first sight seemed adapted from Western classicism was no more Greek than Indian. It belonged to the ancient West Asian artistic pool that nourished both Greece and India."[16] The stakes of that phrase "no more Greek than Indian" within the context of colonial and postcolonial discourse and literature and in the context of arguments about European identity are high, and these concerns are picked up by Hyder in *River of Fire*, her own very liberal translation from and rewriting of her Urdu novel *Ag ka Darya*—a book that is often referred to as the greatest Urdu novel of the twentieth century. Hyder's dubbing this her "transcreation" gestures to the creativity of any translation while marking the particular license she takes with the Urdu text, which she rewrites substantially. The novel(s) span(s) several millennia, structured around stories set in different historical periods: the first set in the period of the expansion of the Mauryan empire in the fourth century BCE and the last around 1947, dramatizing the period that led to Indian Independence and tracing the social unraveling that followed as a result of Partition. Between these are stories placed in the historical periods of the end of the Lodi dynasty and the beginning of the Mughal Empire, followed by the late-eighteenth-century moment of the East India Company leading into the consolidation of the British Empire by the 1870s.

Early in *River of Fire*, Hyder includes an episode that sets up a major theme in this quietly powerful text about the terrible violence, social ruptures, and historical erasures unleashed by Partition. A Hindu prince, who has converted to Buddhism, momentarily passes as a Greek traveler who has a conversation with a Hindu named Gautam, which is, of course, also the name of the Buddha:

> The stranger smiled impishly. "Yes, I am Harius Sancarius at your service." He bowed from the waist in an outlandish manner. Gautam was mystified then he said, "Oh, a Yavana!" He had never seen a mleccha (a dirty foreigner) before.
>
> "I hail from Ionia and I am in shipping," the Greek informed him breezily. Gautam looked blank feeling like a country bumpkin.[17]

The Prince goes on to say:

> "I have a little Cargo boat I brought from the Gulf to the River Indus. There I left it in charge of my Phoenician crew and decided to explore the land mass to the east. So I bought a horse from a Scythian and . . . may I sit down? First went up to Taxila . . ."[18]

This goes on with the names of peoples and places proliferating. When discovered to be not Greek, the Prince tells the story of his conversion and what he learned in his "brick-like cell" in Taxila, where he had been sent for his education by his father. There, he recounts, he learned of theories of power that led him to confront a moral quandary that anticipates the Buddhist King Ashoka's turning from imperial warmongering to the advocacy of peace: "I faced a dilemma. If I remained in the world of power hungry kings and warlords and politicians, I'd have to kill human beings, whereas now I don't even want to kill animals."[19] He relates that in his subsequent travels he sat around bonfires, heard caravan leaders recount the epics of what he calls Turanian heroes, like Sohrab and Rustom, and heard of the centuries-long Greco-Persian wars and the conquests of Irani emperors. He goes on to say that he encountered people from Soghdia, Cappadocia, and Thessaly.[20]

The invocation of Taxila and the reference to Gandhara locate the novel's world in immediate relation to one of the most important archaeological sites in present-day Pakistan and marks *River of Fire* as a novelistically giddy attempt to undo the violently narrow identity of the Pakistani nation and the Muslimness that is taken to necessitate it. It is, perhaps, significant that Taxila and Gandhara are now used, by critics of Muslim nationalism, to suggest histories that are erased by the nation in the service of distinguishing itself from India.[21] At the same time, Hyder appears to be offering a critique of the rise of Hindu nationalism in the decades that have intervened since the publication of the Urdu text, for Hari Shankar does not appear as a Greek traveler in the Urdu version.

In the Urdu text, Hari Shankar appears wearing the saffron robes of the Buddhist monk, and the color is referred to often. The arbitrariness and irrelevance of origin, so central to Hyder's critique of nationalism and Partition, are invoked using different geographical coordinates:

> "We all have to be born somewhere or other. I could have been born in Memphis and you could have been born in Yawadeep [yavadwipa-ancient Java]," Hari Shankar said with a smile.
>
> "You are from this very place and now you are wondering around as a Buddhist holy man, acting like a stranger."
>
> "We are all eternally strangers to each other."[22]

There is no Greek traveler at this moment, no Ionian garb. The spatial reach is focused on East Asia and North Africa. In her English rewriting of those coordinates and in her extension of the spatial reach Westward, Hyder takes on directly the question of conquest, foreignness, and the historical formation of culture.

It seems that as Hindu nationalism grew in India, saffron, so associated with Hindutva, was less attractive to Hyder. Moreover, Hindutva's claiming of Buddhism as an indigenous religion that could be fit into Hindu nationalist conceptions of indigeneity appears to have made Hyder reach for the Hellenic association in order to perform in intensified manner the very arbitrariness of origin she had suggested in the Urdu text, but which now needed to more explicitly engage with the question of the Muslim presence in India.[23] The changes Hyder makes in the rewriting of the initial encounter between Gautam and Hari Shankar are very much in line with the changes Laurel Steele remarks when she points to Hyder's insertion into the English version of a scene about Faiz Ahmed Faiz's "Freedom's Dawn—August 1947," where the losses and traumatic pain and disappointment of Partition are marked as losses of culture and language—one person has to have Faiz translated from the Urdu.[24]

Perhaps most significant in the English exchange quoted above, is the use of the term "Yavana" to refer to the prince who is passing as Greek. According to Romila Thapar, "Muslim" does not occur in Indian records of early contact with the new arrivals: "The term used was either Turuska, referring to the Turks, or geographical, Yavana, or cultural, mleccha. Yavana, a back formation from *yona*, had been used since the first millennium B.C. for Greeks and others coming from West Asia."[25] Derived from "Ionian," the term "Yavana" referred to the Hellenistic dynasties that were in control of large swathes of Afghanistan and northwestern India in the second century BCE.[26]

That a word that was used to refer to the Greeks of Asia Minor could later be applied to the Muslims is perhaps most significant for Hyder in this episode. Greek could function thus as a precursor of Muslim (as West Asian, Turkic, etc.—speaking also to the Hellenic presence in Asia minor), while elliptically enabling an address to elements of foreignness and conquest in the formation of culture and history. The word "Yavana" brings Muslims into this meditation on the impossibility of historical purity and the problem of Indian authenticity right at the inception of the novel.

I would speculate, moreover, that in the intervening years, Hyder had read the poems of Cavafy, whose geographical reach covers the same expanse as Hyder's in her transcreation and for whom places like Bactria, Syria, and Egypt are simply part of a pan-Hellenic, but not nationalist, historical sweep. The following lines from "Orophernes" seem a particularly likely candidate in this regard, containing as they do an ironic reflection on the relation between "heart" and garb, identity and space:

> As a child they cast him out of Cappadocia,
> out of the great paternal palace,
> and they sent him away to grow up
> in Ionia, to be forgotten among strangers.
>
> O these rapturous Ionian nights
> when dauntless, and entirely *a la grecque*
> he came to know the fullness of pleasure.
> In his heart, always an Asiatic:
> but in his manners and in his speech Greek,
> adorned in turquoise, in Greek dress.[27]

It is significant, given my suggestion that Hyder might have read the poem and been playing with it in her rewriting of this section, that the poem's spatial referents include Cappadocia, Ionia, and Syria and that we read a little further down that Orophernes recalled he was "himself almost a Seleucid." For the Seleucid Empire stretched from Thrace to the borders of India and went to war with the Mauryans—Chandragupta Maurya (known as Sandrocottus in Greek accounts) is said to have married Seleucus's daughter Helen.

To understand the relation between knowledge, origin, space, and historical loss in Hyder's writing, it is important to turn to a moment in the *River of Fire* where, having skipped millennia, we are in the British colonial period. Here, unlike the swirling space of India and West Asia circa 300 BCE, we are in a rigidly taxonomized world, and a character called Cyril Ashley stands and shouts at a ferryman, "Hello! Abdul. Listen," and the narrator goes on to say: "All lower grade Mussalmans were called Abdul by the firangis (foreigners). This was one of their arrogant habits after they became victorious."[28] So ingrained does this colonial structure of naming and typing—where every Muslim and Christian and Hindu is the same as every other of his perceived kind—become that a hundred years later in an upper-class household:

> Gulfishan's cook was called Hussaini—most cooks were called that. Washermen were known as Nathu; all bearers answered to the name of Abdul. Syces were usually Gunga Din. Night club violinists were known as Tony, fathers had such names as Syed Taqi Reza Bahadur or Aftab Chand Raizada.

We have already learned that

> there were many houses like Gulfishan down the road. The same kind of exceedingly refined people lived in them. They all had motor cars and their daughters went to convent schools and I.T. college and their sons studied for the competitive examinations of the Imperial Covenanted Services.[29]

Hyder's multimillennial span is thus a challenge both to colonial ethnoracial construc-
tions and hierarchies and to the nationalist and identitarian bloodletting of Partition that
are themselves predicated on those stabilized taxonomic structures. Such typologies are
an aspect of colonial discourses concerned with positing a Greek origin for motifs found
in ancient Indian architecture and sculpture, very much in line with a Hegelian notion of
Greece as a source of subjective art and an essential origin for the Germano-European
culmination of history. This approach to history is performed quite directly in the novel
in the form of an anonymous "Conscientious" Englishman's letter to the *Calcutta Gazette*, in which Salamis in 470 BCE, Plassey, 1757, the Reformation, Roman ruins, and
cathedrals that replaced Roman temples get pressed into an inexorable, if slightly comic,
teleology, in the service of asserting the divine providence upholding English colonialism
as destiny:

> I do believe that the superiority of Europe over the Asiatics was decided for all time to
> come when Persia was defeated finally in the long drawn-out war against the Greeks in
> 470 B.C. at Salamis. The victory of Plassey in 1757 is only a recent example. . . . What
> India also needs is a Reformation of the kind we had in Europe in the 16th century. But
> given the complexities and very ancient roots of their superstitions, one cannot visualize
> it happening here. All of the Roman Empire became Christian. All over Europe Roman
> temples were pulled down and cathedrals built over their ruins.[30]

The acanthus and honeysuckle motif with reference to which I began this section is,
thus, part of the colonial, nationalist, and now *antinationalist* debates in the subcontinent
regarding the historical significance of Gandhara, Taxila, and the pillars that are said to
bear Ashokan edicts, carrying as they do a complex Buddhist history and suggestions of
an Indo-Greek relation. These debates are themselves produced out of a structure of epistemic colonial rigidity composed of simplified (and simplistic) taxonomies and an equally
simplified providentialism. In the episode of the Greek traveler, the novel's double move
is to interrogate the Greekness of European teleology and press a different temporal-spatial
notion of Greekness into service against religious nationalism. At stake are the way in
which colonially stabilized conceptions of what constitutes a Hindu or a Muslim led to
the Partition of the subcontinent, and the claims of religious identitarianism upon the
identities of both Pakistan and India. Unsurprisingly, then, if Nehru was a proponent of
Ashoka in the service of Indian secularism, Hindutva is not keen on him.[31]

That Gautam, the Hindu, has the same name as the Buddha suggests both a fluidity of
identity and a commonality of origin for Hindus and Buddhists and the interchangeabil-
ity of names/epithets for Bactrians, Indo-Greeks, and Muslims. The exchange between
Hari Shankar and Gautam thus carries both critique and possibility. For the suggestion is
that the religious and national divisions of the postcolonial period were not inevitable. Yet
in the shift from the Urdu novel to the English text, Hyder increases the emphasis on the
arbitrariness of origin, presented as assertion and extended philosophical debate in *Ag ka
Darya* but made more concrete both in Hari Shankar's dress and in the framing of the
narrative in *River of Fire*, as the "Bactrian-Greece Buddha-heads of Gandhara" are mentioned at the end.[32]

If Mitter is particularly interested in colonial and postcolonial debates regarding Asho-kan pillars and in the colonial investment in their originary Greekness and thus in their source lying in the West, Hyder, too, seems aware of these art historical debates and ap-pears to engage them in a section on ruins later in the novel, where we have been trans-ported a few thousand years into the future of the same space (around 1500 CE). In an episode that shows her interest in historical ruination and the loss of meaning over time, she mentions Ashoka and the unintelligibility of Indian antiquity to later inhabitants (including Muslim invaders) of India:

> A full moon sailed over the extensive ruins. All was eerily quiet. Moonbeams lit up the
> faint decorative designs on the floor of a roofless house. A trident, a lotus, a wheel, "a
> pillar of fire." . . . What did those remote people mean by such symbols, Kamal wondered,
> yawning and lay himself down upon an elephant head made of stone.[33]

As she engages quite explicitly in the interpretation of the sculptural and architectural motifs and their origin, she intervenes in and against the production of colonial knowl-edge. This is particularly obvious in her treatment of the statue Gautam sculpts, to a discussion of which I shall turn in the next section.

The swirling space of the episode of the Greek traveler, like the spatial referents of Cavafy's poems, suggests networks and circulations of knowledge that undermine mod-ern borders, both national (India and Pakistan) and continental (Europe and Asia), and the narratives and taxonomies that underpin them. These networks have yet to find an adequate engagement in postcolonial studies.

Moreover, the postcolonial engagement with the problem of European colonial power and its discursive structures can lead to casual ratification of Europe as idea. One might think here of Edward Said's using Aeschylus as a precursor of Orientalism because of his manifestation of a "European imagination" in *The Persians*.[34] Such an example accepts the European production of history (in this case as canon), which reads repetition as continu-ity and continuity as destiny, forgets the historical circumstances of power at the time, and concedes the "conscientious" Englishman's historical conscription of Greece—simply providing a dark mirror to European teleology. In such moments, postcolonial studies risks hypostatizing the fiction of Europe even as it seems to critique it.[35]

The Muteness of Statues

River of Fire is full of recurrences—of rivers, seekers, and travelers (wandering mendi-cants, Sufis, yogis, bhikshus), and artistic production—which repeatedly push through the layers of time, giving the novel's different periods and overall structure the quality of ar-chaeological strata and the recurrences those of archaeological shards. As an attempt to encompass the range would lead to discursive chaos, I focus here on one example. One of the most intriguing subplots (expanded from the Urdu version) in *River of Fire* is of a statue that the novel follows from creation in ancient India to curation in the post-Partition subcontinent. We see Gautam as he sculpts it, and it then keeps turning up in the novel's different eras, an emblem of ruination and of the illegibility of one historical moment to another.

Hyder uses the statue's muteness to dramatize historical loss. In the museum we see the way in which the story, known to the reader of the novel, is lost to the characters who view it in the museum: "Excavated recently from the ruins of Shravasti," the caption read, "circa 4th century B.C." Hyder goes on to present a description of the sculpture filtered through the narrative perspective of the twentieth-century viewer:

> The lady stood cross-legged. She had a puffy face, arched eyebrows and pointed chin. With one arm she had bent the bough of a kadamba tree over her elaborately coiffed head. She looked strong and earthy. She was bare-breasted and wore heavy ornaments. "The ancients liked rotund women, and they didn't wear saris," Mons. Raoul commented with glee.[36]

An Orientalist scholar, Dr. Hans Krammer, writing a book on Gupta sculpture, can only turn this encounter into a list of clichés on the stasis of Indian time and regarding "the Indian mind":

> "Wish we knew the name of the sculptor who created this girl under the kadamba tree. But in India history has no meaning. Events are not important. Reality, myth and tradition all get mixed up. Historical time does not exist. The moment is eternal, man remains nameless. His creations get lost in this ocean of eternity. No crisis affects the Indian mind because crisis is also part of time and time has no meaning," Dr. Krammer intoned. "That is why the artists of the East hardly ever bothered to inscribe their names."[37]

The description of the figure's "puffy face," Mons. Raoul's prurient glee at its naked roundness, and Dr. Krammer's platitudes about Indian time, so at odds with the sophisticated way the same sculpture and Indian philosophy and creativity have been presented at the beginning of the novel, figure history as a kind of forgetting, violent in its casual imperviousness. The revelation of the violence of history, which can so dismiss a complex human narrative, militates against the triumph inherent in any teleological account. We are confronted with the loss in the transformation of past forms and the leaching from them of their own affect and meaning, confronted instead with the *indifference* of history. In this subplot, the quietness of the loss is less dramatic than the catastrophic repetition of historical ruin, which one can also find in the novel and which critics have seen as aligned with Indian conceptions of reincarnation and committed to a more indigenous conception of time and form.[38]

It is perhaps worth remarking that Hyder's literary practice seems to incorporate an awareness that the inevitable repetition of historical ruin can sometimes seem as only the other side of a redemptive vision of history, leading in her work to some tension and doubleness. As a result, the statue's survival over time is both testament to the inevitability of historical loss—that is, of the loss of human meaning to time and of the mortality of humans and their stories—and to the *persistence* of some human stories, which cut across time. The execution of the subplot focuses attention on the *process* of that loss and at the same time performs the entirely paradoxical persistence of the story. In this, it is an instance of what Kumkum Sangari describes when she suggests that theories of decline and fall such as T. S. Eliot's vision of a once monumental Europe as reduced merely to debris which had "to be spatially reassembled" or Spengler's view of "cyclic decline" "are noted and startlingly inverted in the novel in which becoming modern is both old and new, heartbreaking but still promising."[39] Moreover, the story of the statue functions archaeologically to produce an understanding of the epistemic transformations of time, which counter the nation-state's eradication of past histories. Of these histories, the statue is (illegible) evidence, hinting at alternative futures. In other words, its illegibility—which is available to the reader as the multiplicity of now inaccessible ways it has been legible in the novel—inscribes both loss and possibility.

At the same time, Hyder's use of ekphrasis is at odds with the tendency of Western aesthetics to set up a competition between words and pictures. She thematizes, instead, that tension, making words complicit in the violence of history. The muteness of the statue becomes thus a testament to that violence, reinforcing the recurrent skepticism about language and its capacity to betray, present throughout the novel, which in the ending of the English transcreation, substantially altered from the much more humanistic one in Urdu, culminates with the sentence, "The silence became absolute":

> The yatris' wooden sandals produced an awesome, rhythmic sound on the cobbled path. Slowly the clip-clop, clip-clop receded in the depth of the primeval jungle. The silence became absolute.[40]

Contrast this with the ending of *Ag ka Darya*, which I render here in translation as literally as I can, in which Gautam, while hearing religious chants, imagines himself as

> The world's eternal man, tired, joyful, hopeful, the human who is in God
>   and who is himself God. He smiled, came down and opened his eyes.
> May the wakefulness of those waking be blessed.
> Blessings on the promulgation of the law.
> Blessings on peace in the land.
> Celebration of the dominion of the people
> to whom peace is available.
> Shakyamuni had said . . .
>   He climbed off the parapet, took a long, deep breath and walked slowly toward town.[41]

Sangari has suggested that Hyder's understanding that "all things pass" may have been a way to gain a certain "poise and distance" from the bloodletting of Partition, indeed to reclaim the subcontinent from the violence by producing a "consoling civilizational *longue durée*." Such a position could, according to Sangari, both "mourn a loss and demand a future."[42] Although I think "consoling" seems not quite precise about Hyder's practice and her emphasis on the presence of betrayal in every aspect of being in the Urdu text as well, it does seem that in *River of Fire* the humanistic and social hope present in the ending of the Urdu text (he walks *toward* human habitation) was no longer available. So, in the

English ending all that appears to be left is the loss that is already beyond mourning and recedes into "absolute silence."

The statue's silence and opacity are an aspect of this loss, but within the narrative the statue is also a reminder of a different history. Recent discussions of ekphrasis, such as W. J. T. Mitchell's in *Picture Theory*, have sought to align the act of ekphrasis with the muting of the subaltern. In this alignment the writer is to the object described as the colonizing subject is to the subaltern. However, Hyder's use of ekphrasis stands in significant contrast to the alignment of the muteness of aesthetic object with the subaltern in Mitchell's work. For Mitchell, the act of ekphrasis presents the silencing of the subaltern because words are made to impose themselves upon the object in the very act of ekphrasis. But Mitchell disturbingly aligns object with person, thereby ironically objectifying the subaltern and reproducing the very silencing of the subaltern that he invokes critically. Hyder, by contrast, prises apart the relation between object and person: Language, aesthetic object, and aesthetic creation/creator *all* have the potential to betray the person, so that when Gautam encounters the woman who inspired the work of art, her aging, bodily reality is too difficult for him to assimilate, and he can only flee the truth of the female body that cannot conform to an aestheticized idealization.[43] The violence done to Champak is able to reveal alternative histories and thus subaltern narratives—not in the retrieval of the story of a highborn lady from antiquity, but instead in the creation of the possibility of a different thinking of history and, thus, of forms of living and being.[44]

The Present of the Past

As I turn to Myrivilis's *The Mermaid Madonna*, a caveat is in order: Apart from an occasional engagement with a word or a sentence in the original language, in this section I work with or refer to translated texts, which means that this reading is of a mediation and has all the limitations thereof. As a result, the Myrivilis I refer to here is himself partially a fiction of translation. Yet even in translation, the texts make available a certain reflection on the themes with which this essay is concerned.

In the novel, Myrivilis presents a description of a painting, its creator, and its effect on the characters. His ekphrastic practice, though different, as might be expected, in its execution from Hyder's, shares her investment in the arbitrariness of origin as a counter to the predestinarianism of nation as History, which must first posit an origin that can lead with causal certainty to whatever is perceived as the set of characteristics constituting the nation. For Myrivilis, the inability to accept or even understand the arbitrariness of origins and the absence of certainty at its heart leads to a pervasive and socially constitutive gendered violence in which a young woman becomes a repository for an entire village's anxieties.[45]

The novel tells the story of refugees from Asia Minor, who start arriving in a fishing village, based on Sikamnea, on the island of Lesvos in 1914 after the Balkan Wars and before the formalized transfers of the Lausanne Convention. The novel is, in some measure, a portrait of the (re)constitution of the village by the refugees. Within this social portrait, comprising not just the interconnection of the lives of several characters but also a web of tales and myths, a child, Smaragthi, is found and raised by a couple in the village. She is presented as uncannily beautiful and so desirable and inclined to independence that she can only be perceived as monstrous by the inhabitants of the village. As her origins are unknown, all kinds of tales can be imposed on her, compounding the vision of her monstrosity. The violence of the desire imposed upon her is everywhere in the village, from her adoptive father's attempted rape to a young man, Lambis's, stalker-like obsession with her and the fact that almost all the men seem (exhaustingly) to want her.

In the first chapter we learn of a man called Captain Lias, who might be from Anatolia, who paints a strange painting—part mermaid, part Madonna—on the wall of a relatively new chapel on a rock. A mysterious figure, he leaves in 1914, the day before the first refugees start arriving. The relationship between the refugees and the locals is characterized by skepticism and even some hostility—in a relatively muted echo of *The Schoolmistress of the Golden Eyes* (*I Daskala me ta Chrysa Matia*).

Smaragthi attempts to assert her independence but, finally overcome by grief and guilt at Lambis's suicide, dedicates herself to the Mermaid Madonna, the icon of the chapel. Her dedication comes with the rejection of the sea, which she has loved with a passion that makes her relationship with it seem emblematic of her freedom. The icon to which she goes to pray every day remains wrapped in "mystery and silence," powerful in its enigmatic solicitation of all manner of projection.[46]

The violence done to her, which she comes to embrace in her sacrificial dedication to the icon, can be seen as a result of her illegibility to the village, which is, in part, a consequence of her being a foundling. She can become a screen, free of origin, and thus her own tales and myths, on which other tales and myths and desires, tales and myths *as* desires, can be projected. This interest in projected desire and its relation to female inaccessibility is evident in the way Sappho is perceived and treated by fellow villagers in *The Schoolmistress with the Golden Eyes* and is, of course, also very much a component of the protagonist Leonis Drivas's hostile desire for her, which is itself part of that novel's equation of masculine desire, violence, and warmongering nationalism.

The Mermaid Madonna's very first chapter sets up the troubling of origin, executed through a representation of Captain Lias's dismissal of questions about where he is from and in the ekphrasis of his painting. The villagers (and readers) never learn where Lias is from:

> Nobody knew where this man came from. Among the old residents of Mouria who got to know him, some said he was from Tchesme but others said he was from Alatsata. He himself never spoke of his life. Once when someone thoughtlessly asked him about his origin, he was silent for a moment then, looking off into the distance replied: "I am of this world you see, my son. So, you see, we are fellow country men."[47]

Lias's refusal of the necessity of declaring origins is matched by the narrator's description of the Captain: "He was nicknamed the *dedes* [the hermit] because he lived there in solitude like a Moslem ascetic in his cell."[48] It is perhaps important here that a literal translation of the Greek reads: "He was nicknamed dede because he lived alone like a Muslim monk in a 'teke.'"[49] I have left the two words that are significant for my argument untranslated here. "Dede" is a title for Sufis of a certain standing in orders, such as the Bektashi and Mevlevi, which were spread across Anatolia and the Balkans. Moreover, the Greek "teke," a declension of "tekes," is of Turkish origin. The Turkish "tekke" (which can be transcribed as "teke" and has as variants "tekije" and "tekkiye"), refers to a place of gathering for Sufis—also known as a "khanqah" (Persian) and "ribat" (Arabic) in other geographical areas and Sufi contexts.[50]

It is significant that the villagers *casually* give him a Muslim title in a novel concerned with the aftermath of the Balkan Wars, refugees, and population resettlement, indeed, with the consequences of unmixing, serving as a pointed and ironic reminder of the presence of the language, the historical intimacy of Turks and Greeks, the physical proximity of Anatolia, and the difficulty of ascertaining the difference between "Turk" and "Greek," which emerge as confessional designators that do not line up with borders and space.[51]

Lias's departure before the first refugees from Anatolia arrive suggests a mystery (that is never to be resolved in the novel) regarding his presence in Lesvos giving rise to rumors that there is someone from Anatolia he did not want to meet. The mystery foregrounds the question of his origins all the more as the possibility of having it resolved recedes, even as Lias's commitment to the irrelevance of origin and insistence that we are all sojourners suggests that the villagers' nickname might unknowingly be accurate and that he is indeed a wandering dervish: "Wherever we go, we are sojourners. Let us be sure that our bundle is tied and ready for departure at any minute and that we have a knife to cut the mooring quickly."[52] Myrivilis's play on these words, and equally and somewhat in the opposite direction his explanation of a Sufi as a Muslim monk (in a Christianizing translation into Greek of a Muslim title/description), reveals the mutual influence within this intimacy, which has in addition a spatial ground in the practice of shared religious spaces between Christians and Muslims in the Balkans and Macedonia.

It is this mysterious, determinedly unplaceable man, who paints:

> The most remarkable Madonna in Greece and in the whole of Christendom.
> Her head is done in the conventional, familiar Byzantine style—a dark-complexioned face, sensitively drawn, with an expression of reserve, rounded chin, almond eyes, and a small mouth. A purple pallium surrounds the upper part of the body and covers her head down to her eyebrows. There is also the golden halo, as in all the icons. Her eyes are extraordinarily wide and green in colour. But from the waist down, she is a fish with blue scales; and in one hand she holds a ship and in the other a trident like that of the ancient sea god Poseidon.
> When the fishermen and the villagers first saw this painting, they stood in wonder before it, but it did not seem odd to them.[53]

This is a new deity, but it is presented as aligned with the villagers' spirit and aligned with the Greek "race," which is how Abbot Rick translates "fili," which also has the sense of nation. The latter meaning may be less confusing in the context. The combination of the Byzantine icon and Greek antiquity, of the Madonna with a mermaid, comes across as an attempt to give visual form to a continuity of history. But that attempt also suggests a monstrosity to the demand for continuity in a teleological conception of history. So the painting, a new icon, can both represent the violence of the Great Idea (*Meggali Idhea*) as it sought to merge Byzantium and antiquity into a whole, that could become the raison d'être for a nationalist project of war and imperial reconstruction and, at the same time, represent the possibility of a flexible and expansive notion of history and identity. It could, after all, just be an image painted by a Sufi with no commitment to the Great Idea, but who, in Sufi "syncretic" fashion, was taken with the possibility of merging the sacred figures. This latter vision militates against a hostile Europeanized conception that demands a geographically shrinking straight line to antiquity with all intervening history erased or simply scooped out and put away and all connection to Asia, Islam, North Africa eradicated.

The ambivalence, quite literally the double valence, of the force of the Mermaid Madonna in the novel is perhaps best understood by working with a passage in which Stathis Gourgouris engages Cavafy in the context of a discussion of the place of Greece in Europe and "the international order." My point is not at all to conflate Cavafy and Myrivilis, nor to forget Myrivilis's ideological mutation over the course of his career, but rather to think with his ekphrastic spatialization of time. Gourgouris argues:

> Cavafy was arguably the first in Neohellenic culture to delineate a decentered vision of its history, pointing to the absolutely confining predicament that any culture's significational reliance on "the barbarians" (of one kind or another) guarantees. In this Cavafian sense, Greece must externalize and exceed itself, as it were, beyond its geographical boundaries to its historical ones—which is to be understood not at all as a neo-Byzantinist imperialist fantasy but as an internal upturning of what is basically nationalist insularity.[54]

What Myrivilis seems to perform in the representation of painting and its creator is the destructiveness of the geographical fantasy that underpinned the Great Idea, which is also a result of the spatialization of "History," leading to war, devastation, and the "draining of vitality" of the people, a retreat from that geographical fantasy, *and* the (receded) mixedness and geographical reach of the history from which it drew.[55] He seems to engage, thus, in an "externalization" (to use Gourgouris's term) where origin is irrelevant, perhaps irretrievable, and certainly arbitrary.

The melancholy of the novel issues from the triumph, defeat, and perhaps triumph in that defeat of the former vision, powerfully exemplified, in my view, by Smaragthi's dedication to the Madonna at the end. The only way Smaragthi can get her freedom is to renounce all the things that she loved, so she can be free of the masculine attentions she does not desire. The power of the Mermaid Madonna is such that she can appear to command a sacrificial dedication that mirrors that of her "monk"-like creator but remain utterly mysterious in her enigmatic silence. She is iconic, thus, in the manner of sacred icons, but her auratic power is revealed in the novel to come from the powerful and profoundly arbitrary act of her creation and the sacral authority with which the villagers invest her.

Both the creation and investiture are secular acts. As such, the destructive power of the painting, as evinced in Smaragthi's renunciatory dedication, reveals the irredeemability of history. For what else is the attempt to envision history as continuity—represented by the painting as a monstrous beauty—but an effort to match the telos of Germanicized Europe with a reconstituted imperial destiny that can claim antiquity as more properly Hellenic, and thus produce Neohellenism as the Hellenic telos, both absorbing along the way and finally trumping the claims of Philhellenism? It is significant that the Madonna is "effaced" by the "salt sea air": its fading attesting to the inevitable erosion of all grandeur. Smaragthi's dedication to the Madonna becomes a metaphor for the absence of redemption at the heart of any idea, however grand its vision and scope, smitten with a teleological drive.

W(h)ither Europe?

Focusing on the emergence of the nation and the violence of the unmixing that attended it, even in the context of the constitutive porosity of Europe and West Asia, risks confirming Europe in its separateness, if we do not also attend to the violence of Ottoman imperial dissolution and the emergence of the Turkish nation-state—that is, if we see Ottoman-Turkish violence as separate from that of Europe. If the iconicity of Myrivilis's painting, indeed its auratic power, and the novel's unfolding of its destructive capacity expose, on the one hand, a local, internalized violence and, on the other, a national and neo-Byzantinist imperialist violence to be connected, Myrivilis is nonetheless restrained regarding the Turkish role in the homogenization of the Anatolian border and regarding the violence visited on the Greeks of Asia Minor. The most powerful evocation of their loss is the representation of the pathetic exaggerations of the refugees' nostalgia. That this novel follows the critique of nationalist war he had so powerfully presented in *Life in the Tomb* (*I Zoe en Tapho*), and *The Schoolmistress with the Golden Eyes* makes this quiet both unsurprising and powerful.

Yet it is no less important to the broader reflection that Hyder and Myrivilis enable, that, on the Turkish side, the ethnic and religious homogenization of Anatolia was achieved both through the resettlement policies regarding non-Muslim populations and the "assimilation" of non-Turkish Muslim communities. The population and resettlement policy entailed transfers under what Taner Akçam calls the "ambiguous framework" of population exchanges with countries such as Greece, Serbia, and Bulgaria, and the "unilateral expulsion and deportation" of the Armenians.[56] The fate of the latter would, of course, famously prove enough of an inspiration to Hitler to cause him to remark on the eve of the invasion of Poland: "Who still talks nowadays of the extermination of the Armenians?"[57]

In this historical context, Angela Merkel's overtures to Turkey in the context of the refugee situation in the Mediterranean, in which Lesvos is once again the recipient of an influx of refugees that the present Greek government has inadequate resources to handle, are particularly ironic. An opportunistic alliance with an authoritarian leader in Turkey could, perhaps, be used to suggest that Europe is attempting to overcome its Islamophobia as it finally might admit Turkey; it seems, instead, to reveal that accepting this Muslim majority country is the price the EU might be willing to pay to keep the migrants out. Turkey could thus function as a better gatekeeper than Greece, making Erdogan's authoritarianism useful in the brutal management of migrants while at the same time enabling Germany to keep presenting itself as the welcoming and *rightly* hegemonic face of Europe. The erasure of Greece, in the process, reveals the complexity of the drama of self and other being enacted in Europe. In this drama, an inconvenient aspect of the self can be violently erased or attacked while the imagined former other is recuperated, revealing itself to be a face of the self after all.[58]

At the same time, the current situation exposes the astonishingly simple calculation that authoritarianism (secular *or* religious) and neoliberalism are comfortable, perhaps necessary, bedfellows. It appears easier for Germany to accept an alliance with an authoritarian Islamist government than to countenance a left-wing Greek government's demand for an end to the austerity measures being used to punish Greece. That the economic confrontation has converged with the refugee situation means that the question of the "un-" and "re-" mixing of populations, and their imbrication with authoritarian institutional structures, is a matter of renewed urgency. A rethinking of people and space, of demos and topos, and their relation to conceptions of time and thus to the possibility of conceptualizing livable futures, is tied to the very question of the sustainable organization of planetary space.

Postcolonial studies has yet to engage the networks I have attempted to chart here, in an admittedly preliminary way, in the fullness of their possibility and *recalcitrance*. To do so, would be to confront empires that were in competition (but also implicated) with European colonialism. Such complicities are inadequately confronted in postcolonial engagements with Europe and the "West." Moreover, the engagement with the problem of European colonial power and its discursive structures can lead to casual ratifications of Europe as idea—an instance of which, as I mentioned earlier, occurs in Said's invocation of classical Greek literature as a precursor of Orientalism—which can lead, in turn, to an obviation of a more complex understanding of global complicities of power and authoritarianism.[59]

A "provincialization" of Europe cannot mean letting it retreat into an insular and willfully embattled fortress but instead requires recalling how tangled it is with the planet its discourse attempts to keep at bay.[60] It is not mere polemic to point out, then, that a postcolonial project such as mine that seeks to perform a critical operation that might be related to provincialization upon Europe, that simply disregards the fact that the Ottoman Empire was also a European empire—both in territory and population—would be remiss, for in so doing it would merely accept the deracinations of the European fiction.[61] That fiction demands a narrative of Europe that always subsumes Europe to an exceptional historical destiny, in which space is reduced to time and time evacuated of mess, event, and the social and cultural entwinement of the populations that inhabit that space. A recognition of such an entwinement requires an analogous and equal recognition of the entwinement of the many forces, creeds, ideas, and *violences* that have constituted both "Europe" and its ostensible others.

Postscript, May 2017.

I write this postscript as I complete the final edits on the essay above. The essay, itself, although imagined some years ago as part of a future book project, was written in late 2015 and early 2016, just after the summer when the Greek debt crisis was visibly at its height, SYRIZA was still fighting, and the refugee situation was beginning to garner attention. In June 2015 when I was in Lesvos—an island in which I have been spending large chunks of each summer and the occasional winter since 2007, when the relatively small number of refugees I saw in the village, and with whom volunteers who later became friends worked, were largely Afghans—the people in the villages of Molyvos and Skala Sikamnea were struggling to cope with the situation without much help from the government or from international organizations, while in Athens and Thessaloniki people were primarily concerned with the economic standoff between Greece and Germany and the European Union.[62] Traveling back and forth that summer and meeting SYRIZA officials and adherents, attending the rally in Syntagma square regarding the referendum about whether Greece should accept the brutal conditions being imposed upon it in Athens, I wondered how long it would be before the refugee situation began to get more attention.

Since then, of course, much has changed, the refugees are much more—indeed hyper—visible, Brexit is under way, and Donald Trump has been elected. Germany's ostensible openness to the refugees, the xenophobia powering a great deal (if not all) of pro-Brexit sentiment, and the white supremacist authoritarianism of Trump have combined to appear to redeem Germany and the European Union and to make the Greek debt crisis seem to recede into memory even as the economic violence, now normalized, continues. After thinking about whether to "update" the introduction and conclusion, I decided not to do so, apart from adding Macron's title as president of France to his description. It seems especially important—as a *necessary* critique of the xenophobia and white supremacy driving Brexit is in danger of erasing the violence of the European Union's managerial neoliberalism—that the separate moments and issues in the unfolding drama of Europe and nationalism and the disparate instantiations of suffering, violence, and crisis—in spaces nonetheless connected by the effects of neoconservatism, neoliberalism, the aftermaths of colonialism and Cold war politics, and renewed imperialisms—not be forgotten.

Yet, and very much in keeping with this volume's attention to "historical continuities, repetitions, and reactivations" and colonial aftermaths, we need to think of Brexit in relation to the Greek crisis, for how can we not hear the (misleading) echo of Grexit? I conclude this postscript, then, by imagining a companion essay that engages some of the questions presented by Brexit to the idea of Europe, and of Britain, through a reading of Kazuo Ishiguro's and Aminatta Forna's powerful meditations on memory, atrocity, sectarian conflict between Orthodox and Catholic Christianity (Forna), and imperial loss and ruination (Ishiguro) in *The Buried Giant* (2015) and *The Hired Man* (2013), alongside Julian Barnes's *England, England* (1998), which seems to me an extraordinarily prescient anticipation of Brexit that recognizes the part that the Blairite repurposing of Thatcherism (the Third Way) and, what Stuart Hall once called, the "unresolved psychic trauma of the 'end of empire'" play in the current impasse between nationalist insularity and cosmopolitan neoliberalism on that island off the coast of Europe.[63]

NOTES

I am grateful to Pavlos Andronikos, Andre Gerolymatos, Gerasimos Kouzelis, Dimitris Krallis, R. A. Judy, and Nukhet Varlik for discussing issues of translation and, more generally, the themes and arguments in this essay with me. Thanks also to Helen Theodoratou for introducing me to a number of people associated with SYRIZA in Athens and in New York.

1. "Greece Clash Sparks Fear," *Financial Times*.

2. "The Civil War is not ended: I question whether any serious civil war ever does end." Eliot, "Milton II," 168.

3. My thinking here is very much engaged with and enabled by the work of Iain Chambers, Roberto Dainotto, Stathis Gourgouris, Artemis Leontis, and Vangelis Calotychos. See Chambers, *Mediterranean Crossings*; Dainotto, *Europe*; Gourgouris, *Dream Nation*; Leontis, *Topographies*; Calotychos, *Modern Greece*.

4. See particularly, "Excursus 2: Of Modern Hellenes in Europe," in Gourgouris, *Dream Nation*, 155–74.

5. By "constitute" I mean to invoke a sense of constituent parts rather than to scramble over origins by talking about what the Muslims or Arabs "gave" philosophy, or arithmetic, or the sonnet. I don't mean to dismiss those debates but rather to suggest that what constitutes something can be independent of what it originates or what originates it, and is not in any way contingent upon a resolution of the question of origin—assuming that such a resolution qua resolution is ever possible.

6. Ther, *Dark Side of Nation-States*, 76–77. Curzon is also credited with coining the term "exchange of populations." See also Hirschon, "'Unmixing Peoples.'"

7. Although I read Hyder's English and Urdu texts, I read Myrivilis only in translation. This unequal approach has limitations for which I can offer only an inadequate apology. I hope that this can be rectified in the future. Meanwhile, it is for other scholars to examine and contest the reading offered here. It is worth mentioning—as Dimitri Krallis and Pavlos Andronikos have both pointed out to me—that Abbot's translation simply cuts out many details, at times, it would appear, in the service of making it less politically and historically specific.

8. Taj, "Qurratulain Hyder's *Ag ka Darya*." Many critics have written about Hyder's anti-teleological of time; see, for instance, Sangari, "Joint Narratives, Separate Nations." See also Sangari, "Configural Mode." There is overlap between the two Sangari essays, but they are nonetheless distinct.

9. Hegel, *Philosophy of History*.

10. On the complexity of *topos* for Greece and its many Hellenisms, see Leontis, *Topographies of Hellenism*.

11. Pressner, "Hegel's Philosophy," loc. 4091 of 9780.

12. Dainotto, *Europe*, 160–61.

13. See, for instance, Krieger, *Ekphrasis*, and Heffernan, *Museum of Words*.

14. On Greek modernism more generally, see Tziovas, *Greek Modernism and Beyond*. There is, unfortunately, not terribly much on Myrivilis in English.

15. The challenge of Michael Herzfeld's seminal essay "The Absent Presence: Discourses of Crypto-Colonialism" has yet to be fully taken up. Martin McKinsey raises several pertinent questions regarding Greek literature, Hellenism, and postcolonialism; see Martin McKinsey, *Hellenism and the Postcolonial Imagination: Yeats, Cavafy, Walcott* (Madison, N.J.: Fairleigh Dickinson University Press, 2010).

16. Mitter, *Indian Art*, 14.

17. Hyder, *River of Fire*, 8.

18. Ibid., 9.

19. Ibid., 10–11.

20. Ibid., 10–12.

21. Rafi, "A Case for Gandhara."

22. Hyder, *Ag ka Darya*, 13.

23. Thapar, "Imagined Religious Communities?," See also Sangari, "Configural Mode," 228, on the "abridgment" of this section in translation, which she attributes to the shifting valence of Vedic India in post-Partition "aggrandizing" Hindu discourse.

24. Steele, "Tea and Consequences."

25. Thapar, "Imagined Religious Communities?" 223.

26. Talbot, "Inscribing the Other," 698.

27. Cavafy, *Complete Poems*, 56.

28. Hyder, *River of Fire*, 103–4.

29. Ibid., 197.

30. Ibid., 123.

31. See, for instance, Avari, "Review of *Ashoka*." See also Anupama Rao's essay in this volume on some valences of the issue of Buddhism's Indian indigeneity.

32. Hyder, *River of Fire*, 415.

33. Ibid., 79.

34. Said, *Orientalism*, 56–57.

35. Artemis Leontis's remarks at the conclusion of *Topographies of Hellenism* are salutary here: "More and more frequently, however, scholars hold Hellenism accountable for the West's currently most despised vices: sexism, racism, colonialism, imperialism, metaphysics, the verb 'to be.' Yet little has been said of an obvious oversight in the more than two-hundred-year history of Hellenism's excavation: Hellas illustrates how the modern fetish for the ancient, the defunct, and the exotic operates at the expense of the contemporary Greek world, which has been struggling to control interpretations of its past. As we question the value of Hellenism for the present, perhaps we should consider ways to circumvent this obstacle in our own thinking." Leontis, *Topographies of Hellenism*, 224.

36. Hyder, *River of Fire*, 415.

37. Ibid., 415–16.

38. Biswas, "Narrating National Allegory."

39. Sangari, "Joint Narratives, Separate Nations."

40. Hyder, *River of Fire*, 428.

41. Hyder, *Ag ka Darya*, 480.

42. Sangari, "Joint Narratives, Separate Nations."

43. See the chapter "Ekphrasis and the Other" in Mitchell, *Picture Theory*, 151–82, especially 157. On women in *River of Fire*, see Biswas, "Women in/and History."

44. Indeed, Jini Kim Watson's discussion of ekphrasis, aesthetics, and cinematic representation in this volume suggests the significance of aesthetics and, more specifically, ekphrastic representation for reimagining/revealing the relation of space, social being, and authoritarian structures of power. I am not suggesting that we essentialize ekphrasis as necessarily emancipatory, but instead that such performances as Watson's and my own militate against the claims being made in the name of the subaltern by Mitchell.

45. For a sensitive reading of gender in *The Mermaid Madonna* and *The Schoolmistress of the Golden Eyes*, see Alexiou, "Women in Two Novels of Stratis Myrivilis."

46. Myrivilis, *Mermaid Madonna*, 240.

47. Ibid., 8.

48. Ibid.

49. Myrivilis, *I Panagia i Gorgona*, 11.

50. *Encyclopaedia of Islam*, s.v. "Tekke," by Nathalie Clayer. http://referenceworks.brillonline.com/entries/encyclopaedia-of-islam-2/tekke-SIM_7486.

51. See, for instance, Kofopoulou, "Muslim Cretans in Turkey" and Alexandris, "Religion or Ethnicity."

52. Myrivilis, *Mermaid Madonna*, 9.

53. Ibid.

54. Gourgouris, *Dream Nation*, 174.

55. Myrivilis, *Mermaid Madonna*, 7.

56. Akçam, "Ethnic Homogenization of Anatolia," 260–61. For a quick overview of the situation and an extensive list of sources, see also the website: "The Genocide of Ottoman Greeks 1914–1923," http://www.ncas.rutgers.edu/center-study-genocide-conflict-resolution-and-human -rights/genocide-ottoman-greeks-1914-1923.

57. Anderson, ""Who Still Talked about the Extermination of the Armenians? German Talk and German Silences," 199.

58. A little time after I wrote these lines, President Recep Tayyip Erdogan, asked about his desires for a presidential system in Turkey, cited Hitler's Germany as a precedent. He appears to have been suggesting that such precedents showed that presidential systems were indeed conceivable as shown by modern history. The attempt to clean up the comments led his office to produce a statement claiming that he was citing Hitler's Germany as an example of "bad management." Nick Tattersall, "Turkish Presidency says Erdogan's Hitler Comments Misconstrued," *Reuters*, January 1, 2016, UK edition, http://uk.reuters.com/article/uk-turkey-erdogan-hitler -idUKKBN0UF1T320160101. Turkey's President Erdogan cites Adam Withnall, "Hitler's Germany as Example of an Effective Form of Government," *Independent*, January 1, 2016, http://www.independent.co.uk/news/world/europe/turkey-president-recep-tayyip-erdogan-cites -hitler-germany-as-example-of-effective-government-a6792756.html. See also Kareem Shaheen, "Jailed Turkish Editor slams EU deal with Erdogan's fascist government," *Guardian*, January 19, 2016, http://www.theguardian.com/world/2016/jan/19/jailed-turkish-editor-can-dundar-slams-eu -deal-with-erdogans-fascist-government, as well as letter from Turkish academics protesting the persecution of the Kurds and the crackdown on parts of Turkey with significant Kurdish populations (Beyza Kurai, "Academics: We Will Not Be a Party to This Crime," *English Bianet*, January 11, 2016, http://bianet.org/english/human-rights/170978-academics-we-will-not-be-a -party-to-this-crime).

59. Said, *Orientalism*, 56–57.

60. Chakrabarty, *Provincializing Europe*.

61. Chambers reminds us that in the second half of the nineteenth century the foreign ministries were "full of talk of the 'sick man of Europe'" and poses the trenchant question: "When, why, and how did [Turkey] stop being part of Europe?" *Mediterranean Crossings*, 13.

62. I mention Molyvos and Skala Sikmanea; they are villages in the part of the island where I was staying. Of course, other parts of the island were affected too.

63. Hall, *Hard Road to Renewal*, 2.

BIBLIOGRAPHY

Akçam, Taner. "The Young Turks and the Plans for the Ethnic Homogenization of Anatolia." In *Shatterzones of Empire: Coexistence and Violence in the German, Habsburg, Russian, and Ottoman Borderlands*, edited by Omer Bartov and Eric D. Weitz, 258–79. Bloomington: Indiana University Press, 2013.

Alexandris, Alexis. "Religion or Ethnicity: The Identity Issues of the Minorities in Greece and Turkey." In Hirschon, *Crossing the Aegean*, 117–32.

Alexiou, Margaret. "Women in Two Novels of Stratis Myrivilis: Myth, Fantasy, and Violence." *Modern Greek Studies 2015, Reference Yearbook* 5 (1989): 117–41.

Ambedkar, B. R. *Pakistan, or The Partition of India*. Bombay: Thacker, 1946.

Anderson, Margaret Lavinia. "Who Still Talked about the Extermination of the Armenians? German Talk and German Silences." In *A Question of Genocide: Armenians and Turks at the End of the Ottoman Empire*, edited by Ronald Suny, Fatma Müge Göçek, and Norman Naimark, 199–216. New York: Oxford University Press, 2011.

Avari, Burjor. Review of *Ashoka: The Search for India's Lost Emperor*, by Charles Allen. *Reviews in History*, review no. 1286 (July 2012): http://www.history.ac.uk/reviews/review/1286.

Barnes, Julian. *England, England*. New York: Vintage Books, 1998.

Biswas, Pratibha. "Narrating National Allegory—Marvelous Realism in Qurratulain Hyder's *River of Fire*." *International Journal of English, Language, Literature and Humanities* 3, no. 1 (2015): 497–510.

———. "Women in/and History: Reading the Novel River of Fire." *Muse India* 58 (November–December 2014). http://www.museindia.com/focuscontent.asp?issid=58&id=5302.

Cavafy, C. P. *The Complete Poems of Cavafy*. Translated by Rae Dalven. New York: Harcourt, 1976.

Chakrabarty, Dipesh. *Provincializing Europe: Postcolonial Thought and Historical Difference*. Princeton: Princeton University Press, 2007.

Chambers, Iain. *Mediterranean Crossings: The Politics of an Interrupted Modernity*. Durham, N.C.: Duke University Press, 2008.

Dainotto, Roberto. *Europe (In Theory)*. Durham, N.C.: Duke University Press, 2007.

Eliot, T. S. "Milton II." *On Poetry and Poets*. 168. New York: Farrar, Straus and Giroux, 2009.

Forna, Aminatta. *The Hired Man*. New York: Grove Press, 2013.

Gourgouris, Stathis. *Dream Nation: Enlightenment, Colonization, and the Institution of Modern Greece*. Stanford: Stanford University Press, 1996.

"Greece Clash Sparks Fear over German Power." *Financial Times*, July 17, 2015. http://www.ft.com/intl/cms/s/0/3c65702c-2c81-11e5-8613-e7aedbb7bdb7.html#axzz3iKD3i1QS.

Hall, Stuart. *The Hard Road to Renewal: Thatcherism and the Crisis of the Left*. London: Verso, 1988.

Heffernan, James. *Museum of Words: The Poetics of Ekphrasis from Homer to Ashbery*. Chicago: University of Chicago Press, 1993.

Hegel, G. W. F. *The Philosophy of History*. Translated by J. Sibree. 1956. New York: Dover Publications, 2004.

Herzfeld, Michael. "The Absent Presence: Discourses of Crypto-Colonialism." *South Atlantic Quarterly* 101, no. 4 (2002): 899–926.

Hirschon, Renée. "'Unmixing Peoples' in the Aegean Region." In Hirschon, *Crossing the Aegean*, 3–20.

Hirschon, Renée, ed. *Crossing the Aegean: An Appraisal of the 1923 Compulsory Exchange between Greece and Turkey*. New York: Berghahn Books, 2006.

Hyder, Qurratulain. *Ag ka Darya*. Lahore: Sang-e-Meel Publishers, 2010.

———. *River of Fire*. New York: New Directions Press, 1998.

Ishiguro, Kazuo. *The Buried Giant*. New York: Alfred A. Knopf, 2015.

Kofopoulou, Sophia. "Muslim Cretans in Turkey: The Reformulation of Ethnic Identity in an Aegean Community." In Hirschon, *Crossing the Aegean*, 209–20.

Krieger, Murray. *Ekphrasis: The Illusion of the Natural Sign*. Baltimore: Johns Hopkins University Press, 1992.

Leontis, Artemis. *Topographies of Hellenism: Mapping the Homeland*. Ithaca, N.Y.: Cornell University Press, 1995.

McKinsey, Martin. *Hellenism and the Postcolonial Imagination: Yeats, Cavafy, Walcott*. Madison, N.J.: Fairleigh Dickinson University Press, 2010.

Mitchell, W. J. T. *Picture Theory*. Chicago: University of Chicago Press, 1994.

Mitter, Partha. *Indian Art*. Oxford: Oxford University Press, 2001.

Myrivilis, Stratis. *I Panagia i Gorgona*. Athens: Estia, 1956.

———. *Life in the Tomb*. Translated by Peter Bien. River Vale, N.J.: Cosmos, 2003.

————. *The Mermaid Madonna*. Translated by Abbot Rick. Athens: Efstathiadis Group, 2007.

————. *The Schoolmistress with the Golden Eyes*. Translated by Philip Sherrard. Athens: Efstathiadis Group, 2007.

Pressner, Samuel. "Hegel's Philosophy of World History via Sebald's Imaginary of Ruins: A Contrapuntal Critique of the 'New Space' of Modernity." In *Ruins of Modernity*, edited by Julia Hell and Andreas Schönle. Durham, N.C.: Duke University Press, 2010.

Rafi, Shazia. "A Case for Gandhara." *Dawn*, February 19, 2015. http://www.dawn.com/news/1164469.

Said, Edward. *Orientalism*. New York: Vintage Books Edition, 1979.

Sangari, Kumkum. "The Configural Mode: *Aag ka Darya*." In *Qurratulain Hyder and the River of Fire: The Meaning, Scope and Significance of Her Legacy*, edited by Rakhshanda Jalil, 197–231. Karachi: Oxford University Press, 2011.

————. "Joint Narratives, Separate Nations: Qurratulain Hyder's Aag ke Dariya." *Muse India* 14 (July–August 2014). http://www.museindia.com/viewarticle.asp?myr=2007&issid=14&id=756.

Seferis, George. *Collected Poems*. Translated by Edmund Keeley and Philip Sherrard. Princeton: Princeton University Press, 1995.

Steele, Laurel. "'We Just Stayed on the Ship to Bombay . . .' Tea and Consequences with Qurratulain Hyder." *Annual of Urdu Studies* 23 (2008): 182–95.

Taj, Nikhat. "A Study of the Organizing Principle(s) in Qurratulain Hyder's Ag ka Darya." *Indian Literature* 53, no. 4 (2009): 195–213.

Talbot, Cynthia. "Inscribing the Other, Inscribing the Self: Hindu-Muslim Identities in Precolonial India." *Comparative Studies in Society and History* 37, no. 4 (1995): 692–722.

Thapar, Romila. "Imagined Religious Communities? Ancient History and the Modern Search for a Hindu Identity." *Modern Asian Studies* 23, no. 2 (1989): 209–31.

Ther, Philippe. *The Dark Side of Nation-States: Ethnic Cleansing in Modern Europe*. New York: Berghahn Books, 2014.

Tziovas, Dimitris, ed. *Greek Modernism and Beyond*. Lanham, Md.: Rowman and Littlefield, 1997.

EIGHT

For a Marxist Theory of Waste: Seven Remarks

Vinay Gidwani

"It is more than usually desirable that we should make some slight provision for the Poor and destitute, who suffer greatly at the present time. Many thousands are in want of common necessaries; hundreds of thousands are in want of common comforts, sir."

"Are there no prisons?"

"Plenty of prisons . . ."

"And the Union workhouses," demanded Scrooge. "Are they still in operation?"

"Both very busy, sir . . ."

"Those who are badly off must go there."

"Many can't go there; and many would rather die."

"If they would rather die," said Scrooge, "they had better do it, and decrease the surplus population."

—CHARLES DICKENS, *A Christmas Carol*

Remark 1: The Law of Obsolescence

In 1932, a Russian-born, New York–based real estate broker, Bernard London, proposed a novel economic strategy to fight the Depression: planned obsolescence. His diagnosis of the prevailing economic crisis was one that Marx or Keynes would have recognized. Without so naming, London identified "overaccumulation" and "underconsumption" as the principal causes. "Factories, warehouses, and fields are still intact and are ready to produce in unlimited quantities," he wrote, "but the urge to go ahead has been paralyzed by a decline in buying power." London didn't stop there. The Depression, in his reckoning, had altered consumer behavior, with "people generally, in a frightened and hysterical mood . . . using everything that they own longer than was their custom before the depression."[1] The crux of the crisis, in London's lament, was that consumers had become less wasteful:

In the earlier period of prosperity, the American people did not wait until the last possible bit of use had been extracted from every commodity. They replaced old articles with new for reasons of fashion and up-to-dateness. They gave up old homes and old automobiles long before they were worn out, merely because they were obsolete. All business, transportation, and labor had adjusted themselves to the prevailing habits of the American people. Perhaps, prior to the panic, people were too extravagant; if so, they have now gone to the other extreme and have become retrenchment-mad.[2]

By "disobeying the law of obsolescence," London argued, consumers were unwittingly promoting another form of waste: "untold loss in foregoing the workpower of ten million human beings."[3] London's circular dictum readily lends itself to a Marxist formulation: Without a regular movement of commodities from the domain of use-value to detritus, the circulation of value in its various forms grinds to a halt; capital accumulation ceases or declines; producers whose profit margins are squeezed lay off workers; workers who are now no longer able to able to sell their labor power for a wage cut back on consumption and use already purchased commodities for longer periods; aggregate demand in the economy falls; and the cycle of underconsumption/overaccumulation repeats itself. In a phrase: Speed up the rate at which commodities become obsolete and pass into the universe of waste, and the economic crisis will be cured.

In fact, London's argument is considerably more interesting than that. For example, and again without revealing any familiarity with Marx, London criticizes as detrimental to society the structural asymmetry between the owner of the means of production (capitalist) and those who must sell for a wage the only means of production at their disposal, a power that can be neither stored nor accumulated (laborer): "The man who performed the work received as compensation only enough to purchase comfort and sustenance for a short time, and he must continue to labor if he wishes to go on living. The product of the worker's hand, however, is a semipermanent thing and produces income for its owner for an indefinite period of years."[4] London's policy proposal is to limit the life-span of capital goods and commodities. How?

> I would have the Government assign a lease of life to shoes and homes and machines, to all products of manufacture, mining and agriculture, when they are first created, and they would be sold and used within the term of their existence definitely known by the consumer. After the allotted time had expired, these things would be legally "dead" and would be controlled by the duly appointed governmental agency and destroyed if there is widespread unemployment. New products would constantly be pouring forth from the factories and marketplaces, to take the place of the obsolete, and the wheels of industry would be kept going and employment regularized and assured for the masses.[5]

Remark 2: Commodity as Fetish

London's proposals never achieved traction, but we ignore him at our peril. Scholars before and after London have recognized the social and economic power of obsolescence and waste.[6] In *The Theory of the Leisure Class*, Thorstein Veblen famously asserted that "waste of time and effort" and "waste of goods" are both methods of "demonstrating the possession of wealth."[7] Susan Strasser has evocatively documented in *Waste and Want: A Social History of Trash* (1999) how, in the decades following the Depression, a new consumer culture arose where "having and disposing," wanting "the new and different," became the social norm. In their pessimistic appraisal of this new consumer culture ("culture indus-tries"), Horkheimer and Adorno described a scenario in which consumers were trapped in a "cycle of manipulation and retroactive need."[8] Marcuse in *One-Dimensional Man* char-acterized advertising, public relations, indoctrination, and planned obsolescence as "no longer unproductive overhead costs but rather elements of basic production costs," that is to say, "production of socially necessary waste" as the sine qua non for administering in-dustrial society.[9] In a congruent thesis, John Kenneth Galbraith in *The Affluent Society* ar-gued that once the urgent or intrinsic needs of consumers had been met, firms increasingly resorted to sales and marketing strategies aimed at generating the "craving for more ele-gant automobiles, more exotic food, more erotic clothing, more elaborate entertainment—indeed for the entire modern range of sensuous, edifying and lethal desires."[10] And who can forget Jean Baudrillard's acid verdict on consumerism as the chief form of bourgeois class rule in his 1969 essay (which was included in *For a Critique of the Political Economy of the Sign*)? Observed Baudrillard in that essay:

> Now what must be read and what one must know how to read in *upper class* superiority, in electric household equipment or in luxury food, is precisely *not* its advance on the scale of material benefits, but rather its *absolute privilege*, bound up in the fact that its pre-eminence is precisely not established in signs of prestige and abundance, but elsewhere, in the real spheres of decision, direction and political and economic power, in the manipulation of signs and men. And this relegates the Others, the *lower* and *middle* classes, to phantasms of the promised land.[11]

Although consumer studies scholarship has since rebuked, even rejected, such consumer critiques for treating consumers as "dupes" and divesting them of agency,[12] accusations of planned obsolescence, the affective power of advertising, and consumers' complicity in consolidating a "throwaway" society have all persisted. It was precisely this "throwaway" society, promoted by shifts in production strategies and marketing tactics, which the jour-nalist and social critic Vance Packard cuttingly denounced in *The Waste Makers*. While he lauded "obsolescence of function," when a product becomes outmoded by the introduc-tion of a new product that is functionally superior, he was deeply skeptical of the two other modalities by which products were being rendered obsolete: "obsolescence of quality" (when a product breaks down or wears out) and "obsolescence of desirability" (when an otherwise "sound" product becomes "worn out" because a "styling or other change makes it seem less desirable").[13] Like other consumer critics before him, Packard was taken to task by academics and pro-business publications such as *Barron's*, *Fortune*, and the *Wall Street Journal*. The sociologist Seymour Martin Lipset described Packard as an "old-fashioned conservative" who was wedded to "the simple, primitive, almost poverty-stricken life" and failed to grasp how conspicuous consumption was a democratic way for people to communicate mobility and achieved status.[14]

Yet Packard's critique remains prescient. Joseph Guiltinan affirms Packard's disquiet in a sobering analysis of "destructive creations"—products designed to become obsolete—from an environmental ethics perspective.[15] The "objective of planned obsolescence,"

Guiltinan notes, "is to stimulate replacement buying by consumers" and that the "most direct way to speed replacement demand is to shorten the usable life of a product through one or more . . . physical obsolescence mechanisms."[16] These include limited functional life design (or "death dating"), design for limited repair, and design aesthetics that lead to reduced satisfaction: Each encourages "premature disposal." Physical obsolescence combines with technological obsolescence to foster faster replacement of commodities by consumers. Thus, design strategies that emphasize "fashion positioning" over "durability positioning," or that build in the prospect for functional enhancement through adding or upgrading product features, shape consumer psychology. According to Guiltinan:

> Rapid product improvements can increase the household discount rate (or the "impatience" rate) so that consumers value purchases made in the near term more than the savings from delayed purchase. Moreover . . . more frequent introductions of upgrades may be interpreted by consumers as cues to higher rates of intergenerational improvement, so a policy of "continuous upgrading" creates a heightened sense among consumers that their existing durable is outmoded.[17]

Here we witness a twist on the notion of "consumer sovereignty," where the consumer participates in spurring the process of technological obsolescence—a phenomenon that raises the question, is it the consumer who is sovereign as mainstream economic theory insists or the commodity? Is it the person who owns the commodity or the commodity that owns the person? In Marx's well-known diagnosis, the commodity form's fetish power is revealed as that which possesses persons, commanding them to lose themselves in its pleasure, to forget its human origins, indeed, its genesis in the exploitation and wretched existence of distant others. To grasp this repeating scene of willing subjection, we can take cues from Louis Althusser's cogitations on the subject of ideology: namely, that the subject—in this instance, the consumer—is always doubled. It comes to "know" itself in particular ways and is thereby enabled to act (or desist) as the "author of its initiatives." This is the double sense of "subject" (*in subjection to* and *subject of*) that Althusser posits in his writings on ideological state apparatuses and the reproduction of capitalism.[18] Althusser's theory of the subject has the merit of recognizing the subject as an agent who makes choices even as these choices are generated within a social psychology of relations that the subject inhabits (and which always precede the subject's "coming-to-awareness" of its desires and dispositions).

Remark 3: Waste and the Problem of Surplus Absorption

Although Marx famously begins volume 1 of *Capital* with a discussion of capital's cell-form, the "commodity," his focus is not the domain of consumption; rather it is on establishing how (surplus) value is generated within the production process and ferried in various attires until its realization. The rub is that keeping the cycle of surplus value extraction going—a requisite for capital accumulation—is far from guaranteed (as Marx pointed out; and Luxemburg, Harvey, Saad-Filho, and Henderson, among others, have elaborated).[19] The prospects for breakdown are ever-present, whether in the form of labor shortages or recalcitrant labor, raw material bottlenecks, or creaky infrastructure for production and marketing. But disequilibrium between aggregate supply and demand is the most serious. Capital has a tendency to overproduce in relation to aggregate demand. Weak consumer markets lead to recurrent crises of overaccumulation where the circulatory process so essential to the absorption of surplus value and continued profit making is interrupted.

As we saw, Bernard London proposed legally mandated obsolescence of commodities and capital goods as a cure. Mary Wrenn approaches the issue of product and technological obsolescence, and the sprawling marketing and advertising apparatus that subtends it, as a Marxist economist.[20] Building on Paul Baran and Paul Sweezy's 1966 classic, *Monopoly Capital*, Wrenn points to the ongoing problem of aggregate demand that haunts capitalism. "Because of the insatiability of the accumulation cycle which drives all capitalist systems," she writes, "business interests must constantly and consistently expand production. . . . The problem of ineffective demand plagues modern business, which, coupled with downwardly rigid pricing, forces cuts in productivity and poses the problem of excess capacity or 'capital overhang.'"[21] However, this "excess cannot be used to produce more consumer goods, given the ever-widening inequality of income distribution"; nor "can it be used for investment—i.e., to produce productivity enhancing capital—since this would only compound the problem of excess capacity."[22] Given these limits and loathe to let capital lie idle, monopoly capitalism sustains itself by applying surplus capital to "the production or sale of goods and services that do not meet the needs of the general populace"—in short, what Baran and Sweezy term "waste."[23] Thus, "waste" in their accounting encompasses expenditures on "advertising, market research, expense account entertaining, the maintenance of excessive numbers of sales outlets, and the salaries and bonuses of salesmen," as well as "outlays for such activities as public relations and lobbying, the rental and maintenance of showy office buildings, and business litigation."[24]

Wrenn extends Baran and Sweezy's analysis to include campaign contributions via PACs that aim to consolidate the institutions of monopoly capitalism; she also adds "'new and improved' product differentiations that inundate consumers with choices, creating demand for previously non-essential or unknown options, devices, and accessories."[25] The goal of such market segmentation, she writes (in an implicit rebuke to the consumer studies scholarship), is "to further commodify personal distinction and consumption-driven identities."[26] In short Wrenn, following Baran and Sweezy, embraces a productivist approach to "waste," electing to characterize it as nonproductive expenditures of surplus value that do not substantively enhance society's quality of living. Wrenn mentions in passing how planned obsolescence and "creative destruction" threaten the planet's ecological balance. While the burden imposed on ecosystems by the proliferation of postconsumption waste (as well as the waste that ensues from agricultural activities, industrial production, and construction) is indeed a matter of growing concern, Wrenn commits the common error of supposing that a consumer product reaches its end of life when it is discarded. This truncated understanding blinds her to diverse and ubiquitous nonformal economies that recycle, repurpose, and reprocess a dazzling array of consumer detritus and discards,[27] revealing, on the one hand, the persistence of value in waste matter and, on the other, new couplings of matter and humanity that society remainders.

Remark 4: Where Commodity Detritus Goes to Live

Although Marx did not systematically dwell on the subject of waste, his scattered writings on the topic are nevertheless suggestive. His main observations occur in *Capital*, volume 3, in the chapter titled "Economy in the Use of Constant Capital." To no one's surprise, Marx's comments on waste center on the process of production (or, in a metabolic vein, the consumption of raw material during capitalist production); consumer waste is not a concern, very likely because mass consumption of the sort that preoccupied social critics in the mid-twentieth century is a distant phenomenon when Marx is writing and because it is in "social labor on a large scale" that he finds the germs of a new (postcapitalist) society.

In volume 3, he notes the cost savings associated with economies of scale in production and its positive effect on the profit rate. In describing the "economical use" that such "conditions of production" yield, he mentions "the transformation of the refuse of production, its so-called waste product, back into new elements of production, either in the same branch of industry or in other; the processes by which this so-called refuse is sent back into the cycle of production, and thus consumption—productive or individual."[28] He proceeds to write:

> It is the resulting massive scale of these waste products that makes them into new objects of trade and therefore new elements of production. *It is only as the waste products of production in common, and hence of production on a large scale, that they acquire this importance for the production process and remain bearers of exchange-value.* The waste products, quite apart from the service that they perform as new elements of production, reduce the cost of raw material, to the extent that they can be resold, for this cost always includes normal wastage, i.e. the average quantity that is lost in the course of processing. To the extent that the costs of this portion of constant capital are reduced, the rate of profit is correspondingly increased, with a given magnitude of variable capital and given rate of surplus-value.[29]

Since Marx never specifies what this "so-called waste" consists of (coal ash, metal residues, leftover thread, wood by-products?), it is tricky to unpack his assertion that "waste products of production in common . . . remain bearers of exchange-value." What portion of the exchange value of such "waste products" remains intact after being used in the production process? Is this waste reusable as raw material in future production without further transformation or transportation? Does it require application of new labor to revive or restore its exchange value? Should the "trade" Marx alludes to be considered "productive labor" or simply mercantile acts of arbitrage that add no new value? Would Marx have altered his assessment if he were attentive to the diverse material properties of "so-called waste"? What if Marx had lived in a world saturated with postconsumer waste? I address some of these lingering questions below by considering an urban waste hub in Delhi, India, where commodity detritus of all sorts is recycled, reprocessed, and/or repurposed.[30]

Madanpur Khadar is a large resettlement colony in Delhi's southeast fringe, adjacent to the Yamuna River. Its original residents were relocated here in 2000–2001 after being evicted from slums in east and south Delhi. Since then a steady influx of renters has added to the settlement's population. The settlement is heterogeneous, parts of it resembling a lower-middle-class neighborhood while others have a morphology more closely associated with slums: with tightly packed streets and single-room exposed brick tenements stacked one atop another, as owners and slumlords strive to garnish maximum rent from desperately tiny plots. While the scars of poverty are hard to ignore, they risk obscuring how Madanpur Khadar serves as a diverse economic center, one of many that collectively form the vital human infrastructure that keeps Delhi humming.[31] Madanpur Khadar's residents work as cleaners, sweepers, office helpers, and laborers; large numbers of the colony's women are employed as domestic workers in adjacent upper-middle-class neighborhoods. Madanpur Khadar is also a multiform waste hub, which, like tens of other waste hubs scattered across Delhi and around the country—some specializing in a single waste product, others more flexible in character—daily process thousands of tons of detritus and discards whose accumulation would render urban existence as we know it impossible. One study, for example, puts the total municipal solid waste (MSW) generated in urban India in 2013 at 73.3 million tons per year (TPY) or 200,884 tons per day (TPD), and projects that these figures will soar to 101.6 million TPY and 278,480 TPD by 2021.[32]

As a "pollution haven," a place where pollution-intensive economic activities concentrate, Madanpur Khadar's injured landscape epitomizes the spatiotemporal contradictions of capitalism: of class and ecology, but also caste. Whereas the mineral-rich tribal expanses of central India represent the external frontier of this spatial contradiction as sites of "primitive accumulation," urban nodes like Madanpur Khadar, awash in the quiet violence of neglect, disdain, ill health, and uncertainty are its internal frontier. If the external frontier constitutes the front end of capitalism, where the discourse of "waste" limns a biocultural difference that justifies forcible annexation of territories and their resources, and the displacement of native populations ("primitive accumulation," as we know, has repeatedly invoked "waste" as warrant for projects that dispossess),[33] Madanpur Khadar illustrates its back end, where the waste generated as part and parcel of a capitalist space-economy is interred within stigmatized bodies (who frequently hail from historically vulnerable groups).

Delhi's waste hubs and the pathways of people, objects, information, and money that connect them are the city's lymphatic system, sequestering its waste and inoculating it from lasting damage. The intricate yet undervalued operations, until a moment of breakdown, of this sprawling waste infrastructure—from waste hubs to municipal landfills to sewage pipelines—hinges on the toil, ingenuity, practical knowledge, and risk-taking of several hundred thousand workers, small entrepreneurs, and petty government functionaries. Even as they perform the double function of reproducing the urban economy while inoculating it from the injurious effects of its own detritus, places like Madanpur Khadar and the people who work and reside there are continuously abjected by civil society's propertied estates, which views them with repugnance as a source of crime, nuisance, and contamination. As

I have noted elsewhere: "Resentment of poverty, of the 'rabble' that threatens the productivist core of liberal (and Marxist) thought is the itch that civil society cannot banish." Upper and middle classes in India are gripped by an anxiety that "the poor, unmoored from society's protections, will steal from the propertied and inhibit their enjoyment of ownership."[34] There are dense echoes here with Achille Mbembe's remark in *Critique of Black Reason*, his galvanizing recent book that, "racial danger has been," from the beginning, "one of the pillars of the culture of fear intrinsic to racial democracy."[35]

Mbembe also contends there that for the first time in history "the term Black has been generalized": That is to say, we inhabit a historical moment when an existential condition that was principally imposed on people of African origin—"different forms of depredation, dispossession of all power of self-determination, and, most of all, dispossession of the future and of time, the two matrices of the possible"—are now being "institutionalized as a new norm of existence and expanded to the entire planet."[36] As such, "the systematic risks experienced specifically by Black slaves during early capitalism have now become the norm for, or at least the lot of, all of subaltern humanity."[37] Mbembe terms this emerging state of affairs, with profound implications for our future understanding of race and racism, "the *Becoming Black of the world*."[38] Although it is far-fetched to equate the condition of India's waste workers with the Black slaves who underwrote the West's modernity, it is not difficult to picture them as the new racialized Others of neoliberalizing cities, whose daily toil subtends the aesthetics, economics, and ordinary functioning of these urban formations even as their humanity is denied, their labor devalued, and their claims to dignified existence persistently denigrated.

Remark 5: Wasting Labor's Lease on Life

I have previously mentioned Marx's remarks on "the refuse of production" that is reutilized in future rounds of production, thereby driving down the costs of production with consequent upsides for the rate of profit. Marx also discusses waste in another register, namely the wasting of human material, in *Capital*, volume 3, as well as in *Capital*, volume 1, in the chapter titled "The Working Day." Here is Marx, writing with characteristic sarcasm and sharpness (and I quote at length because his commentary is enormously suggestive):

> The contradictory and antithetical character of the capitalist mode of production leads it to count the squandering of the life and health of the worker, and the depression of his conditions of existence, as itself an economy in the use of constant capital, and hence a means of raising the rate of profit. . . . This economy extends to crowding workers into confined and unhealthy premises, a practice which in capitalist parlance is called saving on buildings; squeezing dangerous machines into the same premises and dispensing with means of protection against these dangers. . . . From the standpoint of the capitalist this would be senseless waste. Yet for all its stinginess, capitalist production is thoroughly wasteful with human material, just as its way of distributing its products through trade, and its manner of competition, make it very wasteful of material resources, so that it loses for society what it gains for the individual capitalist.[39]

Shashank is a contractor in Madanpur Khadar, who runs a large warehouse that employs roughly fifty men, primarily low-caste migrants from eastern Uttar Pradesh.[40] They process the dry, largely paper, waste that Shashank sources from around Delhi. Over thirty of these workers live in the 2,000 square foot compound that houses two pressing machines, which transform the sheets of paper they are fed into tightly packed bundles. They have no fixed work hours; whenever a delivery arrives, they are put to work. Their tasks range from unloading the trucks that deliver scrap paper to operating the pressing machines to, once again, loading trucks that come to fetch the bundled paper. Some of the workers say they have been working at Shashank's warehouse for six to seven years. They earn between INR 6,000 and INR 7,000 ($90–$105) per month but are neither paid overtime nor have any days off. Workers are expected to learn on the job how to operate the pressing machines; no formal instruction is provided. Labor regulations and work safety protocols are absent, and workers seemed unaware of (or were possibly indifferent to) legal protections that apply to them. Inability to work due to illness or family obligations results in loss of pay. In the law's gaze, Shashank's workers don't exist: There is no record of their hiring, no labor register is maintained, the warehouse operates under the radar with the complicity of police and municipal staff, and as such, workers have no basis to mount complaints. They exist only to work. Or as Marx writes in his chapter "The Working Day" in *Capital*, volume 1:

> In its blind and measureless drive, its insatiable appetite for surplus labor, capital oversteps not only the moral but even the merely physical limits of the working day. It usurps the time for growth, development and healthy maintenance of the body. It steals the time required for the consumption of fresh air and sunlight. . . . It reduces the sound sleep needed for restoration, renewal and refreshment of the vital forces to the exact amount of torpor essential to the revival of an absolutely exhausted organism. It is not the normal maintenance of labor-power which determines the limits of the working day here, but rather the greatest possible daily expenditure of labor-power, no matter how diseased, compulsory and painful it may be, which determines the limits of the workers' period of rest.[41]

Indeed, how capital denudes labor's capacities to "be human" is a refrain strewn across Marx's writings. The theft of labor's capacity to be "use-value for itself"—that is, to develop its creative capacities for ends it desires—that are so vividly on display in *Capital*, volume 1, are prefigured in "The Chapter on Capital" in *Grundrisse*. Marx notes there how capitalists demand that workers "maintain themselves as pure laboring machines and as far as possible pay their own wear and tear"[42] or, that "the capitalist likes nothing better than for . . . [the worker] to *squander his dosages of vital force as much as possible, without interruption.*"[43] The daily grind and hazards associated with waste work ensure that most waste pickers age prematurely, their bodies depleted of "life power." Few are able to work into their fifties. Nusrat Begum, a resident of Madanpur Khadar, says she is from Dhubri district, in the northeastern state of Assam. She has been in Delhi for nine or ten years and has been making a living by gleaning recyclable items from garbage from the time she arrived. Her husband, who she guesses is in his forties, has fallen ill and is unable to pick waste these days. She notes that he keeps falling ill. He tries to get some treatment here, in the city, but if the illness persists he returns to their village for treatment.

Pauperism's effects are intergenerational. Nusrat Begum's children don't attend school: They also pick waste, partly to compensate for their father's illness. But Nusrat Begum's unrequited aspirations for her children are apparent when she bitterly remarks: *"Agar ma-baap koode mein rahenge to bacche is se door kaise reh sakte hain?"* ("If the parents live amid garbage, can the children stay away from it?"). Her comment mobilizes the double sense of the word *kooda*. She implies that her children's trajectories can't be otherwise given that *kooda* (waste) is both a source of the parents' livelihood and the squalor or filth that marks their lives. Nusrat's existence is a blunt reminder that women carry the double burden of production and reproduction. Their labor time is never done. After she has finished sorting the day's waste, Nusrat turns her attention to household chores such as cooking the evening meal. Nusrat Begum says that her bones ache and her back constantly hurts; she is unable to sleep at night. It is difficult not to be reminded here of Marx cutting remark that: "Capital is dead labor which, vampire-like, lives only by sucking living labor, and lives the more, the more labor it sucks."[44]

Remark 6: Surplus Matter and Superfluous Populations

The recent accumulation of writings on surplus populations—"wasted lives,"[45] "wasteland of the dispossessed,"[46] a state of "wageless life,"[47] "beyond-populations 'with no productive function,'"[48] the "precariat,"[49] a "floating reserve army,"[50] "revolting subjects,"[51] and "expulsions,"[52]—suggest that we are at an inflection point, a new conjuncture, in the turbulent world history of capitalism, where formal sectors within the capitalist economy are increasingly ill-equipped and disinclined to absorb job seekers. A future without work as we know it may be our new planetary condition in a few short decades.

India offers a sobering example.[53] Based on recent labor force participation rate by age group (an indication of anticipated new entrants into the workforce), the existing backlog of the educated unemployed, and the annual trend in those leaving agriculture for nonagricultural employment, Santosh Mehrotra and colleagues concluded that nonagricultural sectors would have had to create 17 million jobs per annum over the period 2012–17 in order to absorb India's surplus population (not counting the underemployed and the disillusioned).[54] Their prognosis was bleak and, as it transpires, correct. The requisite jobs failed to materialize. In fact, a recent uptick in job losses in vital sectors of the economy (telecom, construction, textiles, and information technology) has led one commentator to proclaim that India is headed for a "demographic disaster."[55] Attempting to explain the phenomenon of "jobless growth" in India, Kunal Sen and Deb Das point out that the manufacturing sector has utterly failed to create jobs, with the employment elasticity of output in manufacturing falling from 0.47 in 1990–99 to 0.05 in 2000–2009.[56] "Particularly disappointing," they write, "have been low rates of job creation in the organised manufacturing sector, which has meant that a vast number of the working poor has been relegated to the low-wage informal sector and agriculture."[57]

Employment statistics constructed from official National Sample Survey Office (NSSO) data offer support to this assessment, indicating an expansion in lower-quality casual employment via two mechanisms, insecure work in the informal sector and "informalization" of previously secure jobs in the so-called organized sector—that is, jobs in the formal economy lacking employment protections and social security protections. According to the NSSO's 68th round (2011–12) survey report, "Informal Sector and Conditions of Employment in India," 80 percent of informal sector employment is based on oral agreement, and 72 percent of those employed receive no type of social security. Depending on how "informal" employment is computed (whether, for example, "casualization" of formal/organized sector jobs is included), the figures for India's economy range anywhere from 78 percent to over 90 percent of the workforce—with informal employment accounting for the vast majority of employment generation in the 1999–2000 to 2011–12 period, that too mainly in micro-enterprises employing fewer than six people on average.[58] In short, India remains a poor, labor-surplus economy with a vast youth demographic that renders the employment challenge all the more daunting.

Informal waste-related work is a major source of job creation. It is estimated that approximately 1 percent of the urban population finds employment in this sector. Even halved, to err on the side of caution, the resultant all-India statistic, 2.12 million people, is telling in its magnitude.[59] The UN's 2014 revision of its *World Urbanization Prospects* report ranks Delhi as the world's second most populous city after Tokyo, with a population of 25 million; this would conservatively place its workforce of informal waste recyclers at 125,000.[60] These workers—stigmatized, undervalued, and highly vulnerable, as I have previously noted—provide critical economic and ecological services to cities by lowering their waste burdens in highly cost-effective ways. Their work is infrastructural: invisible but pivotal for the reproduction of cities. Yet as cities embrace the tide of infrastructure privatization, including management of municipal solid waste (MSW), the livelihoods of these workers is imperiled. Given the health hazards and low incomes characteristic of informal recycling livelihoods, it may seem as though this is not cause for alarm; after all, even advocates concede that "waste picking is a survival strategy rather than an occupational choice."[61] In a labor-surplus economy, with scant employment options, a source of income is better than none at all. As the economist Joan Robinson once trenchantly put it: "The misery of being exploited . . . is nothing compared to the misery of not being exploited at all."[62]

The compulsion to undertake waste-related work has invariably fallen on lower-caste migrants, who come to the city to escape the inherited oppressions of caste. But caste frequently gets a new lease on life in cities by virtue of the matter workers are compelled to handle. The contemporary city with its "world class" imaginary produces new relations of "untouchability," with low-caste workers saddled (yet again, in a grim repetition of historical wrongs) with a double burden: first, a means of economic survival and social being that asks them to dispose waste matter disproportionately generated by affluent households; and second, to bear the ontological burden of "not touching"—physically and figuratively— the urban elite, who consider them dirty by virtue of their daily contact with waste matter.[63] Thus, we witness the rise in postcolonial India of a persistent, if unsteady, relationship between low-caste status and the handling of waste matter, with those who handle organic or wet waste matter (household garbage, slaughterhouse waste, sewage, biomedical waste, human waste) coming to be regarded as more "unclean"—hence, more lowly in the new social relations of (un)touchability that have come to mark the contemporary city—than those who work with dry waste matter (paper, metal, and plastic scrap, glass, e-waste).

Remark 7: Populism and People without Property in Jobs

The world is witnessing a resurgence of ethno-nationalisms, powering the rise of populist, authoritarian leaders in Turkey, the Philippines, and the United States, the latest sign of trouble in the liberal (and neoliberal) global order that has prevailed, with ups and downs, since the mid-twentieth century. One might say that India's 16th General Election in May 2014 was a harbinger of things to come, although it would be rash to equate political developments there to the forces that have propelled recent upheavals in the West. Still, the similarities in the rhetorical platforms that have allowed nativist mobilizations to capture state power across the world, with the notable aid of rural and working-class votes, are striking.

India's Bharatiya Janata Party (BJP) swept to a landslide victory against a background of economic jolts and titanic corruption scandals, on a populist electoral platform built around the promise of good governance, economic growth, and job creation. Unlike the protectionist, anti-free trade, and anticlimate change program espoused by Donald Trump in the United States, the BJP has taken the stand that market liberalization, climate-friendly policies, and bureaucratic reform are the anointed route to employment generation on a mass scale (although it has hedged whether rise in self-employment, historically in informal sectors of the economy, would qualify as a mark of success). In its macroeconomic orientation, the BJP's position is closer in some respects—albeit with significant differences in social policies—to the "Reagan/Thatcher revolution" of the 1980s, than it is to the "alt-right globalism" of Steve Bannon, Donald Trump's erstwhile ideological strategist. The resonances between the BJP's rise and Donald Trump's shock election victory, if one is looking, are to be found in the former's articulation of an economic reform agenda with an unapologetically nativist, Hindu nationalist vision that was able to tap into the majority community's development desires, its religious and sectarian prejudices, its security fears of Islamic terrorism abetted by hostile powers, its accumulated resentment of minority and lower-caste political assertion, its economic and cultural resentment of secular elites, and its wish for a "strongman" leader with the will to rid the perceived buildup of societal rot.[64]

The effectiveness of BJP's political strategy is evident from the electoral outcome: It was able to win 282 of 543 (51 percent) seats in the lower house of the Indian parliament (the Lok Sabha), with its National Democratic Alliance (NDA) capturing 336 of 543 (62 percent) seats. The Indian National Congress (INC) and its United Progressive Alliance (UPA) were wiped out: The INC retained only 44 seats and the UPA, as a whole, 60 seats. The Left Front (LF) alliance, with CPI-M in the lead, won 9 seats and 3.25 percent of the popular vote. How is this connected to the waste of living labor associated with the problem of unemployed and underemployed surplus populations?

As previously discussed, the recent decades have been a period of shockingly uneven, jobless economic growth in India, "making the country look more and more like islands of California in a sea of sub-Saharan Africa," in the words of two prominent economists.[65] The failure to generate stable employment—at least 1 million new jobs are required every month—for an increasingly urban and atomized population, or to allay the severe inequalities of opportunity as well as income, created, well before the recent economic setbacks, a large simmering reservoir of rage and frustration. Many Indians, neglected by the state, which spends proportionately less on health and education than Malawi, and spurned by private industry, which prefers cheap contract labor, appear to have embraced Modi's ideological package; in the words of the journalist Pankaj Mishra, it is "a revolution that will destroy the corrupt old political order and uproot its moral and ideological foundations while buttressing the essential framework, the market economy, of a glorious New India."[66] In short, this bears (cautious) comparison to the Thatcherite playbook so acutely examined by Stuart Hall in a series of writings, most memorably "'The Toad in the Garden': Thatcherism among the Theorists"[67] and later that same year, "Thatcherism and the Crisis of the Left: The Hard Road to Renewal."[68]

Like Thatcherism, the key elements of the ideology that trucks under the name "Moditva" (with "NaMo" filling in for "Maggie" among adulating supporters) have included managerial competence, free enterprise, and individual initiative to spur economic growth and job creation, eliminating bureaucratic red tape and corruption, defending the nation's security, and achieving national glory on the global stage. Less explicit but fully understood is a communal undertone that promises to discipline Muslims, which requires them, among other injunctions, to be "patriotic" and to accept Hindutva as a "way of life" that encompasses all religions.[69] The labile term "development"[70] has done stalwart work in propagating the secular and nonsecular aspects of Moditva to the BJP's diverse constituency.

This constituency includes the hard core of the religious Right (often funded by affluent diasporic communities in the West); wealthy industrialists (represented by the Federation of the Indian Chambers of Commerce and Industry [FICCI]), who want an easing of land, labor, and taxation laws; "intermediate classes" (comprising rich peasants, petty traders, owners of family businesses, and collusive factions of the bureaucracy that implement state regulations); and disaffected segments of the working class—"people without property in jobs," as the sociologist Peter Worsley once described the precariously employed—whose livelihoods have been displaced or put at risk by new regional and global flows of capital.[71]

Still it is prudent to exercise caution in comparing Thatcherism to Moditva. The size of BJP's electoral gains masks sharp geographic variation and the unsettling effects of India's first-past-the-post (FPTP) election system. The BJP's strategy of poll-booth management in states where it won resounding victories appears to have paid rich dividends. In short, although the long-term ideological success of Thatcherism lies in being able to pull mainstream politics in the UK decisively to the right, it is still too early to pronounce on

Moditva's durability: although its ideological inroads across the sociospatial spectrum cannot be ignored, evidence suggests that adept use of political technologies has been as effective in its recent triumphs as the arts of eliciting consent. In short, the BJP *has* made stunning gains in recent years at the national and state levels, but whether or not it has managed to stitch together a hegemonic bloc that will outlive Modi's personal charisma as a leader remains moot. Concessions to social welfare demands, persistent regional violence, suspect gains of its shock "demonetization" initiative, discontent over (and considerable harm from) the rollout of the Goods and Services Tax (GST), and widespread agrarian crises sow seeds of doubt.

What Is to Be Done?

By now it is apparent that modernization has never quite operated in the teleological manner proposed by Western theories. Or, to quote James Ferguson, "The question of rank is de-developmentalized, and the stark status differentiations of the global social system sit raw and naked, no longer softened by the promises of the 'not yet,'"[72] once Euro-American modernity ceases to be the telos. If growing structural unemployment, diminishing opportunities to convert labor power into a commodity, "disposability,"[73] "exclusion,"[74] "slow death,"[75] "abandonment,"[76] "mass alienation,"[77] "expulsion,"[78] "rise of the robots,"[79] and "the *Becoming Black of the World*"[80] are the analytics that capture the racialized dynamics of global capitalism today, then—in combination with climate change—profound questions are raised for the future of humanity and the future of capitalism as we know it.

But to abide by an aesthetics of abjection would be a despairing and imaginatively arid place to end. The contemporary revolution from above, write Stuart Hall, Doreen Massey, and Michael Rustin in *After Neoliberalism? The Kilburn Manifesto*, entails a "restructuring of state and society along market lines" and "the redistribution from poor to rich."[81] Yet, as they also note, "neoliberalism never conquered everything."[82] No matter how desperate their circumstances, the poor people I have met attempt to fabricate meaningful lives. There is, of course, boredom, drudgery, fatigue, sickness, extortion, humiliation, hunger, alcoholism, drug use, and violence that attend the lives of the urban underclasses. But there is *also* anger and contempt for exploiters, cognizance of inequality and injustice, stubbornness and outright defiance, a desire to get ahead[83] combined with unexpected kindness, loyalty, striving for dignity, for autonomy, and cohabitation. The unsettling point for academics and activists wedded to their desired political outcomes is that at certain historical conjunctures, deft demagoguery can cause popular disquiet to coalesce into right-wing populist movements—as appears to be the case in many parts of the world at present. But it possible too for this disquiet to become the political soil in which progressive formations can arise (the early incarnations of Syriza in Greece and Polemos in Spain are testaments).

Mohammad Ashraf, a homeless day laborer who is the protagonist in Aman Sethi's nonfiction account *A Free Man*, has made a living as a butcher and tailor; he's sold lemons and lottery tickets, but in another life he could well have been a philosopher. His musings offer deep insights into the struggle and, poignantly, the solitude of poverty. Trapped by his almost complete lack of power, he's obsessed with exercising the little power he does have. "The maalik owns our work," Ashraf says of his boss. "He does not own us." One way to prove his autonomy is to find work that allows "the perfect balance of *kamai* and *azadi*"—wages and freedom. It is to live fully by spending freely the little money one does have on pleasure, on beedis and boiled eggs and glassfuls of moonshine.

The desire for autonomy pulses powerfully, revealing itself in unexpected sites.[84] My colleague Sunil Kumar and I have encountered waste collectors who gave up waged factory work to enter the hardscrabble world of waste picking, because they resented being bossed around and wanted more control of their own time, even if their newfound livelihood is unstable.[85] What has recurrently surprised us is the "hospitality" and "care" (within limits) that people with uncertain livelihoods extend to each other. For example, I have met longtime waste pickers who are surprisingly accommodating in their attitudes toward Bengali Muslims (politicians and police label them as undocumented "Bangladeshis" in order to gain political mileage and extort them) even though the latter have taken over the lower rungs of informal waste economies in cities like Delhi, Patna, and Srinagar. "They work hard; they toil for long hours. They are trying to exist [*jeena chaha rahe hain*]. Why should anyone resent that?" is a not uncommon refrain. At the Ghazipur and Okhla landfills in Delhi I have witnessed a different sort of accommodation: solicitousness among permanent and contract staff of the municipal corporation, for the families of waste collectors, particularly the children, who scrounge for pickings at these dumps. Hiralal is the municipality's resident *chowkidar* (guard) at the Okhla landfill. He looks out for the children who pick at the dump. He knows the name of every child: who is new and who is old, and who the adult member of each one's family is.

Saskia Sassen claims that we are now at the beginning of a global phase that is "marked by *expulsions*—from life projects and livelihoods, from membership, from the social contract at the heart of liberal democracy."[86] Exaggerated or not, I certainly think that we are passing through an age where capitalism has rewritten the social contract, for example the inclusion promised by earlier instantiations of the "developmental state" or "welfare liberalism." We must accept that working classes who lack "property in jobs" constitute the modal form of employment in India (and increasingly, most of the world). Politically, this implies a departure from the familiar notion of classes as self-evident agents of social mobilization, "since they are not so much social groups as categories which constitute catchment-areas out of which people can be recruited to organized political (and other) activity, and which also throw up associations and organizations which can be 'won over.'"[87] In short, we are back in the world of Antonio Gramsci and Stuart Hall: "politics without guarantees."

The recent, checkered history of waste privatization in India (which I have written about elsewhere) shows a demonstrated bias toward large private firms, overlooking alternative models of *associationism* and *petty proprietorship* involving creative partnerships with waste pickers, waste pickers' organizations, and petty scrap dealers that can leverage their practical knowledge and livelihood needs—in the process quite possibly avoiding the pitfalls and failures of corporate enterprise, while generating safe and sustainable employment for hundreds of thousands. Bangalore's attempt to handle wet and dry waste in a decentralized manner, owing to the efforts, among others, of Hasiru Dala, a waste pickers' cooperative, is one evolving model. Pune Municipal Corporation's arrangement with SwAch, an organization of women waste pickers that has emerged out of the Kagad Kach Patra Kashtakari Panchayat (KKPKP), a registered trade union of waste pickers and waste collectors in Pune, offers yet another alternative.[88] As a consequence of sustained work by several trade unions and advocacy organizations across India, such as Chintan Environmental Research & Action, Transparent Chennai, All India Kabadi Mazdoor Mahasangh, as well as KKPKP and Hasiru Dala, among others, the Government of India's Solid Waste Management Rules of 2016 incorporated recognition of the informal sector's waste networks, repeatedly stressing the need for formal recognition of informal sector workers and their integration into urban waste governance programs. Creative examples from other parts of the world also abound: Melanie Sampson has documented the efforts of Johannesburg's reclaimers to resist waste privatization and secure from city authorities recognition for their rights to and superior knowledge of the waste recycling processes; similarly, Rosalind Frederick's research with Dakar's trash workers reveals "their battle to make their labor manifest and sculpt a vernacular understanding of its worth. Through their conviction that trash work is God's work, and their practical efforts to order the city, the workers demand a remoralization of work and stake claims for a more ethical infrastructure."[89]

A world dominated by people with increasingly uncertain jobs is unsettling. But it doesn't have to be a world without justice. Perhaps it's an opportunity for leftist imaginations to think outside the box, for Marxist political economy and postcolonial critique to enter into a generative quarrel, for ferment and experiment in the worlds of both, theory and practice.

NOTES

Thanks to Sunil Kumar, friend, researcher, and social activist, for invaluable assistance. Joshua Barkan and Rajyashree Reddy provided characteristically thoughtful comments on an early draft.

1. London, *Ending the Depression*, 4.
2. Ibid.
3. Ibid., 5.
4. Ibid., 10.
5. Ibid., 6.
6. Remarks 2 and 3 extend arguments initially developed in Gidwani and Corwin, "Governance of Waste."
7. Veblen, *Theory of the Leisure Class*, 60.
8. Horkheimer and Adorno, "Culture Industry as Mass Deception," 95.
9. Marcuse, *One-Dimensional Man*, 52.
10. Galbraith, *Affluent Society*, 115.
11. Baudrillard, *Political Economy of the Sign*, 62.
12. See Schor, "In Defense of Consumer Critique."
13. Packard, *Waste Makers*, chap. 6.
14. Lipset, qtd. in Strasser, *Waste and Want*, 277.
15. Guiltinan, "Creative Destruction."
16. Ibid., 20.

17. Ibid., 22.

18. Althusser, *Reproduction of Capitalism*.

19. Luxemburg, *Accumulation of Capital*; Harvey, *Limits to Capital*; Saad-Filho, "Abstract and Concrete Labour"; and Henderson, *California and the Fictions of Capital*.

20. Wrenn, "Surplus Absorption."

21. Ibid., 64–65.

22. Ibid., 65.

23. Ibid., 66.

24. Baran and Sweezy, *Monopoly Capital*, 380–81.

25. Wrenn, "Surplus Absorption," 69.

26. Ibid., 68.

27. See representatively, Meyer, "Waste Recycling"; Medina, "Solid Wastes"; Fredericks, "Vital Infrastructures"; Samson, "Waste Management."

28. Marx, *Capital*, 3:172.

29. Ibid., 172–73; emphasis added.

30. The discussion that follows is excerpted with modifications from Gidwani, "Time, Space, and the Subaltern" and Gidwani and Maringanti, "Waste-Value Dialectic."

31. Gidwani and Maringanti discuss the parallel case of Bholakpur, a multispectrum waste hub in Hyderabad, in south India ("Waste-Value Dialectic").

32. Annepu, "Sustainable Solid Waste Management," 145, appendix 2.

33. See Gidwani, "Waste/Value."

34. Gidwani and Maringanti, "Waste-Value Dialectic," 119.

35. Mbembe, *Critique of Black Reason*, 81.

36. Ibid., 6.

37. Ibid., 4.

38. Ibid., 6.

39. Marx, *Capital*, 3:180.

40. Field observations and interviews in Madanpur Khadar were conducted in October 2014 with the aid of social activist and researcher Sunil Kumar. Names of all informants have been altered.

41. Marx, *Capital*, 1:375–76.

42. Marx, *Grundrisse*, 286.

43. Ibid., 294.

44. Marx, *Capital*, 1:342.

45. Bauman, *Wasted Lives*.

46. Sanyal, *Rethinking Capitalist Development*.

47. Denning, "Wageless Life."

48. Smith, "Selective Hegemony."

49. Standing, *Precariat*.

50. Breman, *Informal Economy of India*.

51. Tyler, *Revolting Subjects*.

52. Sassen, *Expulsions*.

53. This discussion draws on Gidwani, "Work of Waste."

54. Mehrotra et al., "Employment Trends," 57.

55. Datta, "No Dividend Here."

56. Sen and Das, "Where Have All the Workers Gone?"

57. Ibid., 114.

58. Mehrotra et al. show that enterprises employing fewer than six workers accounted for 57.7 percent of all enterprises in 2011–12 and those employing fewer than ten workers accounted for 69.6 percent of all enterprises ("Employment Trends," 52, Table 5).

59. Worldometers, India Population, http://www.worldometers.info/world-population/india-population/ from UNEP projections (accessed June 1, 2017). In November 2016, India's total population was estimated at 1.326 billion, of which 32 percent or 424 million was urban. If 0.5 percent of that population is in informal waste-related livelihoods, that would peg the number at 2.12 million.

60. *World Urbanization Prospects*, http://esa.un.org/unpd/wup/Highlights/WUP2014-Highlights.pdf (accessed June 1, 2017). NGOs working with informal waste recyclers in Delhi estimate their population at 250,000–300,000.

61. Chikarmane and Narayan, "Formalising Livelihood," 3640.

62. Robinson, *Economic Philosophy*, 45.

63. See, in this regard, Guru and Sarukkai, *Cracked Mirror*, and Batra, "Untouchable Labor"; see also, Anupama Rao's chapter in this volume.

64. There are intriguing if necessarily imperfect parallels here to Marx's analysis in *The Eighteenth Brumaire of Louis Bonaparte*, originally published in 1852.

65. Sen and Dreze, *Uncertain Glory*, ix.

66. Mishra, "Narendra Modi."

67. Hall, "Toad in the Garden."

68. Hall, *Hard Road to Renewal*.

69. Mohan Bhagwat, the current *sarsanghchalak* (head) of the Rashtriya Svayamsevak Sangh (RSS), the parent organization of the ruling BJP party, said as much in a series of pronouncements in 2014. The proliferation of cow-protection vigilante groups (*gau rakshaks*) in many Indian states and their violent reprisals against Dalits and Muslims suspected of an *intention* to slaughter cows is a sign of the creeping Hindu normativity that is gaining hold in India. As Sawhney asks in a powerful article, "What skewed perspective is it that regards the cow as the only being worthy of protection in all creation; not the exhausted laborer asleep on the roadside, the frail children growing up in the dirt under bridges, or the despairing sick slumped outside hospitals?" ("In Service of Mother Cow," my translation). Also on this topic, see Govindrajan, "How to Milk a Cow in India."

70. Cf. Jini Kim Watson, this volume.

71. Worsley, "Frantz Fanon and the 'Lumpenproletariat.'"

72. Ferguson, *Global Shadows*, 186.

73. Wright, *Disposable Women*.

74. Sanyal, *Rethinking Capitalist Development*.

75. Gilmore, *Golden Gulag*.

76. Povinelli, *Economies of Abandonment*.

77. Harvey, *Seventeen Contradictions*, 24.

78. Sassen, *Expulsions*.

79. Ford, *Rise of the Robots*.

80. Mbembe, *Critique of Black Reason*.

81. Hall, Massey, and Rustin, *After Neoliberalism?* 5.

82. Ibid., 6.

83. Cf. Roberto's story in Jackson, *Wherewithal of Life*, 131.

84. Cf. Forment, this volume.

85. As the French sociologist Robert Castels points out, wage labor was associated with indignity for a very long time in Western societies; it was viewed as sign of compulsion and a site of dependency rather than freedom (*From Manual Workers to Wage Labor*).

86. Sassen, *Expulsions*, 29.

87. Worsley, "Frantz Fanon and the 'Lumpenproletariat,'" 211.

88. See, for example, Chikarmane and Narayan, "Formalising Livelihood," and *Rising from the Waste*.

89. Fredericks, "Vital Infrastructures," 545.

BIBLIOGRAPHY

Althusser, Louis. *On the Reproduction of Capitalism: Ideology and Ideological State Apparatuses.* 1971. Translated by G. M. Goshgarian. London: Verso, 2014.

Annepu, Ranjith Kharvel. "Sustainable Solid Waste Management in India." Master's thesis, Columbia University, Department of Earth and Environmental Engineering, 2012.

Baran, Paul A., and Paul M. Sweezy. *Monopoly Capital: An Essay on the American Economic and Social Order.* New York: Monthly Review Press, 1966.

Batra, Lalit. "Untouchable Labor and Wastewater Infrastructure: The Cultural Politics of Sanitation in Delhi." PhD diss., University of Minnesota, forthcoming, May 2018.

Baudrillard, Jean. *For a Critique of the Political Economy of the Sign.* St. Louis, Mo.: Telos, 1981.

Bauman, Zygmunt. *Wasted Lives: Modernity and Its Outcasts.* New York: Polity, 2004.

Breman, Jan. *At Work in the Informal Economy of India: A Perspective from the Bottom Up.* Delhi: Oxford University Press, 2013.

Castels, Robert. *From Manual Workers to Wage Labor: Transformation of the Social Question.* Translated by Richard Boyd. New Brunswick, N.J.: Transactions Publishers, 2002.

Chikarmane, Poornima, and Laxmi Narayan. "Formalising Livelihood: Case of Wastepickers in Pune." Economic and Political Weekly 35, no. 41 (2000): 3639–42.

———. *Rising from the Waste: Organizing Wastepickers in India, Thailand, and the Philippines.* Bangkok: Committee for Asian Women, 2009.

Datta, Devangshu. "No Dividend Here: The Slowdown in Jobs Shows that India Is Headed for Demographic Disaster." *Scroll.in.* https://scroll.in/article/854211/the-slowdown-in-jobs-shows-that-india-is-not-headed-for-a-demographic-dividend-but-disaster (accessed November 2, 2017).

Denning, Michael. "Wageless Life." *New Left Review* 66 (November/December 2010): 79–97.

Ferguson, James. *Global Shadows: Africa in the Neoliberal World Order.* Durham, N.C.: Duke University Press.

Ford, Martin. *Rise of the Robots: Technology and the Threat of a Jobless Future.* New York: Basic Books, 2015.

Fredericks, Rosalind. "Vital Infrastructures of Trash in Dakar." *Comparative Studies of South Asia, Africa, and the Middle East* 34, no. 3 (2014): 532–48.

Galbraith, John Kenneth. *The Affluent Society.* 1958. 40th anniversary ed. New York: Houghton Mifflin, 1998.

Gidwani, Vinay. "Time, Space, and the Subaltern: The Matter of Labor in Delhi's Grey Economy." In *Subaltern Geographies*, edited by Tariq Jazeel and Stephen Legg. Athens: University of Georgia Press, forthcoming.

———. "Waste/Value." In *The Wiley-Blackwell Companion to Economic Geography*, edited by Trevor J. Barnes, Jamie Peck, and Eric Sheppard, 275–88. Oxford: Wiley-Blackwell, 2012.

———. "The Work of Waste: Inside Urban India's Infra-Economy." *Transactions of the Institute of British Geographers* 40, no. 4 (2015): 1–21.

Gidwani, Vinay, and Julia Corwin. "Governance of Waste." *Economic and Political Weekly* (Review of Environment and Development) 52, no. 31 (2017): 44–54.

Gidwani, Vinay, and Anant Maringanti. "The Waste-Value Dialectic: Lumpen Urbanization in Contemporary India." *Comparative Studies of South Asia, Africa and the Middle East* 36, no. 1 (2016): 112–33.

Gilmore, Ruth. *Golden Gulag: Prisons, Surplus, Crisis, and Opposition in Globalizing California.* Berkeley: University of California Press, 2007.

Govindrajan, Radhika. "How to Milk a Cow in India: Reclaiming Gau-Seva from Gau-Rakshaks." *Wire*, May 1, 2017. https://thewire.in/130617/cow-beef-gau-rakshak/.

Guiltinan, Joseph. "Creative Destruction and Destructive Creations: Environmental Ethics and Planned Obsolescence." *Journal of Business Ethics* 89, Supplement 1 (2009): 19–28.

Guru, Gopal, and Sundar Sarukkai. *The Cracked Mirror: An Indian Debate on Experience and Theory*. Delhi: Oxford University Press, 2012.

Hall, Stuart. *The Hard Road to Renewal: Thatcherism and the Crisis of the Left*. London: Verso, 1988.

———. "'The Toad in the Garden': Thatcherism among the Theorists." In *Marxism and the Interpretation of Culture*, edited by Cary Nelson and Lawrence Grossberg, 35–74. Urbana-Champaign: University of Illinois Press, 1988.

Hall, Stuart, Doreen Massey, and Michael Rustin, eds. *After Neoliberalism?: The Kilburn Manifesto*. London: Lawrence & Wishart, 2015.

Harvey, David. *The Limits to Capital*. Oxford: Basil Blackwell, 1982.

———. *Seventeen Contradictions and the End of Capitalism*. London: Profile Books, 2014.

Henderson, George. *California and the Fictions of Capital*. New York: Oxford University Press, 1998.

Horkheimer, Max, and Theodor Adorno. "Culture Industry as Mass Deception." In *Dialectic of Enlightenment: Philosophical Fragments*, edited by Gunzelin Schmid Noerr, translated by Edmund Jephcott, 94–136. Palo Alto, Calif.: Stanford University Press, 2002.

Jackson, Michael. *The Wherewithal of Life: Ethics, Migration, and the Question of Well-Being*. Berkeley: University of California Press, 2013.

London, Bernard. *Ending the Depression through Planned Obsolescence*. New York: published by the author, 1932. https://babel.hathitrust.org/cgi/pt?id=wu.89097035273;view=1up;seq=1.

Luxemburg, Rosa. *The Accumulation of Capital*. Translated by Agnes Schwarzschild. London: Routledge and Kegan Paul, 1913.

Marcuse, Herbert. *One-Dimensional Man: Studies in the Ideology of Advanced Industrial Society*. 1964. New York: Routledge, 2002.

Marx, Karl. *Capital*, vol. 1. Translated by Ben Fowkes. London: Penguin Books, 1976.

———. *Capital*, vol. 3. Translated by David Fernbach. London: Penguin Books, 1981.

———. *The Eighteenth Brumaire of Louis Bonaparte*. 1852. Translated by Daniel De Leon. Chicago: Charles H. Kerr, 1907.

———. *Grundrisse*. Translated by Martin Nicolaus. London: Penguin Books, 1973.

Mbembe, Achille. *Critique of Black Reason*. Translated by Laurent Dubois. Durham, N.C.: Duke University Press, 2017.

Medina, Martin. "Solid Wastes, Poverty, and the Environment in Developing Countries: Challenges and Opportunities." Working Paper, World Institute for Development Economics Research (WIDER) No. 23. Tokyo: United Nations University, 2010.

Mehrotra, Santosh, Jajati Parida, Sharmistha Sinha, and Ankita Gandhi. "Employment Trends in the Indian Economy: 1994–95 to 2011–12." *Economic & Political Weekly* 49, no. 32 (2014): 49–57.

Meyer, Günter. "Waste Recycling as a Livelihood in the Informal Sector—The Example of Refuse Collectors in Cairo." *Applied Geography and Development* 30 (1987): 78–94.

Mishra, Pankaj. "Narendra Modi and the New Face of India." *Guardian*, May 14, 2014.

National Sample Survey Office (NSSO). "Informal Sector and Conditions of Employment in India." NSS Report No. 557 (68/10/2) (2014). New Delhi: Ministry of Statistics and Programme Implementation, Government of India, 2014.

Packard, Vance. *The Waste Makers*. London: Longmans, Green, 1960.

Povinelli, Elizabeth. *Economies of Abandonment: Social Belonging and Endurance in Late Liberalism*. Durham, N.C.: Duke University Press, 2011.

Robinson, Joan. *Economic Philosophy: An Essay on the Progress of Economic Thought*. London: Penguin Books, 1962.

Saad-Filho, Alfredo. "Abstract and Concrete Labour in Marx's Theory of Value." *Review of Political Economy* 9, no. 4 (1997): 457–77.

Samson, Melanie. "Forging a New Conceptualization of 'the Public' in Waste Management." WIEGO Working Paper No. 32. Cambridge, Mass.: WIEGO, 2015.

Sanyal, Kalyan. *Rethinking Capitalist Development: Primitive Accumulation, Governmentality and Post-Colonial Capitalism*. New Delhi: Routledge India, 2007.

Sassen, Saskia. *Expulsions: Brutality and Complexity in the Global Economy*. Cambridge, Mass.: Belknap Press of Harvard University Press, 2014.

Sawhney, Simona. "Log Gaya Mata Ki Seva Karte Karte Khud Bhediye Ban Gaye Hain" [In claiming to serve mother cow, people have turned into wolves]. *Wire*, May 31, 2017. http://thewirehindi.com/10068/cow-vigilantes-hindu-fundamentalists-and-hinduism/.

Schor, Juliet. "In Defense of Consumer Critique: Revisiting the Consumption Debates of the Twentieth Century." *Annals of the American Academy of Political and Social Science* 611, no. 16 (2007): 16–30.

Sen, Amartya, and Jean Dreze. *An Uncertain Glory: India and Its Contradictions*. Princeton: Princeton University Press, 2013.

Sen, Kunal, and Deb Kusum Das. "Where Have All the Workers Gone? Puzzle of Declining Labour Intensity in Organised Indian Manufacturing." *Economic and Political Weekly* 50, no. 33 (2015): 108–15.

Sethi, Aman. *A Free Man*. Delhi: Random House India, 2011.

Smith, Gavin. "Selective Hegemony and Beyond-Populations with 'No Productive Function': A Framework for Inquiry." *Identities* 18, no. 1 (2011): 2–38.

Standing, Guy. *The Precariat: The New Dangerous Class*. London: Bloomsbury, 2011.

Strasser, Susan. *Waste and Want: A Social History of Trash*. New York: Metropolitan Books, 1999.

Tyler, Imogen. *Revolting Subjects: Social Abjection and Resistance in Neoliberal Britain*. New York: Zed Books, 2013.

United Nations. *World Urbanization Prospects: The 2014 Revision—Highlights*. New York: United Nations, 2014.

Veblen, Thorstein. *The Theory of the Leisure Class*. 1899. Oxford: Oxford University Press, 2007.

Worsley, Peter. "Frantz Fanon and the 'Lumpenproletariat.'" *Socialist Register* 9 (1972): 193–230.

Wrenn, Mary. "Surplus Absorption and Waste in Neoliberal Monopoly Capitalism." *Monthly Review* (July–August 2016): 63–76.

Wright, Melissa. *Disposable Women and Other Myths of Global Capitalism*. New York: Routledge, 2006.

NINE

Goolarabooloo Futures: Mining and Aborigines in Northwest Australia

Stephen Muecke

Writing from a part of the "Global South," whose current conjunctural position is defined historically by old imperial political and economic forces, encourages me to put myself in the position of the Indigenous people. After all, I am writing *with* the Goolarabooloo, and *about* their country. This part of Australia, where the Goolarabooloo people have lived since before memory, is often officially designated as "remote." Sixty thousand years ago when the seas were lower, there was an archipelago of islands stretching from South Asia to the Kimberley, northwest Australia. One theory about the origin of the Australian peoples is that they paddled canoes from island to island and thus entered this huge southern continent at that point.[1] But "remote" makes no sense for the locals at home; this is white people talking from the southern cities for whom the desert center and the far north are still frontier areas, having been colonized about one hundred years after occupation began in Sydney in 1788. Such places may well be remote from government centers and the goods and services now necessary, but "remote" also establishes the affective distance and othering that facilitates continued colonization. This chapter describes how such perceptions of distance have underpinned both old-style dispossession and colonization and the newer corporate colonization associated with mining ventures.

Australia, of course, is a settler colonial society, but its "remote" areas are still somewhat frontier-like, and extractive colonization is strongly in evidence as a get-in get-out industrial-political formation. In large towns such as Broome, where most Goolarabooloo people live, settlement has been in place since the late nineteenth century, but the societal divisions speak of well-marked distinctions among Indigenous locals, locals (born there or long-term residents), and those who are more transient. The last group might comprise mine workers or professionals in administration or education who come to Broome from the city for limited terms. So a place like Broome might be said to exhibit signs of a hybrid colonialism. It is neither fully settled such that Indigenous locals are displaced to the point of no longer having a visible presence, nor is it a temporary outpost of a colonial formation extracting labor or commodities; it shares features of both.

The Indigenous communities of the Broome area retain identity and some political autonomy in that they have institutions (like the Kimberley Land Council) set up to negotiate their interests. Sovereignty (never ceded through a treaty or through explicit military conquest) is sometimes expressed as traditional (i.e., as continual occupation) and sometimes as a struggle against the colonizers. Anne Poelina, for example, is well aware of the historical exploitation of her people in the earlier pearling and pastoral industries, but today, referring to the "neoliberal context, with . . . the ever-increasing threat of massive industrialization . . . by multi-national mining corporations—the new colonisers," pointedly says, "we are all being colonized: it is not a black or white question any longer."[2] This focuses the problem differently from the settler colonial theory (SCT), arguably the dominant model for postcolonial theory in the Australian context. SCT is nationally focused, and it is "an appealing interpretive framework for academics seeking to understand the state's increasingly coercive approach to Indigenous people,"[3] according to Alissa Macoun and Elizabeth Strakosch, and it remains a "largely White attempt" to do so.[4] With its Marxist oppositionality to the state and its intellectual vanguardism, SCT hopes to reveal colonial structures to the colonists themselves, as if they were under some kind of moral obligation to listen or comply. However, on the rare occasions they are forced to listen, the official response is to assert the rule of law (within which the Indigenous colonized must be enclosed) and the popular response is often a version of what Ghassan Hage calls the "white colonial settler *condition*," a kind of reverse racism in which the whites see themselves as essentially good people "forced" to take tough measures against the Others to avoid becoming their victims.[5] No amount of evidence of the oppression of Indigenous people will shake their conviction that these people are in receipt of special benefits, refuse to assimilate, or lazily avoid work.

Now, importantly for the kind of recasting of postcolonial theory I want to sketch is that this "white colonial settler condition" is a globalized discourse that you might find among those besieged by Islamic threats (in France, Israel, or Germany), or any other kind of threat by an Other. Being globalized, it can appear in parallel with the mining companies like the ones Anne Poelina is fearful of—the "new colonisers" working anonymously in "extra-state" spaces created precisely to facilitate the flow of capital and commodities unfettered by fiscal or labor regulation constraints.[6]

Henceforth, I would argue, postcolonial theory will have to come to terms (using on-the-ground ethnographic research) with a globalized neoliberal ideology that is much more anti-state than are the Marxists, now struggling to stay in the picture. Those wielding versions of neoliberal ideology not only have the power of capital investment, they have powerful representation in government to pave their way, and they can mobilize a discourse of moral superiority—what they do is inevitably "good for the economy": They create jobs. And they can masquerade as victims as soon as any Other raises an objection. Although SCT could often be quite good at historical description, it will now have to revise its description of the social spaces in which hybrid colonialisms and global (multi-national corporate) colonialisms do their work. What a local ethnographic description discovers in Broome refers less to the national level (as in SCT) and more to the global networks of which they are instances, that is, the larger context. But the smaller one, by-passing the national level, will focus not on the concept of "society," but on the institu-tions that work toward putting organizational scripts into action. "What is Broome society?" is a question without an answer. But "What institutions have been set up there to do what kinds of work?" is the kind of question an ethnographer can begin to answer. And this is what I shall do: describe what I can see going on in these terms, then come back with a revision of the conceptual architecture that helps us think more generally.

I am engaged in writing an ethnography with the Goolarabooloo and have had a long association with the community. I think I understand the necessary visiting protocols, and I regularly visit from Sydney. For years I was in the habit of meeting the patriarch of the Goolarabooloo community, Paddy Roe, under the old Tamarind Tree where he had his meetings, and now, over a decade after he passed away, I am visiting Broome again. The anthropologist Michael Taussig and I are participating in an experimental documentary called *Sunset Ethnography*, and, having decided that the Tamarind Tree might be a good spot to film a conversation, we install ourselves there as Aaron Burton is doing the cine-matography.[7] Taussig and I are staging a conversation about the theory that is supposed to relate to the workshop on "experimental ethnography" that we were holding with a few colleagues. The following is an extract from the film:

> MICHAEL TAUSSIG: What about a different understanding of the representation of theory itself in its relationship to, aah, call it raw life? That seems to be very important to me, that the theory is not like a . . . flag that's nailed to the experiences, but has a much more . . . sinuous relationship, often barely visible?

FIGURE 9.1. Mick Taussig

STEPHEN MUECKE: Yeah, well, it does, I think. Like, from Michel Foucault I gleaned the idea of the, of the *specific intellectual*. And I found I could immediately say, yeah, well, that's what my friend Paddy Roe is. He's not a *general* intellectual, he's one that works through, um, specific situations, and his technique is a storytelling technique. He persuaded people. He did his politics through seduction, and ah . . . [8]

LOCAL WHITEFELLA: G'day. The woman that owns this block is just inquiring as to what you're doing here.

SM: Teresa?

LW: Yeah, Teresa.

SM: Yeah, she knows me well. Tell her it's Steve.

LW: Steve, Steve's here. Is that all I need to say?

SM: I think so.

LW: Oh, she was a bit miffed. Somebody under the tree, she couldn't see who it was.

SM: Tell her I'm real sorry.

LW: I asked if they got permission, and she said, "I don't know."

SM: I didn't know I needed permission. I worked with old Lulu on this spot years ago, that's why I came back here.

LW: Yeah yeah, no, that's OK. No, nothing else needed?

SM: Tell her I'm sorry.

LW: Yeah yeah, that's all right [He walks off] . . . Steve.

MT: What about the place of, ah, pictures and images in the story, that would seem to me to be important in developing the experimental ethnography?

SM: Yeah, well all I can think about them is their role as mediators. Um, they're not illustrations, they open another window, another mediation, so it's not about . . . "I am interpreting the world," but er . . .

[TERESA ROE walks up]

MT: Hi there, how are you?

SM: How are you?

FIGURE 9.2. Teresa Roe with Stephen Muecke

TR: Heeeey! Good to see you. Good to see you, Steve. [Stephen and Teresa hug.] Been a long time.

SM: Yeah. Only last year I was here. [Stephen introduces Mick.] My friend Mick.

MT: How you doing?

SM: This is Aaron.

Aaron Burton: Nice to meet you. Hi.

SM: Well, we had some good news this week.[9]

Inserted here, this little dramatic episode under the Tamarind Tree records a valuably il-lustrative anthropological mistake—failing to ask permission to come onto land. Teresa, Paddy's daughter, sent someone to interrupt us because of this mistake. She couldn't see who we were, being at some distance, but she sent one of the local whitefellas living on her block, who went back with the message.

As I have been doing fieldwork in and around Broome over many years, I have come to realize that it is through such interruptions that one gets a heightened sense of the real, and what is at stake for participants.[10] It has become something of a fieldwork principle for me, to look for moments when the normal order seems to break down, and the workings of the system become visible. Or as Taussig would say, the system is always "nervous" anyway.[11]

So what is the system, and how well is it working? The system is whatever people are doing to make sense of everything going on around them, but that sense gets interrupted, so you have to do more work to make sense again. But where is the work taking place? Under the Tamarind Tree or in some other institution? There lies all the important dif-ferences; the differing systems are not based on the "same society" or the "same country," but are sustained by organizational differences. If you go online and view more of the exchange with Teresa Roe in *Sunset Ethnography*, you will hear her story about how her people, the Goolarabooloo, have been struggling to protect the country that enshrines their law and culture, what they call *bugarrigarra* in that part of Australia, often glossed as "dreaming." This is the set of institutions they have been seeking to protect ever since Europeans made their incursions into this country, and again, keeping with the analytical vocabulary I wish to continue with, the institutions under attack are economic, religious, legal, moral, and aesthetic. And even if I describe them using these English terms, the organizational differences, compared to the equivalent modern European institutions, are so radical as to cause all sorts of mistranslations. The Goolarabooloo want to protect them because they are their way of making sense in their world; they thus feel a strong sense of responsibility for "the country," to the point of this being a life-and-death issue for them.

So in between the Goolarabooloo institutions and the ones brought and installed by the colonial power, I want to record some of the nervousness among systems, the tenta-tive communications, the clashes, and the reconciliations. It is no longer possible to gaze ethnographically at the others as a culture or a community according to the early twentieth-century models of reconstructive ethnographies. The settler society is embedded, now, having moved from violent dispossession through various forms of liberal accommodation of Indigenous people and their ways of life, without ever fully recognizing Indigenous sovereignty with the instrument of a treaty or a new section of the constitution. The ethnographic description, therefore, will look at "both sides" of the colonial divide but will not see a clear division or battle line, but rather a shifting network of institutional accommodations. It will be necessary to describe the Moderns, as Bruno Latour calls the Europeans, in ways already called for in this context. David Trigger writes, quoting Doug McEachern, that

> work by anthropologists and geographers on the impact of mining upon indigenous peoples, the "cosmology" and "culture of international mining companies" should not be conceived as a "taken-for-granted matter," but should be made as "subject to ethnographic work and critical deconstruction" as other forms of culture.[12]

And what a strange "form of culture" colonialist resource extraction must have seemed to the Indigenous peoples of western Australia. For the first generation of the colonized there was some attraction in station work, getting to know the culture of horses, cattle, and sheep, even if only in exchange for rations, tobacco, boots, and clothing. But the idea of taking the animals away to some invisible market was hard to understand, and if people speared a bullock (on their own traditional lands) to have a good feed, they found out that this was a crime and an opportunity to chain-gang them for hard labor building roads. Mary Durack, descended from early pastoralists, is sanguine about the pearling industry, writing in 1969 about pearl shell extraction:

> The women showed even more enthusiasm than their men and would dive, naked, to a depth of ten fathoms, emerging minutes later, their canvas neck bags crammed to capacity.
>
> By 1868, ten boats operating in and around Nickol Bay had shipped away £6000 worth of mother-of-pearl, mostly procured by native women, and soon the news went forth that there were fortunes for the taking. . . . Traders [were attracted] from China, Java, the Celebes and the Dutch East Indies.[13]

In the early days, these women were enslaved, raped, and murdered at will.[14] And pearling became the most valuable industry in the colony at the time.[15] Europe had not only invented the useful concept of the colony for "shipping away" value using slave labor, but it had also invented the concept of alienable Nature so that stuff like pearl-shell could be seen as coming for free. Having the capital to invest in the necessary equipment gave one the necessary leverage, if not the moral right, to extract both kinds of value. This was the logic of expropriating lands, securing labor, and then extracting resources back to the center of empire, that continues to the present, but now in a more complex form.[16] "Remote" Australia is still a zone of Indigenous-mining conflict, but the flow of power is more complex as Australia is not only a contested territory of resources, but also the corporate headquarters of companies now participating in the colonial extraction of resources in other nations around the globe.

Woodside Energy, for instance, was first incorporated in 1954 in Victoria, a southern Australian state, and now has "exploration acreage" in North-West Australia, Africa, Canada,

Ireland, Peru, and other countries. Now its value accumulates in numbers, translatable to the accounts of an endlessly shifting population of shareholders who might reside any-where, who might not even know that their financial adviser has chosen Woodside for their portfolio. This distance and anonymity were already features of the modern econ-omy that sought to export its conceptual modeling, and are taken to their extreme with the neoliberal economy where locality no longer matters and empire has no center to which to return concrete value. If, in the nineteenth century, "Marvellous Melbourne" was a city built on gold strikes because the wealth extracted stayed in the community, and even in 1972 Conzinc Riotinto could advertise its claim that it was "putting something back" by "building towns, ports and harbours . . . opening up the Australian emptiness; turning hitherto wasted areas into national assets with a future,"[17] then twenty-first-century min-ing finds it harder to plausibly use such nation-building rhetoric, but it tries.

Could this alienation and abstraction of capitalist organization be one of the reasons for its lack of success, so far, in Goolarabooloo country? Woodside has been working in North-West Australia for a long time with a "system" that has these features:

1. The wealthiest shareholders living in comfort a long way away;
2. The natural resources located "out there" and unconnected with any humans involved (water in desert areas is often a scarce resource; pumping up ground water for industry can cause waterholes used by Aboriginal people to dry up. This can be an issue, especially if the waterhole is a *jila*, a sacred place);
3. An organization efficiently installed, with the minimum of infrastructure, ready to pull out and move to another location when the resource runs out;
4. The workers are also alienated from the locality. They might even live in Bali and fly-in fly-out (FIFO).[18] Overlaid on this distance and alienation from localities is,
5. A script that helps sustain the resource-extraction system, the familiar one of "rolling out" a modernist template of progress that is supposed to work everywhere in the same way.

The people living in Broome have seen what has happened in the Pilbara to the south, in places like Karratha and Port Hedland, with huge open-cut iron ore mines, massive in-frastructure, and unfulfilled promises of benefits made to the indigenous people. Some Aboriginal people work for mining companies and related industries are doing well, but it is not the case that whole communities or towns have been able to clearly improve their well-being because of mining. In the film *Heritage Fight*, the parliamentarian Tom Stevens put the case from experience:

> When I was starting my parliamentary career nearly thirty years ago, I listened to Woodside talk about what they were going to do in the Pilbara as they started their gas projects down there. And how they were going to make a significant and positive impact upon the lives of the Roebourne Aboriginal people and the permanent population of the Pilbara. And over those thirty years those commitments, those undertakings, have been breached. They've provided a lot of jobs for a lot of fly-in fly-out workers, a lot of prosperity for the state and nation. They have, in my view—good people though they might

be—broken faith with me as a parliamentarian who was persuaded to support them on the basis of their word that they would do great and grand things for the Aboriginal people of Roebourne and the surrounding areas, and they have not.[19]

So there is some basis for contesting the neoliberal script that it is "only a matter of time" before capital-based industries roll out over the whole country, that what happened in the Pilbara must now happen in the Kimberley, the kind of logic used by the WA government led by Colin Barnett. There is more than one logic; not everyone operates the system or lives in the world of extractive industries. Nowhere is this more visible, in an instructive manner, than on frontiers where Indigenous people and mining companies clash. There are surprisingly different countries, systems, institutions, and worlds, and it is with this pluralism that one can contest the "only a matter of time" narrative.

So when Woodside petroleum looks at Walmadany (JPP), the site on the coast that they wanted to use to build a gas plant and port, their activities institutionalize the site into a quite different world from the one that Paddy Roe showed me decades ago, and different again from the one where the activists situate their base camp for the anti-gas campaign. What elements constitute the Woodside version of Walmadany? The resource they are after, methane gas, is central. They see it as a part of nature, over there, unconnected with us humans; in fact we are alienated from it. (I should add that popular ecological discourses share this same European view of Nature, which is why they too alienate humans from "wilderness.") Woodside's modern institutions set up their outposts here: an Economy, a way of doing Science and deploying technology, and a way of managing an organization. A globalizing Western modernity extends its tentacles here as if it had no connection at all except to extract one part of its Nature, the gas, along the pipeline, which is now a metaphor as well as a technology, a metaphor for an institution that is built to get in and get out with nothing sticking to it. No need to renaturalize, as I like to say now. The call for renaturalization, assuming the possibility of multinaturalism[20] (which I understand to mean that no collective of humans and nonhumans can be reduced to a single nature-culture ontological distinction, that there are multiple variable ontological distinctions in play) unsettles the universalizing (and colonizing) tendencies of the Moderns. But rather than staying with the familiar dialectical opposition of modernization and its critique, the process of renaturalization is reformist.

Once you take the first step, establishing that nature has to be reinstituted, rebooted, and pluralized because the version of nature that European modernity brought with it has hit an ecological wall, then the other institutions have to be readjusted as well. Science, the Law, the Economy, Aesthetics, all have to be reinstituted. They do not have to be completely replaced, because of course there are good things about them, and they have always, in any case, been subject to change. But with my new ethnographic project, I want to specify the changes that might have to be made in the light of Indigenous and ecological local matters of concern.

This project involves practical methods of survival, of persistence rather than opposition and critique. It is about redirecting flows along networks. For this reason, I want the book I will write to speak to each mode of existence (Science,[21] the Law,[22] etc.) on its own terms. The ethnography, the descriptive writing, will follow what it is that keeps the institutions alive as going concerns. These modes or worlds are equally real and are busily and simultaneously composing themselves, with or without our help. They are works in progress, and I hope to expose their more solid attributes as well as their sensitivities. Humans and things interact in the composition of these worlds, they intra-act agentially[23] because this is a process in which human subjectivities are being invented and sustained. Likewise, in what we used to call the "objective world," facts are brought into being and kept alive in their networks of relations. So-called Nature is no longer the privileged site of the real, nor is Society a place for humans alone.

Can't You See the Turtles?

Scientific knowledge, in Latour's account in the *Inquiry*, is elaborated with a mode of existence he calls *reference*. It is what enables bits of knowledge to be passed and maintained across great distances in time and space. It might be born in labs and accumulate in archives, but it needs the collaboration of colleagues, human and nonhuman actors, to sustain it. It, too, is tested against alterity. This would be experimental method. If the same results can be obtained with a repetition of the experiment in a somewhat new context, then the facts are sustained and can continue to exist.

Now, Aboriginal people in Broome don't do this sort of thing, surely not? Where are their labs and archives? Exactly. Although everyone agrees that Aboriginal people have lots of knowledge, outsiders are not quite sure where they are hiding it. It kind of pops up unexpectedly. Let us recall, before going on to a case study, that Latour's philosophical anthropology of the Moderns has successfully "provincialized" Western modernism, and he paid careful attention to the way that Dipesh Chakrabarty did this via the discipline of history.[24] The universalist pretensions of this modernity are now specified and moderated, and have to enter negotiations with all kinds of Others.

So the case of Phillip Roe and the sea turtles is relevant here. Phillip Roe is a key figure in the campaign against mining interests taking over the country that his family has custodianship rights over. Now, at the time of the Woodside Petroleum push to build a gas plant at Walmadany, a team of scientists was engaged by the state government to carry out an environmental survey. Hawksbill and green sea turtles were two animal species on the list to be investigated. The nesting study commissioned for the Department of State Development found only one "old" nest and three false crawls. An independent and peer-reviewed study into marine turtle nesting in the James Price Point area led by University of Melbourne marine biologist Malcolm Lindsay found fourteen turtle nests and thirty-eight false crawls over the 2011–12 nesting season. This independent study was one of a few carried out by "citizen scientists" on different species. They were able to point out flaws in the design of the government report, which, for instance "surveyed only 12 percent of the coastline most threatened by the precinct, overlooking the significant 6 km. strip of important nesting habitat."[25] The scientists doing the government report didn't seek or obtain the help of Phillip Roe, who has hunted turtles and gathered turtle eggs in season all his life. His people have been doing this for innumerable generations. He pointed out to the citizen scientists that turtles around Walmadany often nested on the rocky foreshore. The government scientist hadn't bothered to look there because they "didn't expect" or "would be surprised" to find turtles nesting in a rocky place. Informants were also amazed at Phillip's uncanny ability to point out nests when they couldn't see any traces of a nest in the sand, or, on one occasion, pointing into the ocean and saying the special word, *undud*, for mating turtles. It took my informant a few minutes to see what he was seeing. I found out later that it was Phillip's polarized sunglasses that gave him his "uncanny ability." My Goolarabooloo friends are fond of practical jokes like this.

Alterity introduces the unexpected, disrupting the repetition of the already known that I think characterizes the spread of modernist universals. For the government scientists the science hadn't really extended beyond the lab back in the city and they were closed to the possibility of extending collegiality to Phillip Roe. That the citizen scientists were prepared to do this meant that their lab included more local features of the West Kimberley. It went further in time and space, which is what a referential mode of existence is meant to do, as it discovers and then sustains its forms of truth so that they can be relied on.

A Political Blunder

My ethnographic principle of paying attention to interruptions was fruitful in the mode of existence of politics. Politics, in Latour's account, is about extending representation, in both senses of the word; the politician stands for the people in the electorate and hopes to speak to them and for them in a language in which they can recognize themselves. There would always be some difficulty for a white politician from a capital city far to the south to represent Aboriginal people who may even refuse to vote, but that is a rather general issue.

The more significant thing for my ethnography is the organization of alliances that either builds up or diminishes the number of spheres of influence that are associated, broadly, with the two sides of the gas plant issue. And if I do not want to use the word "society," I can replace it with "association," which means not just associations of humans, but also things, concepts, feelings as these link up to create real worlds.

The interiority of a sphere is constituted by the elements inside breathing the same atmosphere—you can tell that I'm using the language of Peter Sloterdijk here—or having the same values, while being surrounded by a membrane that provides immunity. To this, I would add Latour's idea of partnerships or allies in political causes, and different spheres might be drawn together in political association. Yet these spheres are fragile, and political tactics attempt to redraw the spatial map of associations of different spheres. That the bubble of capitalist confidence is constantly under threat of bursting may not be such an arbitrary metaphor, and it certainly applies in the case of Woodside's tenuous relationship with its joint venture partners. Woodside's bubble finally burst in April 2013 when it announced that it would not continue with the $45 billion gas plant. All along, it was the state government's financial and political support that was urging Woodside on.

Colin Barnett, the head of government, made a major political blunder—one that every-one recalls in Broome—by saying that the coastline at Walmadany was "unremarkable," implying not only remote but empty, and therefore open for industrial development. Sud-denly he wasn't talking the same language as the people he was supposed to represent. For them, the beautiful red cliffs *were* quite remarkable, which is why now I will move from a political mode of existence to an aesthetic one.

But just to conclude this section on politics, you will excuse me, I hope, for complicat-ing the picture with the addition of Sloterdijk's spheres. But they are useful in that they reinforce Latour's rhetorical figure of the circle as that which characterizes the political mode of existence. Politicians talk in circles. They can't be expected to adhere to the truth conditions of scientists whose knowledge is organized to persist over long distances and times. Political talk is true for short periods—as they say, "a week is a long time in poli-tics." It sounds the right note, gathers further allies, and increases its sphere of influence. It will network with institutions and influential individuals to extend its circle, which of course was the case with Barnett's political work in the Kimberley, where the Aboriginal organization the Kimberley Land Council was a key ally. In the end, Barnett's Woodside episode was a failure. In the state election of June 2013, a Green candidate collected 38 percent of the votes in the town of Broome, going against the major parties' trends, and nearly got elected.

The Aesthetic Mobilized

Now, if Barnett blundered politically by saying that the coastline was "unremarkable," then this is a point where the aesthetic crosses the political. The red cliffs are identified with the places people love to go fishing and swimming, which are significant sites for law and culture, which contribute to tourism—nothing much to do with capitalist efficiency, prof-itability, and objectivity.[26] But feelings like "love of country" cannot be ignored if my ethnography is to find out what the core values of the negotiating parties are. You know what the central values are when people will lay down their life for them. The late Joseph Roe said the last thing he would give up in any negotiation is the right to protect law and culture, *bugarrigarra*, whereas his major opponent, the politician Barnett, might say that the last thing he will give up is the right to exploit nature, which probably comes down to (technical) efficiency, (economic) profitability and (scientific) objectivity, core values that never seem to migrate into Indigenous Australians' spheres of influence without threat-ening their very existence as Indigenous people.

I want to give an example of how this love of country was mobilized as political activism in the campaign against the gas plant, and stay within Sloterdijk's "sphereology." Spheres are interiorities that are defined by their passage to the outside through mechanisms of attraction, repulsion, and flow. Sunday, May 13, 2012, in Broome, Mother's Day, pro-vided an "atmosphere" in which the anti-gas protesters tried the charm of love hearts on banners, bouquets of flowers, and so on to lure the police into imitative association and hence into a mutual sphere of protection.[27] The protesters, against all expectations that there would be sporadic violent protests, came up with an unexpected idea. They tried to create a common sphere with the police; they could not assume they were already securely in one (as co-citizens of the nation, for instance). This was a kind of spell exercised in the context of what was remembered as the previous year's "Black Tuesday" when police got quite violent. The rhetoric of this "Platonic love story" seemed to say, "We are all within the charmed circle of mother-love-fertility, within yet another sphere of celebration of the national day for mothers." All this is spatially organized and imitative rather than communicative—they would like the love to be contagious by association.

This unexpected maneuver by the activist campaigners worked: It came as a surprise, another interruption that created the real. Some of the police said they were touched and took flowers home to their mums; the broader community was "charmed" and therefore seduced into sympathy for the campaign; it was coherent with their core beliefs (What do you love about Broome? *The beach, the fishing,* Where do you go fishing? *Up the coast . . .*). Affect and other aspects of an aesthetic mode of existence take on weight here and assert their singular effects. They are strong in themselves; they are not the effect of something else. I have made the point about Barnett's mistake in trying to reduce this mode of existence. By saying "unremarkable" he tried to deflate the aesthetic sphere, so that efficiency and profitability could take over. But by discounting the attachments of the Broome folk who "love the place," he committed the basic political sin. He lost numbers. People moved and attached themselves to the "Save Broome" campaign, which coincidentally was making itself attractive with the Mother's Day campaign.

This spatial tightness, with spheres abutting each other and sometimes dissolving into each other when they find they are swimming in the same atmospheres, breathing the same oxygen, also means that discourses of emancipation don't work so well for the analysis and the writing we might perform. It will not be a question henceforth of cutting ties in order to liberate, but cutting ties in order to engineer further and more productive connections, changing the flow. This has consequences for the writing of ethnographies that work up close with their partners in a critical proximity (immersion) characteristic of forms of fictocriticism, like that of Kathleen Stewart.[28] Critical proximity means not withdrawing to a "perspective" out in that empty space somewhere, that claims overview and impartial judgment. It means a contingent and negotiated "earning the right to participation" in a particular community, as I have elaborated elsewhere.[29]

My ethnographic approach to postcolonial study has necessarily involved fieldwork, including fieldwork mistakes and observations of other organizations tripping up or taking zigzag routes as they try to go about their business. It is not scholarly on historical or theoretical principles like the "largely White" SCT. It tries—with difficulty—to follow and understand various other ways of knowing and maintaining knowledge as these are distributed across Goolarabooloo and Whitefella institutions, and Latour's lead with his *Inquiry* has been useful in providing a kind of framework. Fieldwork leads to descriptive ethnographic writing, but this does not mean that the writing will inevitably remain stranded at some (simple) empirical level. The more one describes, the more one realizes how concepts are part of the description, and are essential in its elaboration toward a negotiable generality. When negotiating parties ask each other what they have in common with controversial matters like industrialization, concepts inevitably come up. Not only are "remoteness," "progress," and "modernity" debatable, but so too is nature, which many nonindigenous people take to be a given, an innocent concept that nevertheless can mobilize fierce passions. For the Goolarabooloo, nature is a whitefella concept that they have had to learn about.

The historicization of "nature"—that it henceforth has to be seen as a European invention—means that it, too, in the context of postcolonial thought, is part of the provincialization of Europe, because decolonization does clearly not pertain to human society alone. The very logic of colonization was ecologically framed. The concept of nature was developed for the purposes of the alienation of the nonhuman world the better to facilitate extraction of materials and their conversion to commodities. Tom Griffiths and Libby Robin deal with some of these issues in *Ecology and Empire: Environmental History of Settler Societies*. A later collection, *Decolonizing Nature: Strategies for Conservation in a Post-Colonial Era*,[30] does not go far enough in its analysis or deconstruction of the central concept of nature. It is Timothy Mitchell, with his "Can the Mosquito Speak?" who directly addresses the role of the nonhuman, opening up the field of postcolonial ecology by emphatically demonstrating that colonization is not just one set of humans dominating another, but the reconfiguring of an ecological system to suit capitalist colonization and commodification.[31] All sorts of complex issues arise from the "liberation" of humans from the yoke of colonization. It is often the case that so-called modernization has "re-naturalized" humans in a new economy and hence made it difficult to undo the damage to the whole ecological assemblage.

So if Nature has to be limited and rebooted, then all the other modes of existence and their ways of knowing have to be adjusted too. The scientist arriving in a place to do an environmental assessment might realize that his or her modern European version of Nature—basically the same everywhere—will no longer cut it. Methodologies might then have to be adjusted too. The kind of scientific reliability Europeans are used to comes through technologies like spreadsheets and statistics, which are fine. But to them the newly arrived scientist might have to add Indigenous colleagues with their nonstatistical ways of knowing. They perform exactly what scientific modes of knowledge are supposed to do—make knowledge persist through the generations and across great distances. We want the sciences to be able to do what they do best, but in a new way adjusted to local conditions for once. Steven Salisbury, an archaeologist working in Broome on dinosaur footprints, collaborates in a way that makes him an exemplary kind of scientist in this way. He is prepared to say, working with traditional owner Richard Hunter, that a dinosaur footprint *is* the Emu ancestor *marala*, not "they believe" it is *marala*.

Writing on postcolonial theory, my friend and colleague Dennis Mischke pays attention to the style of writing—in this case "fictocriticism"—in relation to alterity, and does so within the frame of postcolonial cosmopolitanism, conceived of (following Ulrich Beck), as "the utopian capacity to accept the coexistence of contradictory ways of life in productive dialogue."[32] Mischke agrees with me on two methodological points: that "cosmopolitanism has to start with praxis," and that fictocriticism "constitutes a performative response to the reigning paradox of alterity."[33] This is because the point of writing is to maintain the strangeness of the experience through its translation into a defamiliarized writing, rather than assimilating it to the usual academic genres. Such writing should expect to be surprised by its own material and respond with a new form, in a process that I have called "renaturalization."

Practicing renaturalization in any mode of existence means avoiding the reduction to Nature and looking to institutions as the places where collectivities are formed and organizational scripts are rolled out. Some are very precarious institutions, like Paddy Roe's Tamarind Tree in Broome. We have had a glimpse of how it has provided answers to really important questions like: How do you look after ancestral country without money, without sovereign title, and without a nature-culture divide? I have not been able to paint the picture in full, but it was under that tree that the thinking and organization that slowed the frontier of colonization were begun.

NOTES

1. Veracini, *Settler Colonialism*; Wolfe, *Transformation of Anthropology*.
2. See Anne Poelina's film *Three Sisters: Women of High Degree*, http://majala.com.au.
3. Macoun and Strakosch, "Ethical Demands," 427.
4. Ibid., 426.
5. Hage, *Alter-Politics*, 13.
6. Easterling, *Extrastatecraft: The Power of Infrastructure Space*.
7. Burton, *Sunset Ethnography*.
8. See Benterrak, Muecke, and Roe, "Intellectuals, Power and Truth."
9. Burton, *Sunset Ethnography*, 12:48 to 20:00.
10. Bruno Latour calls these moments "hiatuses," or "passes": "It would be absurd to suppose that this pass would be experienced in the same way by an ethnologist who discovers the new ingredient from the outside, after the fact, as it is experienced by the laboratory director, who has discovered it earlier from the inside and in the heat of action. The surprises registered are only those of the observer: it is she, the ignorant one, who discovers as she goes along what her informants already know. All ethnologists are familiar with situations like this—and they know how indispensable such moments are to the investigation. But the notions of surprise and trial, if we shift them slightly in time, can also serve to define how the informants themselves have had to learn, in their turn, through what elements they too had to pass in order to prolong the existence of their projects." Latour, *Inquiry into Modes of Existence*, 34.
11. Taussig, *Nervous System*.
12. Trigger, "Development Ideology in Australia," 162–63.
13. Durack, *Rock and the Sand*, 11.
14. Bain, *Full Fathom Five*, 19–20.
15. Durack, *Rock and the Sand*, 12.
16. See Law, "Long Distance Control."
17. Muecke and Wergin, "Questions of Value."
18. Greg Bearup, "Lure of the Beach Beats Whack of the Tax," *Sydney Morning Herald*, March 3, 2012, http://www.smh.com.au/world/lure-of-the-beach-beats-whack-of-the-tax -20120302-1u8g9.html.
19. Tom Stevens, recently retired as Member of the Legislative Assembly for the Pilbara, speaking in the film *Heritage Fight*, dir. Eugénie Dumont (Keystone Films, 2012).
20. Vivieros de Castro, *Cannibal Metaphysics*.
21. See Muecke, "Indigenous-Green Knowledge Collaborations."

22. See Muecke, "Earthbound Law."
23. Barad, *Meeting the Universe Halfway.*
24. Chakrabarty, *Provincializing Europe.*
25. "Media Release."
26. Latour, "Recall of Modernity," 14.
27. Muecke, *Mothers' Day Protest.*
28. Stewart, *Ordinary Affects.*
29. Muecke and Pam, *Contingency in Madagascar,* 19.
30. Adams and Mulligan, *Decolonizing Nature.*
31. Mitchell, "Can the Mosquito Speak?"
32. Mischke, "Othering Otherness," 325.
33. Ibid., 326, 327.

BIBLIOGRAPHY

Adams, William Mark, and Martin Mulligan. *Decolonizing Nature: Strategies for Conservation in a Post-Colonial Era.* London: Earthscan, 2003.

Bain, Mary Albertus. *Full Fathom Five.* Perth: Artlook, 1982.

Barad, Karen. *Meeting the Universe Halfway: Quantum Physics and the Entanglement of Matter and Meaning.* Durham, N.C.: Duke University Press, 2007.

Benterrak, Krim, Stephen Muecke, and Paddy Roe. "Intellectuals, Power and Truth." In *Reading the Country: Introduction to Nomadology,* 168–75. Melbourne: Fremantle Arts Centre Press, 1984.

Burton, Aaron. *Sunset Ethnography.* Kurrajong Films, 51:35. November 28, 2014. https://vimeo.com/113130961.

Durack, Mary. *The Rock and the Sand.* London: Constable, 1969.

Easterling, Keller. *Extrastatecraft: The Power of Infrastructure Space.* London: Verso, 2014.

Griffiths, Tom, and Libby Robin. *Ecology and Empire: Environmental History of Settler Societies.* Washington: University of Washington Press, 1997.

Hage, Ghassan. *Alter-Politics.* Melbourne: Melbourne University Press, 2015.

Latour, Bruno. *An Inquiry into Modes of Existence: An Anthropology of the Moderns.* Cambridge, Mass.: Harvard University Press, 2013.

———. "The Recall of Modernity—Anthropological Approaches." Translated by Stephen Muecke. *Cultural Studies Review* (March 2007): 11–30.

Law, John. "On the Methods of Long Distance Control: Vessels, Navigation, and the Portuguese Route to India." In *Power, Action and Belief: A New Sociology of Knowledge?* Sociological Review Monograph, edited by John Law, 234–63. London: Routledge, 1986.

Macoun, Alissa, and Elizabeth Strakosch. "The Ethical Demands of Settler Colonial Theory." *Settler Colonial Studies* 3, no. 3–4 (2013): 426–43.

"Media Release." March 30, 2011. http://www.environskimberley.org.au/wp-content/uploads/2012/02/EKMR-3003121.pdf.

Mischke, Dennis. "Othering Otherness: Stephen Muecke's Fictocriticism and the Cosmopolitan Vision." In *Postcolonial Studies across the Disciplines,* edited by Jana Gohrisch and Ellen Grünkemeier, 323–37. Leiden: Brill, 2013.

Mitchell, Timothy. "Can the Mosquito Speak?" In his *Rule of Experts: Egypt, Techno-Politics, Modernity,* 25–51. Berkeley: University of California Press, 2002

Muecke, Stephen. "Earthbound Law: The Force of an Indigenous Australian Institution." *Law and Critique* 28, no. 2 (2017): 135–43.

———."Indigenous-Green Knowledge Collaborations and the James Price Point Dispute." In *Unstable Relations: Indigenous People and Environmentalism in Contemporary Australia,* edited by

Eve Vincent and Timothy Neale, 252–72. Perth: University of Western Australia Publishing, 2016.

———. *The Mothers' Day Protest and Other Fictocritical Essays*. London: Rowman and Littlefield International, 2016.

Muecke, Stephen, and Max Pam. *Contingency in Madagascar*. Bristol: Intellect Books, 2012.

Muecke, Stephen, and Carsten Wergin. "Questions of Value: Mining and Tourism in Remote Australia." Special issue: "Songlines vs. Pipelines." *Australian Humanities Review* 53 (November 2012).

Salisbury, Steven W., Anthony Romilio, Matthew C. Herne, Ryan T. Tucker, and Jay P. Nair. "The Dinosaurian Ichnofauna of the Lower Cretaceous (Valanginian–Barremian) Broome Sandstone of the Walmadany Area (James Price Point), Dampier Peninsula, Western Australia." *Journal of Vertebrate Paleontology*, no. 36: sup. 1 (2016): 1–152.

Sloterdijk, Peter. *Spheres*, vol. 1: *Bubbles: Microspherology*. New York: Semiotext(e), 2011.

Stewart, Kathleen. *Ordinary Affects*. Durham, N.C.: Duke University Press, 2007.

Taussig, Michael. *The Nervous System*. New York: Routledge, 1992.

Trigger, David S. "Mining, Landscape and the Culture of Development Ideology in Australia." *Ecumene* 4 (1997): 161–80.

Veracini, Lorenzo. *Settler Colonialism: A Theoretical Overview*. Houndmills: Palgrave Macmillan, 2008.

Vivieros de Castro, Eduardo. *Cannibal Metaphysics: For a Post-structural Anthropology*. Edited and translated by Peter Skafish. Minneapolis: Univocal, 2014.

Wolfe, Patrick. *Settler Colonialism and the Transformation of Anthropology*. London: Cassell, 1999.

Buenos Aires's La Salada Market and Plebeian Citizenship

Carlos A. Forment

La Salada, renamed the "poor people's shopping mall" by many of the residents of Cuartel IX (270,000), is a socially stigmatized, economically pauperized, and politically disenfranchised peri-urban district located twenty kilometers from the city of Buenos Aires. It is among the first and largest in Argentina to experience the full force of marketization. Founded in the early 1990s by several dozen undocumented Bolivian immigrants and Argentine street hawkers, by the first decade of the twenty-first century La Salada occupied a central place in Cuartel and beyond. The European Union described it as "emblematic of counterfeit markets" and ranked it among the ten worst of its kind.[1] In studying La Salada and the network of satellite "Saladitas" that have surfaced in hundreds of degraded neighborhoods across the country, I analyze the way the "structural poor" and recently impoverished middle class ("new poor"), in the course of practicing economic informality, paralegality, and noninstitutional politics in everyday life, have transformed themselves into plebeian citizens.

These practices surfaced at different moments and from divergent socio-institutional sites and took three decades to acquire contoured shape and textured form and contributed in Cuartel and across a great many other areas of the Global South to the emergence of what I call plebeian democracy. In order to trace and make sense of plebeianism, I have highlighted the ordinary ethics that constituted and were constitutive of its everyday practices, and structured my argument accordingly. The first section provides an overview of La Salada and Cuartel, the socioeconomic and institutional context from which plebeianism emerged. In the second section, I study the sociolegal and political disputes that surfaced in daily life between La Salada and its critics among public officials and textile firms, with most of the discussion focused on what I term "mimetic branding" and "mimetic consumption." The next section discusses a neighborhood movement that was led by La Salada and Cuartel's residents in support of municipal autonomy. The discussion continues with an analysis of undocumented immigrants in "clandestine sweatshops" and "family workshops" that produce for La Salada and Saladitas. These workers demanded to be recognized as "self-exploited workers" and rebelled against human rights groups that sought to represent them as victims of "slave labor." In my closing remarks, I list the ethical practices that have contributed to the formation of plebeian citizenship as a distinctive form of life.

Thinking Plebeian Democracy in the Global South

In *The Politics of the Governed*, Partha Chatterjee provides one of the most thoughtful and influential accounts of subaltern democracy in the Global South. On his reading, civil society in postcolonial societies has been an enclave for the "privileged few," for citizens who have the capacity to exercise their civil, political, and social rights and can rely on the courts to safeguard them. Political society, in contrast, has been the domain of the "dispossessed many," who have been denied their rights by public officials (and rights-bearing citizens) because they consider the former's penchant for popular forms of religiosity, xenophobia, and illegality a threat to modern democracy. According to Chatterjee, these subaltern groups in political society, far more than rights-bearing citizens in civil society, play a crucial role in repairing the breach that separates democracy and modernity across the Global South.

Public officials define the various groups that inhabit political society (immigrant, indigent, homeless) as "populations" in need of welfare provisions rather than as "citizens" who are entitled to the same set of rights. State officials rely on the particular needs of each group in order to design these welfare policies. In the course of negotiating with officials, each population group revises the various policies and reformulates the administrative categories they now use to construe themselves and in doing so become "governmentalized subjects." These negotiations, on Chatterjee's telling, take place behind closed doors to enable officials to preserve the legitimacy of the democratic state rooted in universal rights and legality.

My study of La Salada challenges all four of Chatterjee's central claims. In the case at hand, negotiations between state officials and plebeian groups occurred in public life, not in smoke-filled rooms, and they included a large cast of characters: public officials, plebeians, rights-bearing citizens in political parties, human rights' groups, and merchants' associations across civil society as well as undocumented immigrants and other pauperized, stigmatized, and disenfranchised groups across political society. As they maneuvered across the public landscape, these plebeians, contrary to Chatterjee's claim, proposed an alternative

vision of democratic life that was broad-minded and multidimensional that went well beyond particularistic claims rooted in basic needs and "survivalism." Moreover, none of
the plebeian groups that I studied relied on state-generated administrative categories to
make sense of themselves.

Whether this study of La Salada can shed light on the emergence of plebeianism in
other parts of the Global South remains to be seen. In any case, those of us who study
this part of the world must now spend more time exploring how subaltern groups become
"ungovernmentalized" and in the course of doing so develop plebeian forms of democratic life.

Socio-Institutional Landscape

Beginning in the 1990s, Argentine officials implemented a series of wide-ranging and radical marketization policies that provoked hundreds of factories to close, disorganized the
labor movement and local unions, and pauperized large and small working-class neighborhoods throughout the province of Buenos Aires. In contrast to other areas that experienced "disaffiliation," in Robert Castel's sense, a great many of Cuartel's now jobless
workers and poor and indigent families refashioned themselves into plebeian citizens.[2]

Stretching over an area the size of twelve football fields, La Salada is a conglomeration
of three markets: Urkupina (1991), Mogote (1994), and Ocean (1995). In 2009 La Salada,
which at the time housed 4,900 stalls, earned US$15 million, nearly twice as much the
eight largest shopping malls in the city of Buenos Aires.[3] This is all the more noteworthy
since La Salada opens only on Tuesdays, Thursdays, and Sundays between the hours of
9:00 a.m. and 9:00 p.m. On any given weekday, 100,000 shoppers flock to the market; twice
as many visit it on Sundays; and on Christmas the crowds swell to half a million.[4] Every
two weeks, no fewer than 36,000 wholesalers from Saladitas across the country organize
"shopping tours" to Cuartel to purchase merchandise and restock their stores (see below).[5]

La Salada provides stable employment and a living wage to almost 110,000 residents
from Cuartel and surrounding areas. The majority of them work in the market as vendors, janitors, security guards, parking-lot attendants, and haulers who accompany shoppers and carry their merchandise. According to the most reliable estimates, there are 12,000
workshops and sweatshops in Cuartel and within a 30 kilometer radius from La Salada
that provide stable jobs to an additional 50,000 undocumented immigrants from Bolivia,
Paraguay, and Peru as well as Argentine-born workers. Many of these workshops and
sweatshops rent or own a stall in La Salada or a Saladita market from which they sell a
significant portion of their output.[6] This socioeconomic boom activity has increased real
estate prices in Cuartel. A square meter of property in La Salada now costs between
US$25,000 and US$50,000, four times more than in Puerto Madero, the most globalized
and expensive area in the city of Buenos Aires.[7]

Cuartel has become the epicenter of plebeian cosmopolitanism. Sixty percent of those
who work in La Salada are undocumented Bolivians; another 30 percent are Argentine-

born citizens; and the remaining 10 percent are either Peruvian or Paraguayan immigrants.[8] On market days, Andean and Argentine bands entertain passersby; rotund matrons serve indigenous and creole dishes; and thieves in hoodies and prostitutes in tight-fitting dresses from every nationality abound. Twice a year thousands of immigrants and Argentines descend on La Salada to render homage to the Bolivian Virgins of "Urkupina" and "Copacabana" and "Gauchito Gil," an Argentine folk saint.

During the heyday of neoliberalism in the 1990s, the municipal government (of Lomas de Zamora) lacked the funds to provide Cuartels' residents with adequate public services. In response to this debacle, La Salada's vendors organized themselves into the Association of Merchants, Professionals, and Industrialists, and used a portion of its funds to pay for public security, street maintenance, and garbage removal, and to supply the local public hospital with bed linens and towels. In addition, the association financed a walk-in clinic and offered health insurance to 400 local families, a soup kitchen, a dozen associations, including "Mothers against Crack," and a technical school that offered courses in sewing, clothes design, and business management.[9] La Salada was authorized recently by the Ministry of Justice and Human Rights to expand its "reentry program" to enable inmates to secure a salaried job in the market.[10]

Plebeian Citizenship as a Form of Life

Plebeian citizenship emerged from the ethico-political practices that surfaced in La Salada and Cuartel in the 1990s during President Carlos Menem's government. Jorge Castillo, the garrulous shoemaker and the administrator of Mogote market, recalled:

> Under Carlos Menem we lost our livelihood, our culture of work and our national industry; it was easier to buy imported goods and machinery than our own products.[11]
>
> We are the darkies ["morochos," sociocultural term rather than a racial epithet] who in the 1990s were left without a job. La Salada enabled us to crawl out from the very bottom of the pit.[12]

La Salada continued to flourish during the "progressive" governments of Presidents Nestor Kirchner and Cristina Fernandez after Argentina began to recover after the state decided to default on its sovereign debt. By 2005, the market was a fixture on the horizon:

> Our market is a place of economic dynamism, social inclusion and honorable work; it provides a large and diverse sector of society an opportunity to learn new skills.[13]

La Salada has flourished in both good and bad times, and cannot be understood as simply a by-product of Cuartel's changing "opportunity structure."

In addition to providing a sense of personal dignity, social justice, and a new "skill set" based on micro-productivism, La Salada incited Cuartel's residents to break with populist, rentier, and human rights conceptions of selfhood that remained dominant across public life.

Between the Lawful and the Unlawful

Under neoliberalism, La Salada and the thousands of workshops and sweatshops in Cuartel were an important source of income for the city government (which still had to pay salaries) and a major provider of public services and jobs for local residents. Municipal authorities now relied on the market to maintain social order and preserve their own legitimacy. The vice-mayor, a Peronist, recalls: "The market was the result of an absent state; for the next 10 years it operated with the complicity of many state agencies."[14] La Salada and the workshops and sweatshops that produced for it paid bribes to city inspectors and members of the police force who now relied on these "tips" to supplement their slashed salaries.

This situation remained more or less unchanged until the second half of the 1990s when La Salada and Cuartel's workshops and sweatshops were reaping huge profits. Local officials demanded an increase in their tips. La Salada's vendors and workers organized a meeting and decided to reject their demands. They organized a series of marches and demonstrations in front of the municipality and police station and contacted major dailies, radio stations, and television stations in order to publicize their cause and win the support of middle-class citizens and public officials outside of Cuartel.

Soon after defaulting on its sovereign debt to the IMF and World Bank, President Kirchner's government, in an attempt to reassert its institutional authority, began pumping monies into city governments, especially those in poor neighborhoods. The president also instructed the governor of the province of Buenos Aires, where a third of the country's taxpayers live, to launch a campaign to pressure citizens to "render unto Caesar." Under the leadership of Santiago Montoya, director of the State's Revenue Service (ARBA), his staff downloaded hundreds of satellite images from Google Maps and cross-checked them with the tax returns warehoused in their databank.[15] Montoya was unrelenting in his pursuit of tax evaders, wealthy and poor alike. He went after transnational and Argentine-owned petrochemical and agro-industrial firms, affluent gated communities, and high-end shopping malls as well as La Salada and Saladita markets.

Between February and July 2007, Montoya led 250 agents on six raids against the market, enabling them to interview a total of 9,000 vendors. Prior to these raids, 90 percent of Salada's vendors did not have a tax number; several months after ARBA's last raid, 77 percent of them were registered, leading Montoya to remark: "Tax evasion is now higher in gated communities than in La Salada."[16] These raids enabled Cuartel's residents to become aware of the relation between taxation and the common good that had been difficult for them to discern when the municipality had not provided them with public services.

Following these raids, ARBA created a tax category named "Special Regime for Gross Income" (Regimen especial de ingresos brutos) to enable La Salada's vendors to obtain a tax number. In return, La Salada agreed to pay its taxes. However, because it did not have a bookkeeping department, the market was unable to comply with ARBA's requirements. Several years later in 2009, Argentina's National Revenue Service (AFIP) established the "Information Regime" (Regimen de Informacion) that was tailored to meet

La Salada's needs. Under the regime, Urkupina, Ocean, and Mogote's administrators were required to submit monthly reports to AFIP with detailed information on each vendor. This piece of administrative technology made it possible for tax officials to cross-check the information of each administrator and vendor to determine the veracity of the other's data. These measures encouraged plebeian citizens to adhere to the rule of law, to become legible to the state, and to construe taxation as a mechanism for advancing the common good.

Vendors and administrators complained bitterly, not because they were required to pay taxes and contribute to the common good, but because state officials, they claimed, were violating their property rights:

> Those of us who are administrators have been transformed into state tax collectors. Every month we are required to file a report on our vendors' commercial activity and the sales tax they paid. We see no reason why we should work for the state; this is not what we get paid to do. The state should assume its responsibility and have its agents do all this work; we even offered to provide them with an office in the market.[17]

From the perspective of La Salada, the state was stealing labor power from them. This dispute remains unsettled. In any case, plebeianism developed its own heterodox account of the mutual duties and obligations that citizens and state officials owed each other.

Wageless versus Informal Life: Workshops and Sweatshops

In the mid-1990s President Carlos Menem liberalized the economy and allowed foreign imports to flood the market, sending the textile sector into a downward spiral.[18] Hundreds of firms went bankrupt. Those that remained afloat did so by downsizing, replacing "formal" with "informal" workers, and by outsourcing the production of garments to family workshops and clandestine sweatshops, including the 12,000 or so that had been established in Cuartel and nearby neighborhoods.[19]

Workshops and sweatshops are similar in some ways. In addition to employing a large number of undocumented immigrants and operating without a license, they are in violation of one or another building and zoning code (their electrical, plumbing, and ventilation systems are a hazard to those who labor in these workshops and sweatshops as well as to their neighbors).

Workshops and sweatshops differ in a fundamental way. A workshop owner describes daily life in his plebeian atelier:

> My family does all the work. We work eight hours daily and stop to eat, but sometimes we≈work ten or more hours when we need to increase our output. After all, we are the owners. We sell all our clothes in our stall [at Salada]; it is of very good quality. We use the same textile material [that is used by brand-name designers].[20]

In contrast, clandestine sweatshops engage in "human trafficking" and "slave labor." Their employees are forced to work fifteen hours daily, and to socialize, eat, and rest in the same cramped, unhygienic room where they work all day. Sweatshop owners routinely confiscate the passports of their workers to discourage them from fleeing.

Most "bon pensant" scholars, especially those who have a state-centered understanding of public life, are reluctant to discuss the subterranean connections between sweatshops and workshops due to the ethico-political dilemmas this raises. After laboring in sweatshops for a year or so, immigrants acquire the technical skills and learn the "trade secrets" of all the firms, brands, and designers that had subcontracted them to produce their garments, enabling these workers later on to produce similar garments in their own family workshops.[21] The Bolivian anthropologist Silvia Rivera Cusiqanqui, founder of the Subaltern Studies Collective in La Paz, is the only scholar who has explored, from the perspective of Buenos Aires's undocumented workers, the ties between sweatshops and workshops:

> They willingly subject themselves to exploitation knowing that they are saving money in order to establish a micro-enterprise that will better the life of their offspring. I would argue against those that claim that life in these sweatshops is based on slave labor.[22]

In contrast to Maussian gift-giving based on face-to-face exchanges among members of the same network, Andean "deferred solidarity" is a multigenerational "virtual" agreement among the dead, the living, and those yet to be born.

Rivera Cusiqanqui's account is, admittedly, troubling to those of us who are against sweatshops and slave labor but committed to improving the everyday lives and socioeconomic opportunities of the working poor without undermining their own forms of life.[23] Because this dilemma defies any simplistic solution, I have refrained from providing any.[24]

Mimetic Branding and Consumer Mimicry versus Counterfeits and Consumerism

In addition, micro-productivism and plebeianism are based on mimetic branding and mimetic consumption. The discussion begins with branding as it occurs inside workshops and sweatshops during the production process, and ends with mimetic consumption as it occurs among shoppers.

Under neoliberalism the process of making clothes, as I noted above, had fragmented into three parts: design, production, and commercialization. Textile firms and brands retained control of the first and third phase, outsourcing the second to workshops and sweatshops. This is where mimetic branding took place. The facts are compelling. Prior to 2005 roughly 90 percent of "counterfeit" garments in Argentina were imported from China, Paraguay, and other countries. Five years later with the sudden growth in the number of workshops and sweatshops in Cuartel and elsewhere, 80 percent of "knock-offs" were now made in the country.[25] Plebeianism had developed its own version of "import substitution" similar to the model used by the populist-developmental state in Argentina and other third world countries during the postwar period to promote industrialization.

What is the difference between a mimetic and original garment? After all, both of them are usually produced by the same set of workers who labor in the same workshops and sweatshops, with similar sewing machines, tools as well as fabrics of comparable quality that were purchased from the same small pool of suppliers. In formal, legal terms, the difference between a mimetic and original garment resides in the label itself. Because the practice of branding is embedded in production and commercialization and remains unarticulated, I will now make them explicit.

I have discerned four types of branding practices. The following two are part of the production process and occur inside workshops and sweatshops.[26] Here is a brief description of each: (1) "Do it yourself": Producers create homemade tags using their own names or the name of a relative (Belen, Filmo); (2) "Adulterated logos": Producers take a well-known brand, for instance, Nike with its upright checkmark, and redesign it while retaining a close resemblance to the original. Many of the sports clothes and caps that are sold in Salada carry upside-down checkmarks.

The next two branding practices occur in the commercialization phase inside La Salada and Saladita markets. (3) "Unbranded": Clothes without logos cost less, enabling Saladita store owners to buy larger quantities of merchandise from their supplier in La Salada. Prior to selling a garment to their clients, the Saladita store owners tag them in order to fetch a higher price. (4) "Generic label": A large number of vendors tag their garments with "Replica" to prevent the police from confiscating them.

I have portrayed these branding practices as static and isolated "acts"; however, recall that a typical workshop or sweatshop laborer toils thirteen hours daily, six days a week, and puts out a garment every half an hour or so.

Let us now examine the demand side of consumer mimicry. Roberto Piazza, an accomplished designer and director of the Institute for Advanced Study of Design, Fashion, and Beauty in the city of Buenos Aires, explains the meaning of consumer mimicry:

> Globalization has made us even more brand fetishists [marqueros] than before, unleashing in us a limitless desire to consume and to be admired. This has heightened our own sense of narcissism and vanity.[27]

Consumer mimicry satisfied the yearning of plebeians for autostimulation, instant gratification, and public self-display. For many, this was the first time that they could afford to dress like middle-class citizens, thereby enabling them to roam freely and visit areas of the city such as malls, movie houses, restaurants, dance halls, and other places from which they had been previously ostracized or excluded. Consumer mimicry made it possible for plebeians to also upgrade their wardrobes, making it easier for them to secure employment in private firms and state agencies that before would have discriminated against them.

Plebeians were drilled in the ethico-political meaning of consumer mimicry. La Salada and Saladita markets launched a countrywide campaign against the rentier model of public life that, they claimed, was promoted by textile firms, designers, boutiques, malls, and other middle-class institutions. La Salada accused all of them of violating the social and property rights of plebeians:

The problem is with the middlemen who charge exorbitant prices for the clothes that are sold in shopping malls and retail stores; they have abused us beyond all reasonable limits. They live stealing from us. The same garment that in the US costs US$33 dollars costs us US$206 dollars. . . . How can this be? . . . [La Salada] has enabled producers and consumers to bypass the middlemen and to deal directly with each other. Designers and retail store owners are just as responsible for the problem; they spend huge sums in branding, marketing and advertising and then make us pay for it. La Salada has exposed all of them for what they really are.[28]

La Salada and Saladita markets across the country encouraged plebeians to buy mimetically branded clothes and to boycott brand-name garments and footwear.

La Salada, Saladita markets, and all those who produced for the markets refused to be described as part of the informal sector, which is how textile firms and designers represented them. Instead, plebeianism identified itself as part of a new moral economy:

Salada is where people without money come at the end of the month in order to make ends meet. Although "brands" portray us as a center for the sale of counterfeits, the market is a social institution. After the "brands" destroyed our economy and robbed us of our jobs, it was the Salada that enabled us "darkies" to crawl out from the bottom of the trash bin.[29]

Salada and the network of Saladitas that had now surfaced across the country encouraged their supporters to act and talk as plebeian citizens.

Cuartel was the epicenter of plebeianism; however, all those who had direct and indirect ties to La Salada, including Saladitas vendors and customers, disseminated its ethico-political practices across the country. According to the Argentine Confederation of Medium Firms (CAME), the number of Saladitas increased from 180 to 500 (278 percent) between 2008 and 2013.[30] These markets, along with La Salada, have made it possible for the recently impoverished middle class ("new poor") to develop an affinity with undocumented immigrants, the working poor, and other similar groups in their rejection of the "rentier" model of public life that was supported by international brands, textile firms, and shopping malls.

Secessionist Networks and Municipal Autonomy

Salada's merchants and Cuartel's residents led a campaign to secede from the municipality of Lomas de Zamora and to establish their own city government.

Cuartel's secessionists developed informal ties to different political parties and coalitions while remaining autonomous from all of them. Secessionists encouraged local residents to break with "ideological" and "party-centered" notions of politics and adopt a "post-ideological" and "issue-centered" stance. The secessionists replaced the venerable figure of the "Peronist militant" and his "loyal client" with that of the "nonpartisan operator." Plebeianism was construed as a radical alternative to traditional populism.

In March 2010 La Salada's Association of Merchants, Professionals, and Industrialists organized a series of meetings with half a dozen church groups and voluntary associations from Cuartel in order to discuss a plan of action. The association outlined the reasons for seceding from Lomas:

> The municipality ignores us; our streets remain unpaved and our public hospital remains dysfunctional. Lomas de Zamora's municipality does not care about Cuartel IX. . . . If we have a municipal government, we would be able to use our taxes to improve public security and our streets. . . . Each year Mogote pays AR$4 million pesos in taxes; this accounts for half of Lomas's income. Nevertheless, it does not provide Cuartel with any services. . . . The only public works that have been done in Cuartel IX were paid with private funds from La Salada.[31]

A longtime local supporter of secession, Ruben Cabanas, president of the Cuartel IX's association, characterized La Salada's role in the movement as "fundamental." In addition to financial clout, the members of the market had the administrative experience that would be needed to manage municipal life.[32]

The association led a grassroots campaign calling for a plebiscite so that Cuartel's residents would be able to secede from Lomas and establish their own municipality. In response to this demand, the governor of Buenos Aires, Lomas's officials, and Peronist party leaders closed ranks and blocked the plebiscite from taking place.[33] If it had succeeded, this would have made it difficult for public officials and party militants to maintain their patronage networks and influence Cuartel's electorate.

Following the failed plebiscite, Cuartel's secessionists devised a new strategy, and decided to make alliances with any political actor that agreed to advance their own cause:

> We still seek autonomy; we don't want to have to beg anymore. We want to be able to resolve our own problems. This is how it should be. This is the reason that we are now inviting Peronists, Radicals and people on the Left to join our cause. We do not care what party you are in; we are only interested in improving our neighborhoods.[34]

Cuartel's secessionists forged alliances with whichever political party or coalition benefited them. Despite its loose structure and nonpartisan character, these alliances placed enormous ethico-political demands on Cuartel's secessionists, requiring them to forgo the material and symbolic benefits (public employment, welfare relief) they had enjoyed as clients of the Peronist party and one or another populist official.

For the 2009 senatorial elections, Cuartel's secessionists organized an association named Militancia y Trabajo, which had its headquarters in Urkupina. In order to generate support among local residents, Militancia's members visited Cuartel's neighborhoods, held public forums, and organized a religio-political gathering in La Salada. Militancia's activism paid off. Its candidate, Quique Antequera, who now had broad support in Cuartel, was invited by the Peronist Party to join its slate. Though a political "outsider," Antequera came in second place in the elections.

Following these elections, Cuartel's secessionists broke with the Peronist Party and allied themselves with the social democratic Coalicion Civica.[35] This alliance made it possible for the Coalicion to make inroads and broaden its electoral base in Cuartel and other poor neighborhoods, while offering the secessionists an opportunity to gain support among middle-class voters in the city of Buenos Aires.[36] In the closing weeks of the campaign, Coalicion's candidate, Alfonso Prat-Gay, former minister of economics, published an editorial in support of plebeian citizenship in the influential daily, *Clarin*:

> It is impossible to favor micro-enterprises yet continue to oppose La Salada. Just because it is an informal market does not make it illegal. We are criminalizing the poor who work in this market. . . . Someone has to defend them.[37]

CAME published a scathing, page-long reply in *Clarin*, *La Nacion*, and other leading dailies accusing Prat-Gay of condoning illegality and demanding that the courts disqualify his candidacy.[38] His sympathetic portrayal of plebeianism altered the way that Buenos Aires's middle-class "progressives" now viewed it.

In September 2012, two hundred thousand Buenos Aires "indignados" filled the Plaza de Mayo in protest against President Fernandez's government.[39] They carried banners denouncing corruption and crime and in defense of the national constitution, which the government wanted to reform to enable the president to run for a third term. The government assigned Lomas's senator, a Peronist militant, the task of discrediting the protesters. He caricatured them by depicting the protesters as "well-dressed members of the middle class who are worried about their dollars which they need in order to go abroad on summer holidays."[40] Coalicion's leader, Lilita Carrio, admitted there were a great many

> well-dressed persons. This is because La Salada has made it possible for the [Argentine-born] poor to dress well. They participated in the march along with many Bolivian and Peruvian immigrants. Our politicians act as if they have custody over all of them. . . . Those who live in shantytowns protested like the rest of us because we are all against crime, robbery, and drugs.[41]

Plebeianism had become a recognizable and respectable political actor among middle-class "progressive" families, many of whom now shop in their neighborhood Saladita market.

Self-Exploited Workers and Human Rights

Undocumented Bolivian immigrants in workshops and sweatshops with ties to La Salada now demanded to represent themselves as self-exploited workers rather than slave labor; this is how human rights groups construed them. This dispute provided another layer of ethico-political meaning to plebeianism.

On March 26, 2006, a fire broke out in a textile sweatshop in Caballito, a middle-class neighborhood in the City of Buenos Aires, taking the lives of six Bolivian immigrants. In the weeks that followed, city inspectors and police, under pressure from middle-class citizens from all walks of life, raided 365 sweatshops and accused 138 of them of engaging in slave labor.[42] These citizens also organized street marches and public forums to discuss the situation of undocumented immigrants and other aspects regarding the continued informalization and deregulation of everyday life.

Two views predominated. La Alameda (hereafter Alameda), a human rights' organization, accused La Salada and Saladita markets of engaging in slave labor, maintaining ties to sweatshops, undermining the rights of workers, and contributing to the spread of the informal economy. In contrast, the Asociacion Civil Federativa Boliviana (hereafter ACIFBOL), the unofficial representative of immigrants in Buenos Aires, argued that the thousands of family workshops that produce for La Salada and Saladita markets provide their "paisanos" with dignified work in a city that remains exploitative, exclusionary, and racist.

ACIFBOL and the network of thirty or so radio stations that are linked to it provide immigrant families, the majority of whom live in shantytowns, with a variety of services.[43] In the words of ACIFBOL's president, Alfredo Ayala, they

> visit our radio station when they need assistance to bury their dead, give birth, undergo surgery or feel threatened; in these cases we then organize demonstrations. We are organized and have the support of many brothers (and sisters) in the community. If the Bolivian consulate performed his job and fulfilled his duties, then we would not have to take them on ourselves.[44]

"Constelacion," "Metropolitana," "Favorita," and the other stations exert an enormous influence on immigrants, especially those who spend most of the day hunched over a sewing machine inside their workshops. In addition to late-breaking news, musical programs, and information on employment and housing opportunities, these radio stations contribute to the ethico-political cohesion of the community over issues such as police brutality, racism, and human rights.[45]

ACIFBOL and its network of radio stations derive legitimacy from defending immigrants against police brutality and raids against their home-based workshops. In December 2009 ACIFBOL led a funeral march from Cuartel to the Plaza de Mayo, symbolic center of the human rights movement, in honor of a Bolivian immigrant who had worked in La Salada and had been shot by a "trigger-happy" policeman. When the marchers reached the plaza, they heckled and interrupted a gathering of the "Abuelas" that was being televised in order to call attention to their situation.[46]

Beginning in 2011 the police launched a series of raids against family workshops in several shantytowns. Fidel Colque described the raid against his workshop:

> It resembled a witch hunt; our families were terrified. The police smashed the front door, entered our house and ordered us to lay flat on the ground; they forced our children to do the same. They respected no one.[47]

Instead of targeting sweatshops, city inspectors attacked workshops owned by Bolivian immigrants, which reaffirmed their belief that the municipal government is racist and discriminates against them.

ACIFBOL and its radio stations led 15,000 workers through the streets of Buenos Aires in protest against these raids. One of the participants, Carlos Jimenez, a workshop owner, recalls,

The fear had become widespread. This is the reason that so many of us participated in the protest. The textile firms that we work for were surprised and confused. They had no idea of what was going on; how did we come together; where had we come from; how could we organize such a large demonstration? We had finally woken up, all of us needed to be heard.[48]

In contrast to sweatshop owners, who can afford to bribe policemen and inspectors, undocumented immigrants rely on street marches, radio stations, and community groups to protect their workshops. According to ACIFBOL, human rights groups such as Alameda are perpetuating racism under the guise of defending human rights.

ACIFBOL also accused La Alameda of denying immigrants the right to represent themselves. In the words of a workshop owner,

[Vera and Alameda's members] treat Bolivians as if we were idiots. He thinks we are incapable of knowing whether we are getting exploited or not.[49]

Bolivian immigrants sought to represent themselves as self-exploited workers rather than as slave labor as La Alameda portrayed them:

Vera [La Alameda's director] is a liar and a cheat. We are not slaves, we are workers, and if we work as hard as we do it is because we want to earn more money.[50]

In seeking to defend Bolivian undocumented immigrants, La Alameda violated their "right to have rights," in Hannah Arendt's sense.

These immigrants have developed their own idiom based on notions of self-exploitation, moral economy, and so on in order to represent themselves.

Concluding Remarks

Salada and the countrywide network of Saladitas brought the newly impoverished middle class in contact with the urban poor and undocumented immigrants, reconfiguring each others' ethico-political practices and notion of selfhood, and contributing to the emergence of a new form of life: plebeian citizenship. In the remaining pages, my aim is to summarize in a highly stylized manner its key features as they were experienced by vendors, buyers, and producers in La Salada and Saladitas, Cuartel residents, and undocumented immigrants in workshops and sweatshop.

In the course of resolving legal administrative disputes with municipal officials, tax collectors, and members of the police force, plebeian citizens developed their own ethico-political understanding of the rule of law, property rights, and the common good, contributing to making themselves legible to each other.

The many thousands of undocumented immigrants and Argentine citizens who toiled daily in workshops and sweatshops and practiced mimetic branding and mimetic consumption succeeded in exercising their right to have rights though they had far fewer material and symbolic resources than their rivals—textile firms, shopping malls, and international brands. The ethico-political campaign that the former launched against the latters' rentierism made it possible for the recently impoverished members of the middle class, undocumented immigrants, and working poor to develop their own conception of moral economy and to reject those who sought to portray them as lawbreakers and part of the informal sector.

The secessionist movement led by La Salada in Cuartel added a new layer of ethico-political meaning to plebeianism. This neighborhood movement encouraged local residents to break with populism long identified with the Peronist Party and rooted in patron-client relations, ideological militancy, and a party-centered conception of politics. Plebeianism instilled in members a pragmatic, issue-centered, and post-ideological conception of politics rooted in daily life and needs. This approach encouraged plebeian citizens to break or develop ties, as the case might be, with any and all parties and coalitions as long as they contributed to the secessionist cause. This pragmatic stance might strike some readers as opportunistic and devoid of ethical content; however, as I noted earlier, this was not so. Those plebeians who broke away from populism did so knowing that they would no longer have access to any of the material and symbolic resources (public employment, welfare relief, access to influential city officials) they once had.

Bolivian undocumented immigrants in workshops that produced garments for Salada organized a series of street marches in the city of Buenos Aires. These immigrants demanded to represent themselves as self-exploited workers and rejected the way Alameda and other human rights portrayed them as enslaved laborers. Bolivian immigrants also challenged the "Abuelas of the Plaza de Mayo," the country's leading human rights organization, as well as municipal officials, the police, and city inspectors. According to immigrant groups, all of them to varying degrees employ the idiom of human rights and legality in order to energize and reaffirm the xenophobic practices that remained dominant and widespread in the city of Buenos Aires, especially among the middle-class "progressive" sectors of society.

Despite its momentary setbacks and long-lasting reversals, plebeianism has already left thick material and symbolic residues across Argentina's public landscape, providing a significant number of poor and impoverished middle-class families an alternative to rentier and populist models of democratic life. Similar processes are taking place in other countries of the Global South. Whether or not plebeianism is able to create an alternative set of institutions the way that the working class and middle class of nineteenth-century Western Europe and North America were able to do (citizenship, civil society, mass markets, public sphere, political parties) remains to be seen. Under neoliberal conditions, in places like Latin America, postcolonial thinking needs to move beyond an overemphasis on center-periphery relations or state power in the Global South. A case like La Salada provides an opportunity to better understand popular experiments in plebeian forms of democracy. These emergent practices displace familiar debates about whether politics in the Global South are either derived from European examples or are wholly indigenous.

NOTES

This essay is based on a revised version of my article "Ordinary Ethics and the Emergence of Plebeian Democracy across the Global South: Buenos Aires' La Salada Market," *Current Anthropology* 56, no. 11 (2015): 116–25. Miriam Ticktin, Andreas Kalyvas, and Bryan Turner were generous and insightful critics, as were the members of the year-long seminar organized by CUNY's Committee on Globalization and Social Change under the directorship of Gary Wilder and Jini Kim Watson.

1. European Union, http://trade.ec.europa/doclib/docs/2006/.

2. Castel, *Manual Workers to Wage Workers*; Merklen, *Pobres Ciudadanos*.

3. Barral, "La Salada vende más que los shoppings"; Dewey, "Taxing the Shadow," 2.

4. Girón, *La Salada*, 33.

5. CAME, "Argentina Ilegal."

6. Peralta and Novillo, "Talleres ilegales."

7. Sainz, "En La Salada, el metro cuadrado es más caro que en Puerto Madero."

8. Monjonnier, "La Salada."

9. Ossona, "El Shopping de los Pobres"; Eleisegui, "Si usted tiene problemas con su cobertura"; Schiavo and Rodriguez, "Informalidad e inclusion social"; "Quique Antequera entregó 3000 pesos a Centro de Jubilados," www.militanciaytrabajo.com. As of 2013, most of these social programs no longer exist.

10. "La Salada dice tener la solución para la inseguridad."

11. Castillo, "Esclavitud es lo hacen las grandes empresas y los sindicatos."

12. *Hacerme Feriante* [Becoming a vendor], directed and produced by Julián d'Angiolillo, 2010.

13. "Administrador de La Salada destaca el rol en la economía."

14. Girón, *La Salada*, 152.

15. "Montoya busca evasores con el Google."

16. "Montoya se sumo a la polemica por La Salada: Quinto operativo de Rentas en La Salada," *En Blanco* 2, no. 10 (August 2007).

17. "La provincia no hace un relevamiento."

18. Sanchez and Butler, "Productivity Levels, Growth and Dispersion."

19. De Vincenzi and Torres, "Esclavitud Fashion."

20. "La Salada en manos de bolivianos."

21. Including information on clothes design, fashion trends, the quality and types of fabric, local suppliers, and so on.

22. Colectivo Situaciones, *De chuequista y overlocks*, 14.

23. "Guaraschi Mamani, Tito y otros," Juzgado Federal, Secretaría #7, Capital Federal, Causa 26.083-10733 (November 20, 2007). In a well-known case against a sweatshop-textile firm accused of slave labor, Judge Norberto Oyarbide twisted Cusiquanqui's account by arguing that "working and living together" is an "ancestral custom" among Bolivian workers.

24. Montero, "Neoliberal Fashion." The "Center for Clothes," in the neighborhood of Barracas in the city of Buenos Aires, houses a dozen textile cooperatives that employ ex-sweatshop workers. Although a promising alternative, the center has not received broad and strong support from most workers.

25. Soler, "Crece la falsificación"; Sainz, "El modelo La Salada se multiplica."

26. This typology is based on fieldwork I undertook in Salada from May to August 2013 and on the market's webpage: www.puntamogotes.com/indice_anunciantes.php.

27. Barral, "La Salada vende más que los shoppings."

28. Selén, "Y cuánto vale la ropa nueva?"

29. "Desde la Salada reconocieron que el 40 percent de la mercancia es falsificada."

30. CAME, "Argentina Illegal."

31. "La Salada quiere ser una ciudad autónoma."

32. "Arturo Illia, El municipio de La Salada," www.econblog.comm.ar.

33. Lucesole, "Intendentes se oponen a reclamos de autonomía."

34. "La Salada quiere ser una ciudad autónoma."

35. "Quique Antequera."

36. Rosenberg, "Carrio desembarca en el conurbano"; "Acto."
37. Prat-Gay, "En defensa de La Salada."
38. Cornide, "La Salada es indefensible."
39. Rosenberg, "Un masivo cacerolazo de protesta."
40. "Los ecos de las cacerolas."
41. "Entrevista: Elisa Carrio," *A dos voces*, aired September 19, 2012.
42. Santiago and Krell, "Bolivia en Buenos Aires"; Lipcovich, "Entre el gobierno porteño, talleristas bolivianos y empresarios coreanos."
43. Caggiano, "Desiguales divergentes."
44. Colectivo Situaciones, *De chuequista y overlock*, 53.
45. Cantor, "Entramados de clase y nacionalidad."
46. Videla, "Que paso realmente en la Plaza."
47. Guibelalde, "Como opera la patota de los talleres."
48. Santiago and Krell, "Bolivia en Buenos Aires."
49. Tomás Eliaschev, "Trabajo sucio," *El Argentino*, June 10, 2010.
50. "Trabajadores textiles bolivianos exigieron precios justos."

BIBLIOGRAPHY

"Acto: Militancia y Trabajo." *Diario del Sur*, October 14, 2010. www.diariodelsur.com.
"Administrador de La Salada destaca el rol en la economía." *El Dia*, February 11, 2011.
"Arturo Illia, El municipio de La Salada." www.econblog.comm.ar.
Barral, Patricia. "La Salada vende más que los shoppings." *Perfil*, May 9, 2011.
Caggiano, Sergio. "Desiguales divergentes." Berlin: Interdependent Inequalities in Latin America, 2013.
Cantor, Guillermo. "Entramados de clase y nacionalidad." *Migraciones Internacionales* 7, no. 1 (2013): 197–234.
Castel, Robert. *From Manual Workers to Wage Workers*. Translated by Richard Boyd. Rutgers, N.J.: Transaction Press, 2002.
Castillo, Jorge. "Esclavitud es lo hacen las grandes empresas y los sindicatos." *Políticas del Sur.* politicasdelsur.com.ar.
Chatterjee, Partha. *The Politics of the Governed*. New York: Columbia University Press, 2006.
Colectivo Situaciones. *De chuequista y overlocks*. Buenos Aires: Retazón, 2011.
Confederacion Argentina de la Mediana Empresa (CAME). "Argentina Ilegal." Buenos Aires: Working Paper, August 23, 2013.
Cornide, Osvaldo. "La Salada es indefensible." *CAME*, March 31, 2009.
"Desde la Salada reconocieron que el 40 percent de la mercancia es falsificada." *La Nacion*, March 3, 2011.
De Vincenzi, Jorge, and Gustavo Torres. "Esclavitud Fashion." *Revista Zoom*, April 1, 2008, 12–15.
Dewey, Matías. "Taxing the Shadow: The Political Economy of Sweatshops in La Salada." Cologne: Working Paper, 14/18, Max Planck Institute, 2014.
Eleisegui, Patricio. "Si usted tiene problemas con su cobertura." *IProfesional*, January 16, 2010.
Eliaschev, Tomás. "Trabajo sucio." *El Argentino*, June 10, 2010.
"Entrevista: Elisa Carrio." *A dos voces*. Aired September 19, 2012.
Girón, Nacho. *La Salada*. Barcelona: Ediciones B, 2011.
Guibelalde, Juan. "Como opera la patota de los talleres." *Bolivia te Amo*, August 29, 2011.
"La provincia no hace un relevamiento." *Politica del Sur*. politicadelsur.com.ar.
"La Salada dice tener la solución para la inseguridad." *Diario Crónica*, September 21, 2012.
"La Salada en manos de bolivianos." *La Razon*, April 23, 2012.

"La Salada quiere ser una ciudad autónoma." *Contexto*. San Miguel de Tucumán. February 16, 2010.

Lipcovich, Pedro. "Entre el gobierno porteño, talleristas bolivianos y empresarios coreanos." *Página 12*, April 7, 2006.

"Los ecos de las cacerolas." *Página 12*, September 17, 2012.

Lucesole, Maria José. "Intendentes se oponen a reclamos de autonomía." *La Nación*, October 4, 2004.

Merklen, Denis. *Pobres Ciudadanos*. Buenos Aires: Gorla, 2010.

Monjonnier, Laura. "La Salada." *Argentine Independent*, December 15, 2010.

Montero, Jerónimo. "Neoliberal Fashion: The Political Economy of Sweatshops in Europe and Latin America." PhD diss., Durham University, 2011.

"Montoya busca evasores con el Google." *La Nación*, February 21, 2007.

"Montoya se sumo a la polemica por La Salada." *Perfil*, April 7, 2009.

Ossona, Jorge L. "El Shopping de los Pobres." Toulouse: University of Toulouse, Conference June 30–July 3, 2010.

Peralta, Elena, and Pablo Novillo. "Talleres ilegales." *Clarín*, April 9, 2006.

Prat-Gay, Alfonso. "En defensa de La Salada." *Clarín*, April 3, 2009.

"Quinto operativo de Rentas en La Salada." *En Blanco* 2, no. 10 (2007).

"Quique Antequera." *Politica del Sur*, April 14, 2009. www.politicadelsur.com.ar.

"Quique Antequera entregó 3000 pesos a Centro de Jubilados." September 10, 2012. https://lomasdigital.blogspot.com.ar/2012/09/quique-antequera-entrego-3000-pesos-de.html.

Rosenberg, Jaime. "Carrio desembarca en el conurbano." *La Nación*, January 4, 2009.

———. "Un masivo cacerolazo de protesta." *La Nación*, September 14, 2012.

Sainz, Alfredo. "El modelo La Salada se multiplica." *La Nación*, March 28, 2010.

———. "En La Salada, el metro cuadrado es más caro que en Puerto Madero." *La Nación*, December 6, 2009.

Sanchez, Gabriel, and Ines Butler. "Understanding Productivity Levels, Growth and Dispersion in the Textile Sector in Argentina." *Revista de Economía Política de Buenos Aires* 4, no. 7–8 (2010): 49–102.

Santiago, Silvana, and Tamara Krell. "Bolivia en Buenos Aires." *La Nación*, April 28, 2006.

Schiavo, Ester, and Sergio Rodriguez. "Informalidad e inclusion social." Recife: University of Recife, Conference Congreso Latinoamericano de Sociologia, 2011.

Selén, Leandro. "Y cuánto vale la ropa nueva?" *Miradas al Sur*, November 25, 2011.

Soler, Paula. "Crece la falsificación." *La Nación*, March 10, 2009.

"Trabajadores textiles bolivianos exigieron precios justos." *La Nación*, April 6, 2006.

Videla, Eduardo. "Que paso realmente en la Plaza." *Pagina 12*, December 20, 2009.

ELEVEN

The Speed of Place and the Space of Time:
Toward a Theory of Postcolonial Velo/city

Peter Hitchcock

The present is increasingly characterized as one of acceleration, the epoch of the nanosecond, as James Gleick avers. Politically and theoretically this represents a complex array of possibilities that I consider below in terms of the aesthetics of variable velocity in postcoloniality. Understanding speed is vital to postcolonial critique, from how to read rates of ecological catastrophe (Rob Nixon's *Slow Violence*) to unpacking the scalar profusions of disjuncture and difference (Arjun Appadurai's *Modernity at Large*). I am particularly interested in the cultural representations of the postcolonial urban that distill and problematize the notion that all compressed modernization is simply an expression of speedup and the will-to-hegemony of neoliberal desire. Speed is at the heart of every city, but how does an understanding of velocity enable critique to think the city as postcolonial? Is decolonization measured by the rates in which urbanization is lived? To address such possibilities, I propose two concepts that correlate rather than codify time and space for the postcolonial city, a geopolitics of the aesthetic that cognitively maps, to borrow from Fredric Jameson, the contradictory unevenness of the speed of change in decolonization. From capital circulation to public transportation, the modern city appears to encapsulate the terrible beauty of speed, yet the grammar of velocity is undertheorized, and no more so than when the urban space of postcolonial delinking is at stake. It is not that the new megacities of the Global South are learning to catch up, to be faster in their modes of socialization, as if the whole notion of postcolonial velocity rests on a false binary of fast and slow. The problem pivots principally on the logic of change itself, and how one cognizes the scales of difference between the economic, the political, and the cultural. As Fanon notes in his conclusion to *The Wretched of the Earth*, the point is neither to chase the North nor to assume that the people of the South are inherently slow. The question is not about appropriating a paradigm of velocity, but of creating one.

Speed has a provocative purchase on contemporary cultural theorization. On the Left the idea of acceleration is greeted with the usual pessimism of the intellect and optimism of the will but, given the perceived diminution of radical global alternatives to capitalist neoliberalism (the largest Communist Party in history now commands arguably the world's largest capitalist economy), the vain hope is that what is actually at work is the acceleration of contradiction on a world scale that will no longer need states, parties, or any form of International to foment a postcapitalist future. Historically, of course, challenges to capitalism, like those to colonialism, have often benefited from the speed of insurrection: Here the interest is not in the doxa of velocity necessarily, but its symptomatic specificity, its role in the temporal logic or eventness of postcoloniality, which helps to shape and is shaped by the literariness of postcolonial expression in the current conjuncture. In literary studies speed is pinned to the abstruse processes of modernization, with modernism as its strongest concretization.[1] The literary genre most inclined to examine the logic of accelerating existence (its effulgence and/or entropy) is science fiction, whose speculative critique, as Steven Shaviro has underlined, often opens up the fault lines in neoliberal fantasies of speed tuned to the eternal now.[2] But just as neoliberalism struggles to articulate ideological consistency, so logics of speed appear contradictory in their cultural expression. Rethinking velocity has become a vital arena for challenging the inertial force of modernity as simply the prevailing condition of an ever-faster world, and this cannot but inflect the fraught relationship of postcoloniality to its project.

When James Gleick offers genealogies of speed as a form of cultural abundance, he quotes from Milan Kundera's fiction: "Speed is the form of ecstasy the technological revolution has given to man," a provocative declaration in a world where the speed of neoliberalism appears to have outrun the social capacity to transform it.[3] Kundera—Communist Party member, expelled from Party, readmitted to Party, expelled from Party—is a living testimony to the kinds of constitutive antinomies in twentieth-century Communism that riddled (and ridiculed) the communist hypothesis and was answered by so many countries of Central and Eastern Europe becoming postcolonial states. The Kundera quote comes from his first novel in French, *La Lenteur* (*Slowness*), and a longer excerpt throws light on the problem of speed for modernity's meaning:

> Speed is the form of ecstasy the technical revolution has given to man. As opposed to a motorcyclist, the runner is always present in his body, always obligated to think about his blisters, his exhaustion; when he runs he feels his weight, his age, never more conscious of himself and of his time of life. Everything changes when man delegates the faculty of speed to a machine: from then on, his own body is out of play, and he gives himself to a speed that is noncorporeal, non-material, pure speed, speed itself, ecstasy speed.[4]

Kundera's fiction here can be read biopolitically, as a moving contradiction of the capitalist body, but also in terms of geopolitical divisions of technology that calibrate speed for hegemony. Like Kundera, Gleick is circumspect about a faster world, but Gleick's somewhat breathless investigation is only partly about acceleration and is more about the construction of temporal scales (see, for instance, his discussion of "real time"). Indeed, it is how a seemingly faster world striates our sense of measure that is increasingly problematic, the logic in which velocity varies that has critical purchase on the way we think difference as the production of the social.

In this regard, the eventness of postcoloniality is not just about rates of change (the impress of decolonization, for instance), but simultaneously about the speed of coexperience, the capacity for co-being in what makes an event "postcolonial" in the first place.[5] This idea, in part inspired by Bakhtin, thinks of I/Other relations in being as participatory, yet also as forms of consciousness highly dependent on the time of recognition. True, for Bakhtin the logic of event, eventness, is primarily a metric of the aesthetic act,[6] but part of the suggestion here is that such sense is overdetermined by the velocity of modernization that enables or disables its cognition as an event, as a meaningful act. We might say modernity attempts to regulate the time of aesthetic cognition with difference and repetition compounded by speed. Faster does not necessarily undo cognition in politics or art but accentuates why changes in velocity are also a way to scale postcoloniality, as historical, eventful, and living.[7] At this level speed becomes a critical heuristic that connects time and space, temporality in place, and the dynamics of modernity to their economic and cultural coordinates. As a conceptual link, however, speed is hardly settled in its theorization, and, as we shall see, its implications for postcolonial critique are never less than vexed.

Benjamin Noys, for instance, who coined the term "accelerationism," offers an erudite if not always thicker description of speed's role in modernity in *Malign Velocities: Accelerationism and Capitalism*. He identifies accelerationism less with a movement and more as a sensibility, which for him is an intensely mediated affect in which delinking from speed in capitalism would require, among other things, a refusal of work that yet enables sustainability, and a de-commodification that permits pleasure beyond circuits of production and consumption (both elements are, of course, germane to living postcoloniality).[8] Eschewing all forms of socialist nostalgia, Noys suggests countering fantasies of speed with a little friction in fiction, a project that "involves attention to the aesthetics of these moments of friction, which encode the tension accelerationism wishes to dissolve."[9] The frictionality in fictionality is only partly about slowness and is more critically focused on the transnational division of temporality, variable velocities that fiction can both foreground and fracture. Again, the point is not to suggest the world should be apprehended simply as speed, but that forms of velocity reveal imaginaries to which fiction attends and to a significant degree creates. On the one hand, this is certainly consanguine with the *longue durée* of modernity itself; on the other hand, the compressed modernization of the twentieth century has made reading for speed vital for its disjunction in the twenty-first, as if understanding velocity might help us to live speed at optimum levels of community and planetarity, a species being of speed in struggle. This is where two critical concepts for postcolonialism, the "speed of place" and the "space of time," might usefully be elaborated.

If we can say globalization performs a matrix of speeds, both calculated and often unintended, the speed of place refers to the ways in which the local reproduces and resets such velocity, creating not so much lines of flight but alternative rhythms of worldly integration. Locality is not globality in disguise but always asks, is globalization also this? Place may situate globalization yet does not guarantee it. But globalization is never uncontested, so even if place is interrogative of globalization's sway, it might also be read as consistent with what we already know of the unevenness of the world system as such. Put another way, the developing world is often burdened with a temporal lag (like that in the phrase, "developing world"), as if the imaginaries of the South are in search of a Symbolic that globalization provides. Needless to say, this idea sounds suspiciously like the old saw the West proposes however the Rest disposes. One answer to this assumption has been to pluralize globalization so that it can mean more things to more people. Another response has been to differentiate its forms from what constitutes it as a horizon, so that the world moves toward globalization. In both cases, a shortfall is implied that the study of place can indicate without necessarily fulfilling. Speed here may not correspond to a formula for velocity, but place gives direction to its magnitude, meaning to its coordinates. The idea at issue both refers to rates of change and to how place creates a metric for that measure. Clearly, however, if speed is perspectival and experiential, even with the outer body split that Kundera invokes, then the speed of place is almost impossible to differentiate: It becomes minimally descriptive, unable to sustain a single example beyond the broadest generalizations about mobility and technology. Velocity gives to speed direction, and therefore it is a vector quantity that requires more than one attribute or number. Accelerationism, invoked above, often assumes that a change in velocity is an increase in speed, but changes in direction are not necessarily the same thing. Here we are noting, by contrast, the tensions and contradictions between the objective conditions of speed and how it is perceived in place (*a* place, but also situated). Lived relations are always moving, so if place is to be a useful index of variable velocity, it requires another dynamic dimension that is also divisible as both objective and experiential.

The space of time is derived both from Marx and from Bakhtin's thoughts on chronotope. Readers of Bakhtin will know chronotope is hardly formulaic, but it is vital to his aesthetic constellation (along with dialogism, carnival, and the grotesque). Typically, Bakhtin can find a time/space even in a void—think of his exploration of "adventure time," which is narratological nonspace where objective time, or what he calls "real duration," is suspended. Such an imaginative grasp is the very impress of a chronotope (in this case, of the classical Greek romance). So, in chronotope ratios of time and space are at stake but they also come with a *ratio* (rationale) in which such perceptions are formed. In a more dialectical mode, when Jameson writes of postmodernism as the cultural logic of late capitalism, he sets the terms for a certain chronotopic critique. For Jameson, the key "antinomy of postmodernity" is its crisis of time. For me, the concept of the space of time adjudicates literary time/space in its time/space, in the coordinates of a particular literary example. Second, however, it attempts to measure the very logic of that appreciation, the critical act, from the time/space of its articulation (or as Jameson reminds us, dialectics is itself subject to dialectics). Speed only means something within chronotopic coordinates, but obviously not all chronotopes need accentuate velocity in their articulation. For postcolonial critique the speed of place and the space of time open up the logics of literary scales. Rather than abstractions on the world, they are distillations of it. But *how* are they useful? How are they even relevant? And isn't this another baleful example of killing post-colonial studies by conceptualizing it, or perhaps flogging a horse already dispatched by Vivek Chibber? Is there a way to return a little flesh to the bones?

The first vector of velocity discernible for postcolonial literary study exists in the logic of the country and the city that together constitute horizons for themselves and each other. Long histories are available about the materialization of such relations, but they offer a particular valence regarding postcolonial conditions and conditionality. Briefly, colonialism must satisfy a number of requirements to establish dominion, and one is to figure the logic of power between the country and the city specific to a colonized space; indeed, the depth of this understanding turns space into place for colonialism, despite the fact that place (space with meaning) clearly preexists colonial adventures and occupations. How exploitation will proceed is a complex set of calculations, from what is a defensible settlement to how to manage subjugation, from identifying extractable resources to developing trade routes and protecting distribution hubs (often port cities, but not exclusively so). Colonialism is both an episteme and specific modes of praxis, each requiring variable velocity between the country and the city. The familiar binary—the country as slow, plodding, traditional, rudimentary, simple and the city as hyperkinetic, vigorous, complex, intelligent, now—fails to articulate variable velocity, which must also account for capacities of movement and strategies of position (in postcolonial parlance, these include wars of position) that determine to a significant degree the success or failure both of colonial predations but also, crucially, anticolonial resistance and insurrection (one might use scalar thinking across several discourses of technology, culture, and politics as the vigor of the countryside in surrounding the city, or as the slow uprising in everyday urban sabotage, the patience of autonomous network building, the building out of infrastructure, etc.). Colonialism and its sublation take time, but the speed of change (in any direction) necessitates the negotiation of velocity by calibrating its intensity (since some moves necessarily prove easier than others). One caveat for materialist critique is accounting for indeterminacy in the relation of the social interests of speed to politics rather than by allowing speedy positivism to replace metonymically how contradiction actually moves. On this level, variable velocity for postcolonialism marks a structural antinomy in the forms of state possible while also indicating a scene of critical tension whenever speed is a hermeneutical pivot.

A second vector of velocity rests on a kind of generic inconsistency: the ways in which speed is rendered culturally expressible (or not). At a basic level, one can think of this in terms of any mode of socialization in all of the mediatory functions; yet beyond this, a postcolonial concern at once foregrounds the politics of form and genre in the clash of, for instance, local cultural embeddedness *and* the accoutrements of cosmopolitan, worldly pretensions (that have made the novel, for instance, so vibrant and contradictory in narrating decolonization). Today such schisms are often deemed superfluous: Even if a novel believes itself to run narrative faster than a griot, technology asks all to bow before its dominance, as if the instantaneity of social media has artfully decided on the difference between speed thrills and speed kills. Again, velocity is about a rate of change in its direction, but that necessarily invokes modernization's acceleration thesis. The issue here is close to aura in modernity for Walter Benjamin: Velocity is a logic of cognition and *Jetztzeit* (now-time) an intimation of temporal disjunction. Benjamin thought mostly about the time and place of apprehension and less about the speed of technological reproducibility itself—the difference between a dialectical image and the time it takes to develop an image as photograph, for instance. The difficulty is thinking different levels of affective speed simultaneously when immediacy and duration have both objective and subjective correlatives. Benedict Anderson, for whom Benjamin's philosophy of time is crucial, uses the concept of "meanwhile" as a heuristic of the nation form, an interpretive mode that seems to work much better for colonial and decolonizing states than it does for nations whose form is preimagined in the immediate aftermath of the Peace of Westphalia. For both, however, processes of serialization are key, and how fast nowness can be generated in serialization (whether in newspapers or continuous newsfeeds) is an important barometer of identities and their discontents. Serial thinking imagines the bounds of nationness, and velocity is a measure of the relative efficiency in its circulation. Yet using Anderson's terms, empty time has never been so full, and bounded seriality has never been so unbound. This is another reason postcolonialism can appear out of time.

A third frame for understanding postcolonial velocity concerns accumulation, the economics of speed in the production and maintenance of states both colonial and decolonizing. To some degree, this is a basic measure of infrastructural capacity in which production and growth facilitate value extraction and distributed good. Yet again, however, such brute economic logic has to be supplemented with an understanding of its lived relation. One reads Marx, for instance, not just because of his articulation of British industrialization in the nineteenth century under the sign of capital, but precisely because of his reading strategies, the ways he reveals the abstract as lived. In postcolonial studies such insight encourages closer attention to the economics of the actualized and the living of the possible—the economic as itself a dream of difference both within and against accumulation. Variable velocity of the economic appears most easily graphed (as Thomas Piketty has recently proved again), and yet as lived it can be illegible, unexpressed, or nonrepresentational, problems that postcolonial theory (although clearly not only postcolonial theory) has sought to address.[10]

Capital, of course, exists in different compositions but is marked by dynamism. Even constant capital for Marx refers to a process of production inputs, and fixed capital is only relatively so, especially when fixed assets (plant, buildings, machinery, and the like) can now be unfixed and shipped across the planet. Since decolonization and globalization are conditions of the same dialectical impasse, how capital moves and at what rate is worth considering in more detail. As Marx puts it in Notebook V of the *Grundrisse*, "The circulation of capital constantly lights itself anew, divides into its different moments, and is a perpetuum mobile."[11] What Marx examines as the speed or slowness of capital circulation "itself forms one of its intrinsic moments." In the *Grundrisse* such analysis is often tied to what Marx refers to as the "space of time" (*Zeitraum*—literally, time/space), a specific dimensionality between production and circulation.[12] Marx keeps coming back to this term, especially when he is attempting to elaborate the four moments of capital in production and circulation. The space of time allows Marx to differentiate money and commodity as conditions of production and the movement of capital between product and money. He comments, "The frequency with which capital can repeat the production process, self-realization, in a given amount of time, evidently depends on the speed with which this space of time is run through, or on its duration."[13] Obviously the first circle of Marx's inquiry in this section of Notebook V is calculation, the actual measurement of surplus as value, but he is also attempting to fathom the abstract conditions of the speed of circulation itself that are not fully expressed as number alone (for these also contain a "qualitative process of value").[14] Although there is no space here to consider the extraordinary implications of this mode of critique for political economy, coordinating the space of time with the speed of circulation leads Marx to perhaps his best-known statement on the subject and its logic:

> The more production comes to rest on exchange value, hence on exchange, the more important do the physical conditions of exchange—the means of communication and transport—become the costs of circulation. Capital by its nature drives beyond every spatial barrier. Thus the creation of the physical conditions of exchange—of the means of communication and transport—the annihilation of space by time [den Raum zu vernichten durch die Zeit]—becomes an extraordinary necessity for it.[15]

Viewed in this light, the production of place, the speed of place, is the scene of a mighty temporal struggle, not just within the abstract confines of capital circulation but in the rhythms of the everyday, the calculation of the working day, the production of leisure, the infrastructural necessity of the domestic production and reproduction of social life, how to make days longer, consumption constant, and so on. Time's space, the space of time, has both geographic proportions and a degree of unrepresentability as relation. David Harvey has usefully accentuated the "molecular processes" of capital accumulation, and again the question is about how to scale such practices in critique not as an adjunct to the aesthetic but as the conditional detail that appears even in the escape velocities of the aesthetic. Vectoring speed as variable velocity highlights these practices within a great number of critical methodologies well beyond the impress of Harvey's, but for postcolonial studies, is this methodological emphasis a purposeful provocation?

Fanon reads the problems of native bourgeoisies in postcolonial states as stemming from their small business proclivities. With such accumulation strategies, he notes, "it would take centuries to set on foot an embryonic industrial revolution."[16] Fanon's essay on violence is replete with an understanding of the implications of variable velocity; for example:

> Since July, 1954, the question which the colonized peoples have asked themselves has been, "What must be done to bring about another Dien Bien Phu [the Viet Minh defeat of the French in 1954]? How can we manage it?" Not a single colonized individual could ever again doubt the possibility of a Dien Bien Phu; the only problem was how best to use the forces at their disposal, how to organize them, and when to bring them into action. This encompassing violence does not work upon the colonized people only; it modifies the attitude of the colonialists who become aware of manifold Dien Bien Phus. This is why a veritable panic takes hold of the colonialist governments in turn. Their purpose is to capture the vanguard, to turn the movement of liberation toward the right, and to

disarm the people: quick, quick, let's decolonize. Decolonize the Congo before it turns into another Algeria. Vote the constitutional framework for all Africa, create the French Communauté, renovate that same Communauté, but for God's sake let's decolonize quick. . . . And they decolonize at such a rate that they impose independence on Houphouët-Boigny [he is referring to the Francafrique of the first president of Côte d'Ivoire].[17]

Clearly this is only one dimension, the rate of change in struggle, but it has been a central dynamic in decolonization. Indeed, the cultural suasion of velocity in postcolonial studies is already a rich and diverse resource. In *Secular Devotion*, Tim Brennan reads decolonization with socialism as the possibility of "the pleasures of a slower pace."[18] When work is unhinged from the necessities of capital accumulation, music can be enjoyed to a different beat. Benita Parry in her work on Wells's *Tono-Bungay* registers "the social and psychic turbulence" of the text, but Wells is unable to intimate this "vortex" in anything but descriptive terms.[19] It is as if, facing the new speeds of financial capitalism, Wells refuses to believe they can be interiorized, in the same way the internalization of imperialism in England at the time seems to have no psychological correlative. "The End of an Age," a title Wells had considered for his novel, is an apt way to describe a book caught between two modes of narrative velocity, in which one cannot engage the differential dynamism of the other (an impasse also seen in its rendering of colonial relations).

The most pointed invocation of speed in postcolonial studies is one I have already mentioned, Rob Nixon's *Slow Violence*, which for me generates all kinds of accelerational insights and contradictions. Nixon, like Brennan, is quick to admit the impress of Edward Said, whose philological deliberation and deep cultural reflection preternaturally refused the more hurried corners of academic exchange. Here is Said, for instance, prefacing *Orientalism*:

Rather than the manufactured clash of civilizations, we need to concentrate on the slow working together of cultures that overlap, borrow from each other, and live together in far more interesting ways than any abridged or inauthentic mode of understanding can allow. But for that kind of wider perception we need time and patient and skeptical inquiry, supported by faith in communities of interpretation that are difficult to sustain in a world demanding instant action and reaction.[20]

This is not a refusal of accelerationism per se but a poignant warning about making critical inquiry commensurate with the velocity of its object or assuming the instant is decisive. Again, I would emphasize that the variability in velocity is more important than absolute speed. There are times when instantaneity is of the essence, and patience might step back from the "real state of emergency" that Benjamin advocated. Thus, Nixon learns from Said's careful contemplation but appreciates that slowness in another key, environmental degradation for instance, might necessitate more immediate intervention.

Of course, there are fast targets for Nixon's polemic about the international division of toxicity and environmental disaster (Lawrence Summers being the most obvious), but in general the pertinence of Nixon's approach is how perceived gradualism, "attritional violence," is a pernicious dimension when it comes to the long-term effects of pollution and global warming on the peoples of the South and is demonstrably "urgent." I do not have space here to go into every element of the quiet calamities Nixon explores, but one is left in no doubt that neoliberalism, the fossil fuel industry, the geopolitics of dams, and the cultural logic of tourism overlap and slowly work together (to recall Said) in their deleterious effects. Yet two points in particular are also germane in this regard. One concerns the arc of illumination—that is to say, how what is slow, invisible, and violent becomes "dramatic enough to rouse public sentiment and warrant political intervention." Nixon clearly defines the dilemmas of the poor and of the "empty-belly environmentalists," yet the logical structure of the book shifts from this to their representation among writer/ scholar activists, then to the metacritique of the one who collates them. The process, we say, is inevitable: This is not a testimonial, and even it were one, the actually existing antinomies of representation would still obtain. What I am pointing to, however, is that the method of deliberation here does not necessarily work against the harm slowness itself is read to mask.

If we place the emphasis on communities of interpretation, then *Slow Violence* clearly participates in several (postcolonial studies, environmental studies, and American studies, to name but three), but the speed of place is indicated not just in the reference to environmentalism in the book's title but also to the poor. True, as Nixon indicates, an elaboration of the environmentalism of the poor can be found in the work of subaltern studies, and Ranajit Guha in particular, but "poor" is a mischievous signifier that will not sit still (poor in one place does not perform its function isomorphically with poor in another). Nixon admits "poor" is subject to "almost unlimited local variation" while also being complicated by other identifying markers (race, gender, ethnicity, class, religion, etc.). The problem of resource-poor environmental activists and the variable velocity of violence in place is one of visibility in slowness, seeing the poor in their situation. The difficulty of this perception is in its distance, not necessarily in Nixon's own (although this would need further clarification), but in the poor's perception of its position (relative to what? relative to whom? How is the existential position and plight of the poor being finessed by its visibility in slowness?). "Poor" is often a solution to a critical problem unavailable in other registers. Vijay Prashad, for instance, writes of "poorer nations," but he has a clear sense of capitalism's role in making them, and he historicizes the many attempts they have organized to resist it (which includes internal resistance to those local class formations who view the poor as a necessary evil in the concentration of their own wealth). In Nixon's critique "the poor" is a floating signifier that permits passionate opprobrium about the environment but has no function in political economy or in theorizing the state. This is somewhat ironic given that one of the writers discussed is Abdelrahmin Munif, whose *Cities of Salt* quintet (*Mudun al-Milh*) is about how an elite can produce a state of obscene wealth and structural inequality with few parallels in the age of oil. Nixon rightly resists Munif's tendency to romanticize the oasis as a pre-petroleum environment innocent of exploitation, but it is noticeable that the poor are barely legible in such analysis. There is no discussion of how the poor shape the social democratic debates in the region, inspire all kinds of communist and other hypotheses, or affect how the power of oil has also constituted a Southern disruption (what Prashad reads within a Third World Project). The ethical claims advanced over environmentalism are unimpeachable, and few writers can match the acetylene accentuation of Arundhati Roy, whose work is foregrounded in Nixon's book, but she has a theory of the state, of shifting hegemonies, of radical resistance, and thus one understands the insidious aspects of growth as degradation in a more extensive range of its contradictory dynamics.

The second comment relates to the first, which is to say that at no point in *Slow Violence* are the material dynamics of the sociopolitical seen to constitute a theoretical problem for the "slowness" arrayed. There is no theory of speed in this conjuncture, just that the violence of climate change is slow. Between the Saidian emphasis on reflection and the urge to understand variable velocity in postcolonial studies, this is a missed opportunity. Nixon is careful to acknowledge radical critiques of decolonizing processes, but he avers that the thinkers he mentions in passing elide "socially resurgent environmentalism."[21] One could, therefore, invoke different thinkers on the subject, like John Bellamy Foster, Joel Kovel, Jane Bennett, or a more sustained engagement with the work of Vandana Shiva—the political schisms among these thinkers would throw light on the production of slowness and the profound unevenness in its disarticulation. A long time ago Joseph Schumpeter told us "a stationary capitalism would be *contradictio in adjectio.*" This, of course, has its own realm of contradiction, but even Nixon's use of "turbo-capitalism" (originally coined by Edward Luttwak, a senior fellow at the Center for Strategic and International Studies in Washington, D.C.) fails to acknowledge how differing rates in the movement of capital produce discrepant or counterintuitive environmentalism (conservation as an accumulation strategy, or carbon credits, or the price manipulation of solar panels by dumping, etc.). Similarly, the use of the neologism "the Chimerican Age" (a term first proposed by Moritz Schularick and Niall Ferguson) to describe a moment of U.S./China dominance in world markets falls short of understanding the second "scramble for Africa" (I am thinking here of C. K. Lee's work on copper mining in Zambia, for instance) and needs some concept of decision in dynamism. All of this aside, the main problem in cross-referencing the environmental humanities and postcolonial studies is the reproduction of culturalism in the very place where the material dynamic of variable velocity is otherwise composed. One can suspend entirely a critique of slowness but still wonder whether the culturalist bent of Nixon's framework (which, by the way, is hardly true of the writers included) mystifies the material conditions of those excluded in their name. Can one invoke the cultural dimensions of such materiality without displacing it or undermining speed's purchase on postcoloniality per se? Let me suggest one element of an alternative critique in this regard.

Velo/city. To think the city in terms of speed is hardly a new idea; indeed, the modernist novel made of this a consummate art. There are, however, significant difficulties in the elaboration of the postcolonial city, not just in the aesthetics of the novel but in the critical practices deemed adequate to their articulation (works I have found useful on this question include Jacobs's *Edge of Empire*, King's *Postcolonial Cities*, Varma's *The Postcolonial City and Its Subjects*, and essays by Ananya Roy, Simone, Triulzi, and Yeoh). My aim here has been to foreground primarily why the materialization of speed might be of greater interest to postcolonial analysis, and aspects of this are refracted through the writing and reading of postcolonial urban spaces. I am only going to mention those parts of the approach that build on the concepts indicated so far, perhaps in deference to the fact that so much evidence for the city as postcolonial has previously come from the social sciences, urban studies, and human geography. In the same way speed and acceleration invite exaggeration, however, there is a certain hyperbole that attends the urban/postcolonial conjuncture, so that being everywhere it becomes, analytically, nowhere (pointedly, the latest *Blackwell Companion to the City* drops all reference to postcolonialism and the only essay that took postcolonial studies as its central focus). A brief example may help accentuate the dialectical contradictions of speed for the city in its postcoloniality.

Jeet Thayil's first novel, *Narcopolis*, is at once a fiction that confirms postcolonial obsolescence while giving it a place. It ends in contemporary Mumbai (a Shanghai-aspirant, maximum city), but the final word is, like the first, "Bombay," which is to say that however its contemporary speed of place is represented as frenetic, hyper, ecstatic (to recall Kundera), it has a *longue durée* steeped in the scales of chronotopic colonialism (Thayil knows that the use of the old Portuguese name remains controversial). Velocity itself constructs the city as a time of intoxication, but whereas such warp-speed cosmopolitanism is almost automatically linked with methamphetamine, cocaine, Ritalin, or caffeine, Thayil writes the city anachronistically in its variable velocity as a center for the distribution of opium (a specific reference to the work of the East India Company in Bombay in the early nineteenth century and its "special" relationship with China—readers may find Amitav Ghosh's *Ibis* trilogy more explicit on this topic). It is a historical novel only to the extent that without this genealogy, Bombay as place makes no sense, although we have to hold in tension intoxication as itself a historical method so that in much of the novel, history wafts like so much pipe smoke. A drug novel always invites you into its imaginary with a drug as its handmaiden (Burroughs has been read to rule the genre, although comparisons with Mohsin Hamid's *Moth Smoke* may be more germane, regionally and genealogically); here, different levels of intoxication are indicated, and any trace of historical foundation is dangerous, viewed as something of a "bad trip." Although reviewers often point to Thayil's own struggles with alcohol and opium/heroin in the early eighties as the source of the novel's authenticity, I find it more interesting to think of its questioning the very terms of authenticity (minimally in what constitutes a novel and maximally about postcoloniality and the city).

The first sentence, of six and a half pages, is less designed to invoke Molly Bloomisms as it is to foreground the specific problem of invoking place in kinesis. On one level, place is marked clearly as city-space, although what the narrator navigates to is Shuklaji Street, a street of drug dens, prostitutes, and crime, a location that must be erased at the scale of a forward-looking city, tech central, media hub, and Bollywood babble. The ostensible narrator, Dom, has been kicked out of one city, New York, on drug charges (which seems like a pot casting aspersions on a kettle) yet wants Bombay not for its shiny modernization but for its "human and animal debris," "the poor, everywhere the poor," "the working-class suburbs," and "the more than poor . . . the invisible entities without names or papers or families"—both the "victims of a failed experiment, the Planned Socialist State of India" and the underside of neoliberal rationality, an unaccountability that leaves so many unaccounted.[22] Indeed, the speed of Mumbai is precisely the production of these nonspaces as an unrecognizable history, Bombay. Opium permits Dom to jump scales in the city, between consciousness and nod, between participation and exotopy, and between hurried work and the "bliss . . . that renders velocity manageable."[23] The opium pipe itself is a marvel of variable velocity. Dom is taught how to pull hard on the pipe to prevent the opium from burning but, in order to maximize the lungs' capacity for absorption, he is encouraged to take short pulls in succession which, if done well, will sweep away his night in "dreaming eyes," a realm of perception where he is no longer certain what is his own memory as distinct from the opium's eye/I, and the pipe as narrator, the "other I." Using a drug experience to almost literally frame a city is not a novel conceit, but it does allow the imagination to figure its contours as relevant or not to the experiential, to the affective, to locatedness itself.

If we can say postcolonial studies has long since moved beyond obsessing over its hyphen, what is its provenance in the city and specifically in the dreamworld of *Narcopolis*? Just as Bombay existed outside colonialism (as Kakamuchi), is the postcolonial peripheral to how the city is imagined in Thayil's novel? To some extent postcoloniality is external to the ontological sense of the city, something of the "elusiveness" in the way Nuttall and Mbembe, for instance, think Johannesburg. It is the vector of what Mbembe terms "the postcolonial event," or here "eventness," the structural logic in which the city takes place, imbricated but not synonymous with how it is told. Now it would seem odd to claim this for *Narcopolis*, since its event is principally smoking opium in a dark interior that, as one critic would have it, could be anywhere. Indeed, Dom's drug-induced languor is not quite what Walter Benjamin offers as dialectics at a standstill, even if Benjamin's own hashish heuristics offer a provocative correlative. What should be emphasized is not the novel's perspective *as* postcolonial but its reading *of* it, the articulation of a space of time in which the very idea of the postcolonial is materialized, concretized in its relation to locale, to history, and to imaginative capacity. Dom's sense of Bombay is not Mumbai but is insistently postcolonial in that gap, in the logic of that disjunction, in the space of time as méconnaissance. Drug taking may make for the novel's essential event, yet its eventness appears in the texture of its contradictory measures of living the city otherwise, by eschewing its normative registers of time, mobility, and architecture.

Dimple, a hijra and under the employ of Rashid, the owner of the opium khana Dom frequents, is a better-drawn character than either opium or Bombay in the novel while she also indicates the limits of velocity as a postcolonial analytic. Much of what she is is highly sensitive to the rhythms of location but troubles its coordinates in important ways. Castrated at an early age, Dimple feels neither male nor female (pertinently, the Indian Supreme Court recognized hijras as a "third gender" under law in 2014), which does not free her from abuse or gendered exploitation yet nevertheless shapes the narrative within a whole range of discourses (including Islam). What is provocative in her representation for the current discussion begins in her voracious reading, which works to explode the otherwise limited confines of her existence. Much of the critique of speed within modernist studies does not move beyond technological determinism with artists as veritable myna birds, singing the machine electric. In *Narcopolis*, Dimple's reading seems to catalyze a typically postmodern referentiality, whether it is a novel, a weekly magazine, a newspaper, or S. T. Pande's *New Textbook for Non-Christians*—all inscribe the city's surfaces in their circulation as media and meaning.

Yet again, however, the colonial lineaments of the narrative interrupt its postmodern profusions, so that each story within a story (place as a series of fragmented frames) seems to fold back further and further into a past as present (this is the friction in its fiction). On this level Thayil's experiments are not unproblematic, as if the conventions of the opium den make appropriate historical invocations ritualistic performance pieces. Indeed, an opiated chronotope is at once contradictory, evincing a passionate addiction to the slow modern, while yet miming the logic of its obsessive high speed. The working day of the addict is rigidly determined, and the den is its abject distillation, a space annihilated by opium's time. More than this, however, the faith in fractured framing produces troubling historical excursions, like the story of (and stories by) Mr. Lee, from Canton, a Chinese migrant, exile, pipe purveyor, and Dimple's father figure. For those who doubt the possibilities of the orientalized orientalizing, book 2 of the novel comes as a significant challenge. The retelling of the story of Zheng He, a Muslim made a eunuch in the early Ming who eventually became an admiral of China's imperial treasure fleet, is a provocative counterweight to the exploits of the East India Company but presses too hard on the China/India connection to the point that Zheng is rumored to be buried in the environs of Bombay. The question is not really one of historical accuracy, although the narrative seems to shy from the hurt such history conjures. Lee's subsequent recollections of his parents in China before and under communism (see, for instance, the representation of Mao's Yenan talks or Lee's recollections of his father's stories of Ah Chu, presumably to echo Lu Xun's Ah Q) play well with historical fact but inevitably unpick the novel's stronger claims for reading Bombay in the rest of the book. Lee may allay Dimple's back pains, but the place of his fabulation provides a discomfort all its own, perhaps because of or despite Thayil's early education in Hong Kong. When Dimple asks why she is learning to swear in Cantonese, one also begins to question the aesthetic capacities of nod.

There is much more to the novel than this (even in the Lee sequences), and the speed of place in Thayil's Bombay only begins in Dimple's cognitive mapping of its streets in her opium dreams and, of course, in the stark contrast offered with the new Mumbai that Dom paints upon his return in 2004 of cocaine and ecstasy (a lesson for Kundera, perhaps, in designer speed). It is a city dominated by poverty but one drawn ever more sharply in the hues of compressed modernization: "It was still a conglomeration of slums on which high-rises had been built. There were new highways but all they did was speed you from one jam to the next. Everything was noise and frenzy, a constant beat, like house music without the release."[24] Such observations are overly practiced in narrating megacities, but here they are complicated in two ways. First, Thayil returns us to Shuklaji Street, which on one level conforms to the anxious syntax of creative destruction—the brothels and opium dens are gone, and the space is edged with glass and steel office buildings and the obligatory McDonald's. Yet he also emphasizes the crazed web of market stalls, spaces of individual entrepreneurial striving where subsistence is made honorable because it is yours, productive spaces that regiment time in openings and closings, where the drug is consumption itself.

If this is never only postcolonial, it is yet a frangible postcolonial condition, the slow violence in the high speed of circulation, the revenge in enterprise itself. Second, the city reinvents itself, not just in the intense labor influx its economic activity encourages, but also by closing off spaces according to the whims of conservative Hindu nationalism, typified in the fast violence of the riots in Mumbai in 1992 and 1993 over the destruction of the Babri Masjid in Ayodhya (Appadurai's *Fear of Small Numbers* is an extended analysis of this moment). Thayil reads this as a turning away from a more creative if still agonistic cosmopolitanism, and here his work bears comparison to the Bombay of a previous generation, like Rushdie's. Indeed, that genealogy should remind us of another troubling dimension, the contemporary Indian writer found in the impress of transnational literary competitions. *Narcopolis*, for instance, languished under the weight of dismissive reviews in India, but once it was short-listed for the Booker Prize, its circulation and esteem reached entirely new velocities, a process consonant with the city that is its subject.

If we are indeed in the age of acceleration, then this can illuminate but not encapsulate the articulation of postcolonial conditions, in the same way that literary horizons can inform but not constitute ontology as such. What I have been suggesting are some possible parameters and protocols for thinking variable velocity as a literary analytic appropriate to the material dynamics of space, place, and time. As is well known, advantages in speed were crucial to the forms and location of colonial acquisition. That these rates of speed were subsequently internalized in colonizing states as territorial extensions waned or were challenged is a more complex hypothesis that finds support in Virilio's concept of endocolonization and in critiques influenced by it.[25] In the initial period of delinking and decolonization, this would suggest the colonial hegemony over speed left with the colonizer, but this is only partially true, especially if it is thought of as more than technological superiority and assumed control over orders of time. In terms of culture, literacy, and bureaucratic efficiency, specific logics of speed remained in place even as they were overwritten by the imperatives of autonomy and a creative velocity that preexisted colonial adventures. Yet on the order of a developed dependency, the former colonizer would export its speed efficiencies as a way to profit from building out postcolonial infrastructure and as a means to gain special preferences within the new transnational architecture. Of course, to think postcolonial spaces is also to confront the advantages in velocity of the Global South not just for capital and labor circulation and accumulation, but also as a template for new alliances in the world order. Indeed, the metrics of speed have been changed by these shifting conditions, so much so that specific critical paradigms feel themselves to be overreached. For obvious reasons, I do not believe that to be automatically the case, although change can seem much faster if one is standing still. Nevertheless, significant problems remain in the articulation of the speed of place and the space of time for literary critique, and here I will mention a couple of them. First is the constitutive antinomy of distance. The incommensurability between the time/space of the literary and the time/space of critique is often thought of as distance; indeed, distance is characterized as the basis for contemplation, the kind of measured reflection we have noted in Said. Distance, however, can also mean a studied disengagement, the variation advanced in Franco Moretti's distant reading that permits knowledge in the form of pattern recognition. To embrace speed, however, Enda Duffy suggests rejecting distance in the main currents of Western rationality (he is thinking of Kant, but I would argue even there we see contra-indications) and proposes instead an "adrenaline aesthetic," in the spirit of modernism's greatest shock, which was to portray speed as the death of distance as such. If this only gets us so far (!), it is because the time/space of critique has a different order of measure than its object. However much adrenaline you pump (which already seems to displace the narcotic in my primary example), what is metaphorical in one may not be literary in another. Like Nixon's slow polemic, Duffy's fast one has no conceptual bridge between the perception of speed and the material conditions that make such appreciation possible. And yet even by introducing this dimension or its constellation (dimensionality), distance, like the horizon, remains. A second problem builds out of the first, which is to say that rereading an Anglophone Indian novel using variable velocity as a hermeneutic only begins to address its dialectical implications for materialist critique and/as postcolonial studies. *Narcopolis*, for instance, can quite easily be discussed as a tale of personal catharsis mediated with the conviction of redemptive memory, the eventness of coming clean, as it were. But even by cleaving to the interpretive frame I have suggested, there is much more that could be said, about migration to Bombay, about the production of specific spatial fixes between novel and city, about the mystification of the country and its political and aesthetic possibilities (again, Arundhati Roy is particularly provocative on this question in an Indian frame), about Mumbai's developed externality, its city-stateness in comparison to representations of New Delhi (a contrast redolent in the writings of Dasgupta and Prashad, for example, but a significant question about the global city in a number of cultural formations), and about the concomitant challenge for postcolonial studies of generic inconsistency as itself a symptom of accelerationism in cultural critique. The proof of chronotope is as much in the time of its elaboration as it is in the space in which it takes place. In *Phenomenology*, Hegel notes that "distance and velocity are ways of being, *or* of representational thinking, and either of them can exist just as well without the other."[26] In the age of acceleration, it has become more rather than less necessary to investigate this division in its moving contradictions, which is a critical challenge in reading postcoloniality and a vital materialization of its horizon today.

NOTES

1. See, for instance, Duffy, *Speed Handbook*; Kern, *Culture of Time and Space*; and Tichi, *Shifting Gears*. The idea here is not to discount modernism's aesthetics of speed but rather to read these as also, whatever else they are, materializations of colonialism and its contradictory "progress."

2. For Shaviro, science fiction imagines the end of capitalism in ways that seem foreclosed in its nonfictional existence. Like Jameson, he is not proposing an aesthetic solution to what is properly a problem of political economy, yet the invocation of speed itself in such work brings us closer to what constitutes capitalism as a dynamic, as abstract and concrete moving contradictions.

3. Kundera, *Slowness*, 6.

4. Ibid., 2, translation modified.

5. The eventness of postcoloniality refers to the cultural logic of decolonization not just as a shared experience and memory of anticolonial struggle, but as a principle of divisible moments in the way postcoloniality, consciously or not, is expressed. The "post" in this sense is less about an "after" colonialism but is about the articulation of divisibility itself.

6. Bakhtin, *Toward a Philosophy*, 1.

7. If we think of postcolonialism as waning, this has less to do with the actual diminution of colonial conditions per se (which is debatable on a number of levels) and is more a symptom of difficulties in cognizing the scales of postcolonialism, in apprehending its substance across different modalities of time and space.

8. The subject of accelerationism is beyond the scope of this essay, but the basic thesis, to catalyze rather than restrict capitalist speedup in the cause of accelerating its dysfunction to the point of collapse, is hardly outside the profound contradictions redolent in the development of the contemporary megalopolis. My invocation of accelerationism here is to indicate the extent of speed's theorization in the present. The challenge of accelerationist thinking intensifies in Nick Srnicek and Alex Williams' manifesto "#Accelerate" in *#Accelerate: The Accelerationist Reader*, ed. Mackay and Avanessian, as does the list of detractors in the same volume, notably Nick Land.

9. Noys, *Malign Velocities*, 216.

10. The economics of postcolonialism in the age of neoliberalism are complex, but certain characteristics, like the process of accumulation by dispossession that David Harvey elaborates (building on Marx's discussion of primitive or original accumulation), have changed the ways in which the speed of development (and immiseration) is experienced. That forms of capital, even "fixed" capital, can move faster is undeniable. Part of my point here is to understand how this is legible in cultural expression.

11. Marx, *Grundrisse*, 516.

12. Ibid., 271.

13. Ibid., 518.

14. Ibid., 524.

15. Ibid.

16. Fanon, "Trials and Tribulations," 112.

17. Fanon, "On Violence," 31.

18. Brennan, *Secular Devotion*, 167.

19. Parry, *Materialist Critique*, 150.

20. Said, *Orientalism*, xxii.

21. Nixon, *Slow Violence*, 251. Although, Marxism does not appear relevant, and major activist decolonizers like Fanon and Césaire are seen to offer little or no inspiration for activism in the present.

22. Thayil, *Narcopolis*, 2.

23. Ibid., 4.

24. Ibid., 265.

25. Endocolonization is discussed in Virilio's *Pure War*. When the state is in crisis, Virilio argues, it turns to colonizing its own people. As both an urbanist and a theorist of speed, Virilio's concepts have pointed implications for how one might reframe the projects of postcolonialism.

26. Hegel, *Phenomenology*, 94; emphasis added.

BIBLIOGRAPHY

Anderson, Benedict. *Imagined Communities*. New York: Verso, 2006.

Appadurai, Arjun. *Fear of Small Numbers*. Durham, N.C.: Duke University Press, 2006.

———. *Modernity at Large*. Minneapolis: University of Minnesota Press, 1996.

Bakhtin, M. M. "Forms of Time and of the Chronotope in the Novel." In *The Dialogic Imagination*, translated by Caryl Emerson and Michael Holquist, 84–256. Austin: University of Texas Press, 1982.

———. *Toward a Philosophy of the Act*. Translated by Vadim Liapunov. Austin: University of Texas Press, 1993.

Benjamin, Walter. "Theses on the Philosophy of History." In *Illuminations*, translated by Harry Zohn, 253–64. New York: Schocken, 1969.

Brennan, Tim. *Secular Devotion*. New York: Verso, 2008.

Chibber, Vivek. *Postcolonial Theory and the Specter of Capital*. New York: Verso, 2013.

Dasgupta, Rana. *Capital: The Eruption of Delhi*. New York: Penguin, 2015.

Duffy, Enda. *The Speed Handbook*. Durham, N.C.: Duke University Press, 2009.

Fanon, Frantz. "On Violence." In *The Wretched of the Earth*, translated by Richard Philcox, 1–51. New York: Grove Press, 2005.

———. "The Trials and Tribulations of National Consciousness." In *The Wretched of the Earth*, translated by Richard Philcox, 97–144. New York: Grove Press, 2005.

Foster, John Bellamy. *Marx's Ecology*. New York: Monthly Review Press, 2000.

Gleick, James. *Faster: The Acceleration of Just About Everything*. New York: Vintage, 2000.

Guha, Ranajit. *Elementary Aspects of Peasant Insurgency in Colonial India*. Delhi: Oxford University Press, 1983.

Hamid, Mohsin. *Moth Smoke*. New York: Riverhead, 2012.

Harvey, David. *The New Imperialism*. Oxford: Oxford University Press, 2005.

Hegel, G. W. F. *Phenomenology of Spirit*. Translated by A. V. Miller. Oxford: Oxford University Press, 1979.

Jacobs, Jane. *Edge of Empire: Postcolonialism and the City*. New York: Routledge, 1996.

Jameson, Fredric. "Cognitive Mapping." In *Marxism and the Interpretation of Culture*, edited by Lawrence Grossberg and Cary Nelson, 347–57. Urban/Champaign: University of Illinois Press, 1988.

———. *The Cultural Turn*. New York: Verso, 2009.

Kern, Stephen. *The Culture of Time and Space*. Cambridge, Mass.: Harvard University Press, 2003.

King, A. D. *Postcolonial Cities*. New York: State University of New York Binghamton, 2009.

Kovel, Joel. *The Enemy of Nature: The End of Capitalism or the End of the World?* London: Zed Books, 2007.

Kundera, Milan. *La Lenteur [Slowness]*. Translated by Linda Asher. New York: Harper Perennial, 1997.

Land, Nick. "Teleoplexy." In Mackay and Avanessian, *#Accelerate*, 509–20.

Lee, C. K. "Raw Encounters: Chinese Managers, African Workers and the Politics of Casualization in Africa's Chinese Enclaves." *China Quarterly* 199 (September 2009): 647–66.

Mackay, Robin, and Armen Avanessian, eds. *#Accelerate: The Accelerationist Reader*. Falmouth, UK: Urbanomic, 2014.

Marx, Karl. *Grundrisse: Foundations of the Critique of Political Economy*. Translated by Martin Nicolaus. New York: Penguin, 1993.

Moretti, Franco. *Distant Reading*. London: Verso, 2013.

Munif, Abdelrahmin. *Cities of Salt*. Translated by Peter Theroux. New York: Vintage, 1989.

Nixon, Rob. *Slow Violence and the Environmentalism of the Poor*. Cambridge, Mass.: Harvard University Press, 2013.

Noys, Benjamin. *Malign Velocities: Accelerationism and Capitalism*. London: Zero, 2014.

Nuttall, Sarah, and Achille Mbembe, eds. *Johannesburg: The Elusive Metropolis*. Durham, N.C.: Duke University Press, 2004.

Parry, Benita. *Postcolonial Studies: A Materialist Critique*. New York: Routledge, 2004.

Piketty, Thomas. *Capital in the Twenty-First Century*. Cambridge, Mass.: Belknap Press of Harvard University Press, 2014.

Prashad, Vijay. *The Poorer Nations*. New York: Verso, 2014.

Roy, Ananya. "Postcolonial Urbanism: Speed, Hysteria and Mass Dreams." In *Worlding Cities: Asian Experiments and the Art of Being Global*, edited by A. R. Ong and Ananya Roy, 307–335. Oxford: Blackwell, 2011.

Roy, Arundhati. *Power Politics*. Cambridge, Mass.: South End Press, 2002.

Said, Edward. *Orientalism*. New York: Vintage, 2003.

Schumpeter, Joseph. *Capitalism, Socialism, and Democracy*. New York: Harper, 2008.

Shaviro, Steven. *No Speed Limit: Three Essays on Accelerationism*. Minneapolis: University of Minnesota Press, 2015.

Shiva, Vandana. *Making Peace with the Earth*. London: Pluto Press, 2014.

Simone, A. "On the Worlding of African Cities." *African Studies Review* 44, no. 2 (2001): 15–41.

Srnicek, Nick, and Alex Williams. "#Accelerate Manifesto: for an Accelerationist Politics." In Mackay and Avanessian, *#Accelerate*, 347–62.

Thayil, Jeet. *Narcopolis*. New York: Penguin, 2012.

Tichi, Cecelia. *Shifting Gears*. Chapel Hill: University of North Carolina Press, 1996.

Triulzi, Alessandro. "African Cities, Historical Memory and Street Buzz." In *The Post-colonial Question: Common Skies, Divided Horizons*, edited by Iain Chambers and Lidia Curti, 78–91. London: Routledge, 1996.

Varma, Rashmi. *The Postcolonial City and Its Subjects*. London: Routledge, 2014.

Virilio, Paul. *Pure War*. Translated by Mark Polizzotti and Brian O'Keefe. New York: Semiotext(e), 1988.

Yeoh, Brenda, S. A. "Postcolonial Cities." *Progress in Human Geography* 25, no. 3 (2001): 456–46.

TWELVE

The Wrong Side of History: Anachronism and Authoritarianism

Jini Kim Watson

The Meritorious Dictator

Partha Chatterjee has noted how, in the latter part of the twentieth century, the Bandung principles of nonaggression, cooperation, and mutual benefit among the nonaligned Third World gave way to development focused on "a rapidly growing, principally capitalist, modern industrial manufacturing sector," and that such a "transformation has been brought about everywhere in Asia."[1] Arguably, the authoritarian capitalist sites of South Korea, Taiwan, and Singapore were the first to signal this profound shift away from a decolonizing, "third way" of development toward high-growth capitalist development. Under the present dominance of neoliberal capitalism—and as other developing nations have followed suit—such a model has been widely legitimized and confirmed as the correct one. This essay examines two texts that demand a return to the complexities of such authoritarian capitalist states. In her film from 2013, *To Singapore, with Love*, the documentary filmmaker Tan Pin Pin tackles the question of Singaporean political exiles living outside the exceptionally well managed but famously still authoritarian city-state. Hwang Sŏk-yŏng's 2000 novel *The Old Garden (Oraedoin Chŏngwŏn]* meanwhile chronicles the aftermath of the South Korean military's crushing of the 1980 Gwangju Uprising, raising questions about that country's period of simultaneous political repression and remarkable economic growth. Both texts allow us to linger with the ongoing aftermath of authoritarianism and dwell on the ambivalent social memory of regimes that are often viewed with admiration for their economic achievements. They also help refute a common story of East Asian or Southeast Asian postcolonial capitalist success, instead revealing the complex imbrication of decolonization, development, and the Cold War.

First, some brief introductions to the texts and the conceptual questions guiding this essay. Tan Pin Pin is an acclaimed documentary filmmaker from Singapore. Her films—such as the award-winning *Singapore Gaga* (2005), *Invisible City* (2007), and, most recently, *In Time to Come* (2017)—have explored the city's soundscapes, stories and spaces that lie beyond official histories. In *To Singapore, with Love*, Tan returns to several foundational moments in Singapore's postcolonial history. Her film's subjects—a variety of political activists, trade-unionists, and former Malayan Communist Party members—were forced to leave Singapore as a result of intense state repression during "Operation Coldstore," the 1963 elimination of leftist political forces, and subsequent government crackdowns directed at suspected communist student leaders and activists. At these moments, the state employed the indefinite detention powers of its notorious Internal Security Act (ISA), in place since the end of the colonial era. The film profiles the former student leader and successful human rights lawyer Tan Wah Piow; the surgeon Ang Swee Chai, who was exiled with her late husband, the democracy activist Francis Khoo; Ho Juan Thai, a former Chinese-language proponent; the journalist Said Zahari, who was imprisoned for seventeen years; and a number of former Malayan Communist Party (MCP) members who were then living in Thailand. Intercutting scenes and interviews of the exiles in their various locations—London, Southern Thailand, and Malaysia—the film is less a documentary investigation into the repressive mechanisms of the People's Action Party (or PAP, Singapore's only ruling party since independence) and more a reflection on the personal struggles, memories, and experiences of Singaporeans who have lived much of their lives in exile. The film opens, for example, with Ho Juan Thai at his home in London, cooking Singaporean-style noodles and prawns and explaining, "You still try to cook your own Singapore food" in order "not to feel defeated."

In a fictional narrative mode, Hwang Sŏk-yŏng's *The Old Garden* brings to life the repression of the radical Left under South Korea's long years of military dictatorship (1961–87). Hwang himself is perhaps South Korea's best-known dissident writer. Born in colonial Manchuria in 1943, he made his name writing workers' literature in the 1970s as well as an extended allegory of the Park Chung Hee (Pak Chŏng-hŭi) dictatorship. In 1985, he published a scathing account of South Korea's role in the Vietnam War, and in 1989 took an unauthorized visit to North Korea for which he spent five years in prison upon his return to the South. Drawing—we can assume—on his own experiences of the Gwangju Uprising in 1980, *The Old Garden* is narrated by two voices: The first is that of political activist Oh Hyun Woo (O Hyŏn-u),[2] who has just been released after eighteen years' imprisonment for his involvement in a left-wing antigovernment organization. The other, in the form of her posthumous diaries and letters, is that of his former lover Han Yoon Hee (Han Yun-hŭi), who dies two years prior to Hyun Woo's release. Hwang's novel is especially interested in reconstructing the complex political climate of 1979–80 when the South Korean military regime saw the transfer of power from Park—whose two-decade rule ended with his assassination in 1979—to General Chun Doo Hwan (Chŏn Tu-hwan). Told from the novel's diegetic present of the late 1990s, Hyun Woo and Yoon Hee's story addresses political repression and authoritarian rule through a reflection on extended periods of imprisonment as a kind of internal exile. Both Tan's and Hwang's texts raise larger questions of how to think about the past violence of postcolonial states that, in comparative developmental terms, are often viewed as "success" stories and overdetermined by discourses of "Asian Tigers," "miracle economies," and the like. In that sense, the dissenting subjects of Tan's and Hwang's works are anachronistic remnants from the "wrong side of history": from the side that appears to have been mistaken about the alternatives to capitalist development in the former Third World, or the postcolonial world. In "looking back" at authoritarianism through the tropes of exile, homelessness, and anachronism, Tan and Hwang offer powerful critiques not just of authoritarianism, but of the very space and time of model postcolonial development.[3]

Such overdetermined narratives of "success" and "model" can make it difficult to think about the relationship between repressive authoritarian governments and economic development.[4] The critic Paik Nak-chung clarifies the conceptual problem at hand in his recent essay, "How to Think about the Park Chung Hee Era":

> It has by now become a platitude to say that, while Park must be condemned as a dictator and gross violator of human rights, he deserves praise for leading the country out of poverty and building a strong, industrialized nation. How do we go beyond this all too facile "striking of a balance" and particularize the manner in which the two contrasting appraisals are to be combined, specify the precise weight to be given to each, and *determine the actual relationship* between the two aspects?[5]

Paik goes on to describe General Park's regime as "meritorious service in unsustainable development"—unsustainable both in terms of its "unabashed environmental destruction" and because Park's militaristic rule "could not go for long."[6] He concludes by warning against the "Park Chung Hee nostalgia of our day."[7]

This essay aims to go beyond "striking a balance" with regard to the problem of "meritorious dictatorship." I do this by engaging with texts that invite us to reckon with state violence and repression from "the wrong side of history"—from the perspectives of political dissidents, communists, and student leaders whom (neoliberal) history can only view as misguided, anachronistic, or superfluous to the triumphant narrative of capitalist modernity. At the same time, I want to view both Singapore and South Korea as emphatically *postcolonial* formations, despite the fact that they do not conform to our postcolonial paradigms of the day. If postcolonial studies has attempted, in profound and productive ways, to critique the legacies of Eurocentrism and racialism as they have been embedded in teleologies of modernity, certain East Asian and Southeast Asian sites complicate many of the field's assumptions. How might the Asian "Newly Industrializing Countries" expose the fault lines between postcolonial narratives of liberation and a dominant Cold War writing of history that has reduced those energies to developmental revolutions? How do these texts open up conceptual space for imagining other forms of postcolonial liberation beyond the advantageous insertion of the nation into circuits of global capitalism?[8] These texts are valuable precisely because they necessitate a conceptual return to, and reassessment of, a particular configuration of decolonization, authoritarianism, and development at a moment when other futures were imaginable; these are those "futures past" in the historian Reinhart Koselleck's phrase.[9] How, I ask, do Tan's and Hwang's texts map the unresolved continuities between an apparently "past" moment of decolonization and the formation of economically successful, authoritarian states?

Exiles of Modernity: Tan Pin Pin's To Singapore, with Love

All of the documentary subjects in *To Singapore, with Love*, in differing ways, attest to the heartbreak of exile in terms of a fierce nationalist identity and tenacious love for Singapore—hence the film's title. In accordance with Edward Said's poignant 1984 essay on exile, the "essential sadness" of exile emerges as a set of paradoxes:[10] Most distinctly, it is dialectically entwined with nationalism "like Hegel's dialectic of servant and master, opposites informing and constituting each other."[11] On one level, such nationalist devotion seems at odds with both the peripatetic, cosmopolitan lives they have been forced to live and the deep criticisms they have leveled at the Singaporean state. Ho Juan Thai, who fled the country in 1977 after he was accused of inciting violence as a "Chinese chauvinist," dreams of nothing more than giving his two young sons Singaporean citizenship so that (somewhat surprisingly) they can fight in the Singapore Armed Forces. The surgeon Ang Swee Chai, who fled around the same time, describes how her life in the UK has been one of struggle, due to the hardships she and her husband faced as refugees and her own homesickness. She recalls, in an interview with the off-screen filmmaker, desperately wishing to be working as a doctor back in Singapore: "Oh how I wish[ed] I was operating on *Singapore* patients!" The exiled democracy activist and lawyer Tan Wah Piow explains that now that his livelihood in England is secure, "the real problem is how to get back to Singapore." Even the former militant Malayan Communist Party members speak fondly of their ties to Singapore. The married couple Tan Hee Kim and Yap Wan Pin, who now run a small noodle factory in Thailand, refuse to give up their communist beliefs, a condition that the Singaporean state insists upon if they want to return. Nevertheless, as Tan Hee Kim says, "We long to go back to Singapore." This sentiment is confirmed by their pile of Chinese-language newspapers from Malaysia and Shanghai through which they keep abreast of all things Singaporean.[12]

At a superficial level, the film is staged around the binary of what Ang Swee Chai says in her interview, "see[ing] things in term of Singapore/non-Singapore." Notably, there is only one scene in the entire film shot in Singapore, which is the moment Ho Juan Thai's wife and sons arrive at Changi Airport for a family celebration. Ho himself is stuck in a hotel in Johor Bahru on the other side of the causeway that connects peninsula Malaysia to the island-nation, where he participates in his mother's ninety-fourth birthday party via Skype. Shots of him looking wistfully over the narrow passage of water to Singapore's skyline are the film's purest visual expression of the aesthetics of exile. Not surprisingly, this scene is used as the film's publicity still: the lone figure defined by his longing for homeland and loved ones.

FIGURE 12.1. Ho Juan Thai looks toward Singapore from Malaysia. Image courtesy of Tan Pin Pin.

Said notes that exilic nationalism is precisely the ideology that "affirms the home created by a community of language, culture and customs; by so doing, *it fends off exile*, fights to prevent its ravages."[13] And yet "the exile's nationalism is constructive of an *alternative*: it is active."[14] What deserves attention, then, is the fact that the film's exilic subjects continue to desire Singapore, but do so in terms of radically *competing versions* of the postcolonial nation: of its national culture(s), its political and economic orientations, and its very borders. Ho Juan Thai, for example, was persecuted for his advocacy of the Chinese language—the linguistic heritage of many Singaporeans—at a time when affiliation with China was dangerously equated with Communism. Among other activities, Francis Khoo (Ang's husband) protested against the Vietnam War, and by extension, Singapore's complicity with U.S. imperialism, while Tan Wah Piow fought against worker exploitation at the massive Jurong Industrial Estate. At an earlier moment, the MCP members resisted the PAP suppression of the Barisan Sosialis, or Socialist Front, the party that emerged after the PAP purged its left-wing members in 1961. Such contestations thus range from workers' rights, cultural and linguistic policy, foreign relations, and Cold War alignments.

Presented collectively in the film, these dissidents form their own alternative territorial figuring *and* political imagining of Singapore, offering national, regional, and global imaginaries far more complex and multilayered than the binary of Singapore/non-Singapore. Indeed, Tan's curating of these disparate exilic lives constitutes something like an archipelago of alternate Singapores, a political and spatial alternative to the Singaporean state's monological and insular narratives of success. Such a logic is reinforced at the formal level. In the film, similar scenes or cities are occasionally juxtaposed with a slight delay in identifying titles, leaving the viewer momentarily disoriented as to whether or not we have left one location for another. For example, the film cuts suddenly from a scene of Tan Wah Piow walking down a London street to Yap Wan Pin negotiating with a taxi driver in Hat Yai, Thailand. These simultaneous filmic and geospatial disjunctures produce a concatenation of spaces, a series of discontinuous but interpenetrating islands of exilic space.

The film not only challenges the unitary spatial imaginary of Singapore, but emphatically questions its temporal underpinnings. The progressivist, teleological logic of Singapore's success has been well captured by the longtime prime minister and founding father Lee Kuan Yew in his best-selling memoirs, *The Singapore Story* (1998) and *From Third World to First* (2000). His writings helped legitimize the national myth of the tiny colonial trading port that made the incredible leap to become Asia's model "world class" city and oasis of First World modernity.[15] In contrast, in *To Singapore, with Love*, London, Hat Yai and Betong in Thailand, and Johor Bahru and Shah Alam in Malaysia function as multiple external vantage points through which to contest Singapore's smooth temporal narrative of postcolonial modernity. The London office of the lawyer Tan Wah Piow holds a veritable library of Singapore's (authoritarian) political history, just as Yap Wan Pin and Tan Hee Kim's unassuming noodle shop in Yat Hai doubles as a reading room for contemporary Singaporean affairs. He Jin and Shu Shihua's house in Bangkok holds a photographic archive of the MCP's long and forgotten struggle in the Thai-Malaysian jungles. Such personal archives—comprising photos, memories, newspaper clippings, and musical recordings—effectively function as anachronistic counterarchives to Singapore's official histories. One way to read the film's aesthetics of exile, then, is to see these anachronistic lives and memories as challenging the PAP's hegemonic spatial-temporal logic, which has claimed its own path of development as the *only* possible form of decolonization for the vulnerable city-state.[16]

In part, the difficulty of examining other histories—and their futurities—beyond the overriding "Singapore Story" is due to the prevalence of what Sharad Chari and Katherine Verdery call a "Three-Worlds ideology."[17] Such a paradigm has too neatly bounded off the Third World—the region dealt with by postcolonial studies—from the Second World, which has come under the remit of postsocialist studies. Instead, they contend that "Cold War representations of space and time have shaped knowledge and practice every-

Was this taken when we were about to leave the jungle?

FIGURE 12.2. He Jin and Shu Shihua reminisce about their time in the jungle. Image courtesy of Tan Pin Pin.

where"[18] and argue that a more "integrated analytical field ought to explore *intertwined* histories of capital and empire . . . and the ongoing effects of the Cold War's Three-Worlds ideology."[19] Two particular effects of the Cold War era are notable: first, the "domination of modernization theory in western social sciences" epitomized by W. W. Rostow's stagist theory of economic growth from 1960[20] and, second, "decades of censorship (including self-censorship) of a Marxist intellectual tradition," especially pronounced in the United States and those aligned with it.[21]

In a similar spirit, Chen Kuan-Hsing has recognized that in East Asia and Southeast Asia, the urge to "de-cold war" may be more relevant that the task to "de-colonize." He notes that "Cold-war structures in East Asia have been weakened, but by no means dismantled."[22] Consequently,

> Just as the formal end of colonialism did not lead overnight to a dissolution of its cultural effects, so the subjectivities formed during the cold war remain within us. Our worldview, political and institutional forms, and systems of popular knowledge have been deeply shaped by the cold-war structure.[23]

The goal of Tan's film, therefore, is not merely to recuperate the personal costs of political activism, nor to "strike a balance" in acknowledging the less savory side of the Singaporean miracle.[24] Rather, it opens a space for us to reflect on the way the now celebrated "Singapore Story" was *predicated on* a number of specifically Cold War political, economic, and temporal assumptions. As such, the decades following formal independence may be less structured by the familiar postcolonial idioms of resistance to colonial power and its cultural hierarchies. The anthropologist Heonik Kwon usefully notes that the history of the Cold War is "about a particular power structure of domination, *invented and realized* along the bipolarization of modernity."[25] Such a structure precipitated certain forms of modernization and attendant ideologies of freedom, and not others. A nuanced understanding of the *global* cold war emphasizes "the unequal relations of power among the political communities that pursued or were driven to pursue a specific path of progress within the binary structure of the global order."[26] In one memorable scene in Bangkok, for example, former members of the MCP, He Jin and Shu Shihua, reminisce over photos taken in the jungle in Betong, where the movement maintained a stronghold until 1989. They hold up a photo of a smiling couple in outdated military fatigues against a jungle backdrop. The average viewer cannot but be slightly unmoored when He Jin remarks that the photo was taken "just before" they left the jungle, probably in the late 1980s, a period when Singapore was already gaining worldwide attention as a "first world oasis" in Southeast Asia, and Malaysia was ascending the ranks as a "second-tier" industrializing nation. Such a scene destabilizes Singapore as a paragon of uncontested capitalism as frequently read through the linear timeline of modernization theory.[27] Rather, Singapore's modernity must be understood both in terms of the foundational role of regional Marxist movements at decolonization and the prolonged socialist ideologies with which it aggressively competed until 1989.[28]

In another of the film's memorable scenes, Chan Sun Wing, a former MCP member, sits in small, neat, but slightly dingy courtyard in Hat Yai, Thailand. Framed by overflowing

Reluctant, for it is not that I don't love Singapore

FIGURE 12.3. Chun Sun Wing reads a poem to Singapore. Image courtesy of Tan Pin Pin.

potted plants and a washing line, the elderly man sits down on a plastic chair in the center of the frame, unhurriedly takes out a piece of paper, and reads the following poem in Chinese:

Thoughts on Changing Citizenship: 17th May 2006

I changed my citizenship!
Born and bread a Singaporean
Who would've thought I'd leave home for half a century
And spend 12 years stateless in Thailand, despite being a nation builder
Today, I became an IC-carrying Thai citizen
Reluctantly, yet gratefully
Reluctant, for it is not that I don't love Singapore
Grateful, for the generosity of the Thais
My smallpox vaccination from the colonial times is still on my left arm
Kretya Ayer, Cross Street, Ang Siang Hill, Tanjong Pagar, Pasir Panjang, Clifford Pier
Our youthful stomping grounds
How can we forget?
In Upper Cross St where the Japanese drop the first bomb
Of both sides of Temple Street lay bodies to be collected, along with their stench
The white flags raised, we surrendered
The Japanese dogs leave, the British monkeys return
The Union Jack rises once again
In the old Kallang airport, thousands cry "Merdeka!"
Amidst the wind and rain we surged
from self-governed to Independence
All these things I have seen
The History that I have witnessed
I still have so much to tell you

Singapore, oh Singapore
If only you knew
How your present and your future still preoccupy me every day.

Written on 25th May, 2006, South Thailand,
Hat Yai Chan Sun Wing

It is, of course, another iteration of the poetics of exile, specifically framed by the anguish of taking another country's citizenship. When I asked the filmmaker about how this striking scene came about, Tan explained,

> He wrote the poem in 2006. When I read it, I had to find a way to have it in the film. It explained his life story and his decisions in a succinct and moving way, better than any interview could have done. I had conceived of *To Singapore, with Love* as love letters to Singapore by the exiles. I saw the poem as a letter by a lover to his ex-love on why he had to take on a new lover. So it made sense for Chan Sun Wing to read his apologia to camera, to us, he whom we are unlikely to ever meet.[29]

Indeed, in Chan's poem, the anguish of exile is figured as betraying a loved one: "it's not that I don't love Singapore." Notably, his poetic recitation is the only time in the film when a subject directly addresses the viewer rather than the filmmaker offscreen, and we never learn any more details of his life outside this scene. The poem's vivid intersections between quotidian personal memories and the larger sweep of twentieth-century history are therefore all the more striking. Starting with "My smallpox vaccination from the colonial times," Chan reminisces about the spaces of his childhood in British Singapore: "Kretya Ayer, Cross Street, Ang Siang Hill, Tanjong Pagar . . . ." He then provides an abridged version of World War II and the struggle for decolonization: "The Japanese dogs leave, the British monkeys return." The moment of liberation—signaled by the Malay word for independence, "Merdeka"—resonates across the archipelago, and is an event poetically attuned with the forces of the natural world: "Amidst the wind and rain we surged/from self-governed to Independence." The poem reaches a crescendo in the last few lines: "All these things I have seen/The History I have witnessed/I still have so much to tell." The poem's poignancy is produced in the gap between the speaker and an unwilling, absent, or lost interlocutor: "I still have so much to tell you [*jiang bu wan*, literally: the telling cannot be completed]."[30] It is not simply that Singapore is spatially absent or removed, but that the Singapore that *could have heard* and assimilated Chan's version of nationalist attachment—his time in the jungle, the MCP experience, his twelve years of statelessness—no longer exists. It must be summoned via Chan's memory and the poetic figure of apostrophe, "Singapore, oh Singapore," while the memory of this future continues to exert psychic and physical pressure on the present: "How your present and your future still preoccupy me [*guadu qianchang*, literally: anxiety hangs in my belly] every day."

Chan's memory of national independence thus remains at odds with that of the "Singapore Story" narrative and prompts unanswered questions: What should independence have meant for this exiled MCP fighter? Anachronistically, how can we remember the future of Singapore he imagined in 1963?[31] Chan's alternative poetic rendering of Singapore's decolonization and its possible futures thus indexes the suppression of an entire political imaginary. Syed Aljunied notes, "In Singapore, as in Malaya (later Malaysia), leftist activists were cast as 'fanatics,' 'extremists,' 'communists' and 'radicals' who sought to challenge the moral economy of the ruling regime. They were construed as wishing to stunt 'progress' and 'development' through their outright refusal to submit to the rule of capital that colonialism set in place."[32] Such anachronistic remainders force us to recast Singapore's independent development as a complex and contested product of Cold War decolonization rather than the unproblematic start date of the always anticipated "Singapore Story." Diverging from teleological state narratives, Chan's scene works to return the island-nation—so often extracted and abstracted by its exceptionality—to its regional archipelagic location and its Cold War formation, as well as to open up room for transnational relations and perspectives.

We might say that Tan's documentary subjects and her remarkable film archive historical imaginaries of *other futures* of Singapore beyond the pragmatist, hypermodern city-state we know today. Her exploration of the dialectics of inside/outside, exile/nationalism, Third World/Cold War, island/archipelago, decolonizing history and globalizing present raises crucial questions around the politics of remembering postcolonial authoritarianism, via memories that emerge from the "wrong side of history." As Gary Wilder puts it in his recent study of seminal anticolonial thinkers Aimé Césaire and Léopold Senghor, to look back on unrealized projects for emancipation beyond the event of independence involves "remembering futures that might have been."[33] But such reflections do so not only in the name of liberal democracy or to offer a "balanced" assessment of the meritorious dictator. Nor do they simply affirm the clichéd notion that postcolonial modernity can only be authoritarian. Rather, they offer up such imaginaries in the name of alternative visions of collective life that persist in the multiple and competing desires for a homeland.

Dictatorship and Homelessness: Hwang Sŏk-yŏng's The Old Garden

In turning to Hwang Sŏk-yŏng's novel *The Old Garden*, we must reckon with significant differences between it and Tan's film. To start, the PAP's targeted anti-leftist purges of the 1960s and '70s must be contrasted with the generalized violence that followed the Chun Doo Hwan military coup of 1980, as well as the different landscapes of public memory in contemporary Singapore and South Korea.[34] Unlike the prompt 2014 banning of Tan's film in Singapore, representations of the 1980 Gwangju Uprising and the broader 1980s democracy movement that followed it have, by now, become mainstream in South Korea. By the 1990s, citizens' eyewitness accounts and government documents surrounding the event in the southwestern capital of Chŏlla Province had surfaced, and much subsequent political and historical analysis has attempted to fully determine the causes and events of the uprising and the government's brutal reprisal. Such perspectives have revealed it was a complex, ten-day affair that initially began as a student protest against General Chun and in particular his arrest of Chŏlla opposition politician (and later president) Kim Dae

Jung. The violence escalated after elite paratroopers—apparently specially trained for anticommunist combat in North Korea—were sent in to restore order, waging indiscriminate violence on the demonstrators. The citizens retaliated, staged mass street protests of 20,000–30,000 people, began arming themselves, and managed to hold the city for five days before the military entered the city with a heavy arsenal of tanks to crush the uprising. The most conservative estimates put the death toll at around 500, with another 3,000 injured.[35] As Jang Jip Choi puts it, "Not since the Korean War had the civilian population been so brutally victimized by the military."[36] The Gwangju 5.18 People's Uprising (*o-il-p'a minjung hangjaeng*), or the Gwangju 5.18 Democratization Movement (*o-il-p'a minjuhwa undong*) as it is officially known, is now memorialized by public monuments, a museum and a yearly memorial service in Korea. In the process, however, the multivalent struggles of workers, farmers, and students of which it was composed—like the larger 1980s anti-government movement—have tended to be conscripted by the liberal, linear narrative of the "democratization movement".[37]

If Singapore's dominant narrative has been the "Singapore Story" of postcolonial pragmatism and miraculous development, South Korea's self-narrative is somewhat more complicated. On the one hand, it shares Singapore's bootstrapping exit from colonial subordination and wartime poverty, albeit with Japan as its former colonial master and the United States as direct neocolonial power. Yet unlike Singapore, it is one site in the larger so-called "transition to democracy" political map of Asia in the 1980s and '90s alongside the Philippines, Taiwan, Indonesia, and Malaysia. Largely figured in the West as a political zero-sum-game between a receding authoritarianism and an awakening popular democracy movement (with the United States as its often paradoxical model and guide), the democracy "transition" story tends to privilege the moment of free elections (1986 for the Philippines, 1987 for South Korea, 1991 for Taiwan, and so on), occluding a myriad of historical complexities and persisting injustices.[38] In South Korea's case, it especially misses the Cold War episteme whereby the domestic dictatorship of the South was set up, with the blessing of the United States, in direct competition with the North. Some of these broader effects of Cold War bipolarity come into focus as we "look back" at South Korea's authoritarianism of the 1970s and '80s.

Hwang's novel sets out in a different direction from much 5.18 scholarship and collective memorializing which, while filling in the historical record and honoring its victims, has attempted to recast peripheral Gwangju as central to the "transition to democracy" narrative.[39] His layered and polyvalent account of 5.18 prevents the uprising's assimilation into an evolutionary narrative focused on the arrival of electoral democracy.[40] *The Old Garden* does this by pushing the direct experience and events of the 5.18 event to the background and presenting a wider account of the period focalized through his two main protagonists, Hyun Woo and Yoon Hee, both eccentric to the massacre itself. Indicating that 5.18 both is and isn't the focus of the novel, the center of narrative gravity becomes the tiny hamlet of Kalmae (Kalmoe) in the mountains of Chŏlla province where Hyun Woo is forced to go underground during the anti-leftist crackdown that followed the uprising. Yoon Hee—always ambivalent regarding radical politics—is a local schoolteacher who is drawn into helping him; they eventually fall in love and spend a secluded, blissful summer in their mountain retreat. Kalmae therefore operates as a kind of space of internal exile, a space both inside and outside the nation, a retreat from politics, but also its place of reimagining. In this sense *The Old Garden* might be read as the spatial inverse of *To Singapore, with Love.* Where the latter takes place outside the formal territory of the nation, *Garden* unfolds both from the nonplace of prison, the black hole at the center of the South Korean military regime, and from the politically insignificant village of Kalmae.[41]

The novel's supple rendering of 5.18 is partly achieved through the formally complex arrangement of different perspectives and voices. One plot strand involves Hyun Woo's antigovernment radicalism, his organization's clandestine work around Seoul, his meeting Yoon Hee in Chŏlla Province, and eventual arrest and eighteen years of imprisonment. Told through Hyun Woo's first person narrative, this arc consists of a series of flashbacks from the novel's diegetic present of around 1999—not long after the 1997–8 Asian Financial Crisis and South Korea's humiliating IMF bailout.[42] Yoon Hee, who dies of cancer two years prior to Hyun Woo's release, tells her own intersecting, meandering story through the letters, diaries, and notebooks that Hyun Woo finds when he returns to their former residence in Kalmae. Despite sharing narrative space on the page, the two lives are adjacent and asynchronous, rather than connected. One effect of Hwang's temporally disjunctive narrative is that the novel refuses to present the 1980s in terms of a unified political character; thus, "we see the 1980s in Korea through the eyes of a political activist and of an ordinary citizen [*p'yŏngbŏmhan sosimin*] at the same time."[43] Hwang's fragmented narrative form has the further advantage of incorporating multiple voices beyond the main protagonists[44] and disrupting the typically gendered hierarchy of "political actor" versus "love interest." During Hyun Woo's long years in prison, his world narrows to the slow-moving microdramas of prison life, while it is Yoon Hee who goes on to live a life inflected by all the contradictions of Cold War South Korea. Unmarried, she bears their daughter Eun Gyul (whom Hyun Woo is unaware of until his release); returns to graduate study; runs her own art school in Seoul; is swept up in the 1980s antigovernment student movement; and eventually moves to Berlin to study art, the latter section offering a comparative Cold War lens through which to read the Korean peninsula.

Let's look more closely at Hwang's intricate staging of narrative voices and its temporal effects. In a much commented upon passage in the novel, Hyun Woo and Yoon Hee look down over the city of Gwangju, one year after the massacre, and hold an impromptu memorial service for its victims. In this scene, I argue, the present can only be perceived as a moment out of time. Yoon Hee records the episode in her diary, addressed in the second person to Hyun Woo.

> We opened a bottle of soju and poured some into the lid of the rice bowl, and we knelt down next to each other. I was a little embarrassed—your somber silence made me feel uneasy. . . . You took out a piece of paper and began reading out loud. You started with a year and a month and date, some long sentences that I can no longer remember. But I do remember the last sentence, about longing for a new, different world.[45]

In a melancholic tone, Yoon Hee goes on to observe: "The classic revolutionary age [*kojŏnjŏgin hyŏngmyŏng ŭi segi*] was already finished" (184; 1:215).[46] The scene is nevertheless imbued with a "longing for a new, different world" (184), and an invocation of a united peninsula: in Hyun Woo's recorded words, "From Baekdoo [in the North] to Halla [in the South], I can see the beautiful land of Korea as one. But you are all gone now. What kind of world did you picture in your mind? [*dangsin dŭrŭn ŏtdŏn sesangŭl kŭrida kasyotnayo*, literally: what kind of life had you been drawing when you passed away]" (184; 1:215).[47] The "longing for a new, different world" is circumscribed both by geopolitical boundaries and a sense of postcolonial belatedness: The age of "classic" revolutions has been foreclosed by a bipolar world order. Note that at the formal level, the scene is marked by an unusually convoluted narrative temporality. Yoon Hee's diary entry is narrated in the second person ("You [*dangsini*] took out a piece of paper. . . . You started with . . .") while its addressee, Hyun Woo, is himself addressing the absent victims of Gwangju. Yet he is privy to Yoon Hee's written account only some years after she has died. The point of such a layered narrative construction with its multiple addressees and temporalities, we might surmise, is that the significance of 5.18 cannot be wholly relegated to any one historical moment: It resides neither in Hyun Woo's flashbacks of the antigovernment struggle, nor in the novel's diegetic present of the late 1990s. Rather, the out-of-sync, second person address of Yoon Hee's belated diary entry is an attempt to collate the discrepant desires and temporalities that point both forward *and* backward to a "new, different world."

The past and present are conjugated slightly differently in one of Yoon Hee's earlier notebook passages, in which she meditates on her father's life. Yoon Hee knew him only as an alcoholic, broken man who was cared for begrudgingly by Yoon Hee's hardworking and thrifty mother. Only when he is close to death does she come to understand his past political passions and unrealized dreams, as well as the lifelong persecution he suffered in the South as a result of his leftist commitments. She relates his story of returning from his studies in Japan (the colonial metropole) and joining both the Preparation Committee for Founding the Nation (*Chosŏn kŏn'guk chunbi wiwŏnhoe*) and the Communist Party in the heady postliberation milieu where youth and political groups of all stripes flourished.[48] The next few years, however, saw the hardening of political ideologies in the lead-up to the Korean War, particularly through events like the Taegu uprising of 1946 and the mass violence on Cheju Island in 1948.[49] Her father eventually fights for the North in the civil war, is taken prisoner, and very narrowly escapes death.

Yoon Hee's father's story attests to the nonlinear historicity of the peninsula's tumultuous decolonization, division, and subsequent authoritarianism. The year 1972—the year of Park Chung Hee's notorious Yusin ("Revitalizing") reforms—is usually known as the beginning of the state's more repressive and overtly military rule;[50] correspondingly, it is the year of radicalization for many of Hyun Woo's generation. But as Yoon Hee's narrative reveals, it is also the year that a new "Law of Society's Safety" (*sahoe anjŏn pŏb*) mandates that "anyone who once infringed on the Anti-Communist Law . . . be reinvestigated,"[51] imperiling Yoon Hee's father and the family anew. To secure a sponsor and avoid imprisonment he must beg for the support of his powerful but despised brother-in-law, a conservative lawyer. In another section of her posthumously read diary, Yoon Hee imagines what her father would have gone through:

> Ah, I can picture that day, my father meeting my mother at the market and together going to my uncle's law office to beg for clemency. I can imagine my father's return home. After sending my mom back to the market, he walks down the busy, unheeding street in the middle of the day, in the world where no one believes in his future. On the grand avenues full of government buildings, where the whole street would freeze during the daily ceremony of lowering the national flag, my father tries to breathe and wander around the dark corridors of foreign bookstores and used bookstores. And he buys the book on Goya for me, feeling the same way he did when he first saw the Goyas in Tokyo as a young man from a colony. Those black-and-white images are like fearful groans issuing from war and oppression.[52]

Yoon Hee's father, a former colonial subject, nationalist, and communist, walks the streets of Seoul as an outsider, "in the world where no one believes his future" [*i sahoi esŏnŭn amudo chasin ŭi jangnae rŭl midŏjuji annŭn . . . gŏri*, 1:92]. He is spatially *and* temporally at odds with the symbols and aspirations of the rapidly rising and militarized nation, with its "grand avenues full of government buildings" and flag ceremonies. Reprising his existence as a colonial subject in Tokyo, he is the anachronistic remnant of a decolonizing desire that has been eliminated for the smooth functioning of the capitalist developmental state. In this scene of urban alienation, vividly reimagined by his artist daughter, the only legacy her father passes on is the intensity of aesthetic engagement.

The couple's impromptu memorial service in Kalmae and Yoon Hee's imaginative reconstruction of her father's experience in downtown Seoul share several features. Both point to the way that responses to authoritarian political repression demand a critique of Cold War decolonization as much as opposition to politically repressive state forms. In other words, the development rationality of postcolonial South Korea simultaneously *represses and reactivates* anticolonial liberationist desires. Like *To Singapore, with Love*, the novel deploys a temporal layering through the use of anachronistic subjects and their memories. But unlike Tan Pin Pin's literal examination of exile, *The Old Garden* proceeds through a series of affiliated moments when the postcolonial nation itself becomes estranged territory, blurring the boundaries between colonial, decolonizing, and postcolonial time.

There is one more important parallel with Tan's film. This is the pronounced role of the aesthetic, specifically, the rhetorical figure of ekphrasis, usually understood as the verbal description of a work of visual art.[53] It is no coincidence that the character of Yoon Hee is an artist; as she writes in one diary entry, "A painting is a way of looking."[54] As already mentioned, Hwang mobilizes a multiperspectival and analeptic narrative structure that incorporates Hyun Woo's and Yoon Hee's consciousnesses in overlapping but discrepant fashion. The novel's most striking expression of discrepant subjectivities is the portrait Yoon Hee paints of Hyun Woo during their brief summer together—at the very moment, he only later realizes, when she was newly pregnant with their child.

Although she originally paints the portrait of Hyun Woo during their summer in Kal-mae, in the last years of her life Yoon Hee inserts her own self-portrait onto the canvas to create an impossible, asynchronous representation of the couple. Having come across it after her death, Hyun Woo attempts to decipher its meaning through this extended ekphrastic description:

> Her high cheekbones, the little lines under her eyes and the gray in her hair, her cheeks painted with overlapping colors, together they betrayed her withering youth and her solitude. But her eyes were calm and collected, and there was that mysteriously tender smile. Here were a thirty-two-year-old man and a woman in her forties, depicted in different colors and distinctive tones, standing side by side and watching the world beyond the canvas. She was right behind me, not looking at what was right in front of her but staring at something far away, over my shoulder. Where was I looking, so nervous and pained? And where was she looking years later, with the hindsight of her age? Which way in the world were we going?
>
> In our garden, asters and cosmos began to bloom. Yoon Hee's school was about to start again. Our friends in Kwangju, those who had somehow survived and gone through humiliating trials, were released from prison on the thirty-sixth anniversary of the liberation [August 1981], some pardoned, others paroled. . . . Around that time, Yoon Hee was almost done with my portrait. It became all that was left of my youth.[55]

The painting, with its intimate connection to the political events of 1980, stands as a fig-ure for what the novel seeks to perform in its looking back at 5.18. Yoon Hee's portrait poignantly refracts political time through biological time, as the "hindsight of her age" promises insight into the meaning of both Hyun Woo's long years in prison, as well as the meaning of the country's anniversary of liberation from Japan. It stands in not only for the tragedy of broken lives and sundered families, but also the discomfiting temporal leg-acy of those who fought for another kind of future, made unavailable by the time of the novel's present. The portrait indexes the disjunctural temporality of Cold War postcolo-niality against the simple arithmetic of the "thirty-sixth anniversary of the liberation."

If the overthrowing of dictatorships in the postcolonial world is often told as a narrative of "political liberalization" and "transitions" disconnected from decolonial formations, *The Old Garden* defiantly refuses such neat evolutionary trajectories. It shows, instead, how the energies and sacrifices that brought the military government to an end were also critiques of a Cold War logic that produced what Paik Nak-chung has called the "division system," resulting in authoritarian structures on *both* sides of the 38th parallel.[56] Like Chan Sun Wing's poetry recitation in *To Singapore, with Love*, the moment of explicit aestheticiza-tion plays with the strictures of narrative time. Yoon Hee's portrait is thus irreconcilable with dominant redemptive histories of the liberalizing nation, although neither does it allow for an "unreflecting identification with these protagonists."[57] It redeems neither the couple's love nor the political radicalism of the era. Rather, it poignantly raises the problem of the hindsight of age—of looking back at dictatorships—as a profound object of intellectual and aesthetic inquiry, demanding new and revised ways to answers the enduring question, "Which way in the world were we going?"

Postcolonialism in Three Worlds

Sandro Mezzadra and Federico Rahola have noted that postcolonial studies is not beholden to "an absolute persistence" of colonial power. On the one hand, the field is interested in the persistence of "vertical" threads of domination and exploitation and, on the other, "the ambivalent role played by the failure of a set of real, historically enacted projects of liberation from those very forms of domination and exploitation."[58] Put otherwise, the failures of liberation projects have produced their own regimes of repression and suffering. This is one of the intractable political and conceptual problems of our time, and one that the "postcolonial contemporary," as conceived in this volume, attempts to grapple with. And yet what does this equation look like if the "historically enacted projects of liberation" have been beset not by failure, but by Cold War–driven developmentalist successes? Following Chari and Verdery and a number of other scholars, I suggest that a critical task for postcolonial studies is to interrogate incomplete decolonization and the repression of radical anti-imperialist energies by developmentalist, anticommunist security states.[59]

In revealing such complexities, Tan's film and Hwang's novel reject the notion of authoritarianism as a preparatory stage to be passed through on the way to a fully developed capitalist democracy. Instead, their figures of anachronism and exile trouble the Cold War logics of time and space and reveal how these states are complex products of decolonizing desires, colonial reactivations, and bipolar geopolitics. This is especially relevant for our current moment of neoliberal orthodoxy when the rising NICs and BRICs obscure the conflicts of decolonization and foreclose imaginings of self-determination or justice beyond a teleology of capitalist development.

Finally, I hope my analysis also works toward unsettling the temporality of the "post" itself as a prefix that supposedly separates distinct epochs: postauthoritarian, post–Cold War, postcolonial. For Singapore, the exemplary postcolonial narrative of national independence and development yields to an alternative, nonlinear temporality produced by unrepentant exiles beyond the illiberal city-state. In South Korea, despite the violent intersections of decolonization, U.S. militarization, and the Cold War, residues of other imagined futures remain persistent and unresolved components of the present. Both South Korea and Singapore invite a reckoning with postcolonial studies' assumed *post*–Cold War epistemology: first on the question of independent but authoritarian development, and second on the ongoing repression of leftist anticolonial energies.

I conclude by returning to the opening of *The Old Garden*, in which we find Hyun Woo recently released from prison and struggling with unfamiliar modern technology. He is confounded by cell phones—the "small object that looked like a transistor"[60]—as well as elevators and new high-rise architecture. In so many ways, he functions in the narrative as a living anachronism, a fairy-tale character who has awoken with astonishment to find the world changed, precisely in order to allow us to see this world anew. Through their respective techniques of disjunctive narratives, Tan's and Hwang's works stage and archive the incompatible temporalities of liberation that subtend postcolonial development and modernity. In their formal attentiveness to experiences of exile and dislocation, they present us with subjects of suffering and sacrifice from the wrong side of history, who emerge unredeemed, unvindicated, and unassimilated by a neoliberal historical reckoning. These anachronistic figures carry with them energies and demands not just for another world that was never realized, but for the ongoing right to help define our political futures.

NOTES

This essay benefited greatly from feedback I received from Gary Wilder and the other contributors to this volume, as well as from Daniel O'Neill, who gave generous comments on a version presented at Berkeley in Fall 2016. I am also grateful for invaluable research help from Bomi Woo.

1. Chatterjee, "Empire and Nation Revisited," 488.

2. For proper names from Hwang's novel, I use the Romanization employed in Jay Oh's translation of *The Old Garden*; however, I use the McCune-Reischauer system for clarifications and other transliteration.

3. Let us briefly recall that Singapore and South Korea have long held anomalous status in comparative studies of the postcolonial or developing world. As two of the original "Asian Tiger" or "Newly Industrializing Countries" (NICs), they are important precursors to today's "BRIC" (Brazil, India, and China) nations. From the 1960s to 1980s, along with Taiwan and then-British Hong Kong, the Asian Tigers confounded the trend of Third World underdevelopment by becoming models of successful export-led industrialization. Andre Gunder Frank and other dependency theorists also early identified the Tigers as models for a (then) new kind of industrial development based on export-led growth and anticommunism (*Crisis*, 100). The key features of such development are a cheap and disciplined labor force, rapid urbanization, and manufacturing export orientation supported by foreign loans or foreign direct investment. Indeed, Singapore has now become a leading exporter of its urban-economic management recipes, selling know-how and advice to hundreds of cities in the Global South through the Singapore Cooperation Enterprise and the "World Bank-Singapore Urban Hub." South Korea, which has moved rapidly from the Asian Tiger manufacturing model to a high-tech, neoliberalized flexible market, boasts the world's eleventh largest economy, is the fifth largest exporter, and a major investor in China, Southeast Asia, and beyond.

4. I have written elsewhere of the way that such developmental states were the result of a particular Cold War configuration, and decolonizing desires were recruited toward the "urgent national task [of] accelerated economic development." Watson, "Aspirational City," 174.

5. Paik, "Park Chung Hee Era," 87–88; emphasis added.

6. Ibid., 89.

7. Ibid., 91. The logic of nostalgia for South Korea's authoritarianism can be clearly seen, for example, in the bootstrap narrative of the wildly popular film *Ode to My Father* [*Kukje Shijang*] (dir. Je-kyoon Yoon, 2014).

8. I am, of course, paraphrasing Partha Chatterjee's argument: "Conservatory of the passive revolution, the national state now proceeds to find for 'the nation' a place in the global order of capital, while striving to keep the contradictions between capital and the people in perpetual suspension." Chatterjee, *Derivative Discourse?* 168.

9. See Koselleck, *Futures Past*.

10. Said, *Reflections on Exile*, 173.

11. Ibid., 176.

12. Such dialectical tensions resonate with Sophia McClennen's observations that "exile is personal/individual and political/collective; . . . exiles write about the past and also about the future." McClennen, *Dialectics of Exile*, 39.

13. Said, *Reflections on Exile*, 176; emphasis added.

14. McClennen, *Dialectics of Exile*, 26; emphasis added.

15. We can recall the broad outlines of its "exemplary" development: Following decolonization and its separation from Malaysia in 1965, the PAP—under the leadership of the late Lee Kuan Yew—quickly decided the only way to become a viable city-state, cut off from its Malaysian hinterland, was to develop new labor-intensive manufacturing export industries, to rapidly modernize its urban fabric and infrastructure, eliminate any vestige of the socialist anticolonial movement, and to open itself up to investment by multinational capital to attract CEOs from around the world to set up shop.

16. The oft-cited vulnerability of Singapore is neatly evoked in the political language of the "little red dot"—the tiny spot on the world map that must ever be wary of being swallowed up by larger neighbors. See Chua Beng Huat's discussion of state survivalism in *Liberalism Disavowed*, 32–35.

17. Chari and Verdery, "Thinking between the Posts," 12.

18. Ibid.

19. Ibid., 19; italics added.

20. Ibid.

21. Ibid., 23.

22. Chen, *Asia as Method*, 119.

23. Ibid.

24. Paik, "Park Chung Hee Era," 87.

25. Kwon, *Other Cold War*, 4; emphasis added.

26. Ibid., 2.

27. Fierce anticommunism in both Singapore and South Korea was integral to the repression of labor utilized in their emerging manufacturing industries, in forming alliances with the U.S. military and capital interests, as well as providing the rationale for the single-minded obsession with national development and security. However, Chari and Verdery also note the role of actually existing socialisms as a competing model for social production and consumption. Hence, South Korea's comprehensive land distribution occurred not despite, but in competition with, the North's socialist planned economy, and Singapore's far-reaching social housing provision was also a response to the socialist development from which the state rhetorically distanced itself. See Chua Beng Huat's *Liberalism Disavowed*, 74–97.

28. It is for these reasons, I wager, that the film has been banned in Singapore, earning a "Not Allowed for All Ratings" classification in 2014. Ironically, this has caused *To Singapore with Love*—as Tan has noted in her response to the ruling—to also "be in exile."

29. Tan Pin Pin, personal correspondence, July 8, 2015.

30. My sincere thanks to Laurence Coderre for the nuances of this translation.

31. This scene may be compared with that of Ang Swee Chai speaking of her humanitarian work with Palestinians, with whom she identifies as they are an entire nation "in exile." Chan— the unrepentant, unredeemed communist speaking from the wrong side of history—can be contrasted with Ang's redemptive, humanist story of exile. Chan's declarations of love for Singapore remain an apologetic, almost jealous, attachment in contrast Ang's successful "working through" along the lines prescribed by Said, which would "transcend national and provincial limits." Said, *Reflections on Exile*, 185.

32. Aljunied, "Political Memoirs," 516.

33. Wilder, *Freedom Time*, 12.

34. Interestingly, both countries have been led by the children of former longtime authoritarian leaders, that is, Lee Kuan Yew's son Kuan Hsien Loong and Park Chung Hee's daughter Park Geun-hye, deposed in March 2017, raising questions of both political and biological genealogies.

35. Shin, Introduction to *Contentious Kwangju*, xvii.

36. Choi, "Political Cleavages in South Korea," 35.

37. Notable fictional representations of 5.18 beyond Hwang's novel include Lee Chang-dong's powerful 1999 film *Peppermint Candy* (*Bakha satang*), Han Kang's 2014 novel *Human Acts* (*Sŏnŏyni Onda*, or "The Boy Comes") and, most recently, Jang Hoon's 2017 film *A Taxi Driver* (*T'aeksi Unjŏnsa*).

38. For example, Paul Y. Chang represents the "dark ages" of Korean democracy as a single period stretching from Syngman Rhee's rule (1948–60) until 1987. Chang, *Protest Dialectics*, 2.

39. In 2011, the "May 18th Democratic Uprising against Military Regime in Gwangju" was included in UNESCO's Memory of the World Register, under the category "Human Rights Documentary Heritage."

40. Another complexity missed by the broader Asian liberalization narrative is the *increasing* anti-Americanism that occurred after 5.18, which focused on the complicit role of the U.S. armed forces in the civilian massacre, as the occupying military force on the peninsula. In that sense, the United States, as Gi-wook Shin has argued, was the not the model of democracy but rightly perceived as restraining it. See Shin, Introduction to *Contentious Kwangju*, xxiv.

41. Critics have debated the role of Kalmae as either a place of utopian promise or merely an apolitical place of refuge and exile. See Kwŏn, "Recognition of Survival Reality," 208–11.

42. On the 1997 bailout and its repercussions in South Korean society, see Jesook Song, *Debt Crisis*.

43. Kang, *Novel Education*, 39.

44. Two examples come to mind: first, the eyewitness accounts of the 5.18 violence that enter the novel via a political pamphlet Yoon Hee finds herself typing up, and, second, a blow-by-blow account of a valiant factory workers' strike that is incorporated in the form of long letters from her activist friend Mi Kyung. Ibid., 429–41.

45. Hwang, *Old Garden*, 184.

46. I use the first page numbers to refer to Jay Oh's English translation of the text; the second refers to the Korean original—the volume number precedes the colon, and the page number follows the colon.

47. Recall, of course, that any engagement with the communist North was (and still is) ferociously proscribed by the South Korean state. The literal severing of geographical home-land—a spatial by-product of decolonization that effectively turned South Korea from peninsula to island—was a central object of critiques in the important Minjung [People's or Popular] Movement of the 1970s and 1980s. On the Minjung movement, see Namhee Lee, *Making of Minjung*.

48. Hwang, *Old Garden*, 129.

49. For an overview of the period, see Choi, "Political Cleavages."

50. Chang, *Protest Dialectics*, 41.

51. Hwang, *Old Garden*, 79.

52. Ibid., 79.

53. See Sadia Abbas's essay in this volume for her analysis of ekphrastic tropes in novels by Qurratulain Hyder and Stratis Myrivilis. Abbas stresses the anti-identitarian possibilities of ekphrasis, but I stress its temporal ambiguity.

54. Hwang, *Old Garden*, 99.

55. Ibid., 218.

56. Paik, "Coloniality in Korea," 76–78.

57. Holden, "Postcolonial Desire," 353.

58. Mezzadra and Rahola, "Postcolonial Condition," n.p.

59. See Woo-Cumings, "Introduction: Chalmers Johnson and the Politics of Nationalism and Development," 9, for an overview of the East Asian developmental state.

60. Hwang, *Old Garden*, 15.

BIBLIOGRAPHY

Aljunied, Syed Muhd Khairudin. "Political Memoirs as Contrapuntal Narratives." *Interventions: International Journal of Postcolonial Studies* 18, no. 4 (2016): 512–25.

Amin, Samir. *Re-Reading the Postwar Period: An Intellectual Itinerary.* Translated by Michael Wolfers. New York: Monthly Review Press, 1994.

Amrith, Sunil S. "Asian Internationalism: Bandung's Echo in a Colonial Metropolis." *Inter-Asia Cultural Studies* 6, no. 4 (2005): 557–69.

Chang, Paul. *Protest Dialectics: State Repression and South Korea's Democracy Movement, 1970–1979.* Stanford: Stanford University Press, 2015.

Chari, Sharad, and Katherine Verdery. "Thinking between the Posts: Postcolonialism, Postsocialism, and Ethnography after the Cold War." *Comparative Studies in Society and History* 51, no. 1 (2009): 6–34.

Chatterjee, Partha. "Empire and Nation Revisited: 50 Years after Bandung." *Inter-Asia Cultural Studies* 6, no. 4 (2005): 487–96.

———. *Nationalist Thought in the Colonial World: A Derivative Discourse?* London: Zed Books, 1986.

Chen, Kuan-Hsing. *Asia as Method: Toward Deimperialization.* Durham, N.C.: Duke University Press, 2010.

Choi, Jang Jip. "Political Cleavages in South Korea." In *State and Society in Contemporary Korea,* edited by Hagen Koo, 13–50. Ithaca, N.Y.: Cornell University Press, 1993.

Chua, Beng-huat. *Liberalism Disavowed: Communitarianism and State Capitalism in Singapore.* Ithaca, N.Y.: Cornell University Press, 2017.

———. "Singapore as Model: Planning Innovations, Knowledge Experts." In *Worlding Cities: Asian Experiments and the Art of Being Global,* edited by Ananya Roy and Aihwa Ong, 29–54. Chichester: Wiley-Blackwell, 2011.

Frank, Andre Gunder. *Crisis: In the Third World.* New York: Homes and Meier, 1981.

Hobsbawm, Eric. *The Age of Extremes: A History of the World, 1914–1991.* New York: Vintage, 1994.

Holden, Phillip. "Postcolonial Desire: Placing Singapore." *Postcolonial Studies* 11, no. 3 (2008): 345–61.

Hwang Sŏk-yŏng. *The Old Garden.* Translated by Jay Oh. New York: Seven Stories Press, 2009.

———. *Oraedoin Chŏngwŏn.* P'aju: Changbi, 2000.

Kang Jinho. "Sosŏl kyoyukgwa t'aja ŭi jip'yŏng" [Novel education and the horizon of the other]. *Munhak kyoyukhak* [Literary education] 13 (2004): 33–62.

Kang Yonghun. "Hwang Sŏkyŏng changp'yŏn sosŏl e nat'anan kwihan ŭi ŭimi: *Chang Kilsan* kwa *Oraedoin Chŏngwŏn* chungsim ŭro." [A study on the meaning of return in the novels of Hwang Sŏk-yŏng: *Chang Kil-san* and *The Old Garden.*] *Han'guk moonye pip'yŏng yŏn'gu* [Criticism and research in Korean literature] (2007): 259–83.

Koselleck, Reinhart. *Futures Past: On the Semantics of Historical Time.* New York: Columbia University Press, 2004.

Kwon, Heonik. *The Other Cold War.* New York: Columbia University Press, 2010.

Kwŏn Kyŏngmi. "Chisikin chuch'e ŭi sangjon hyŏnsil insik kwa chŏhang ŭi sŏsa." [The recognition of survival reality of the intellectual subject and the narrative of resistance.] *Han'guk munye ch'angjak* [Korean Literary Creative Writing] 1, no. 27 (2013): 207–35.

Lee, Namhee. *The Making of Minjung: Democracy and the Politics of Representation in South Korea.* Ithaca, N.Y.: Cornell University Press, 2007.

McClennen, Sophia A. *The Dialectics of Exile: Nation, Time and Language in Hispanic Literatures.* West Lafayette, Ind.: Purdue University Press, 2004.

Mezzadra, Sandro. "How Many Histories of Labour? Towards a Theory of Postcolonial Capitalism." *Postcolonial Studies* 14, no. 2 (2011): 151–70.

Mezzadra, Sandro, and Federico Rahola. "The Postcolonial Condition: A Few Notes on the Quality of Historical Time in the Global Present." *Postcolonial Text* 2, no. 1 (2006).

Paik Nak-chung. "Coloniality in Korea and a South Korean Project for Overcoming Modernity." *Interventions: International Journal of Postcolonial Studies* 2, no. 1 (2000): 73–86.

———. "How to Think about the Park Chung Hee Era." In *Reassessing the Park Chung Era, 1961–79: Development, Political Thought, Democracy, and Cultural Influence*, edited by Kim Hyung-A and Clark W. Sorensen, 85–91. Seattle: University of Washington Press, 2011.

Said, Edward. *Reflections on Exile and Other Essays*. Cambridge, Mass.: Harvard University Press, 2000.

Shin Gi-wook. Introduction to *Contentious Kwangju: The May 18 Uprising in Korea's Past and Present*, edited by Gi-wook Shin and Kyun Moon Hwang. Oxford: Rowman and Littlefield, 2003.

Song, Jesook. *South Koreans in the Debt Crisis: The Creation of a Neoliberal Welfare Society*. Durham, N.C.: Duke University Press, 2009.

Tan Pin Pin, dir. *To Singapore, with Love*. 2013.

Watson, Jini Kim. "Aspirational City: Desiring Singapore and the Films of Tan Pin Pin." In *Interventions: International Journal of Postcolonial Studies* (forthcoming).

Wilder, Gary. *Freedom Time: Negritude, Decolonization, and the Future of the World*. Durham, N.C.: Duke University Press, 2015.

Woo-Cumings, Meredith. "Introduction: Chalmers Johnson and the Politics of Nationalism and Development." In *The Developmental State*, edited by Meredith Woo-Cumings, 1–31. Ithaca, N.Y.: Cornell University Press, 1999.

Yeo, Kim Wah, and Albert Lau. "From Colonialism to Independence, 1945–1965." In *A History of Singapore*, edited by Ernest C. T. Chew and Edwin Lee. Oxford: Oxford University Press, 1991.

ACKNOWLEDGMENTS

This volume emerged out of a collective conversation about the status of postcolonial thinking in relation to contemporary political challenges and scholarly debates. It began with a small symposium titled "Critical Horizons: Beyond Marxism vs. Postcolonialism," organized by the Committee on Globalization and Social Change at the CUNY Graduate Center in April 2014. The event included a group of innovative scholars from diverse fields working on different geographic areas, at various stages in their careers, whose work implicitly or explicitly challenged the idea that there was some kind of choice to be made, or tension, between Marxist and postcolonial criticism.

We thus discussed papers by Vinay Gidwani on the dialectics of waste and value in northern India, Anne-Maria Makhulu on the affinity between financialization and the domestic strategies and practices of urban squatters around Cape Town, South Africa, and Jini Kim Watson on the dynamics of modernity and desire in, and in relation to, contemporary Singapore. Another set of presentations by Peter Hitchcock, Anjuli Fatima Raza Kolb, and Anupama Rao reflected on the stakes and implications of an ongoing commitment to postcolonial critique in the current theoretical and political landscape. The discussion was skillfully moderated by Ruth Wilson Gilmore, who also offered a powerful set of closing remarks. These memorably began with a pointed question, which we paraphrase, *Why would any of us assume that the majority of Marxists in the world are, or have ever been, white or Euro-American?*

Several months later we decided to collaborate and extend our discussions into a volume, conceived more broadly as a set of reflections on the state and stakes of postcolonial thinking in our contemporary conjuncture. We hoped that the project would continue to be shaped by a set of collective conversations. The "group" gradually enlarged to include scholars who attended but did not present at the original symposium and others who were in some way connected to the participants involved or issues in play, while some initial participants did not end up submitting essays to the volume but continued to be involved in the project. As part of our process, members of the group offered extensive comments on each of the papers and we had collective conversations about the larger themes, questions, and dilemmas that we hoped the volume would frame in productive and open-ended ways. Given that we were formed as scholars within the larger project of postcolonial theory, we also understand this project to be an exercise in self-criticism.

We would like to acknowledge Anjuli Kolb, Anne-Maria Makhulu, and Ruth Wilson Gilmore whose work does not appear in this volume, but whose incisive contributions to the original symposium helped launch the conversation that led to this volume. We owe special thanks to all of the contributors who agreed to share their work despite the longer than usual editorial process we proposed. Thomas Lay at Fordham University Press not only supported this project from the start, but engaged substantively with the work and offered invaluable feedback, and we owe him our deepest thanks. The Committee on Globalization and Social Change at the CUNY Graduate Center provided the intellectual and material support for the initial symposium, and NYU's Abraham and Rebecca Stein Faculty Publication Fund generously supported this volume. We are especially indebted to Shela Raman, for her extraordinary editorial assistance throughout. We are also grateful for the wonderful editorial and production team at Fordham Press.

Finally, we thank our colleagues, students, and family members whose ongoing assistance and support—in so many ways and forms—were crucial to this project.

SADIA ABBAS is an associate professor in the English department at Rutgers-Newark. She is the author of *At Freedom's Limit: Islam and the Postcolonial Predicament* (co-winner of the MLA first book award for 2014) and numerous essays on subjects ranging from Renaissance poetics to the Greek crisis to contemporary theorizations of Muslim female agency. She is currently working on a book on Greece and the idea of Europe and co-editing a book on Shahzia Sikander's work with Jan Howard for the RISD museum. Her first novel, *The Empty Room*, will be published by Urvashi Butalia's Zubaan Press in early 2018.

ANTHONY C. ALESSANDRINI is a professor of English at Kingsborough Community College-CUNY and the program in Middle Eastern studies at the Graduate Center of the City University of New York, where he is also a member of the Committee on Globalization and Social Change. He is the author of *Frantz Fanon and the Future of Cultural Politics: Finding Something Different*; the editor of *Frantz Fanon: Critical Perspectives*; and the co-editor of *"Resistance Everywhere": The Gezi Protests and Dissident Visions of Turkey*. He is on the faculty of the Brooklyn Institute for Social Research and is a coeditor of *Jadaliyya E-Zine*.

SHARAD CHARI is an associate professor of geography at the University of California, Berkeley, and a research fellow at the Wits Institute for Social and Economic Research (WiSER) at the University of the Witwatersrand, South Africa. He is the author of *Fraternal Capital: Peasant-Workers, Self-Made Men, and Globalization in Provincial India* (Stanford University Press, 2004) and is finishing a monograph called "Apartheid Remains" on the remains of racial capitalism and revolution in South Africa. He works collectively with the Berkeley Black Geographies Project and the Submergent Archive, and is formulating work on the southern African Indian Ocean region.

CARLOS A. FORMENT is an associate professor in the Departments of Sociology and Politics at the New School for Social Research, New York City, and Research Professor in the Division of Human Studies at the Universidad Nacional General Sarmiento, Buenos Aires. He is the author of *Democracy in Latin America, 1760–1900*, vol. 1 (University of Chicago Press, 2003); *La Formacion de la Sociedad Civil y la Democracia en el Peru*

(Editorial Universidad Catolica del Peru, 2012) and coeditor of *Shifting Frontiers of Citizenship: The Latin American Experience* (Brill, 2013). He is working on two book manuscripts: "Everyday Forms of Nationhood in Nineteenth-Century Latin America" (in contract, University of Chicago Press) and "The Remains of Citizenship: Post-Democratic Life in Buenos Aires in the Wake of Marketization."

VINAY GIDWANI is a professor of geography and global studies at the University of Minnesota, Minneapolis. He is the author of *Capital Interrupted: Agrarian Development and the Politics of Work in India* (University of Minnesota Press, 2008). He studies the entanglements of labor and ecology in agrarian and urban settings, as well as capitalist transformations of these. His ongoing research, employing oral histories, is on the lifeworlds of informal sector workers in India's cities.

PETER HITCHCOCK is a professor of English at Baruch College and the Graduate Center of the City University of New York, where is also the associate director of the Center for Place, Culture, and Politics. He is the author of five books, including *The Long Space: Transnationalism and Postcolonial Form* (Stanford University Press, 2010), *Imaginary States: Studies in Cultural Transnationalism* (University of Illinois Press, 2003), *Oscillate Wildly: Space, Body, and Spirit of Millennial Materialism* (University of Minnesota Press, 1999), and an edited volume (with Jeffrey Di Leo), *The New Public Intellectual* (Palgrave Macmillan, 2016).

LAURIE R. LAMBERT is an assistant professor of African and African American studies at Fordham University. She is completing her first book-length manuscript, "Forms of Survival: Black Feminist Revisions of the Grenada Revolution."

STEPHEN MUECKE is Jury Chair of English Language and Literature in the School of Humanities at the University of Adelaide, South Australia. Recent publications include *The Mother's Day Protest and Other Fictocritical Essays* (Rowman and Littlefield International, 2016), a special edition of *New Literary History* ("Recomposing the Humanities—with Bruno Latour"), 2016, and a new edition of Paddy Roe's *Gularabulu: Stories from the West Kimberley* (UWA Publishing, 2016).

ANUPAMA RAO is TOW Associate Professor of History, Barnard College, Columbia University; senior editor, *Comparative Studies in South Asia, Africa, and the Middle East*; and associate director of the Institute for Comparative Literature and Society at Barnard College, Columbia University. She is the author of *The Caste Question* (University of California Press, 2009). She is working on a book on the political thought of B. R. Ambedkar, as well as a project titled "Dalit Bombay," which explores the relationship between caste, political culture, and everyday life in colonial and postcolonial Bombay.

Adam Spanos is a Harper-Schmidt Fellow and Collegiate Assistant Professor at the University of Chicago. He has forthcoming work in *Alif: Journal of Comparative Poetics* on the politics of translation in the Arab anticolonial movement. His research concerns the rhetoric of sincerity in postcolonial literature.

Jini Kim Watson is an associate professor of English and comparative literature at New York University. She is the author of *The New Asian City: Three-dimensional Fictions of Space and Urban Form* (University of Minnesota Press, 2011) and is working on a book project that examines aesthetic engagements with Cold War authoritarianism in East and Southeast Asia.

Gary Wilder is a professor in the PhD programs in anthropology and history, and the director of the Committee on Globalization and Social Change at the Graduate Center of the City University of New York. He is the author of *Freedom Time: Negritude, Decolonization, and the Future of the World* (Duke University Press, 2015) and *The French Imperial Nation-State: Negritude and Colonial Humanism between the World Wars* (University of Chicago Press, 2005).